The Church
in an Age
of Negligence

The Church
in an Age
of Negligence

*Ecclesiastical Structure
and Problems of Church Reform
1700-1840*

Peter Virgin

James Clarke & Co.
Cambridge

For Kitson

A don of old
With lungs of brass
And heart of gold

James Clarke & Co Ltd
P.O. Box 60
Cambridge
CB1 2NT

British Library Cataloguing in Publication Data

Virgin, Peter
    The Church in an age of negligence
    1. Great Britain. Christian church, history
    I. Title
    274.1

ISBN 0-227-67911-3

First published in 1989 by James Clarke & Co

Printed in England by
Bookcraft Bath Ltd.

Preface

In Georgian England, men spoke easily and naturally of the alliance between church and state. Two centuries later, in an era of semi-disestablishment, the conjunction seems puzzling, even confusing; but this bewilderment, far from challenging the validity of eighteenth-century perceptions, does no more than bear witness to the profound changes that have taken place in modern England. The influence of the church and clergy within English society has declined since 1840 to a point where it is virtually unrecognisable. The fact of this decline is not debated, but its time-scale is contentious. One of the main arguments in this book is that the era of reform, ushered in by the repeal of the Test and Corporation Acts in 1828 and completed by the ecclesiastical reforms of the mid- and late-1830s, was the decisive period: one when the clergy, it will be claimed, reached the peak of their affluence and power. The view from the summit was not enjoyed for long. Soon after 1840, or possibly a little before, they were to begin the long descent.

Although contemporaries readily agreed that the Georgian church was important, historians have been slower to recognise this. Books on eighteenth-century politics abound; those on the religious establishment are few and far between. Indeed, during the course of the twentieth century, only two major works have been published. First was Norman Sykes, *Church and State in England in the XVIIIth Century* (1934), a pioneering account of, primarily, episcopal administration. This was followed, thirty years later, by G.F.A. Best, *Temporal Pillars. Queen Anne's Bounty, the Ecclesiastical Commissioners, and the Church of England.* The title is not fully indicative of the content. Although purporting to chronicle development of the church's centralised machinery of self-government, *Temporal Pillars* encompasses a great deal more. The position of the church within eighteenth-century society is discussed and documented, and problems of church reform are outlined and analysed. Best's work is invaluable. Where he has led, I have striven to follow.

Neither Norman Sykes nor Geoffrey Best tackled the issue of ecclesiastical structure. The reader of *Church and State*, as of *Temporal Pillars*, will come across many examples of neglect of clerical duty during the Georgian period, but neither work states how frequent neglect was. Assessment of the situation is the primary objective of this book. The beneficed clergy, it will be argued, were rising very fast indeed; their wealth was increasing, and their social status was improving too. The task is to quantify the forward movement, and then to explore the ramifications, for the church and for a predominantly rural society, of an increasingly rich and aristocratic clergy: the impact upon patterns of clerical residence and upon the associated problems of church reform; the significance of this development for local government, particularly the role of the clergy within it; the change in relationships between incumbents and their employees, the curates, and the like. These are broad themes, and they are also important.

This is a general study of the wealth and status of the clergy in the late eighteenth and early nineteenth centuries. How things were in Cumberland or Kent is, of course, pertinent, and space is given to a consideration of local variables; but these are placed, wherever possible, in a national context. What matters most about the situation in a locality is whether it confirms, or runs counters to, overall trends. A sense of the whole is what has been attempted; details of rich diversity are there, but they are given second place. The problem is that the map of the eighteenth-century church lacks clarity and coherence. Even an issue as apparently simple and straightforward as the number of clergy, both beneficed and non-beneficed, has never been adequately analysed. There is no definitive study of ecclesiastical patronage; research on benefice incomes is fragmentary; and the clerical magistracy is still without its historian.

Two major reasons for this neglect can be identified. Interest in the eighteenth-century church was stifled by the clergy of the mid-Victorian period. Self-confident and self-assertive, they developed a mythology about their Georgian predecessors, and this mythology has held sway since then. The point is well put by another historian. 'Churchmen in the middle years of the [nineteenth] century', he states, 'had feelings comparable to those of a patient miraculously cured of a mortal sickness, grateful for the deliverance and determined to avoid contagion again' (Brian Heeney, *A Different Kind of Gentleman*, p.9).

The second reason for neglect has to do with the nature of the evidence. The diocesan archive of the eighteenth century is vast, unwieldy, and often in poor condition; nor, to make matters worse, did parliament show any interest in publishing nationwide data regarding the state of the church until after 1800. The historian is heavily dependent upon the facts presented in the 1835 Report - the most detailed survey of the English church since Henry VIII's *Valor Ecclesiasticus* three centuries earlier. This is not a dependency that is necessarily to be envied. Geoffrey Best offers a forthright judgment on the subject. After estimating some episcopal incomes, he makes the following comment. 'These figures', he says, 'have been extracted, not without difficulty, from the 1835 report. I have no doubt they can be disputed. So hard is it to get the facts out of that report, and so far devoid of rhyme and reason was the whole ecclesiastical system, that nothing less than the personal co-operation of scholars side by side will ever bring their sums to the same answers '(*Temporal Pillars*, p.197, note 2). This neatly defines the problem.

The present work has been twenty years in the making, inordinately long by any reckoning. I can only plead in my defence fairly persistent interference, ever since 1974, from work. However, even incompetence has its compensations. Books, like wines, mature with age. The text, one hopes, becomes with time less dense; and the book is allowed to breathe. I have tried to make each paragraph clear and fluent, and have also, as a matter of policy, pared down the amount of information. The tables, a crucial part of the argument, have been detached from the text.

Modern works of scholarship are, in a direct sense, the product of community. The pattern of ideas is woven from a thousand strands. A chance remark by a colleague, long submerged in the mind, can well up into an apparently fresh and glistening spring of thought. Acknowledgment of the source is never, in such circumstances, an easy task. With others, the contribution to this book is more palpable. None of them is responsible for the use, or misuse, to which I have put their help.

Pride of place belongs, in many ways, to David Newsome, Master of Wellington College. His generous and unstinted encouragement, way back in 1968, played a critical role in forming that foundation of self-belief without which authorship is impossible.

I am also indebted to the Master and Fellows of Trinity College, Cambridge for awarding me a Research Scholarship. During tenure, from 1970 until 1973, the groundwork of this book was laid.

It was my pleasure and privilege to have as supervisor for five years the late George Kitson Clark. Kitson's prowess as a teacher was formidable. Always positive, he stretched his pupils in the direction of the outer limits of their possibilities.

Kitson was succeeded as supervisor by David Thompson of Fitzwilliam College, Cambridge. He has seen the present work through several drafts, making a wealth of acute comment. *The Church in an Age of Negligence* is, because of him, a better book.

Assistance has also come from a number of other scholars. Owen Chadwick, Edward Norman, the late Gordon Rupp and Alec Vidler have all discused the project with me at different stages of its development, and their comments have helped to shape the work. There has also been a detailed correspondence with F.C. Mather. Robert Robson read the final draft, and put me right on several points. W.R. Ward kept me in touch with other work being done in the field, as did John Walsh and Stephen Taylor. J.C.D. Clark, Geoffrey Best, and John Beer have given encouragement, and I have benefited from the sage advice of Geoffrey Rowell.

The bulk of the research for this book was done at Cambridge University Library. I am grateful to the staff there, especially those working in the Rare Books Department. Helpfulness has also been the watchword at other places; I refer, here, to the British Library, the Public Record Office, the Bodleian, the Norfolk County Record Office at Norwich, and the libraries at Trinity College, Cambridge and Magdalene College, Cambridge. The staff at the Church Commissioners have well exceeded the call of duty, especially D.A. Armstrong. Tracing admissions to Cambridge colleges in the Georgian period was not one of my easier tasks, and it would not have been possible without access to records given by the Librarians at Corpus Christi, Jesus, Queen's and St John's. For Downing, information was generously supplied by

P.J. Barnwell.

Friends have lent a hand. Arnold Harvey was very informative on the subject of ecclesiastical patronage. Francis Witts, my colleague at Morgan Grenfell, made me aware of the voluminous diary of his namesake and great-great-grandfather, rector of Upper Slaughter in Gloucestershire. Anthony Watkinson read part of an early draft, making useful comments. Christopher Coulter was ready with an apt anecdote, as was that great conversationalist, Revd John Bruce. Gavin Punter-Sorrell, with much greatness in his heart, let me have use of his magnificent house on the island of Skiathos; part of the book was written there. Finally a special word of thanks must be offered to two men. Peter Beer read through the whole of the final draft; I place much trust in his fine eye for grammatical detail. Nigel Howe, a scholar of the highest repute, did the same; his remarks were always lucid, and never long-winded.

Checking the accuracy of footnotes and shaping the bibliography were laborious tasks. They were done with speed and efficiency by Graham Goodlad of Magdalene College, Cambridge.

Typists have there been more than one. Mention must be made of Kay Ward, Grace Collins and finally, last but by no means least, my former wife, Marjory. The fact that my writing is reasonably clear should not be taken to imply that it is necessarily decipherable.

My publisher, Adrian Brink, has assisted in innumerable ways, most notably by keeping faith in the project. The structure of the book is better because of him. Adrian has been ably supported as copy editor by Richard Burnell.

Finally, there has been the glorious incomprehension of my colleagues at Morgan Grenfell Securities. Under the charismatic leadership of John Holmes, they have provided the happiness and fulfilment which have made the completion of this book possible. I am deeply grateful to them, both for the supportive power of their wit and humour, and for the breadth and depth of their tolerance. I wish them all that is well.

Peter Virgin

September 1988

20 Finsbury Circus
London E.C.2.

Contents

Abbreviations

A.H.R. - Agricultural History Review
C.U.L. - Cambridge University Library
D.T.P. - Dawson Turner Papers
E.H. - Economic History
E.H.R. - Ecónomic History Review
E.R. - Edinburgh Review
G.M. - Gentleman's Magazine
H.O. - Home Office Papers
J.B.S. - Journal of British Studies
J.E.H. - Journal of Ecclesiastical History
J.R.S.S. - Journal of the Royal Statistical Society
N.R.O. - Norfolk Record Office
P.P. - Parliamentary Papers
Q.A.B. - Queen Anne's Bounty

1

Continuity and Change

i. *The Medieval Inheritance*

England, it is often said, is not a land given to change: a generalisation to which many exceptions can be found, but which has, nonetheless, an undeniable poignancy when applied to almost every aspect of the structure of its established church between the Restoration and 1800. The church of the late seventeenth century, and of the eighteenth century, was a slow-moving institution, its characteristic forms deeply influenced by the past and compounded of constant compromise mixed with seemingly perpetual precedent. Most of the permanent changes made in the ecclesiastical system after the medieval period were carried through during the sixteenth century, and even these were scarcely extensive. An especially pressing problem inherited from the Roman dominion was the random nature of diocesan geography. To palliate the situation, Henry VIII created five new dioceses, raising the total from twenty-one to twenty-six; he also consecrated thirteen suffragan bishops, an example followed by Elizabeth I, who added a further three. Some of these changes were neither especially elegant nor particularly clever. The newly-created see of Bristol, for example, was for some strange reason allocated Dorset rather than Somerset or Gloucestershire, a decision effectively isolating the bishop from the clergy in his charge. After Elizabeth's death, ecclesiastical reorganisation entered a period of prolonged quiescence. No sees were created between the 1530s and the 1830s: Elizabeth appointed her third suffragan bishop in 1592, and the next new suffragan bishop was not consecrated until 1870.[1]

It had been Henry VIII who, once again, had tried to improve another aspect of the church's medieval inheritance - the gross financial inequalities all too easily discernible among the ranks of the clergy. An act of 1529[2] laid down that two livings could not be held together if either was worth more than £8 a year; and, to give force to this enactment, a comprehensive survey of benefice values was carried out, with the results being incorporated in Henry's *Valor Ecclesiasticus*, henceforth known as the Kings' Books. The survey required constant revision in order to prevent it from becoming outdated; but this mammoth task was not, unfortunately, attempted. What Henry VIII had decreed, no Stuart - or, for that matter, early Hanoverian - monarch saw fit to modify. Incongruously, a Georgian incumbent holding two or more livings still had to refer to Henry's *Valor* in order to test the legitimacy of his pluralism. Not surprisingly, any such perusal was an academic exercise; the rise in benefice values during the intervening centuries had long deprived the King's Books of any significance they may once have had.

Between 1600 and 1800, the only important changes to the laws governing pluralism were made in James I's new Canons of 1604. Under the forty-first of these, all livings - including those worth less than £8 a year - were subject to regulation. Benefices held in plurality must not be more than thirty miles apart; no dispensation to hold them together could be given to any incumbent who had not attained the status of Master of Arts; and all pluralists must reside in each of their livings for 'some reasonable time in every year', as well as appoint lawful preachers to instruct the flocks deserted in their absence.[3] These vague regulations met, with the passage of time, that same fate of obdurate and casual non-observance which had likewise rendered innocuous the Plurality Act of 1529.

In Cromwellian England the problems of the church were tackled 'root and branch', but all the reforms which were put into effect were swiftly reversed at the Restoration. In the year of Charles I's death, the royal revenues from the ecclesiastical taxes of first-fruits and tenths - Papal exactions appropriated by Henry VIII at the Reformation - were summarily withdrawn from the Crown. The income in both cases was handed over to trustees, who used it to give financial assistance to poor preachers, ministers and schoolmasters. As Cromwell gained in power, the whole basis of the economic settlement which had emerged at the Reformation came under attack. The Protector returned to a Puritan clergy what had previously been acquired by an Anglican laity. Tithes impropriated during the sixteenth century by lay owners were taken from them; the same happened to advowsons and glebes which had passed into lay hands; and the proceeds of all of these were applied to much-needed augmentation of poor parishes. Cromwell achieved what Laud had tried, but failed, to do; after 1649, the laicisation of the church - such a dominant feature of the English Reformation - was decisively overcome. But this victory over lay interests proved short-lived. The Restoration of 1660 restored, in every respect, the ecclesiastical *status quo* of 1640. Cromwell's radical economic reforms were abolished, 'confiscated' ecclesiastical property was returned to lay owners, and even the modest measure of 1649, whereby the Crown lost its income from tenths and first-fruits, was done away with.[4] Charles II, it will be little surprise to learn, was not minded to alter what had already been altered before; no alleviation of the church's economic problems was effected during his reign. His brother, James II, did concede a little ground, however; he discharged livings valued at under £30 a year from arrears of tenths. This arrangement was continued under William and Mary. It was not until the reign of Anne that something imaginative was decided upon: the foundation, in 1704, of Queen Anne's Bounty. Under statutes of 1707 and 1708, livings up to £50 a year were permanently discharged from payment of tenths and first-fruits.[5] The Crown gave up revenue bringing in about £17,000 a year, and the Bounty was instructed to use this sum to augment poor livings.[6]

The list of permanent improvements made between the Reformation and the end of the eighteenth century is not impressive. Five new dioceses; a sixteenth-century, unamended, statute restricting pluralism; an updated version of Canon Law; the foundation of Queen Anne's Bounty: it is a rather random selection of changes, leaving central problems largely untouched. A little had been done, but there was still much to do. Pluralism remained rife, lay patronage was not restricted, diocesan geography was without any sense of order, clerical discipline was not effective. The situation which had developed was not inevitable, nor was it defensible, but it was very real nonetheless.

One of the major themes in this book is what happened to the church, venerable and medieval institution that it was, when the pre-industrial rural order began to give way to the predominantly urban life which has replaced it. The church of Joseph Butler, of Warburton, of Gibson and of Hoadly was pretty well continuous with the church of Burnet, of Laud, of Andrewes and even of Hooker; and it was this church which was destined to come face to face with all the difficulties, and all the problems, unavoidable in any society striving to work its way through a period of profound change and equally profound discontent.

ii. *Industrialisation*

The essence of the industrial revolution[7] was novelty; before it happened it was not anticipated, and while it was happening it was not understood.[8] The breakdown in understanding is, at first glance, surprising. After all, the leading characteristic of the emerging society was visibility. There it was, in road, canal, railway; there it was, in a myriad of smoking chimneys and a muddle of sprawling back streets; there it was, in every line and every lineament, of the various Coketowns spread across the land. Not only was the new society visible, it was also visibly growing, very quickly indeed. Coketown, as Dickens reminds us, had 'come into existence piece-meal, every piece in a violent hurry for some one man's purpose'; it was like 'an unnatural family, shouldering, and trampling, and pressing one another to death.'[9] 'Violent hurry' is not an expression which springs immediately to mind when thinking of early Georgian England: the language used by Dickens would not have been explicable to Defoe.

Why, then, did men fail to comprehend what was happening? Two main reasons can be advanced. The first is psychological. The arsenal of the human mind is, it may be argued, disagreeably defensive; it seemingly bristles with ammunition, all too readily used to repel the onrush of novel ideas and to deny the reality of momentous events. How could it be that traditional pastoral society - the only society most men either knew or could conceive of - was destined slowly to lose its dominance; and that in its place a new order of life, with its own rhythms, landscapes, and institutions, was being painfully born and was as painfully growing towards maturity. This had never happened in any human community before; why, went the refrain, should it happen, in England, now? The second reason has to do with the fact that industrialisation was, in its earliest phase, confined to localities. It was possible, as with Jane Austen, to be the daughter of a well-off Hampshire parson and to live a life that was entirely undisturbed by the shock of the new. Modernity did not, suddenly and without struggle, replace age-old patterns of human community. Even in places where the pace of industrial advance was fastest, most people continued to live in rural societies - it has been calculated that, in the West Riding of Yorkshire, in 1811, only about one quarter of the population was to be found in urban areas.[10]

The industrial revolution provides matter for intense controversy among historians: some writers stress change, others continuity. The former, typically, would locate the origins of industrialisation in a single decade, the 1780s, collecting evidence in support of this contention from the explosive growth in the cotton industry which took place then. The latter, more cautious, emphasise the economic growth achieved earlier in the century, and point out that cotton, although growing exponentially, represented only a minute fraction of gross national product.[11] It is, fortunately, unnecessary to choose between these two schools of thought. As so often in historical debates, both sides are right in what they affirm, wrong in what they deny. The cotton industry did take off in the 1780s; on the other hand, it is equally true that much of the groundwork for change was already laid. To deny the importance of the novel economic events which occurred at the tail-end of the eighteenth century is as misleading as to suggest that industrialisation was not, ultimately, a continuing and developing process, also to be found in earlier decades and, probably, the previous century.

Industrial growth was associated with, and arguably partly fuelled by, demographic growth. The nature of the causal link is uncertain: the study of population is an emerging historical discipline. As far as Georgian England is concerned fresh evidence has overturned old views, requiring, as a consequence, revisions to the perception of eighteenth-century society. It used to be thought that the population was roughly static between 1700 and 1750, started to rise in the 1750s, 1760s, and 1770s, and then accelerated sharply as from 1780. No longer is this held to be the case; historians now pencil in a figure of around five million in 1700, moving forward to close on six million by 1750, and then reaching a figure approaching nine million by the century's end.[12] Rural population grew, but urban population grew quicker. Over the course of the eighteenth century, one estimate would have it that the urban population went up by 181%, the rural population by 46%.[13] The faster urban growth is traced back, at the very least, into the later decades of the seventeenth century.[14]

Population growth in the early nineteenth century outstripped that in the eighteenth. This is clear from examination of national census returns, an exercise in statistical ingenuity that was first attempted in 1801 and was, with commendable perseverance, repeated regularly each decade thereafter. The early chroniclers of the demographic record tried hard but lacked precision: they might choose March as the due date, or they might choose June; there was under-registration of young children; and members of the armed forces, as well as of the merchant marine, were omitted. Modern historians have made strenuous efforts to make good these imperfections. According to one estimate the population of England, when appropriately adjusted, registered an increase from 8.66 million in 1801 to 15.11 million in 1841, a rise of 74% within four decades.[15] Where industrialisation went ahead rapidly, nationwide statistics sink into insignificance. Bradford, at the turn of the nineteenth century, was little more than a large market town - its inhabitants then numbered 6,393. By 1841, there were 34,560.[16] Leeds over the same period nearly trebled, from 53,000 to 152,000;[17] and the London parish of St Pancras quadrupled, from 32,000 to 128,000.[18] Such was the cataclysmic nature of the demographic revolution that overwhelmed parts of England in the early nineteenth century.

Most of the inhabitants of the new industrial towns did not show any great enthusiasm for the services of the Church of England. This, in the circumstances, was just as well; had they all decided to attend, there would have been nowhere to put them. The seriousness of the shortage in church accommodation was made clear by a set of parliamentary returns that came out in 1818. In that year, there were 1,220,000 people in the diocese of London, with church-room for only 336,500 (28%); while in Chester, which encompassed Lancashire, there were 1,250,000 to cram into places for 325,000 (26%).[19] Locally, the shortfall could be far greater - St Matthew's, Bethnal Green had 33,000 inhabitants, with room in churches for only 1,200 (4%).[20]

It is tempting, on the basis of this evidence, to conclude that urbanisation led to mass defection from religious observance. Temptation, at any rate in this instance, is to be resisted. For if there were many absentees from Anglican worship in the towns, there were also - at least in some areas - many absentees in the countryside.[21] This was a matter which Georgian bishops were understandably anxious to keep quiet about. The church, after all, claimed to be the church of the nation. Discovering that it was no such thing was unlikely to be productive of confidence. Typical of the reticence of the episcopal Bench on this topic was John Butler, Bishop of Hereford. He moved to the diocese in 1788 from Oxford, and shortly afterwards sent out some visitation queries. The results were not encouraging. Indeed, they were so discouraging that Butler decided not to publish them. The Bishop made enquiries about the number of communicants at the great festivals, comparing figures for 1789 with those at a visitation held just over forty years earlier, in 1747. All that he could bring himself to say was that 'Communicants in the year 1747 appear to have been many more, so many more, than those reported in the year 1789, that I am unwilling to recite the numbers'.[22] He was worried about the present, and he was even more worried about the future: 'if', he went on, 'we were to continue in the same declining state, which God forbid! the appearance at our Sacraments would, forty years hence, be extremely deplorable'.[23] It is tantalising that the Bishop of Hereford failed to be more specific; the deafening quality of his silence is what we have to be content with. What holds for the diocese of Hereford holds for other dioceses also; there is a paucity of statistics to do with religious observance in the Georgian countryside.[24] This renders particularly valuable a survey, published in 1800, summarising the situation in an admittedly small sample of 79 parishes, drawn from the diocese of Lincoln. Population was 15,042; adults over fourteen were reckoned at 11,282; congregations were believed to average 4,933 (33%

5

of all inhabitants); and communicants were thought to be 1,808 (16% of all adults).[25]
For an established church in a pre-industrial society these were not good figures.
Interestingly, they dovetail well with our own analysis of two deaneries in Norfolk at
the same period.[26]

Although the church was less than spectacularly successful in some parts of the
countryside, few people commented upon the fact. Problems in the towns, on the other
hand, were harder to conceal. Not only was pastoral ministry blighted by the sheer
scale of population increase, there was also a further severe difficulty to contend with.
Most ancient corporate towns - Cambridge and Bristol are good examples - were
divided into several parishes, but the same was not true of many of the new towns that
were springing up as a result of the industrial revolution. Leeds was still a single parish,
as was Bradford. If pastoral ministry was not to become hopelessly ineffective,
something had to be done. At this point, however, a further problem presented itself.
Each parish was a legal entity as well as a unit of ecclesiastical administration; parish
boundaries had been fixed by law, and it was only by law that they could be changed.
It was characteristic of the eighteenth century that such an apparently simple matter
could only be achieved through the complex procedure of a local act of Parliament.
In the eyes of many churchmen, it was legislative action which held the key to many
of the problems posed by industrialisation.

iii. *War*

Just as the new industrial society was beginning to crystallise, England became
embroiled in twenty years of warfare with France. The Revolutionary and Napoleonic
Wars were a transitional phenomenon - something of the methods of modern conflict
mixed with a little of the decorous manners characteristic of an earlier age. France
introduced - for the first time - the totalitarian idea of conscription, which has since
proved singularly unproductive of the intended quick result; while, on the other hand,
it remained part of the unwritten constitutional law of warfare that generals (being
gentlemen) were not to be shot at, a tacit agreement that Wellington and Napoleon had
a mutual self-interest in upholding. (Captains of warships were not quite gentlemen,
and did not therefore enjoy similar immunity, as Nelson found to his cost). Although
this 'genteel' style of conducting military operations lasted into the First World War
- not, of course, beyond it - it was already under pressure. The Napoleonic and
Revolutionary Wars were quite unlike eighteenth-century experience of conflict;
nothing in the War of the Spanish Succession, or of the Austrian Succession, or in the
Seven Years War was remotely comparable. The length of the war against Napoleon
is not the main point. What was happening was that modern industrial technology -
iron in place of sweat - was beginning to have military applications; the art of warfare
was being turned into a science. Guns, manufactured more rapidly, were becoming
deadlier and more costly. An income tax was first levied in England in 1797, while
wartime inflation reached levels of unprecedented seriousness.

War creates a situation of domestic scarcity which leaves farmers with little to complain about, and the hostilities with France, far from being an exception to this general rule, furnish potent evidence in support of it. The farming community was already doing well when conflict began. The Georgian enclosure movement had been set in motion, some advances had been made in agricultural techniques, and population growth had begun to increase domestic demand; but these were as nothing in comparison with the impetus that Napoleon's Continental System, aided and abetted by a series of bad harvests, was to give. Agricultural production rose, cereal prices kept ahead of the domestic inflation rate, the enclosure movement accelerated, and the total area under cultivation was rapidly expanded. The peak was reached with the abundant harvest of 1813. Quite soon afterwards, there was peace; and with peace came depression. As is usually the case when a boom breaks, the initial reaction - during 1814-16 - was the most severe; but English farmers also faced periodic difficulties throughout the next twenty years.

Good times for farmers were good times for clergy, and bad times for farmers were bad times for clergy. The explanation of this somewhat strange harnessing of fortunes is the tithe system. The beneficed clergy depended upon tithes for income, and the monetary value of tithes depended upon agricultural production, being sensitive to both price and volume. The enclosure movement therefore put more money in the pockets of the clergy, advances in agricultural techniques put more money in the pockets of the clergy, and - by way of blackened blasphemy - war put more money in the pockets of the clergy. Equally, of course, the postwar agrarian depression took some money out of the pockets of the clergy. The conclusion which needs to be drawn is both simple and fundamental: the Georgian church was profoundly affected by events in the rural economy. The interaction between agrarian change and church reform is an important part of what this book is about.

iv. *Social Unrest*
Local 'rows', as they were known, were frequent in eighteenth-century England. The tinder did not have to be material as combustible as famine; something drawn from the canon of everyday events - an unpopular decision by a local magistrate, for example - could do, on occasion, quite as well. The same continued to be true in the years after 1800; but now there was the difference that industrialisation and war had given a new dimension to traditional unrest: a dimension summed up in a single word, Luddism.[27] For those engaged in trade the most disturbed period was towards the close, and just after, the Napoleonic Wars. Between 1811 and 1817 there was a series of Luddite outbreaks. Worst affected were the Midlands, and also parts of Lancashire, Cheshire, and Yorkshire. Attacks upon machinery were prefaced by a simple yet impressive ritual, designed to brace friend and frighten foe. This ritual had four main elements - blackened face, nightly drill, a threatening letter, the muttered rumour of impending fire. Where Luddites were strongest they were boldest, smashing in broad daylight the much-hated heralds of a strange modernity. Industrial Luddism was a solemn protest against an unknown society.

'Captain Ludd' was not without his rural counterpart, the sinisterly named 'Captain Swing'. Linking them is appropriate. In each case the motives of rebellion were the same - threats to patterns of traditional livelihood and fear of mass unemployment. The object of attack was also similar in both instances. Swing, like Ludd, marshalled his forces against property rather than the person, against the artefact rather than the artist; and the chief artefact in the countryside was the threshing-machine. Since this device was in short supply in early nineteenth-century England, unrest was generally restricted to a narrow geographical compass; it also tended to be sporadic. Only twice was authority seriously worried. In the spring of 1816 there occurred the East Anglian 'bread and blood' riots, an outbreak fairly small in scale and concentrated in area, though nonetheless at times intense in ferocity.[28] Rather later, in the winter of 1830-1, broke out what has become known as the Last Labourers' Revolt, an outburst of Luddite feeling at once more widespread but less violent.[29] East Anglia was, once again, in the thick of the fray, as were many other southern, midland and western counties.

Social unrest affected the Georgian clergy in three main ways. It could happen that an incumbent became a victim. He might, for instance, receive a threatening letter, or be forced to make a 'contribution' to rioters; one of his hay-ricks could be burnt; he could be mobbed or jostled; lastly, and most rarely, he could suffer serious assault to property or person, either being beaten up or, as happened at Littleport in Cambridgeshire in 1816, seeing his parsonage wrecked in front of his eyes.[30] Secondly, and more subtly, unrest inflamed relationships - even at the best of times uneasy - over tithe. Farmers might refuse to pay at all, or plead for time, or - most ominously of all - they might combine with labourers to enforce reductions. Thirdly, disturbance highlighted, in a way that was far from comfortable, the fundamental contradiction implicit in the dual role of the clergyman as pastor and as preserver of rural order. Free, now, of the taint of Jacobitism, well advanced in social status over his predecessors, and enjoying, as against many of the gentry, a reputation for both learning and assiduous attention to duty, the late-Georgian incumbent stood a good chance of being co-opted on to the local Bench, particularly if his parish was located in an outlying district, where there was a paucity of suitably qualified squires. In 1831, one incumbent in every six was also an active magistrate.[31]

In the voluminous Radical literature of the period, the clerical magistrate is depicted as harsh and over-zealous, harsher indeed, and more zealous, than his fellow justices. The clear implication is that the clergy had, as a group, a distinctive attitude towards magisterial work: that they separated themselves - as a matter of policy - from other members of the Bench, forming a discrete body, a kind of 'moral police', characterised by a dedication beyond the call of duty in the preservation of law and order. Few things are further from the truth. The Georgian clergy were not a separate social caste; on the contrary, they were mixed and blended with the society of which they were a part. It follows that the behaviour of the clerical magistracy, far from being distinctive, reflects the behaviour of the Bench generally: there was, certainly, 'zeal' in some districts, but there was, equally, much less 'zeal' in others. This merging of the clergy within the magistracy is a social fact of some importance. It is therefore helpful at the outset of our enquiry to reveal, with the maximum degree of clarity and coherence, the falsity of the contemporary Radical view.

The easiest way of doing this is by examining events in the winter of 1830-1. Some clerical magistrates were prominent in putting down insurgence; on the other hand, others exhibited a degree of leniency verging upon the supine. Robert Wright, rector of Itchin Abbots in Hampshire, must be firmly placed in the former category. The district in which he lived was disturbed during the month of November, 1830. Throughout this period, Wright arranged for 150 tenants to bivouac, nightly, in the grounds of Avington House, the country seat of the local magnate, the Duke of Buckingham. The expenses of this exercise were met by Wright out of his own pocket.[32] His money was not wasted. When a crowd of labourers, estimated at three hundred strong and intent upon destroying the Duke's threshing machines, approached Avington House on the 24th of the month, they were met by the rector and two policemen at the head of one hundred special constables, armed with bludgeons. Between forty and fifty prisoners were taken, and the rest of the labourers were put to flight. Needless to say, so notable an example of clerical bravado made the headlines in numerous London and provincial newspapers.[33]

Another belligerent clerical JP was Edward Cove, vicar of Brimpton in Berkshire. He master-minded an extremely effective confrontation with a group of labourers on Brimpton Common, on Thursday, 18 November. The 'mob', according to Cove, advanced three abreast. Some were armed with sledge-hammers, others carried with them iron balls, typically weighing between twelve and fourteen pounds. The latter were fearsome weapons; originally part of the frames of threshing machines, they had been forcibly removed and fastened to sticks. Cove did not flinch. When the labourers approached, he met them head on, flanked by his clerical son and supported by a strong contingent of tradesmen and farmers. In the ensuing 'battle' several farmers were slightly hurt, but most of the labourers quickly fled across a ditch, leaving eleven of their number to be escorted to Reading jail.[34]

Wright and Cove, it could be argued, did no more than was their duty; but John Lafont, rector of Hinxworth in Hertfordshire, indisputably exceeded it. His own district was quiet, but there was, early in December, restiveness among the labourers of Stotfold, across the border in neighbouring Bedfordshire. Lafont went on the offensive. On the morning of Saturday, 4 December, he crossed the border; he then called upon a number of JPs, helped to gather two large groups of special constables - one numbering over a hundred and the other about seventy - and was present at the arrest of ten ringleaders. In correspondence between the Home Office and the local magistracy, Lafont was singled out for his 'excellent conduct'. The rector of Hinxworth seems, however, to have felt that his zeal deserved a somewhat larger measure of recognition: a few months later, we find him writing to Earl de Grey, lord lieutenant of Bedfordshire, that he had 'saved all this side of Herts., Beds. and

Cambs. from insurrection',[35] by any reckoning a wild and preposterous claim.

Not all clerical JPs showed the mettle of Robert Wright, Edward Cove, and John Lafont. Ageing Dr Newbolt, rector of Morestead in Hampshire, certainly did not. At lunchtime on 19 November, he received a message that a mob estimated at 1,400 was gathering at East Stratton, eleven miles or so from his home. Being, as he described himself, a 'cripple' incapable of riding - the doctor was nearly sixty - he ordered a post-chaise and met the mob at Sutton Scotney, parleying with them from his carriage. It would, perhaps, be more accurate to say that they parleyed with him. The ringleaders were peremptory, demanding wages of 12s per week for married men and 9s for unmarried. Newbolt, according to his own account, felt far from comfortable. Uttering a 'tremendous oath', one of the mob had told him, 'You shall not leave this spot till you have ordered us 9s a week'. Some of the labourers were armed with sledge-hammers, others were intoxicated, several clutched at the carriage door, a few wanted to drag him out and 'destroy' him. In the face of these threats, he had recommended farmers to pay what was demanded. Melbourne, as Home Secretary, was not impressed, informing the learned doctor in fine lapidary prose that 'conditions extorted by force upon the one hand, and acceded to by fear upon the other, are not likely to be long adhered to by those who have submitted to them, or be long satisfactory to those who have imposed them, and therefore that the tranquility which has been so purchased is likely to be of a very treacherous and uncertain character'.[36]

Dr Newbolt did not do particularly well, and the Revd Fulwar Craven Fowle - the second Christian name is, in the circumstances, peculiarly apt - did no better. Fowle was vicar of Kintbury in Berkshire. Towards the end of November, the Kintbury labourers started to roam the countryside, demanding 'subscriptions' and smashing threshing machines. This was difficult to prevent because they were better organised than rioters in other districts, being ably led by 'Captain' Winterbourne, a blacksmith. Order was eventually restored on the evening of Thursday, 24 November, but until the launching of this successful counter-attack it was Fowle's task to face the Kintbury labourers alone. The experience had not been pleasant. To Charles Dundas, MP for Berkshire, Fowle confessed three acts of leniency. He had connived at Dundas' own threshing machines being taken into the main street of Kintbury and broken up, he had paid the labourers a 'contribution' of £2, and he had promised to do 'all in his power' to persuade local farmers to raise wages to 12s a week, the amount settled on by other justices at Hungerford.[37] Other, more serious, charges were made by Frederick Page, deputy lieutenant of the county. He alleged that Fowle had been reluctant to parley until the intervention of Job Hanson, a stone mason and Wesleyan district preacher; the clerical magistrate had, 'to a certain degree', promised the labourers an indemnity; and he had 'induced' Lord Craven, a local magnate, to part with £10.[38] To these allegations, Fowle made no formal or detailed reply, being content to affirm that his advocacy of a wage rise was conditional upon a return to work.[39]

Robert Wright, Edward Cove, and John Lafont would also have found it difficult to comprehend the actions of the North Walsham Bench. On 24 November, the justices in this part of Norfolk issued a remarkable document, well worthy of quotation. They wished, in their own words, 'to make it publicly known that *it is their opinion* that ... disturbances principally arise from the use of Threshing Machines, and to the insufficient Wages of the Labourers. The Magistrates therefore beg to *recommend* to the Owners and Occupiers of Land ... to *discontinue the use of Threshing Machines, and to increase the Wages of Labour* to Ten Shillings a week for [the] able bodied'.[40] They also took a decidedly relaxed view of the threat that machine-breaking posed for maintenance of public order; it was, quoting the document once again, the magistrates' 'Full Conviction, that, *no severe measures will be necessary*'.[41] These words - a flagrant incitement to incendiarism, as some would doubtless describe them - were written by three laymen and five clergymen.[42] The North Walsham Bench, moreover, was as good as its word; just three days later, on 27 November, thirty machine breakers were discharged.[43]

The winter of 1830-1 has a further importance. The events which took place made a major contribution towards a growing sense of clerical unease and loss of confidence, thus helping to ferment the panic felt by many of the clergy during the Reform Bill crisis, which broke shortly afterwards. One rural parson spoke for many of his brethren when he told a friend, in December 1830, that 'I anticipate better times - when I may leave home with the confidence that my premises may not be burnt before I return. This is a calamity to which we are nightly subject'.[44] The experience of Fairfax Francklin, rector of Attleborough in Norfolk, was not unrepresentative. He was 'requested to attend' a vestry meeting, at which at least 300 labourers, armed with large sticks, were also present. The labourers, according to Francklin's account, were rough and threatening, and yelled 'Down with tithes'. Down is, indeed, the operative word: a reduction of 50% in the rector's exactions was demanded, but refused. Francklin was kept for four hours against his will, before being rescued, 'in an exhausted state', by friends. One of his machines, a chaff-cutter, was then broken up by the mob.[45] Incidents of this kind occurred, with varying degrees of frequency, in most disaffected areas. Usually, the main aim of those who were opposed to the clergy was to force down tithes. 'Solicited' or 'unsolicited' reductions were negotiated in many parishes throughout southern England and the midlands - there are, for example, at least fourteen instances in Kent[46] and twelve in neighbouring Sussex.[47] Clerical unpopularity, on the scale witnessed in the winter of 1830-1, was without recent precedent, and opened psychological wounds which were not easily healed.

v. *An Age of Enquiry*

With industrialisation, technology began to advance along a broad front, and among the processes which were revolutionised were paper production and printing. The first paper-making machine was introduced into England in 1803, and it brought great changes in is wake. Whereas the old hand-mills could only produce 50 or 60 lb of paper a day, the new machines could turn out up to 1,000 lb; by 1824, in consequence, the price of some kinds of paper had fallen by a quarter or even a third.[48] The major innovation in printing was invention of the power-driven press. As with paper production, work was now carried on at an altogether different pace, bringing very large economies of scale - the hand-worked press had had a maximum capacity of around 250 impressions an hour, but a power-driven one, introduced by *The Times* in 1814, could roll off 1,100 in the same time. A four-cylinder press, in operation in 1827, was even more efficient; it had a capacity of 4,000 sheets an hour, more than fifteen times as many as the old hand-driven machines had been able to produce.[49]

These advances accelerated the growth of an already well-established newspaper industry. Foreign visitors were struck by the interest in newspapers shown throughout all ranks of eighteenth-century English society. Not until 1777 was it possible for a Parisian to start each day by reading his newspaper; a Londoner began enjoying the same privilege three-quarters of a century earlier. By 1769 there were six metropolitan daily newspapers, as well as a further eight evening papers, all appearing tri-weekly; and by 1783 the number of dailies had risen to nine, with ten tri-weeklies in the evening.[50] Expansion of the metropolitan press continued - *The Times* dates from 1788, *The Observer* from 1791, and *The Sunday Times* from 1822. Outside London, daily newspapers did not manage to establish themselves, but provincial weeklies were very successful indeed. By 1832 there were 130 in all, and by 1842 there were 225. In 1837, Sheffield boasted four, Manchester had five, and Liverpool had eleven.[51]

In the spring of 1802, just a year before the introduction into England of the first paper-making machine, a young clergyman, Sydney Smith (then only thirty-one) started toying with the idea of producing a literary review. For help, he turned to three friends, all of them younger than himself, and all sharing his Whiggish turn of mind. All three were, like Sydney Smith, obscure men from obscure backgrounds. One of the three was Francis Jeffrey, married, penurious, and diminutive; another was Francis Horner, later a reputed political economist; and the third was the insatiably energetic polymath, Henry Brougham. The *Edinburgh Review*, the first publication of its kind, was launched later the same year. Only 'Young Men in a Hurry' would have ventured upon so bold a plan, using as their base the city of Edinburgh, at that time isolated from main-stream English literary society. The plan nevertheless succeeded. After only three issues, contributors to the *Review* were able to command fees of ten or twelve guineas a sheet, a rate of payment which encouraged Brougham to write a phenomenal total of eighty articles, most of them well over 25,000 words long, in the first twenty numbers.[52] The Whigs now had their 'organ', as the infelicitous contemporary phrase had it; and later - with the appearance of the *Quarterly* (1809), and then with *Blackwood's* (1817) - the Tories had theirs. It is difficult, now, to appreciate how influential these Reviews were; but any reader of Georgian political biography cannot but be struck by the seriousness with which the interminably long, and often bitingly sarcastic, unsigned articles were taken.

With the fall in the cost of paper, and with the rise in the speed of printing, it would be natural to expect a popular press to grow strongly. This was certainly a train of thought that occurred to government; through the agency of the Stamp Acts, it was official policy to prevent this unwanted development by the simple expedient of keeping the tax on newspapers at a high level. This policy worked well during the Napoleonic Wars, but then, only a month or so after Waterloo, Liverpool's Tory administration overreached itself, raising stamp duty to 4d.[53] High levels of taxation concentrate minds; in this case that of the Radical, William Cobbett, who decided in the autumn of 1816 to avoid stamp duty by publishing leading articles from his *Political Register* in the form of addresses. Cobbett's initiative was an instant success. The first issue, an *Address to Journeymen and Labourers*, sold 20,000 copies within a fortnight and 200,000 within a year; the price was only 2d each or 12s 6d a hundred.[54] Soon other popular publications, also in pamphlet form and also therefore avoiding duty, appeared on the streets. Two of the notorious Six Acts of December 1819 sealed up the loophole[55]; only three of the unstamped, one of them Cobbett's *Register*, survived, and the cost of survival was, in each case, a doubling in price. Radicalism was now on the decline. Editors were arrested, sales fell away, and by December 1826 the death-knell of the legal unstamped was sounded.[56]

The popular press was not suppressed for long. A seismic shift in the structure of political power in England now occurred: the Test and Corporation Acts were repealed in 1828; Roman Catholic emancipation followed a year later; the Last Labourers' Revolt began in the autumn of 1830; and, in March 1831, the Reform Bill passed its second reading in the House of Commons by one vote only to be defeated in committee.[57] There was a dissolution of Parliament, and at the ensuing general election the Whigs were returned to power after fifty years of almost continuous Tory rule. It was now the 'Age of Reform'. The popular press took full advantage of the new situation. No longer was it on the defensive, seeking to remain within the perimeter of the law by exploiting legislative imprecision; it was now on the attack, openly flouting the law by appearing as both illegal and unstamped. Advertising improved, and novel methods of distribution were thought out. One Radical, Richard Carlile, had an address printed on cotton handkerchiefs.[58] Several hundred unstamped and illegal publications were floated between 1830 and 1836, of which seventy-odd were Radical.[59] Stamp duty was then reduced from 4d to 1d, and the unstamped press soon disappeared.

The years after 1800 were also an age of information. The first census was completed in 1801, and parliamentary papers were first put on sale in 1835. It was, moreover, in the 1830s that a number of agencies and societies, all of them destined to become influential, were founded - the statistical department of the Board of Trade in 1832, the Royal Statistical Society the next year, and the department of the Registrar General in 1838. Select committees of both Houses of Parliament examined hundreds of witnesses, asked thousands of questions, and printed their findings in thick volumes. What, they asked, was the state of agriculture in Cornwall and Kent? What were conditions like in the factories of Rochdale? Why was the policing of the metropolis ineffective? Were many labourers unemployed in Wiltshire? Was there an agrarian depression in Devon? Bolstering this inquisitiveness was a seemingly boundless confidence in the power of human reason: knowledge, it was thought, would inevitably bring improvement in its train. Thus it was that 'diffusion of knowledge' became a catch-phrase. Societies, political parties, philanthropic bodies and religious pressure groups, all used similar tactics. 'Information, then agitation', was their watchword and their plea. This was the method adopted by Benthamites in their attempts to change society, and it was also the method adopted by Evangelicals in their crusade against slavery and the slave trade. Much early nineteenth-century statistical material was partial and piecemeal, and a good deal of it lacked a solid theoretical base, but these limitations must not be allowed to obscure the fact that a decisive change in attitude towards society and its problems was taking place. This new attitude was to produce abuses - the outlook typified by Mr Gradgrind is a prime example - but it also brought immeasurable benefits: greater concern over problems of sanitation; a quicker response by government to discovered social ills; factory legislation; street lighting; and a host of other blessings.

There were clergy, crusted with old ways, who rued the day the power-driven press had been invented. To those who thought in this way, the numerous publications which issued from the presses of early nineteenth-century England were an unmitigated evil. Everything, it seemed, was now open to inspection; and, upon inspection, was found wanting. Ecclesiastical diehards certainly had a lot to complain about. Upon opening their newspapers, they discovered a volume, and a range, of censure which induced severe alarm and acute despondency. The bishops and beneficed clergy were accused by the press of pastoral slackness and flagrant neglect of duty. They were held to be arrogant and ostentatious. Their sporting amusements, worldliness, and political involvement, were held up to ridicule. Instances of nepotism were eagerly seized upon. It was also widely asserted that they were inordinately wealthy, and that the building of their castles of comfort was being undertaken, at least in part, by their own employees among the race of curates.

The sharpest spears were thrown by the unstamped. The Radical press of 1816-19 was caustic and ironic, eagerly devouring dainty morsels of scandal. A coroner's inquest had shown that a seventy-three-year-old clergyman had died of an apoplectic fit in a brothel in the neighbourhood of Oxford Street; 'a few years back', when another brothel in Chandos Street was gutted, a parson had been burnt to death.[60] The anti-clericalism of the early 1830s was less restrained in its tone and less precise in its detail, broadening out into a generalised attack upon 'priestcraft' and 'corruption'. Of the seventy-odd Radical publications of these years, two were wholly devoted to anti-clerical propaganda; one of these was the *Episcopal Gazette*, and the other was *Slap at the Church*, which soon changed its title to the *Church Examiner*. To describe much of this anti-clerical literature as vitriolic is not an overstatement. 'That huge, hideous, and lubberly leviathan, the *law-church*, is almost at its last gasp', gasped the *Church Examiner*; 'the events of the last few years have armed a million hands against its foetid existence'.[61]

There were clergy who lamented the invention of the power-driven press, and there were also clergy, often enough directly threatened themselves, who lamented the contemporary thirst for statistical enquiry. But like Mrs Partington with her broom, they were helpless to resist the incoming tide. If it was necessary to investigate rotten boroughs, bastardy, the wages of Wiltshire labourers or the conditions in Rochdale's factories, it was also necessary, as was rightly felt, to investigate the church. There was, needless to say, much to find out. How many incumbents held two livings, and how many had three? What was the level of the clergy's pay? Were most parsonages adequate? Did incumbents pay their curates enough? Was clerical non-residence a widespread problem? It is questions such as these that gave constant exercise to the mind of every conscientious late-Georgian bishop.

The Radicals, unsurprisingly, had their own version of statistical enquiry, published in 1820 as the *Black Book*; it contained lists of incumbents who were pluralists and non-resident. A *Supplement to the Black Book* appeared in 1823, and the *Extraordinary Black Book* came out in 1831. Information was also gathered at an official level. There are statistics on the residence of the clergy from 1805 onwards (the earliest returns are extremely crude and incomplete, but as from 1809 they are more helpful); figures on salaries paid by incumbents to their curates begin in 1810; the state of parsonages was surveyed in 1818; the amount of church accommodation available in towns was made known the same year. It was recognised, however, that all this material, while useful and informative, was not sufficiently comprehensive. Grey, as Whig prime minister, set about remedying the situation. In 1832, he appointed a body which has become known as the Ecclesiastical Revenues Commission, but whose full title, explanatory of its purpose, was the Commission of Inquiry into the Ecclesiastical Revenues of England and Wales.[62] The twenty-four commissioners worked for three years, and then produced a voluminous report over 1,000 pages long, stating the value of every bishopric, cathedral post and living throughout the land. The report also contained a mass of supplementary information, in fascinating detail. This was the first comprehensive ecclesiastical survey since Henry VIII's *Valor Ecclesiasticus* three centuries earlier. The findings of Grey's Commission of Inquiry form the bed-rock of this book.

vi. *The Church of the Nation?*

The church, according to classic eighteenth-century theory, was a pillar of the constitution; and as such it was part and parcel of the system of law,[63] as well as being the partner - some said ally - of the state. Well protected by the great and powerful, the church was held in its accustomed social place by a complex legal apparatus. Part of this apparatus was financial - payment of church rate (for the upkeep of the fabric of the parish church) by every householder, irrespective of his religious affiliation; part was sacramental - baptism and marriage, if desired by any member of the population, only in Anglican churches, burial in the parish churchyard only by Anglican clergy using an Anglican Order of Service; and part was educational - exclusion of Dissenters and Roman Catholics from degrees at Cambridge, and from even matriculating at

Oxford. In practical terms, it was this legal apparatus which sustained many of the major privileges enjoyed by the Anglican church as an establishment.

Part of the inheritance of the Henrican Reformation was the authority of Parliament in church affairs. Parliament had the power to fix Orders of Service, regulate clerical residence, change the laws governing pluralism, create new bishoprics, reduce, if it thought fit, the number of cathedral posts, and even to alter the system of clerical discipline. It looks, on the face of it, as though the Georgian church suffered the thraldom of a thoroughgoing Erastianism. This, however, was not the case. The true position has been accurately stated by Edward Norman. 'It is', he says, 'important to notice that it was the interdependence of Church and State, and not the dependence of the Church upon the State, that formed the basis of the eighteenth-century view'.[64] It did indeed, as was amply shown by the reaction in England to events in France during the 1790s. The 'alliance' between the English church and the English state ceased to be a hypothesis and became a reality.[65] As the French Revolution unfolded, it seemed to those on this side of the channel that a religious establishment was politically essential. Without the moral basis that only such an establishment could provide, the centre would not hold and everything would split apart. Crown and church would fall together, and the tremors caused by their mutual collapse would turn to dust and rubble the edifice of a civilised life, too. As one contemporary put it: 'We, who live in the present age, have had the most awful and instructive lessons presented to our experience, written in blood and heightened by every human misery. We have seen that Law, Science, and Civilization, - Liberty, Wealth, and Order, may all sink under the want of Religious and Moral Principle'.[66] Elevation of the role of religion involved elevation of the role of the clergy. This, at any rate, was the conclusion reached effortlessly - perhaps, rather too effortlessly - by one contemporary clerical pamphleteer. 'A harmonious society', he wrote, 'has been powerfully compared to a bundle of sticks, the united strength of which, defies any effort to break them. May I not liken the Clergy to the ligament which keeps the whole bundle together?'[67]

Although the political importance of the established church was widely recognised, relations with the state were not without tension. The difficulty was that parliament's powers, already extensive, also covered two as yet uncharted territories. It could if it chose make grants for the relief of clerical poverty, and it could try to do something about the failure of the church building programme to keep pace with the increase in population. Here were two cruxes of the alliance between church and state; and here, too, were inherent weaknesses which threatened to precipitate its breakdown. Any parliamentary grant, either to augment clerical stipends or to quicken the pace of church building, raised awkward doubts about the limits of state obligation. These, to opponents of establishment, seemed potentially limitless. Where, they wondered, would state help end? How much exactly would, or could, be given?, both pertinent questions to which the classic theory of establishment made no answer. It was also important that parliamentary support for the church should be well timed. It would have been best if help had been given while opposition to the alliance was still weak, but this did not happen: apart from founding Queen Anne's Bounty in 1704, parliament gave the church no direct financial assistance throughout the eighteenth century. Then, in the space of only fifteen years, a hurried effort was made to atone for past sins of omission. First of all, in 1809, a grant of £100,000 was made to the Bounty to help it in its campaign to raise the values of poor livings. This was arguably indiscreet, but then parliament proceeded to compound its indiscretion, renewing the £100,000 grant every year until 1820, except in 1817. The total sum given to the Bounty in this way was £1,100,000. Lack of sufficient church accommodation in towns was dealt with more expeditiously: a lump sum of £1,000,000 in 1818 was followed by another lump sum of £500,000 in 1824. Between 1809 and 1824, assistance given to the church amounted to £2,600,000. Never had the church received direct financial support on such a scale; nor was it again to receive such support, on the same generous terms, on any scale at all. Only in the field of education has the church received parliamentary grants since the 1820s, and these, without exception, have always been shared either with Dissenters or with Roman Catholics. The church building grant of 1824 marks the end of an epoch.

Parliament's tardy generosity towards the church was open to the criticism that it weakened the church's position, by presenting opponents of the religious establishment with a much-needed stock of live intellectual ammunition. It did this, moreover, at a time when most religious groups outside the Anglican communion were gaining greatly in numerical support, and thus in confidence. The reasons behind expansion of non-Anglican forms of faith were varied but, from the church's point of view, the effects were remarkably similar: a decline in allegiance pledged to the national church, with a consequent diminution in its power and influence.

As far as English Roman Catholicism is concerned, the main impetus to growth was political: the transformation wrought by the influx into England of successive waves of Irish immigrants following the Act of Union. In the eighteenth century, Roman Catholic faith was largely a family matter, centred around the households of scattered gentry. The religious practice of these households was unobtrusive; Mass and baptism were private, a priest was kept as a domestic chaplain, and often enough the outward garb of conformity to the dominant Anglicanism, satisfied by regular attendance at the parish church, was worn as well. Eighteenth-century Roman Catholicism was rural and regional, strong in the north of England (apart from Cumbria and the West Riding), in Worcestershire and Warwickshire, East Hampshire and Sussex, and parts of Monmouthshire, but weak elsewhere. The situation after 1800 was different. Middle class support did begin to form, but the main source of expansion came from the allegiance of numerous Irish immigrants, predominantly labourers, who came to England after the Act of Union. Their religious practice was poles apart from the aristocratic Roman Catholicism of the previous century, public rather than private, self-assertive rather than tactful, and urban rather than rural. Although the exodus after the famine of 1845 greatly strengthened this new form of Roman Catholic faith, it was already gaining ground in the earlier decades of the nineteenth century.[68]

17

English nonconformity, meanwhile, was being transformed by the Methodist revival. From an old trunk, vigorous new branches were putting on substantial growth. The largest denomination among the Methodists was the Wesleyans. Their expansion, in the early nineteenth century, was spectacular: figures of absolute membership soared, and membership relative to population also soared. The statistics make, indeed, impressive reading. In 1801, adult Wesleyan membership amounted to 87,010, equivalent to 1.6% of the adult population; and in 1841 membership was 305,682, or 4.5% of adult population.[69] The relative strength of Methodism within English society was now greater than at any time either before or since.[70] The Primitive Methodists also did exceptionally well. Not formed as a separate denomination until 1811, they managed to increase membership from 16,394 in 1821 to 75,967 in 1841.[71]

Methodism breathed life into the bones of English Dissent. Not only did the Wesleyans and Primitive Methodists do well, but other denominations which were outside - although influenced by - the Methodist revival were also invigorated. The Congregationalists, for instance, claimed a membership of 35,000 in 1800; by 1838 this had surged to 127,000, over three and a half times as many. Remarkably similar was the achievement of the Particular Baptists: a membership of 24,000 in 1800 was turned into one of 86,000 in 1838, a rise this time of 250%.[72] It would, indeed, be true to say that virtually all the denominations of English Dissent were going from strength to strength in the late-Georgian period; virtually all, but not all. Two important exceptions are to be made. Numerical support for the Quakers had declined during the eighteenth century, and the fall continued until the middle of the nineteenth. In 1680 membership had been just under 40,000; in 1800 it was down to under 20,000; in 1840 it was less than 16,000; and in 1860 the figure levelled out, at just over 13,000.[73] Secondly, English Presbyterianism was falling apart, with many congregations becoming either Unitarian or Independent. This was a sad blow for Presbyterianism, but was not significant in the context of nonconformity as a whole.[74]

In some places, growth of Dissent revolutionised traditional religious geography. Of nowhere, probably, was this more true than of Wales. Another historian, describing the situation there in the early years of the nineteenth century, has asserted that Dissent was then able to claim the allegiance of only a 'very small minority' of the Welsh people. He then extends his analysis, by examining in detail the data to be found in the religious census of 1851, concentrating attention upon the three westerly shires of Carmarthenshire, Pembrokeshire, and Cardiganshire. On census Sunday, 30 March 1851, no more than 21% of worshippers in the three shires attended the services of the Church of England; the remainder went elsewhere. Elsewhere, in this context, largely means nonconformist places of worship. By 1851, West Wales had been won over from church to chapel, especially to Baptist sects and the different brands of Methodism.[75]

England was becoming a religiously pluralistic society. The virtual hegemony enjoyed by the Anglican establishment over many areas of eighteenth-century English life was now almost a thing of the past, a distant memory, and a more religiously varied, but also fragmented, society was emerging. Of the reality of this kind of society there came, gradually, to be little room for doubt, and its existence was tacitly admitted when, in 1828, Parliament repealed the Test and Corporation Acts. Before this, Dissenters could only sit in Parliament and in city corporations by favour of the annual Indemnity Act; now they could sit there as of right. Within a year, with the passing of a further Emancipation Act, political rights were extended to Roman Catholics. Although Jews still remained outside active political life, a wide breach had been made in the walls of establishment.

Antagonism between churchmen and nonconformists was not alleviated by repeal of the Test and Corporation Acts; indeed, the opposite is true. Christians outside the Anglican church remained half liberated; they were still confronted by the ever-present reality of the legal apparatus of the establishment - exclusion from taking degrees at Cambridge, and from matriculating at Oxford, payment of church rate, baptism and marriage customarily in Anglican parish churches, and burial in the parish churchyard using only an Anglican Order of Service. The result of partial liberation was predictable. In towns up and down the country - in, for instance, Manchester, Birmingham, Leeds, and the more radical districts of London - dissenting agitation, principally against church rate, became in the early and mid 1830s a marked, and also bitter, feature of local political life; but despite much nonconformist effort, the legal apparatus of establishment remained substantially intact.

Nonconformist opposition to payment of church rate was part of a broad-fronted attack mounted against the 'alliance' of church and state during the early 1830s. Tension and animosity were at their most severe during the Reform Bill crisis. On 8 October 1831, the second version of the bill was thrown out by the House of Lords, by a majority of forty-one. Only two Bishops - Maltby of Chichester, appointed by Grey in some haste a short time before, and Bathurst of Norwich - voted for reform, with twenty-one voting against, and a further six episcopal abstentions.[76] 'The Bishops have done it', exclaimed a prominent Radical, 'it is the work of the Holy Ghost'.[77] For a time it was not pleasant to be a bishop. Gray's palace at Bristol was burnt down;[78] the Archbishop of Dublin, whilst passing through Birmingham, found his coach surrounded outside a hotel by 'a dense mass of squalid and lowering faces;'[79] and Edward Copleston of Llandaff had a round hat and a brown great coat in readiness for a quick escape if informed of an impending attack on his residence.[80] Strong anti-episcopal feeling persisted into 1832; in August of that year various missiles, including brickbats and cabbage stalks, were hurled at the coach of the Archbishop of Canterbury.[81]

There were no recent precedents for such behaviour towards bishops. Coming as it did on top of so much else - repeal of the Test and Corporation Acts, the Last Labourers' Revolt, renewed activity of the popular press, the return of the Whigs to power - leading churchmen began to panic. The days of the Establishment were 'numbered';[82] it was 'impossible that the Church (in so far as it is of human institution)' could 'go on as it is';[83] 'no human means' were 'likely to avert' its overthrow;[84] 'no human power' could 'preserve it'.[85] Language such as this was not calculated to sustain calm in rectory drawing-rooms; bishops were striking apocalyptic notes, sounding the trumpet of doom. It was a far cry from the self-confidence of the eighteenth century, when the church had been sure of its position as a 'pillar of the constitution', the necessary support of all rationality, harmony and order. Many bishops, as they surveyed the political scene in 1832, feared that the church's ally of only a few years ago - an ally who had, after all, recently come to the church's aid with grants of £2,600,000 - was in the process of breaking the alliance, turning instead with relish to a new role as the Arch-fiend, the Great Despoiler. Although episcopal fears were grossly exaggerated, it was certainly true that the parchment on which was written the old treaty between church and state, on the old terms, now had a deathly pallor, and it would take little to turn its fragile membranes into that dust, and those ashes, which are the common end - as well as the common destiny - of all things of purely human enactment.

vii. *Church Parties*

If the church was being threatened from without, it was also being renewed from within. As from about 1780 the Board of Queen Anne's Bounty, quiescent and inert since the 1730s, began stirring itself. At first, renaissance took the ambiguous form of proposals for action rather than action itself: it was not until the new century that any major initiatives were put into effect. Once the governors were firmly set upon a path of reform, however, they did not look back. From its inception, the main function of the Bounty had been relief of clerical poverty. Procedures for achieving this were now streamlined, and a special effort was made to raise the values of those livings that were poverty-stricken; more importantly, the eleven parliamentary grants, made in the years 1809-20, were, as already noted, entrusted to the Bounty's care. The governors, when administering these, opted to set up a new fund - the Parliamentary Grants Fund - alongside the older Royal Bounty Fund. For this new fund, moreover, it was decided to have new rules, the main hall-marks of which were flexibility and effectiveness. With formation of the Parliamentary Grants Fund, confidence was regained; the Board began to expand the sphere of its operations, most notably by becoming heavily involved in plans to increase provision of parsonages.

The 1780s were also an important gestation period for the as yet embryonic Evangelical movement, which was destined in the next century to contend with its main adversary, the Oxford movement, for the leading place among church 'parties'. Evangelicalism crystallised and clarified around a small group of like-minded friends; it drew its strength from theological conviction, explored novel methods of enlisting popular support, and was inspired by deep dissatisfaction with the ecclesiastical *status quo*. The church, Evangelicals argued, had severed itself from its roots in the theology of the Reformers, and was desperately in need of spiritual renewal. The existing ecclesiastical structure, furthermore, was unsuited to the society that was emerging. There must be new standards of clerical duty, new theological imperatives, and new methods of spreading the Gospel: new men, new thinking, and new life.

When William Wilberforce became an Evangelical in 1785, he joined a tiny minority within the church. The active core of the group - clergymen and laymen, men and women - probably did not number a hundred. The leaders were a few men of influence - Sir Richard Hill, an MP with a country seat in Shropshire, the well-known London merchant, John Thornton - and about forty or fifty clergy. Only two of these held London livings, with the rest scattered about in obscure rural parishes.[86] Wilberforce, one of Pitt the Younger's closest friends, increased Evangelical influence and gave much-needed leadership. His *Practical View*, published in 1797, was widely read and respected. Wilberforce made Evangelicalism vigorous, and gave it a sense of direction. One of the key tokens of 'real' faith as opposed to merely 'nominal', Wilberforce argued, was its visibility, its conspicuousness in action. The Scriptural man not only had to be 'serious' and 'earnest', he had to be seen to be both of these. Such a view required self-confidence, and at the same time developed it. The early Evangelicals were nothing if not prominent. From Clapham, the campaign against the slave trade, and later against the institution of slavery itself, was orchestrated - the monster public meetings, the parliamentary petitions, the voluminous literature, the popular appeals. The Evangelically-inspired Proclamation Society entered the arena of political debate, initiating prosecutions against publishers and booksellers who printed, or sold, the works of Tom Paine; cheap tracts and pamphlets flowed from the pen of Hannah More; the Church Missionary Society was set up. Evangelical laity active among the urban masses judged their own effectiveness by the number of free Bibles distributed, of visits made, and of souls saved.

The early Evangelicals encountered a great deal of instinctive hostility, particularly from many of the clergy. Opposition was strongest in the period between the fall of the Bastille and the close of the Napoleonic Wars. Evangelicals were accused of everything distasteful to a cultured mind: they acted with overmuch zeal, summed up in the single comprehensive term 'enthusiasm'; they were ill-bred; they held to a fanatical Calvinist theology; they fraternised with publicans and sinners, otherwise known as Jacobins and Dissenters. But opposition did not prevent Evangelicalism from spreading. It was a conscious decision of Evangelical policy to concentrate upon developing support in localised areas. One such locality was Cambridge. In the 1770s, of the twelve pulpits in the town, only one was occupied by an Evangelical - capacious Samuel Ogden, incumbent of the Round Church - but by 1836, the year of the death of their acknowledged Cambridge leader, Charles Simeon, six were at their disposal, while a seventh, Great St Mary's, was shared between an 'orthodox' vicar and an Evangelical curate.[87] The power and influence of the movement, as measured by representation on the episcopal Bench, also grew. In 1800 an Evangelical bishop was not even a remote possibility; but by the late 1820s there were three - Henry Ryder, brother of Dudley, first Earl of Harrowby, elevated to Gloucester in 1815; J.B. Sumner of Chester (1828), destined to become the first Evangelical Archbishop of Canterbury; and Sumner's brother, Charles Richard, raised to Llandaff a little earlier, in 1826.

Early Evangelicalism was a predominantly urban movement; its centres were places like Clapham, Cambridge, Cheltenham and Hull.[88] Leaders in less well known strongholds also concentrated their efforts upon urban mission. Mention can be made of Daniel Wilson, later Bishop of Calcutta, who was at St Mary's, Islington, from 1824;[89] of Hugh Stowell, Manxman and ultra-Protestant, in charge of Christ Church, Salford, as from 1831;[90] and of W.W. Champneys, builder of new churches and ragged schools, founder of an East End shoeblack brigade, and originator of the Church of England Young Men's Society, chosen as rector of St Mary's, Whitechapel in 1837. There was a scattering of Evangelical country clergy by the 1820s and 1830s - one thinks, for instance, of William Sharpe, vicar of Cromer in Norfolk, whose curate, William Andrew, is the subject of Owen Chadwick's delightful *Victorian Miniature*; but, despite the occasional rural beacon, most Evangelical light shone out from the dense mass of the towns.

The high church counterpart of the Clapham Sect was a group of clergy and laity known as the Hackney Phalanx, active from roughly the turn of the nineteenth century onwards.[91] Although relatively small in size, the Phalanx was ably led by Joshua Watson, a wine merchant and government contractor turned philanthropist. Several of the Phalanx's members were related to Watson by ties of either blood or friendship. There was Joshua's brother, John James, rector of Hackney; and there was, also, Thomas Sikes of Guilsborough, a brother-in-law. One of Joshua's closest friends was William Wordsworth's clerical brother, Christopher;[92] another was William Van Mildert, later Bishop of Durham;[93] and thus the list goes on. As with the Clapham Sect, many of the members of the Hackney Phalanx were from well-to-do middle class families with business interests. A further similarity is that the Phalanx strongly believed in the importance of efficient organisation. It was Joshua Watson who perfected the 'Park Street technique', gathering friends at his London home to form a pressure group. As with the Clapham Sect, the Phalanx exercised an influence out of all proportion to its size. It benefited from the active encouragement of Charles Manners-Sutton, Archbishop of Canterbury from 1805 until 1828; it had, as was only natural, its own 'organ', the *British Critic*;[94] it managed to attract *literati* of the stature of Wordsworth and Southey; and it could rely on the instinctive support - although not, admittedly, the active interest - of many clergy. Direct influence upon pastoral ministry was slight, but the Phalanx did help to formulate church policy, especially towards education and church building.

Joshua Watson's circle of 'sound and sensible' men found little favour with a group of bold and brave young spirits, coming to maturity at Oxford in the late 1820s and early 1830s. Newman and his friends had little patience with the work of committees; they thought Watson weak and ineffectual, and had no intention of modifying their views in order to avoid offending Protestant sensibilities. The decision, in 1833, to begin publishing the notorious *Tracts for the Times* was a victory for donnish tactics; Watson, typically, wanted the *Tracts* to be edited, a wise foresight, but he was overruled. Following publication of the *Tracts*, the group gathered around

Newman became known as Tractarians, an apt description. In the 1830s, the version of Anglicanism emerging at Oxford was a movement of mind, centred upon Newman, his teaching and his personality. It is a pardonable exaggeration to claim that the number of beneficed clergy advocating Tractarian principles at this period could be counted on the fingers of a single hand. John Keble at Hursley in Hampshire springs immediately to mind, as does W.F. Hook at Leeds;[95] but extending the list soon becomes difficult. The Oxford movement did not greatly influence church life in the years before 1840.

Differences, alike in theology and in pastoral practice, divided early Evangelicals from members of the Hackney Phalanx; and the latter, for their part, did not always see eye to eye with Tractarians. There were, nonetheless, wide areas of agreement between the three groups. They shared one vital thing in common: a vision of spiritual renewal. Clerical reform, and church reform, was their watchword and their prayer. There was, in each case, a determination to increase the clergy's pastoral effectiveness, to improve standards of preaching, and to strengthen clerical discipline. A concerted attack was mounted against the old ideal of the 'squarson', of the clergyman who combined within himself the duties of local parson and local squire. In place of this, a more functionally distinctive (and also more socially self-conscious) conception of the clergyman's role was popularised and propagated. The jostle of the hunt, the suspense of the card-table, the merriness of the port decanter, were all to be eschewed. Evangelicals demanded 'seriousness'; orthodox high churchmen aimed to increase the clergy's 'influence'; Newman spoke of 'magnifying' the clerical office;[96] but whatever the emphasis, the effect was the same. The clergy were bidden to become more 'spiritual', to forsake worldly amusement - and worldly duty - for the professedly harsher demands of prayer-desk and pulpit, of daily parish round and evening cottage meeting. Such was the significance for pastoral ministry of early Evangelicalism, of the work of the Hackney Phalanx, and of the genesis of the Oxford movement.[97]

viii. *Pamphlets on Church reform*
After 1800, the more conscientious kind of churchman began to have a new worry on his mind: the 'state of the church'. This, indeed, was the title of a long pamphlet that came out in 1809, with a second, even longer, edition the next year. All was not well. It was becoming increasingly evident that something had to be done about a number of matters - the prevalence of sinecure posts in cathedrals, the lack of church accommodation in towns, the stark contrast between the pay of incumbents and that of their employees, the curates, the widespread non-residence and pluralism among the clergy, the dilapidated condition of numerous parsonages, and so on. It had not occurred to most eighteenth-century parsons to think or write about such things, but from the first decade of the nineteenth century interest was awakened. One of the first influential pamphlets has already been mentioned. A little later, in 1815, Richard Yates, chaplain of Chelsea Hospital, brought out a work with the provocative title, *The Church in Danger. The Basis of National Welfare*, again from Yates's pen, followed

in 1817. The next year, the Chancellor of the Exchequer referred to the 'very useful publications of Mr Yates' in a speech introducing the Church Building Bill.[98] Church reform was a subject which could now be discussed in public.

Before 1820, few churchmen put pen to paper. The first spate of pamphlets on church reform dates from 1822 and 1823: a series of clerical responses, in differing tones, to an aggressive article in the *Edinburgh Review* for November, 1822.[99] The sparks which set fire to the tinder were, on this occasion, political: Peterloo and the trial of Queen Caroline. Later, the vivid incandescence of the Reform Bill gave an urgent glow to the dormant ashes of a more widespread clerical eloquence. Writing of the events of 1832 and 1833, one cleric later recalled how every vicarage dining-table had been, as he put it, 'covered with pamphlets, many of bulky dimensions'.[100] Excluding charges and sermons, we have come across fifty-one contributions to the church reform debate of these two years. This was the high water-mark; between 1834 and 1836, as far as we can judge, only eleven pamphlets on church reform were published. Discussion centred around the proposals put forward by two reformers - Lord Henley, an Evangelical layman, with his *Plan of Church Reform*, and Thomas Arnold's much more controversial *Principles of Church Reform*. Dissenters largely stood aside from the fray, although one of their number, R.M. Beverley, was among the most prolific authors on topics of church reform in the period.[101] Some Evangelical clergy seceded, and then gave their reasons; but the great majority of pamphlets were written by those, usually incumbents, who stayed within the church.

The heat of debate generated many ideas, some quaint, some novel, and most long-forgotten. A few notions, if adopted, would have radically changed the church for the better. Into this category comes the suggestion that preferment should not be permitted until clergy had been in Orders for some years, an innovation which would have stifled some of the worst excesses of private patronage.[102] Equally sensible, as well as far-reaching in its potential effects, was the proposal of a graduated tax on livings, in order to even out disparities in clerical income.[103] Alternatively, a plan was put forward for the Treasury to make loans to poor livings in private hands.[104] Cathedrals, with their handsome revenues and equally handsome sinecures, attracted a great deal of attention; two of the most popular proposals were to turn them into either parish churches or diocesan theological colleges.[105] One of the quaintest suggestions was that clerical discipline should be strengthened by the introduction of an ecclesiastical equivalent to the Court Martial.[106]

Some pamphleteers, the so-called 'ultras', rejected change in any shape or form. They were particularly severe on any version of what they termed the 'levelling' principle; needless to say, schemes to tax wealthy livings came within this category, as did proposals to reduce pluralism. The arguments marshalled by one anonymous author offer, in their variety and scope, illuminating access to the inner workings of the 'ultra' clerical mind. His first foray was pedestrian enough - it would be 'impolitic' to equalise clerical incomes, because so revolutionary a change would lower the standard of clerical learning and decrease the clergy's 'moral influence', an argument found in pamphlet after pamphlet.[107] He then became more original and imaginative. If, he mused, the clergy were still supported by that 'awfully eloquent power', the ability to work miracles, they could safely throw away the crutch of 'earthly station'; but since the 'awfully eloquent power' was no longer theirs the use of more mundane supports was vital and necessary. No one, he affirmed, was prepared to listen to a 'hedge preacher' or a 'strolling expounder of the Holy Volume', no matter how inspired his speech might be.[108] The clergy, he went on, ought to be 'courteous, considerate, affable and well mannered'; they ought, in a word, to be 'gentlemen'; and this simply would not be possible if their stipends were reduced to £200 or £250 a year.[109] 'In ninety-nine cases out of a hundred' it was the parents who chose 'the Church' as a suitable profession for their sons, and the nobility would rightly want a reasonable provision to be made for their children.[110] To lower clerical incomes would be to lower clerical 'respectability'.[111] Besides, if 'prizes' were abolished, there would be a most unfortunate increase in clergy who felt 'called' to the ministry, and thus in clerical 'ignorance, fanaticism, and cunning': all of it a code for Evangelicalism.[112]

He also used *ad hominem* arguments. What should concern the public is '*the result*', the '*practical effects*', of clerical endeavours, not the motives which individuals might, or might not, have for their actions; for these are known to God alone, and 'will be revealed to another tribunal than that of man's partial judgment'.[113] The clergy, he felt, would lapse into a 'dull routine', a 'mechanical performance of duty', if their incomes were low and static;[114] the principle of utility, he was arguing, implied maintenance of the inherited system. In any case, those who stood to gain most from operation of the levelling principle - namely, the poor country clergy - did not complain about their lot; they were content to do their duty conscientiously, knowing that 'the few must often suffer for the advantage of the many', and hoping that their 'zeal' would 'deserve the attention' of those in ecclesiastical authority.[115] He really could not understand what all the fuss was about. Even under the unreformed system a clergyman had few opportunities of 'creating a fortune' for himself; and it was perfectly natural that a bishop should wish to provide for his family, since it was his solemn duty to save them from being 'beggared' after his death.[116] The final point left polemical opponents fumbling for a reply: poverty was depressing, and the clergyman, as an exemplar of morals, needed a home 'so replete with domestic bliss and attractive comfort' that he 'should never be induced to desire, even in thought, to wander from it'.[117]

What is particularly important about this body of pamphlet literature is the way in which it marks a critical change in tone. Clergy, whether conservatives or reformers, lacked the confidence of their predecessors. The episcopal panic at the time of the Reform Bill had spread; there was a sense of being stunned and shaken, as after a sudden shock. Loss of popular support could not be concealed. 'Men', wrote one pamphleteer, 'seem to have awakened as out of a trance'.[118] There are, in the literature, recurrent descriptions of the age as 'violent', 'inquisitive', 'wild' and 'restless'. Images of conflict dominate: 'the almost ungovernable tide of a misguided and infuriate people's rage swells around our *beautiful temple*';[119] the Church of England, that 'venerable edifice of Christianity', is 'threatened with temporal ruin';[120] 'the Gaul is at our gates'.[121] Although a certain rough-hewn defiance was not lacking - 'I gaze from the battlements of the Church, upon the enemies who are leagued against her. I behold what our fathers beheld, and overcame - for the battle was the Lord's'[122] - it was not a posture which was easy to sustain for long. A lot of bishops felt harassed and threatened in 1832 and 1833, as did a good many of the clergy.

ix. *Reaction versus Reform*

The Georgian church was torn by contradictory forces, tugging this way and that. There was, on the one side, an innate conservatism, which had been nourished and ripened by a certain kind of ageless immobility within the church. Of nothing was this truer than of the ecclesiastical structure: its foundations had been completed in the medieval period, and men had then forgotten to put up the walls. In place of a strong church there was a strong laity. By gift, or by purchase, the nobles and squires of England had gradually encroached upon the church's patrimony; they had the land, and they had the patronage. Attempts to put the clock back, first by Laud and then by Cromwell, came to nothing. The victory of the laity was also the victory of parliament; and parliament, on thorny issues, generally sided with the army of reaction against the army of reform. There is also the further fact that the clergy's conservatism was in part the result of clerical participation in the burgeoning wealth of the countryside. As the 'agrarian revolution' got under way, tithe-incomes rose steadily; and then, during the Napoleonic boom, rectors and vicars up and down the country had the satisfaction of watching the values of their benefices soar to heights which would have made their predecessors blink in disbelief. A man with much to lose is not, normally, a man addicted to reform. Yet it was reform which became, from the 1780s onwards, increasingly difficult to resist. Industrialisation and urbanisation went forward remorselessly, and made the task of providing adequate church accommodation in towns more difficult by the year. Rural Luddism created problems for clergy. New technology got the wheels of the press spinning faster, and what was spun out did not always please the bishops. The church, even though it was a 'pillar of the constitution', could no longer escape enquiry, and popular support was eroded both by the growth of Dissent and by waves of Irish immigration. To these external pressures were added internal ones. Evangelicals demanded a new 'seriousness', bishops exhorted clergy to reside in their benefices, and there was a veritable flood of pamphlets on church reform.

The way in which institutions react to the ferment of changing times is eloquent of their true nature. Did the Georgian church respond positively to those numerous movements which deeply affected society from the 1780s onwards? Could it adjust its internal mechanisms to meet the challenge of industrialisation? Or did it scowl down from its battlements upon its foes, until that 'violent', 'wild' and 'restless' age, the 1830s, eventually forced its hand? This is a fundamental question, which also has to

26

be asked of other parts of the Georgian body politic - of, for instance, the political system, the armed forces, the legal profession, medicine and local government. For the church, however, it is especially pertinent, because the establishment was forced, in the 1830s, to pass through a crucible for a change of great power.[123] When labourers demanded 'contributions' from rural incumbents, and bishops were hissed in the streets; when copies of the *Church Examiner* were openly on sale, and two platoons of clerical pamphleteers put forward their pet plans for reform; and when Grey, as Whig prime minister, appointed the Commission of Inquiry into the Ecclesiastical Revenues of England and Wales: was the clerical mind wonderfully concentrated upon pressing subjects which had been, perhaps, previously neglected? Put differently, this book is a contribution to the debate among historians over the methods, and means, of historical change in Georgian England: a debate between those who insist that improvement was a gradual process which began in the 1780s, and the views of an older school, now largely discredited, which holds that established institutions successfully resisted the spirit of the times until compelled to make adjustments in the 1830s.

A further aim is to place in perspective the claims and counterclaims made in contemporary polemic. Were the lurid details massed together in the *Black Book* accurate? Did any of those clerical pamphleteers who wrote so interminably, and often repetitively, about church reform have any understanding of the 'state of the church'? Did the publication of official statistics shift the axis of debate? Image is contrasted with reality, impression is set against fact.

Chapter 1 Notes

1. Sykes, *Church and State*, p.141.
2. 21 Henry VIII c.13.
3. *The Constitutions and Canons Ecclesiastical*, p.19.
4. Best, *Temporal Pillars*, pp.11-12.
5. 6 Anne c.24; 6 Anne c.54.
6. For a brief history of first-fruits and tenths, see Best, *op.cit.*, pp.21-8.
7. The evocative description of economic change in England as constituting an 'industrial revolution' was, it seems, adopted in order to forge a link with that other revolution which brought about, in less than a generation, a sea-change in French life, culture, and institutions - see Raymond Williams, *Culture and Society*, p.xiv.
8. D. McCloskey, 'The industrial revolution 1780-1860: a survey', in R. Floud and D. McCloskey, eds., *The Economic History of Britain since 1700, I, 1700-1860*, p.103.
9. Charles Dickens, *Hard Times*, p.75. This novel came out in 1854.
10. John Rule, *The Experience of Labour in Eighteenth-Century Industry*, pp.17-18.
11. See, e.g., N.C.R. Crafts, 'The eighteenth-century: a survey,' in Floud and McCloskey, *op.cit.*, p.1.
12. E.A. Wrigley and R.S. Schofield, *The population history of England, 1541-1871*, Table

A 5.3 (p.577) has a figure of 5.06 million for England's population in 1701, going up to 5.77 million in 1751 and 8.66 million in 1801. This table also contains a number of estimates by other authorities.

13. Figures calculated from P.J. Corfield, *The impact of English towns*, Table I, p.8. There is no easy, or obvious, definition of what constitutes a town. Corfield opts for a demographic description: a town is a place with over 2,500 people.

14. *Ibid.*, p.7.

15. Wrigley and Schofield, *op.cit.*, Table A 6.7, p.595.

16. *P.P.*, 1801-2, VII, 438; *P.P.*, 1843, XXII, 428.

17. *P.P.*, 1801-2, VII, 450; *P.P.*, 1843, XXII, 439.

18. *P.P.*, 1801-2, VII, 208; *P.P.*, 1843, XXII, 221.

19. *P.P.*, 1818, XVIII, 358-9.

20. *ibid.*, 114.

21. This point is strongly made in Edward Norman, *Church and Society in England 1770-1970*, pp.50-1.

22. John Butler, *The Bishop of Hereford's Charge to the Clergy of his Diocese, at his triennial visitation in the year 1792*, p.6.

23. *ibid.*, p. 7. See also R.A. Soloway, *Prelates and People*, p. 50.

24. Exceptions to this rule are two interesting sets of diocesan records edited by Mary Ransome,*The State of the Bishopric of Worcester 1782-1808*, and *Wiltshire Returns to the Bishop's Visitation Queries 1783*. See, also, F.C. Mather, 'Georgian Churchmanship Reconsidered', *J.E.H.*, XXXVI (1985), 255-83.

25. *Report from the Clergy of a district in the Diocese of Lincoln*, p. 6; see also Soloway, *op.cit.*, pp. 50-2. The study of religious observance in Georgian England would make a fascinating book by itself. To get this project off the ground, there is a mass of information among the records of Queen Anne's Bounty, none of which has ever been used. Interesting material on church attendance in the Georgian period can be found in, for instance, W.M. Marshall, 'The Administration of the Dioceses of Hereford and Oxford, 1660-1760', pp.111-12, 119-20; W.M. Jacob, 'Clergy and Society in Norfolk 1707-1806', pp. 315-22, 326-31, and also, especially, Table, p.381; and J.L. Salter, 'Isaac Maddox and the dioceses of St Asaph and Worcester, 1736-1759', pp.44-6.

26. See below, pp. 155-57.

27. Descriptions of Luddite unrest can be found in F.O. Darvall, *Popular disturbances and public order in Regency England*, and in E.P. Thompson, *The Making of the English Working Class*, pp.569-659.

28. See A.J. Peacock, *Bread or Blood*.

29. See E.J.E. Hobsbawm and G.F.E. Rudé, *Captain Swing*.

30. Peacock, *op.cit.*, pp.95-9. The vicar of Littleport was John Vachell, an unpopular magistrate. Vachell was subsequently awarded damages of £708 9s 0d (*ibid.*, p.99)

31. See below, pp. 112-25. See also, below, Table XIV.

32. *P.P.*, 1833, XV, 8.

33. See, e.g., *John Bull*, 28 November 1830; *Bury and Norwich Post*, 1 December 1830; *The Times*, 25 November 1830; *Cambridge Chronicle*, 26 November 1830.

34. Hobsbawm and Rudé, *op.cit.*, pp. 136-7; *Morning Herald*, 4 January 1831; *Kentish Gazette*, 23 November 1830; *Norfolk Chronicle*, 27 November 1830; *The Times*, 22 November

1830; and a letter from two JP's, one of whom was Cove himself, Newbury, 19 November 1830, H.O./52/6.

35. Lord Grantham to Home Office, 5 December 1830, H.O./52/6; Joyce Godber, *History of Bedfordshire, 1066-1888*, p. 419; Hobsbawm and Rudé, *op.cit.*, pp. 149-50.

36. Dr Newbolt to Home office, 10 December 1830, H.O./52/7. The pencilled notes of Melbourne's reply are to be found on the back of this letter.

37. F.C. Fowle to Charles Dundas, MP, 22 November 1830, H.O./52/6.

38. Frederick Page to Home office, 22 November 1830, H.O./52/6. See, in addition, a further letter, dated 24 November 1830, also to be found in H.O./52/6.

39. F.C. Fowle to Home Office, 27 November 1830, H.O./52/6.

40. Italics in text.

41. Italics in text.

42. The five clergy were W.F. Wilkinson, vicar of North Walsham; William Gunn, rector of Sloley; Henry Atkinson, rector of Waston; Benjamin Cubitt, vicar of Stalham; and George Cubitt, unbeneficed.

43. Hobsbawm and Rudé, *op.cit.*, p. 154. See, also, a letter to the Home Office, dated 11 December 1830, from an anonymous inhabitant of North Walsham, in H.O./52/9.

44. Letter, dated 13 December 1830, from William Gunn, at Smallburgh, Norfolk to Dawson Turner, in D.T.P., XXXVIII, 126.

45. Fairfax Francklin to Home Office, 7 December 1830, in H.O./52/9.

46. 50% off at Harrietsham; 25% off at Smarden and Brenchley; 10% off at Birling, Herne, Hartley, Throwley, Snodland, Sturry, Stockbury, Tonbridge and Bredgar; John Austen, rector of Chevening, was willing to accept whatever local farmers thought was reasonable; and John Barton, rector of Eastchurch, cut his tithes by a shilling an acre.

47. At Mayfield, the fall was from between £1,200 and £1,400 to £400; at Rotherfield and Ringmer, tithes came down by half; at Thakeham the reduction was 45%; at Chailey it was 38%; at Itchingfield 33%; at Clayton 25%; at Worth 20%; and at Heathfield 15%. Robert Hare reduced his tithes by 10% at Herstmonceaux, and Robert Hardy did the same at Walberton. The smallest reduction we came across was at Tangmere, where Robert Tredcroft declared himself content with 5% less. As with the illustrations from Kent, this list purports to be no more than a random and incomplete selection of tithe reductions, the details of which have been drawn from local newspapers.

48. G.S.R. Kitson Clark, *An Expanding Society*, p.87.

49. A. Aspinall, *Politics and the Press*, p.7 and note. The four-cylinder press, what is more, could print on both sides, but the hand-worked press only on one.

50. John Wardroper, *Kings, lords and wicked libellers*, pp.2-3, 14; Aspinall, *op.cit.*, p.6.

51. A.P. Wadsworth, *Newspaper circulations*, p.6, 16-18.

52. Hesketh Pearson, *The Smith of Smiths*, pp. 44-60.

53. 55 Geo. III c.185.

54. P. Hollis, *The pauper press*, p.95.

55. 60 Geo. III c.8; 60 Geo. III c.9.

56. Hollis, *op.cit.*, p.98.

57. J.R.M. Butler, *The Passing of the Great Reform Bill*, p.206, 212.

58. A copy of this address can be found in the *Gauntlet*, 28 April 1833.

59. Hollis, *op.cit.*, p.108.

60. *Republican*, III (16 June 1820), 275. We are indebted to our good friend, Revd John Bruce, for this reference. The ambivalent attitude of leading Radicals at this time towards attacks upon religion is described in J. Ann Hone, *For the cause of truth*, pp.332-9.

61. *Church Examiner*, 16 June 1832. Italics in text.

62. Best, *op.cit.*, p.277.

63. See, e.g., J.C.D. Clark, *English Society*, p.380.

64. Norman, *Church and Society*, p. 19. See also P.B. Nockles, 'Continuity and Change in Anglican High Churchmanship', p. 4.

65. N.U. Murray, 'The Influence of the French Revolution', p. 41.

66. Richard Yates, *The Church in Danger*, p. 88; quoted in Clark, *op.cit.*, p. 268.

67. Francis Thackeray, *A Defence of the Clergy of the Church of England*, p. 193.

68. A general discussion of Roman Catholic numbers in the Georgian period can be found in John Bossy, *The English Catholic community*, pp. 77-107.

69. A.D. Gilbert, *Religion and Society in Industrial England*, Table, p. 31.

70. *ibid.*, p. 30.

71. *ibid.*, Table, p. 31.

72. *ibid.*, Table, p. 37.

73. *ibid.*, Table, p. 40, See also W.R. Ward, *Religion and Society in England*, p. 67.

74. Gilbert, *op.cit.*, p. 41; Ward, *op.cit.*, pp. 62-6.

75. David Williams, *The Rebecca Riots*, pp. 122-3. The reference to the 'very small minority' allegiance at the turn of the nineteenth century refers to the Welsh people as a whole.

76. W.O. Chadwick, *The Victorian Church*, I, 25-6.

77. A quip of Richard Carlile's quoted in Butler, *op.cit.*, p.296.

78. A graphic description of the destruction of Gray's palace appears in Chadwick, *op.cit.*,I,27-8.

79. E.J. Whately, *Life and Correspondence of R. Whately*, I, 114.

80. W.J. Copleston, *Memoir of Edward Copleston*, pp.148-9.

81. Chadwick, *op.cit.*, 32.

82. Letter (dated 14 May 1832) by Richard Whately, Archbishop of Dublin, to Edward Copleston, Bishop of Llandaff, quoted in Whately, *op.cit.*, I, 159.

83. C.J. Blomfield, Bishop of London, to William Howley, Archbishop of Canterbury, 11 December 1832; quoted in A. Blomfield, *A Memoir of C.J. Blomfield*, I, 207.

84. Robert Southey to Revd J. Miller, 16 November 1833, in C.C. Southey, ed., *The Life and Correspondence of Robert Southey*, VI, 222.

85. Thomas Arnold to Chevalier Bunsen, 6 May 1833, in A.P. Stanley, *The Life and Correspondence of Thomas Arnold*, I, 317.

86. Ford K. Brown, *Fathers of the Victorians*, p.2. See, also, W.D. Balda, 'Spheres of Influence', p.38.

87. C.H.E. Smyth, *Simeon and Church Order*, pp.136-9.

88. Charles Simeon was partly responsible for this urban provenance. It was the policy of his well-known trust, set up in 1814, to acquire 'permanently accessible preferment in strategic places' - Balda, 'Spheres of Influence', p.264. Balda has written an interesting and illuminating thesis.

89. See Josiah Bateman, *The Life of the Right Revd Daniel Wilson*.

90. See J.B. Marsden, *Memoirs of the life and labours of the Revd Hugh Stowell*.

91. An excellent account of the work of the Phalanx can be found in Alan B. Webster, *Joshua Watson*. See, also, Murray, 'The Influence of the French Revolution', pp.44-79.

92. Christopher Wordsworth was Master of Trinity College, Cambridge, 1820-41.

93. Van Mildert was Bishop of Llandaff, 1819-1826, and of Durham, 1826-36.

94. The *British Critic* was founded in May, 1793.

95. See W.R.W. Stephens, *The Life and Letters of W.F. Hook*.

96. *Tracts for the Times*, I, 4.

97. A very similar conclusion is reached by Heeney, *A Different Kind of Gentleman*, esp.pp.11-12,15,117.

98. *Hansard*, XXXVII (16 March 1818), 1119.

99. 'Durham Case-Clerical Abuses', *Edinburgh Review*, XXXVII (1822), 350-79.

100. Thomas Mozley, *Reminiscences*, I, 297.

101. See, e.g., *A Letter to his Grace the Archbishop of York, on the Present Corrupt State of the Church of England* (1831). This pamphlet reached its seventeenth edition in 1834.

102. See, e.g., [One of the priesthood], *The Outline of an efficient plan of Church Reform*, p.18; and also [A Country Gentleman], *Hints for Church Reform*, pp.31-2.

103. *The Outline*, pp.29-31.

104. G. Townsend, *A Plan for abolishing Pluralites and Non- Residence in the Church of England*, pp.95-8.

105. Parish churches:- [A clergyman of the Church of England], *Safe and easy steps*, p.44; diocesan theological colleges:- E.B. Pusey, *Remarks*, pp.60-72.

106. *Safe and Easy steps*, pp.61-2.

107. *A Letter to the Right Honourable Sir Robert Peel, Bart, MP, on the present condition and prospects of the established church*, p.62.

108. *ibid.*, p.69.

109. *ibid.*, p.64.

110. *ibid.*, p.67.

111. *ibid.*, p.66.

112. *ibid.*, p.68.

113. *ibid.*, p.64. Italics in text.

114. *ibid.*, p.65.

115. *ibid.*, pp.71-2.

116. *ibid.*, p.40.

117. *ibid.*, p.65,70.

118. Pusey, *op.cit.*, p.1.

119. [W. Fletcher], *Church Reform*, p.7. Italics in text.

120. *Plain words addressed to members of the Church of England. By one of themselves*, p. 5.

121. [A beneficed clergyman], *What will the bishops do?*, p.21.

122. Townsend, *op.cit*, p.15.

123. Cf Norman, *Church and Society*, p.95: 'the 1830s were the most significant years for the relations of the Church of England with the State and with society in the nineteenth century'.

2

Sources of Clerical Income

i. *Inequality*

In Georgian England, conventional wisdom held that inequality, far from being a sign of sin, was a proof of virtue. The principle of hierarchy was detected in nature, and it was thought right and fitting that this principle should also be operative in all the affairs of men. Consolidation of hereditary power through primogeniture did not stir consciences nor raise doubts. Taxation was low, and there were no death duties. Over generations, it was easy for a strong landed family to build up vast estates. On the other hand, Georgian England was not a closed society. There was a significant degree of social mobility, which eased the way of many of the richest mercantile families - themselves sharing the common reverence for the stability and sense of permanence given by the ownership of land - into the ruling class.[1] Merchants usually became landed gentlemen, either by buying land themselves or by arranging a discreet marriage for one of their daughters. Even in societies where the principles of hierarchy and heredity are not hallowed, in which taxation of the rich is heavy rather than light, and in which land is not regarded as a personal possession to be prized above all others, history has convincingly shown the strength of the numerous obstacles that stand in the way of achieving equality. In a society constituted as Georgian England was constituted, it is, therefore, only to be expected that among every class, professional as well as non-professional, there would be wide divergences in wealth and status.

The social assumptions which were readily made in the England of the eighteenth century affected the financial standing of the clergy, as did accidents of nature and of history. Every beneficed clergyman was the incumbent of a parish, and the parish as a legal entity was itself the product of a union between chance and ancient law. To study, on a contemporary map, the physical texture of parochial geography in Georgian England, is to confront a bewildering picture. Some parishes were more or less square, others were more or less round; some were neat, others were awkward; a few were huge, a few were miniscule. The strength of the appropriate contrasts is clear from comparison of two East Anglian parishes, Childerley and Doddington, the former as hard to find as the latter was hard to avoid. Childerley lay about seven miles west of Cambridge, through Madingley. Some distance beyond a spot known as Honey

Hill, and just before Two Pot house, lay a cart-track, at the end of which was the sought-for parish. Surrounded by undulating ground, Childerley was a tiny place of only 1,050 acres, with a ruined chapel and a few houses huddled together. Its population in 1801 was 47; forty years later, the figure was just seven more.[2] Very different was the massive Fenland parish of Doddington, where just to 'beat the bounds' was an exhausting day's work. The easiest way to start would be by walking along Twenty Foot river, just north of the town of March. The boundary then drops, in the west, over White Fen, skirting the hamlet of Benwick. Cross, next, Forty Foot drain, and then cut across West Moor. Circle Doddington itself, and move south-east around Wimblington Common and Fen; now follow the boundary due north, around Bedlam Fen, eventually rejoining Twenty Foot river, to circuit again around March. The population of this town, together with the three hamlets of Benwick, Doddington, and Wimblington, was over 7,500 in 1830;[3] and the parish - all 38,240 acres of it - was nearly forty times the size of Childerley.

In urban areas, the size of a parish was important largely as a reflection of population density. This is because the main sources of clerical income in towns were pew rents and 'surplice fees' - payments made for conducting baptisms, marriages and funerals. More people meant, quite simply, more potential customers to rent pews, and also, of course, more baptisms, marriages and burials. The size of an urban parish was historically conditioned. As mentioned in Chapter One,[4] much depended upon whether it was situated in an ancient corporate town (where, in all probability, it would already have been sub-divided), or in a new industrial centre (where it probably would not). The effect of this failure to sub-divide the new industrial towns was catastrophic. By 1841, the population of the parish of Leeds (conterminous with the whole place) was over 150,000, making it the most populous in England. In the denser areas of London, the situation was almost equally farcical - the parish of Marylebone in the same year had over 135,000 inhabitants; St Pancras more than 125,000; St George's, Hanover Square, over 65,000.[5] Population density was also a factor in the countryside - the rector of Doddington did much better out of surplice fees than the vicar of Childerley - but there it was the size and fertility of a parish which were paramount.

The significance of this increase in population for clerical income from surplice fees is made clear by a parliamentary return, detailing the fees received by one hundred London incumbents in 1833. In some parishes, these fees were the major source of benefice income, yielding £1,147 a year at St Pancras, £1,068 at Marylebone, £969 at St George's, Hanover Square, and £883 at Paddington; but in others they were scarcely a benefit at all - only £3 at St Bartholomew the Less, £4 at St Bartholomew by Exchange, and £5 at Allhallows, Bread Street, a neat progression of the negligible. In all, 22 incumbents received £10 or less, while 27 got £200 or more.[6]

Two further factors, one social and the other legal, sharpened problems of inequality. The clergyman was placed, by virtue of his office, within a close network of local relationships, the most significant of which, from a social as well as financial viewpoint, was that with neighbouring gentry. To offend might jeopardise the chances of an improved livelihood; to please might attract a weighty endowment. Wealthy laity, who were often patrons of the livings concerned, made, over the centuries, an enormous number of benefactions, sometimes in cash but chiefly in land. The second factor which widened inequalities among the clergy was the ineffectiveness of the laws supposedly controlling pluralism. The relevant pieces of legislation were outdated, vague, difficult to apply, and frequently evaded; they also failed to cover with enough rigour the capitular clergy - it was legally permissible for a clergyman to be beneficed and simultaneously to hold a post in every one of the twenty-eight chapters in England and Wales.

What matters most is the number of these variables, and the way in which they interlocked. So long as the beneficed clergy continued to derive the greater part of their income either directly or indirectly from the land, the size and fertility of their parish (or parishes) was clearly going to remain a vital matter. To this inherent source of inequality, many others were added: the extent of private benefactions over the centuries; ineffective anti-pluralistic legislation; the strength of each incumbent's social connections; disparities in income from pew rents and surplice fees, and so on. An aged non-pluralist of lowly social origin, holding a small living in a mountainous district, was not likely to be a rich man; a well-connected pluralist, holding several large and fertile livings in tandem with a string of cathedral posts, was likely to be, and quite often was, a decidedly rich man. The common currency of eighteenth-century ideas sanctioned and sanctified inequality: realities of geography, custom, law, history and society ensured that prevailing conditions affirmed rather than denied tenets of contemporary thought.

ii. *Types of Living*

Livings were divided into three categories - they could either be rectories, vicarages, or perpetual curacies. To define the differences it is necessary, first, to analyse briefly the nature of tithe. The basic division was between great tithes and small. Things arising *from* the ground: grain, hay, and wood, for instance, paid 'great' tithes. Things nourished *by* the ground: animals, poultry, were subject only to 'small'.[7] It has often been asserted that rectories were invariably endowed with both great and small tithes, that is, the tithe of all cereals and also of all farm animals; while vicarages were only endowed with small. Reality was more flexible than this rigid distinction would suggest. There were counties - Staffordshire is an example - where tithe of hay was allowed to vicars in a majority of cases, and where it was common for them to hold corn rights, at any rate in part of the parish.[8] These facts blunt the traditional contrast between rectories and vicarages, but the economic advantages enjoyed by the one over the other were nevertheless great. In Derbyshire, the average rectory was worth more than twice as much as the average vicarage by 1830.[9]

The status of the third class of livings, the perpetual curacies,[10] requires more radical revision. The received opinion is that the arrangements made for these were utterly rigid; perpetual curates, according to this view, received no tithes at all, their sole source of maintenance being a fixed money payment or 'pension', paid by the lay holder of both great and small.[11] Local research, again for Staffordshire, has undermined this claim. A quarter of the perpetual curacies in this county, it appears, were supported in part by grants of tithe.[12] Although these did not always amount to as much as the more usual fixed money payment, their existence is nonetheless a further interesting indication of the fluidity which was a marked feature of all things ecclesiastical. In Derbyshire in 1830 the average perpetual curacy was worth just over half as much as the average vicarage, and just over a quarter as much as the average rectory.[13]

iii. *Types of Tithe*

Overarching every other complexity was the tithe system. Based upon Old Testament precedent, and itself the product of an almost infinitely slow process of historical accretion, this system had gradually fragmented. In its simplest form, tithe was a 10% tax on the gross agricultural product, and was taken in kind; but things in the Georgian church were rarely simple. Some land was tithe-free; on other plots fixed payments - called moduses - were levied; tithing in kind could be replaced by a monetary payment per acre, known as a composition; or tithes could be abolished altogether, with the clergy accepting in return either a parcel of land, a corn rent, or cash compensation. This was commutation. One other point deserves emphasis. Not all tithes were paid to clergy, they could be paid to laity also.

Several types of land were tithe-free. Permanent barrenness was one reason for this being the case; and vested interest was another, a principle applying to all forests in the possession of the Crown. Common law could establish freedom from payment - if a tract had been exempt from time immemorial (from before, that is, the first year of English legal memory, namely 1189), then the exemption held. The most contentious category was land previously barren but now fertile; in such instances, it was customary for tithes not to be payable for a few years in order to help reimburse the farmer for some of the costs of reclamation. Then there were two anomalies: plots owned before 1215 by Cistercians, Templars, or Hospitallers; and plots, formerly belonging to monasteries, which had not been paying tithes at the time of the dissolution. The final category, the parson's own glebe, could enlist in its support the force of administrative logic, but also invited retaliatory lay comment.[14]

Lay tithe-owners did not originate with the Reformation - instances can be traced at least as far back as the end of the twelfth century[15] - but it was, of course, upon the revenues of former monastic properties that the fortunes of many families, the Russells and the Cecils to name but two, flourished. With these revenues also went the tithes. A new class of men - lay impropriators - came into being. Some were extremely powerful, with tithe-paying estates scattered across the length and breadth of the land. The situation in the mid-nineteenth century, after the general commutation under the Act of 1836, is clear. At that time, 75% of tithes were held by incumbents and clerical appropriators, 5% by colleges and schools, and the remaining 20% by laymen.[16]

Tithe-free land, and tithes held by laity, were the least satisfactory from the clergy's point of view; but close on their heels came the ancient *modus decimandi*, commonly known as the modus. It could be for cash, or it could take the form of an agreement to take animals in lieu of what they produced - hens, for instance, instead of eggs; it could cover a parish, or it could cover only a farm; it could apply to a range of crops, or it could apply to only one: but the essence was the nominal level of the payment, and the fact that, as with lands exempt from tithe, it was customary, and therefore could not be fully established unless it could be traced back beyond 1189. The legal uncertainty of the modus contained, inevitably, potential for chaos, fully exploited in the famous Cottenham case, where an early nineteenth-century rector of this Cambridgeshire village successfully overturned a modus paid since 1595. Only in 1832, when an Act was passed establishing thirty years' unvarying and continuous payment as a sufficient basis for validity,[17] was this aspect of the law tidied up.

An example from Yorkshire shows how numerous and vexatious moduses could be. The vicar of Brotherton, John Law, recorded in his diary for 1770 the various payments his parishioners were required to make: 'According to an old *modus* with the parishioners of Brotherton a Pidgeon Chamber pays one shilling and threepence, a Dove Coat half a crown, a new milch cow two pence halfpenny, a strip't cow three-halfpence, a foal four pence, every house ninepence halfpenny, a swarm of bees two pence, the old stock a penny ... The Marsh Mill pays an old modus of 2s 6d yearly, and tho' I have agreed to take the same for the Windmill, yet my successor is not obliged to do the same, but may demand the tenth part of the Moultre after all reasonable expenses are deducted'.[18] If he wished to collect all these sums, Law had to ask every householder for the derisory amount of 9½d; he had to visit gardens in search of pigeons and doves, and orchards in search of bees. He was sure it was not worth it.

Modus payments did not bring in much to the clergy. Considering how petty they were, this is scarcely surprising. Probably, they did not make up more than one or two per cent of total clerical income.[19] The failure of moduses to supply an adequate income derives from their fixed and customary nature, and from the nominal sums at which they were set. Clerical distaste for them is easily understood - the Marquis of Waterford was fortunate enough to possess in the early nineteenth century an 8,000 acre estate in Northumberland, paying a modus of £40 a year.[20]

While he was vicar of Brotherton, John Law not only collected moduses; he also took many of his tithes in kind: 'Everyone above the age of sixteen pays two pence as a communicant. Turnips are paid for according to their value, or as they are let. Potatoes are paid in kind if not compounded for. The tythe of Orchards, Pigs and Geese are also paid in kind, if not compounded for. Rape and all new species of vicarial tythes are to be paid in kind unless compounded for, but Hemp and Flax must be paid according to Statute ... The new Shelling Mill built last year in the quarry Holes is also titheable, after it has been so long employed as may be fairly supposed to reimburse the proprietor the expense of the building. N.B. If Clover and Saint Foin stand for seed the Tythe thereof belongs to the vicar, but if it is cut or made use of for Hay, the Tythe belongs to the Appropriators, or Lessee of the Dean and Chapter'.[21]

The severe drawbacks of tithing in kind are clear from this; the parson was turned, of necessity, into a sort of supernumerary farmer, with the added disadvantage that he also had to be an efficient accounts' clerk. He had to keep track of the payments that were due, and he had to gather in his tithes himself. The latter was an arduous task. Produce had to be collected from the fields at harvest, grain had to be threshed, storage barns had to be built, and the parson was faced with all the normal marketing problems which beset the farmer. These operations were costly, especially on labour intensive arable, as well as being time-consuming. Tithing in kind was, nevertheless, a frequent practice in many areas. A survey carried out for Pitt the Younger in the early 1790s mentions twelve counties: Cheshire, Lancashire, and Durham in the north; Shropshire in the north midlands; the county of Huntingdonshire; the adjacent counties of Berkshire and Buckinghamshire; and a wide sweep of countryside running across Kent into Surrey, Hampshire, Wiltshire, and Somerset. To these, several other counties, notably Cumberland and Westmorland, should be added. Although tithing in kind was infrequent elsewhere, its widespread incidence shows that the practice was not confined to agriculturally backward districts.[22]

Taking in kind made acute the already contentious legal problems surrounding tithe. One of the main difficulties was that so many things were tithable - cereals, hay, and wood, farm animals of all kinds, poultry, eggs, and milk - and, in consequence, there was inevitably much room for legal debate. Argument between counsel sometimes entered realms of majestic obscurity. Litigation was particularly complex in cases where the issue centred on the fringes of the untrammelled natural world, which were exempt, and on those parts of that world touched by the hand of man, which were not. A wild duck, it was once decided, was *ferae naturae* and therefore exempt; but what of the eggs, laid by tame ducks, used as decoys to trap the wilder species? These, apparently, were tithable. In a similar vein, bees were held to be tithe-free but not the honey they produced. The case of a fallen apple posed a conundrum of sizeable proportions: did the fact of its fall reclaim it for nature? The courts decided that it did not. Forest and wood also defied logic. In some areas all woodland was exempt, in others only certain trees; or it might be that trunks and branches were exempt, but not the acorns which some trees shed.[23]

The disadvantages of taking in kind were enormous. It was difficult to avoid annoying the local community. The parson entered the harvest field, bearing away with him every tenth stack of corn; he visited farmyards to collect every tenth day's yield of milk; he roamed orchards in search of bee-hives; he checked every litter of pigs, and every new-born calf. All of this, naturally enough, could provoke resistance. The parson would be told curtly to collect his milk every day rather than every tenth day, and to do so early in the morning. Similar tactics were employed over tithe of eggs; the collection of hay and cereals was made difficult; and the breeding habits of the farmyard were kept as secret as possible. Tithes in kind were numerous and their collection costly, yet they could amount to so little that it was almost impossible to draw from them the full Biblical tenth.

Their very vexatiousness could, in certain circumstances, be useful. In cases of dispute, clergy could threaten to take their tithes in kind, and farmers knew that rough words spoken on such occasions were not idle. Normally, taking in kind in such circumstances was no more than a temporary expedient; the ploy, nevertheless, could be effective. Used in this way, it became one move in those complex 'games' of thrust and counterthrust which are part of the warp and woof of litigation. Taking in kind was reality, and it was also a threat.

Compositions were free of many of the pitfalls that went with tithes in kind. They were, basically, agreements to take so much per acre in lieu; as such, they could be arranged separately with each farmer or, as was more likely, on an across-the-board basis for a whole parish. If they took the first form, each farmer compounded for a different sum; and if they took the second, the cost of tithes per acre was the same everywhere. The advantages of this system are obvious. Bickering over definitions of tithe was avoided; each farmer was responsible for paying a single lump sum; payment could be made on an annual basis; and tithe-income became more reliable, no longer dependent upon the uncertainties of the harvest. More subtly, compositions offered a new degree of flexibility. The tithe-owner was in no way bound by them. He could continue with them or, if he wished, he could return to taking in kind; he could arrange them for a given term of years, or he could reassess them on an annual basis; and, as already mentioned, he could compound with each farmer separately, or with the parish as a whole. An annual valuation of each farm was potentially the most lucrative, particularly during an agrarian boom. The major drawback was its expense: the cost of a new valuation, preferably carried out by a professionally trained valuer, had to be deducted from each year's income. The farming community, for equally obvious reasons, preferred agreements to be made for terms of years, because these provided an effective insurance policy against tithes being increased for the stated period. An end to argument over definitions of tithe would come as a relief to both sides; lump sum payments removed a source of constant irritation; and farmers were pleased to see the tithe-owner's tax collectors disappear from their harvest fields.

On the other hand, it would not be true to say that compositions were free from conflict. One source of tension was across-the-board assessments. To charge so much per acre over a parish amounted to the imposition of a system of differential taxation: the higher the crop yield, in monetary terms, the lower tithes became as a percentage of total costs; and, of course, the converse held. Across-the-board compositions, in other words, penalised those farming the less fertile, and consequently less generally remunerative, land. Annual valuations were a further source of difficulty. Farmers argued that they were a 'disincentive' to improvement; every increase in production was followed immediately by a rise in tithe tax. Longer term agreements could also touch veins of anger; in times of distress - poor harvests, high employment, and the like - a tithe bargain struck several years previously could become intolerably oppressive. In these circumstances an 'accommodation', involving mutual compromise, needed to be reached. Compositions eased the burden of tithe payment, and gave in most cases a sense of relative stability, but they did not resolve underlying tensions. They were, however, much more popular than tithes in kind, and accounted for a substantial portion of total benefice income.[24]

Commutation was altogether different. Moduses, tithes in kind, and compositions were all abolished, and in their place either a straight cash compensation was negotiated, or a corn rent agreed upon, or a portion of land allotted. Most clergy preferred commutation for land. The social aspirations of the Georgian clergy are a major fact in the ecclesiastical history of the period. The clergy were a rising social class, a fact of which many of them were only too well aware. Although the process of assimilation into the gentry was far from complete by 1840, it was by then well under way.[25] It came about through marriage, was hastened by rising clerical wealth, and was consolidated by the entry of the clergy into the local magistracy. Commutation fitted neatly into the developing pattern. Land, in the countryside, was the symbol, the palpable insignia, of power; and commutation gave the clergy that power.

Whatever form it took, commutation had much to recommend it. Its essence was its simplicity: no more payments in kind, no more haggling over compositions, no more vexatious moduses. Commutation was, in its way, a social compact: the clergy gained an enhanced degree of financial stability and more social respect; the farming community gained freedom from taxation and relief from petty disputes. With commutation there is, at last, evidence of initiative and will to change - a will that had been fertilised by uncertainty, born of discontent, and nourished by the worries of litigation.

iv. *Threads*

The characteristic shapes and forms of the Georgian church had been crafted with the pen of history. This is why the ecclesiastical structure was complex; and it is also why it was difficult to reform. The influences impinging upon clerical income vividly illustrate these truths. The ancient division of field from field and of parish from parish, often traceable to Saxon times; geographical location and fertility of soil; population density; relationships with the local squirearchy; the status of each parish, as rectory, vicarage, or perpetual curacy; the method of tithe collection, whether in kind, by modus, by composition, or by commutation: all are relevant to the wealth of the clergy.

An indication of the scope of diversity is given by research on benefice incomes in a midlands county around 1830. The sources of income stretch to nine major items: property belonging to the benefice (largely as a result of commutation); compositions; tithes in kind; corn rents; dividends and stock secured to the benefice; stipends and moduses; Easter dues; surplice fees; pew rents. Standing well above the rest in importance are the first two. Nearly 44% of income came from benefice property, and 42% from compositions; tithes in kind were 0.75%; and the other six sources ranged between 1% and 4%.[26] Research for other areas would, doubtless, yield a different result. The explanation lies at hand. Whatever else may be said about it, the Georgian church did not encourage, or develop, any stylised and standardised uniformity.

Chapter 2 Notes

1. On the extent of this mobility, and its significance, the views of historians profoundly differ - see, e.g., Nicholas Rogers, 'Money, land and lineage', *Social History*, 4 (1979), 437-54. Rogers argues (p. 451) that 'the quest for landed status became less compulsive' as the eighteenth century progressed.

2. *P.P.*, 1801-2, VII, 21: *P.P.*, 1843, XXII, 62.

3. The census for 1831 (*P.P.*, 1833, XXXVI, 42) gives the population of the parish of Doddington as 7,527.

4. See above, p6.

5. The census for 1841 (*P.P.*, 1843, XXII, 438) gives the population of the parish of Leeds as 152,054. The figure for Marylebone in the same year was 138,164 (*ibid.*, 220), with 128,479 at St Pancras (*ibid.*, 221) and 66,453 at St George's, Hanover Square (*ibid.*, 224).

6. *P.P.*, 1834, XLIII, 41-154. Nine parishes failed to make returns.

7. J. A. Venn, *Foundations of Agricultural Economics*, p.98.

8. Eric J. Evans, *The Contentious Tithe*, p.7.

9. M.R. Austin, 'The Church of England in the County of Derbyshire, 1772-1832', Table 14, p.170. His figures refer to 1832, and give 30 rectories with an average value of £459 as against 33 vicarages with an average of only £195.

10. On the question of the legal definition of a perpetual curacy, see J.R. Guy, 'Perpetual curacies in Eighteenth-Century South Wales', *Studies in Church History*, XVI (1979), 330-2.

11. See, e.g., Best, *Temporal Pillars*, p.17.

12. Evans, *op.cit.*, pp.7-8.

13. Austin, *op.cit.*, Table 14, p.170. Eighteen perpetual curacies in this county were worth an average of £119 a year in 1832.

14. H.C. Prince, 'The Tithe Surveys of the Mid-Nineteenth Century', *A.H.R.*, VII (1959), 20.

15. Evans, *op.cit.*, p.8.

16. *P.P.*, 1887, LXIV, 532-3. The figures were: incumbents, £2,412,103 14s 4½d; clerical appropriators, £680,030 0s 11½d; schools & colleges, £196,056 15s 0½d; laity, £766,205 18s 2½d.

17. W.E. Tate, *The Parish Chest*, p.139; Evans, *op.cit.*, p.18, 117-8, 122.

18. Venn, *op.cit.*, p.105.

19. In Derbyshire, in 1832, 'stipends, pensions and moduses' accounted for only 2.3% of total clerical income - Austin, *op.cit.*, Table 13, p.167.

20. Evans, *op.cit.*, p.56.

21. Venn, *op.cit.*, pp. 105-6. The total number of Law's payments - moduses, household fees, communicant dues and tithes in kind - was 347, paid by 132 people. Altogether they realised the meagre sum of £28, just over 1s 6d per payment and 4s per person.

22. Evans, *op.cit.*, pp.21-2.

23. Prince, *A.H.R.*, VII, 15.

24. In Derbyshire the figure was 41.6% - see Austin, *op.cit.*, Table 13, p. 167 23.

25. See below, pp.109-12 and Table X.

26. Austin, *op.cit.*, Table 13, p.167. The full figures are: 43.73% for benefice property; 41.59% for compositions; 4.02% for dividends; 2.77% for corn rents; 2.32% for stipends and moduses; 2.28% for surplice fees; 1.31% for pew rents; 1.23% for Easter dues; and 0.75% for tithes in kind.

3

The Sound of Sovereigns

'The Farmers of my Parish are now in the midst of their hop-gathering; but they all complain
how much they have suffer'd by a destructive fly, which attack'd them before they had risen
half-way up their poles. This Circumstance prognosticates to me many long Faces on St Luke's
Day when they pay my Tithes. But I may expect their countenances to brighten a little over the
Punch-Bowl after an ample Dinner which I always set before them. The music of their
sovereigns and Crown pieces, not to mention the pleasing whispers of their Five-pound notes
in piano, will help to keep up the spirits of me and my Curate at the Table of our Morning
Business.'[1]

It is difficult, now, to understand with any degree of cogency either the texture and
quality, or the extent, of the Georgian clergy's involvement in society. The interlacing
of sacred and secular was an intrinsic part of the governmental order - a large number
of incumbents served as magistrates, and many of these clerical JPs were 'active', as
the contemporary phrase had it. Not only did the eighteenth-century rector or vicar
have the experience, somewhat strange for a clergyman, of sitting in judgment upon
his parishioners; he was also intimately involved in many of their day-to-day affairs,
writing correspondence for them, assisting them to overcome their ailments with the
help of his (admittedly primitive) medicine box, and dealing with a host of other
similarly mundane matters. It is indicative of eighteenth-century attitudes that church
and state should have been regarded as linked in unity - both were spoken of as
'temporal pillars' of the constitution. Such thinking profoundly affected the way in
which leading churchmen envisaged the role of the church; to them, church and nation
were synonymous. Nor was the church powerful in theory only. The bishops, sitting
by right of office in the House of Lords, played an important part in government;
while, in the localities, many of the clergy - quite often now with aristocratic
connections - were figures to be reckoned with in rural society.

What was true at a governmental, constitutional, political, and social level, was
also true at an economic level. Because of the tithe system, the clergy's wealth
depended crucially upon the success or failure of the rural economy. Every agrarian
boom, or depression, profoundly affected benefice incomes. Clerical participation in
the rural economy did not end with tithe collection. Whenever a local enclosure was

proposed, the incumbent in his capacity as tithe-owner was involved in negotiations. And if there was a commutation, rectors and vicars had to learn how best to manage their estates. Everything centred upon land: tithe of the produce of land, enclosure of land, management of land. It was land, moreover, which held the attention of the Bounty Board, the governing body of the church's finances, set up by Queen Anne and charged with the task of augmenting the value of the smaller benefices. Augmentations, the governors decreed, were not to remain in cash or to be used to buy government stock, but must be laid out in the purchase of plots of land.

The Georgian clergy were fortunate in their dependence upon the land, because the land could increasingly be depended upon. To begin with, there were advances in agricultural techniques, which gave the term 'Agrarian Revolution' to the language. Secondly, as from the middle of the eighteenth century, the enclosure movement started to make significant headway; agricultural production was given impetus and, in many areas, clergy exchanged the vexations of compositions for the certainties of commutation. Thirdly, improvements were made in clerical estate management. Finally, as the governors of the Bounty Board settled down to work, something began to be done about raising the benefice incomes of the numerous livings incapable of sustaining an incumbent in reasonable comfort. Here, then, is much matter for examination, after which it will be possible to assess the extent of the rise in benefice incomes during the eighteenth and early nineteenth centuries.

i. *Agricultural Advance*

The 'Agrarian Revolution' of the eighteenth century was vaguer in scope, and less dramatic in intensity, than its industrial counterpart.[2] In the towns, there was the steam engine; in the countryside, there was little except the threshing machine. Even the use of this spread slowly. First introduced in Scotland, it had not conquered the southern counties by 1830; it was usually driven either by water, by horse, or by hand; and there is scattered evidence that, in many areas affected by the rural unrest of 1830-1, it was subsequently withdrawn. Lack of an efficient reaper is further evidence of low levels of mechanisation in agriculture.[3]

Rural economic growth had always been steady rather than spectacular. There are many examples of gradual improvement. Enclosures had started under the Tudors; there was extensive reclamation of the East Anglian fens in the next century; turnips were introduced into England during the reign of Charles II, and also the growing of clover as fodder. Innovations, however, made slow progress. This is because advance in agriculture depended - as much else that was important in English society depended - upon the will of landowners up and down the country to accept change. Power was fragmented, there was a high level of local autonomy, and communications were poor.

The haphazard nature of agricultural development is further illustrated by the varying rates at which the inventions and discoveries of the eighteenth-century pioneers were brought into use. Introduction of Jethro Tull's seed-drill and horse-hoe, first recommended in his *New Horse Hoeing Husbandry* of 1733, was slow; so, too, was adoption of new systems of crop rotation - the famous Norfolk Four Course Rotation (wheat, turnips, oats or barley, and clover) took a long time to penetrate outside its county of origin. The stock breeders, notably Robert Bakewell in Leicestershire and Charles and Robert Colling at Ketton, near Darlington, fared better. Long before the scientific basis of heredity was laid by Mendel, Bakewell, by a stoke of genius, hit upon the principle of pedigree breeding and supported it with the use of elaborate genealogical tables.[4] The new methods, sensationally successful, were soon widely copied.

Conditions of change varied from place to place. Hardest to farm, and therefore tending to be backward, were the heavy clays, a soil which predominated in much of the midlands, and also in parts of Yorkshire, Sussex, and Somerset. Three or four horses were needed for ploughing, whereas one or two would do the job on light soils; seed-beds were hard to produce, and did not become strong until after many cultivations of the soil; dampness meant that sowing was late; and crop yields were often low. The best farmed counties, in contrast, usually contained large areas of light soil, and were often, like Norfolk and Suffolk, also centres of ancient enclosure. Essex, another county of old enclosure, had a heavier soil than neighbouring Suffolk, but the standard of farming there was nonetheless high; under-draining, for instance, was known in the county soon after 1700, although the practice had scarcely penetrated to most other districts by 1830.[5]

The peculiar problems of mountain farming deserve special mention. Agriculture in such regions was predominantly pastoral. Farmers customarily left sheep to their own resources, allowing them to roam at will over the extensive commons. In the Cumbrian fells, it was a common practice to salve ewes with butter as a primitive form of weather-proofing, and farmers in this area were happy if they managed to breed to maturity two lambs for every two sheep. In the lowlands, sheep were enclosed; cold and damp posed less severe problems, and here the normal expectation was to breed three lambs for every two ewes.[6] Many of these differences have outlived the context of eighteenth-century farming.

There are, then, several reasons for suggesting that the scope of the eighteenth-century 'Agrarian Revolution' was limited. The pace of mechanisation was slow; change depended upon individual initiative; and there was no equivalent, in the countryside, to the capital formation of early industrial capitalism. These factors do not mean that growth was lacking. Eighteenth-century England was, compared with most contemporary European states, a wealthy society - imports increased in value by over seven times between 1700 and 1800, and exports over the same period rose by almost as much.[7] One of the main characteristics of wealth, a characteristic which it shares with poverty, is its capacity to permeate society; gains in one sector of the economy are transferred to others. The high value placed by eighteenth-century English society upon land - upon the prestige it bestowed, and the wealth it produced - also has relevance. A Georgian merchant was more likely to invest in a country estate than a cotton factory; a fact that had a bearing upon the buoyancy of the land market.

The best guide to movements in tithes during the eighteenth century is movements in rentals. The increases in these between 1690 and 1750 seldom exceeded 40%, and were often less than 15%; but rises in the range of 40% to 50% were typical over the shorter period between 1750 and 1790.[8] A major explanation of the acceleration after mid-century is that agriculture had earlier been held back by a series of depressions. Corn prices were low when the eighteenth century opened; they were low again in the mid 1720s; and they were particularly depressed between the early 1730s and the mid 1740s. As in the more acutely difficult conditions after the Napoleonic Wars, it was the arable farmers on the lighter soils who coped best. Heavy soil went with heavy depression. A particular problem was created for pasture farmers by an epidemic of cattle plague - especially severe in Cheshire, Wiltshire, and parts of the midlands - which broke out in 1745 and lasted for a decade.[9]

After about 1760, agricultural advance was assisted by improved methods of communication, using this word in its widest sense. Improvements in transport - better roads, the canal 'mania' of the 1790s - are only part of the story; the development of the press, and of the publishing industry, is important, too. The leading polemicist for change was Arthur Young. He was Secretary of the Board of Agriculture, founded in 1793, and in this capacity was responsible for many of the Board's official *Reports*. He wrote over a quarter of the forty-six volumes of *Annals of Agriculture*, all of them published during the relatively short period between 1784 and 1809, and he was the author of six *General Views* of the agriculture of various counties. These works were overtly propagandist, designed to spread the knowledge of new techniques, and of new agricultural implements, among the farming community. Young's enthusiasm was infectious, and under his inspiration many counties formed agricultural societies, mostly in the 1790s. At a rather different level, George III read the *Annals of Agriculture* whilst travelling, rejoiced to be known as 'Farmer George', and experimented with stock-breeding on his model farm at Windsor.[10] Coke of Holkham's famous sheep-shearings should also be noted. These were started by him in 1778, attracted much attention, and were used, like Young's books, to propagate new ideas. Similar convivial gatherings were held by the Duke of Bedford at Woburn, and by Lord Egremont at Petworth.[11] Much energy, and much ink, was expended in the cause of reform.

ii. *Special Situations*

There is one group of eighteenth-century livings for which generalisations about agrarian conditions do not hold; these are places where land reclamation took place. Nowhere, perhaps, was the rise in benefice values as sudden, or as steep, as it was in the Fens. The fight to win them over to cultivation was, it must be emphasised, the work of centuries rather than of years. Even after the Napoleonic Wars, the battle was still being fought vigorously. Drainage had by then improved, but large areas still remained liable to occasional flooding. This was because the 'scoop wheels', rather like mill-wheels in reverse, were not yet driven by steam; the first steam-driven scoop, using a Watt engine, was set up at Bottisham in 1820.[12] The reclamation programme then speeded up, but even before the advent of effective mechanisation vast tracts of Cambridgeshire and Lincolnshire countryside had been converted from bog into fertile land.

Clergy tried to take advantage of change, by extending tithe rights and challenging the validity of existing payments. On several occasions, they were successful.[13] At Wisbech, for instance, a composition for tithes was customary, but in 1803 this was challenged by the incumbent, who put in a claim to tithe in kind. The parishioners countered by trying to set up a modus. As was usual in such cases, the Court of Exchequer was called upon to decide. It deliberated for nearly five years - not long by its own standards - and then decided in favour of the vicar. Soon the vicarage, valued at £180 in 1716 and at twice as much in 1775, was approaching £2,000 a year. At Elm, two miles to the south-east, there were comparable difficulties. The parishioners claimed that their payments were, in effect, moduses, and were therefore unalterable; but Jeremiah Jackson, an enterprising new vicar presented in 1825, denied this, arguing, as had the incumbent of Wisbech, for tithe in kind. This time the movements of the Court of Exchequer were positively electric. Within two years, it had decided, as with Wisbech, in favour of the clerical claim to a proper tenth.

Experience at other Fenland parishes was similar. The rectory of Leverington, in Cambridgeshire, was worth the moderate sum of £130 in 1721; this had climbed to £315 half a century later, and to an altogether different amount, £2,099 a year, by 1830. At another Cambridgeshire rectory, Newton, the rise was less dramatic; a value of £190 in 1716 becoming £400 by 1785, and then more than doubling, to £980, by 1810. In 1830 the living was worth £1,135, a rise of five times compared with one of fifteen times of Leverington. A percentage increase between those at Leverington and Newton was recorded at Feltwell, across the border in neighbouring Norfolk; here, £100 a year in 1736 became, within a century, £1,207.

The most dramatic example of all is the Cambridgeshire rectory of Doddington. Its far-flung boundaries, embracing in their progress the town of March as well as three hamlets and 38,000 acres of farmland, have been discussed already.[14] Here, an indication must be given of how it had become, with time, immensely rich. In the 1530s it was valued at £22 5s 0d; but three centuries later the figure had risen to £7,306,[15] more than any other living in either England or Wales. Six bishoprics at this time were worth more, but the other twenty were all worth smaller amounts.[16] The phenomenal rise at Doddington was the result of several factors operating upon each other. One of these was drainage, another was enclosure, and a third,as at Wisbech and Elm, was extension of tithe rights by means of successful law-suits. What happened at Doddington was a solemn warning to English farmers; it showed them how heavy the millstone of tithe hanging round their necks could become. Given such evidence, it is not surprising that they should try to remove it, or at least prevent it from growing heavier.

iii. *The Napoleonic Boom in Agriculture*

It will have been noticed that several Fenland parishes rose dramatically in value during the Napoleonic Wars. The years between the outbreak of war with France in 1793 and the concluding of peace at Vienna in 1815 produced an unprecedented economic situation. It is difficult to overstress the severity of the crisis at this time. The economy was drained as it had never been before: by 1811, 13% of the gross national product was being spent to defeat Napoleon. The National Debt rose by over 240%, from just under £250 million to over £830 million.[17] It would be wrong to claim that the principle of taxation was suddenly discovered - this clever idea, unfortunately, goes back much further; but several additions to the state's armoury were nevertheless made, chiefly through the introduction of income tax. Never had the people of England been taxed so extensively, so rigorously, or so effectively. Their windows were taxed, their servants were taxed, their carriages were taxed, and even their candles were taxed.[18] Such change was rather terrifying. In 1797, when the famous triple assessment was introduced, taxation was running at £18.8 million a year; by 1815 it had reached £69.7 million, nearly four times as much.[19]

Another problem was pressure on domestic consumption, especially severe after the Treaty of Tilsit, since Napoleon then began to enforce the Continental System. In 1806, not a single bushel of grain was exported to England from Prussia, the granary of Europe. Thereafter, the Continental System followed no set pattern - it was tightened in 1807 and 1808, relaxed in 1809 and 1810, tightened again in 1811 and 1812, and then more or less completely collapsed after the failure of Napoleon's abortive Russian campaign.[20]

If war produced inflationary pressures, so did internal stresses. One such was population growth. There was here, as already mentioned, a frightening momentum. Between 1700 and 1750 the population of England rose by about 15%; between 1750 and 1800 it went up by around 50%; and between 1800 and 1840 it rose by a further 75% or so. So great and sustained an increase was previously unknown.[21]

To inflationary pressure from a rising population was added the effect of industrialisation, led by the cotton factories and affecting also the coal and metallurgical industries. All industrial revolutions show in their earliest stages a number of family resemblances, one of the clearest of which is a tendency for prices to rise.[22] In England's case, the inflationary problems resulting from industrialisation were exacerbated by the onset of hitherto unparalleled, as well as prolonged, military commitment in Europe. The ensuing economic confusion was, arguably, made worse by the lack of any effective policy for control of price movements. A clear illustration is the financial crisis of 1796-7. The Bank of England at that time stopped making payments in gold, and did not resume making them until the postwar period. Soon after suspension the money supply started to expand rapidly, and this was probably a major factor in producing the first 'confetti' inflation in English history. During 1797 and 1798 the index of wholesale prices was relatively steady, but in 1799 it went up by around 30%, and between January 1800 and March 1801 it increased by even more.[23]

Peace in 1802 brought deflation - by December of that year, prices were a third lower than they had been twenty months earlier - but this was not to last. Renewal of hostilities was followed by renewal of inflation. This second bout was longer than the first, but its incidence was less intense. Starting from the early months of 1808, prices rose virtually without interruption throughout the next four years, reaching a peak in August, 1812.[24]

The novelty of these economic events cannot be stressed too strongly. Annual inflation rates of 30% appeared, suddenly and unexpectedly, in a society proud of its stability. Inflation had been known in England before - always in wartime, and sometimes, as in several decades during the sixteenth century, in peacetime - but never on the scale of that which threatened the economy during the Napoleonic period.

One section of society saw no reason for complaint. Reduction in foreign competition and the periodic unavailability of imports favoured English farmers, as did the economic ambience of the war years. High government borrowing, especially when combined with inflation, favours rentiers and entrepreneurs; it correspondingly militates against the economic interests of the working community, lowering real wages and pushing up the proportion of income spent on staple food.[25] Farmers also benefited from rising consumer demand, itself the product of population expansion. Figures for domestic consumption of corn are neither easy to compile nor to come by, but it would seem that the increase, in volume terms, was equivalent to about a quarter between 1790 and 1810.[26] This was one factor making for unusually high cereal prices; poor harvests were another. The inflation between January 1799 and March 1801 was partly caused by the disastrous harvest of 1800. Harvests were also very poor in 1795 and 1796, and those in 1809, 1811, and 1812 were little better. All in all, there were fourteen deficient harvests in the twenty-year period 1793-1812.[27] Cereal prices kept ahead of general price movements even in times of chronic inflation; prices for cereals went up by more than 80% between January 1799 and March 1801, and also rose more sharply than those for other commodities during the second bout of inflation between 1808 and 1812.[28]

English farmers always gain from war, largely because the modern English economy is heavily reliant upon food imports, but during the hostilities against Napoleon they did especially well. The Continental System helped them: rising consumer demand from an increasing population helped them; and so, too, did the inflationary effect of poor harvests. With little grain coming into the country, it became essential to cultivate every available acre. Wherever there was land, there too went the plough. There are places, later deserted hillsides, where traces of Napoleonic plough-rig could be seen for generations. To borrow a phrase more often applied to the canal building of the 1790s or the railway building of the 1840s, it could be said that all this activity amounted to a kind of agrarian 'mania'.

What was good for farmers was also good, generally speaking, for clergy. The gains made by benefice incomes during the boom are revealed by some much-neglected returns on property tax, giving the monetary value of tithes in each English and Welsh county. The returns cover the second period of wartime inflation, being for the years 1806, 1808, 1810, and 1812. Within each of these three two-year periods, tithes rose - between 1806 and 1808 by 6.4%, between 1808 and 1810 by 10%, and between 1810 and 1812 by 9.6%. Over the six-year period as a whole the rise was 28.2%. This is impressive enough. However, because of technical factors to do with the make-up of the returns, the increase for tithes is understated: a nationwide rise of 35% is nearer the mark than the recorded figure of 28%.[29]

The returns are ambivalent about the incomes of clergy in mountainous and agriculturally backward districts. In some counties not normally noted for advanced agricultural techniques, tithes did much better than average. The best examples are Hereford, Cornwall and Flint. In Hereford, a fringe county on the English-Welsh border, the rise was over 60%; in Cornwall extended land use helped to push up tithes by a shade over 45%; and in Flint, an area of ancient enclosure, the increase was more than 40%. The situation elsewhere was very different. Worst was Brecon, a mountainous county with much waste and narrow valleys; there the increase was a meagre 0.6%. Figures for those fells walked by Wordsworth and by Coleridge also make depressing reading. For Westmorland the rise was 8%, and for Cumberland it was even less, only 6%.[30] These results are partially explained by special factors - in Westmorland almost a quarter of all property was subject to fixed moduses, and in Cumberland the percentage of tithable property fell by nearly 9% between 1806 and 1812 - but are nevertheless extremely weak. In some places the gap separating rich clergy from poor narrowed during the boom, and in others it widened.

The returns are not a reliable guide to the rise in tithes throughout the war years; besides being short, the period covered by them coincided with the second phase of wartime inflation. Rather broader in its approach is an estimate made by Arthur Young. In 1804, as Secretary of the Board of Agriculture, he sent out a circular to farmers, asking what had been the cost of cultivating one hundred acres of arable in 1790 as compared with 1803; in 1814 he did the same, making enquiries about the previous year. On the basis of the answers given to these circulars, Young told a House of Lords select committee that tithes contributed £20 14s 1d towards the cost in 1790, but that this figure had risen to £26 8s 0d by 1803, and then again to £38 17s 3d ten years later.[31] This is equivalent to a rise of nearly 90% in a little over twenty years.

Young's figures dovetail well with a wide-ranging survey of rentals, based on manuscript sources, included in F.M.L. Thompson, *English Landed Society in the Nineteenth Century*.[32] Thompson studied ten separate estates, drawn from many parts of England. Some were from areas of new enclosure - Northamptonshire, Hertfordshire, Bedfordshire; some from northern England; some from the Kentish Weald; and others from Wiltshire and Devon. The aggregate rental of these estates was large in 1790, in the region of £40,000 a year, and it had grown even larger by 1815, to over £80,000 a year. Only on one estate - Orlebar in Bedfordshire - was a rise of under 50% recorded; on five it was over 100%, and the average works out at 112.6%.

Tithes probably increased by about 100% during the war years. The fact that they generally lagged a little behind rentals would, in the context of F.M.L.Thompson's figures, suggest this; Arthur Young's evidence before the House of Lords select committee points in the same direction; and an improvement of this magnitude is broadly compatible with the adjusted figures of a rise for tithes of about 35% between 1806 and 1812. Increases were not the same everywhere; probably most fell within the range of 50% to 150%. At the upper end of the scale there are some figures for compositions in Cambridgeshire, showing a rise of 100% between 1790 and 1804.[33] The general picture is one of a strong move forward over a wide front, leaving some laggards and spearheaded by some leaders.

iv. *Depression*

Modern warfare - the warfare of mass conscription, mass destruction, and mass death - does many things to human communities. It breaks loyalties, shatters relationships, disrupts families; it acts, also, as a powerful levelling influence within society. This is mainly a levelling down rather than a levelling up - some wars improve the living standards of some workers, but it is the rich whose fortunes change the most. While war lasts, contradictory forces operate. High levels of personal taxation - income tax, introduced during the Napoleonic Wars, rose from 1s 8d in the pound in 1914 to 6s in 1918, and from 7s 6d in 1939 to 10s by 1941[34] - make for a larger measure of equality. On the other hand, landowners stand to gain from the inevitable stimulus to agriculture, while those with capital to spare can finance, at high rates of interest, the expanding National Debt. The postwar period is less ambivalent. Ancient empires may break up - Austria-Hungary and the Ottoman Empire in 1918 - and landed estates can meet the same fate; taxation remains high; and speculative possibilities dry up. Those with capital may win the war, but they invariably lose the peace. The aftermath of the Napoleonic Wars was no exception to this general rule. Inflation gave way, towards the end of 1813, to severe deflation. For May 1813 the index of wholesale prices stood at 177.0; for December 1813, it was 158.6; and for December 1815, it had fallen to 118.7.[35] This represents a fall in prices of 33% in two and a half years. Banks, especially country banks, often could not stand the strain - there were 206 bankruptcies between 1815 and 1830.[36] Money lost value, and those who suffered most were those who had gained most from wartime inflation: speculators first, landowners second.

The plight of English agriculture was acute in the postwar period , but it is important not to over-emphasise the degree of distress. Deflation was periodic, being most virulent in 1813-15 and then again in 1819-23. Comparisons must also be made between different areas and types of soil. Worst hit were the heavy clays; light soils fared best. During the boom, corn had been king, with cattle and sheep being, so to speak, merely courtiers; but after 1813 the roles were reversed. Cereal prices, especially for wheat, fell sharply, while those for livestock held up better.[37] Another important point is that arable farmers cushioned the fall in their profits by increasing yields. Illuminating in this context are notebooks kept by surveyors working for two Liverpool firms, and containing crop-cutting data collected over a wide area. These show that, between 1815-19 on the one hand and 1832-6 on the other, yields of wheat increased, despite the depression, by 16%.[38]

Evidence presented to the frequent parliamentary committees on the state of agriculture supports these findings. Everywhere the heavy clays were in difficulty. Thus it was at Doncaster, near the border between West Yorkshire and Nottinghamshire; and so, too, in the Kentish and Sussex Wealds. One farmer, with five hundred acres of arable, at Bapchild in Kent, told the House of Commons select committee of 1821 that he had made a loss during the past two years. Other farmers in the same area had been in trouble somewhat earlier, in 1814 and 1815, but no land had been abandoned.[39] Across the border in neighbouring Sussex the situation was worse. The Weald running from Horsham towards Guildford was in a depressed state as late as the early 1830s; at the same period the heavy clays on the Hampshire-Sussex border were returning to grass.[40] Sussex and Kent were counties of ancient enclosure, but even in counties of new enclosure there were comparable problems. Complaints that the heavier soils were being allowed to return to grass came from many counties - for instance, Berkshire, Buckinghamshire, and Hertfordshire, and also Bedfordshire, Oxfordshire, and Northamptonshire[41] - but, despite the gloom, farmers in many places responded positively to prevailing conditions. Interesting, here, is evidence submitted to the House of Commons select committee of 1836 by Thomas Neve, who farmed at Benenden in Kent. Neve confirmed that farms on the heavy clays of the Kentish Weald between Tenterden and Tunbridge Wells were in a depressed state due to a succession of wet summers, but also emphasised that farmers were combating the ill effects of damp by undertaking extensive schemes of new drainage.[42]

In areas where light soils predominated, there were fewer signs of distress. One such example is Norfolk. This county, according to a witness before the 1833 Committee, was in a state of 'progressive improvement'. A number of farms had been in a bad condition prior to 1818, but few now were, principally because clay was scarce. Some land had suffered as a result of overcropping during the boom, but no arable - at least around Aldeburgh - had been given up, despite the 'immense' increase in the area under cultivation between 1800 and 1813.[43]

In outlying counties infertile land, pressed into service during the boom, was now abandoned; but otherwise conditions do not seem to have been too bad, particularly in areas of subsistence farming and extensive livestock production. North Wales staged a strong recovery between 1816 and 1821. Shropshire, much of which was given over to livestock, also fared quite well.[44] The Lake district is one of the best examples of a subsistence economy. Everyone there, farmer as well as labourer, lived on a strictly staple diet: barley bread, potatoes, milk, a little bacon. Fresh meat was almost unknown, except perhaps on Sundays, and milk mixed with water was more likely to be drunk than beer. It is significant that distress in Cumberland and Westmorland was only severe in those areas brought suddenly under cultivation during the boom, chiefly large tracts of commons of poor quality. Where these had been given over to wheat production, they were now given up, but good land remained very profitable; indeed, one witness before the 1833 committee claimed that he had 'no doubt' but that 'the produce from the lands of the first quality' in Cumberland 'is not only as great at this moment, but greater than it ever was'.[45]

Statistical evidence of the depression's affect upon rents is more authoritative. It is possible to find examples of rentals which went down as soon as the boom broke, following the abundant harvest of 1813, and then stayed down, but these are few and far between. One such is the Belsay estate, in Northumberland, where rents brought in £7,600 in 1810, but rather less - only £6,800 - ten years later.[46] A lot of other evidence, however, points to a more optimistic conclusion. In some places there was zero growth for a period, soon followed by a return to partial prosperity. Such were Lord Darnley's estates in north-west Kent. The rents on these rose by nearly 100% between 1788 and 1820, from £2,229 a year to £4,404. For the period between 1805 and 1811 the annual growth rate was 5%; between 1812 and 1815 it was nil; and during the next five years it recovered to 3%.[47] More impressive are areas where rentals fell, only to stage such a strong recovery that former levels were surpassed. One example is an estate in Norfolk where income went down from over £6,650 a year in 1813 to only £4,029 in 1815; but by 1818 a resurgence was fully under way, and income had climbed past the previous high, to over £7,500 a year.[48] Most impressive of all are places where depression was scarcely even felt. There is a large sample in this final category - sixteen estates, comprising 65,000 acres, dispersed across Lincolnshire, Essex, Hereford, and parts of North Wales. On these, rents continued to rise after 1815: the average annual rental between 1806 and 1810 was 11s 7d an acre, but for the next two five-year periods it was 14s 7d and 15s 2d respectively.[49]

For tithes, as for rentals, the situation in the 1820s and early 1830s was unfavourable. Nevertheless, it is difficult to find instances of severe reductions in receipts; in most places, the worst that was encountered was the modest loss of some of the enormous advances made during the boom. Derbyshire is a good example. The sample from this county covers 63 benefices - 30 rectories and 33 vicarages. Between 1824 and 1832 the average worth of the rectories declined by £15 a year from £474 to £459, while that of the vicarages fell by £2 from £197 to £195.[50] This suggests that, over the period from 1813 to 1836, the rectories may have lost about £30 or £45 a year (6% to 10% of their value), and the vicarages about £4 or £6 (2% to 3%).

On a far larger scale, there are two valuable sets of parliamentary returns. The first of these, indicative of the chaotic state of much episcopal administration, is in fact a conflation, bringing together information supplied by the bishops to the Bounty in 1810 with further facts set before parliament in 1815.[51] The second return, much tidier and more precise, is a table in the Report of the Ecclesiastical Revenues Commission. Both sources give details of the number of benefices in each diocese where the value did not exceed £150 a year. The comparison between 1810-15 on the one hand, and 1829-31 on the other, is interesting indeed. In the earlier period there were 4,361 livings worth £3 a week or less, among a total of 10,421 parishes making returns;[52] in the latter, no more than 3,528 among 10,478. The reduction works out at 833, equivalent to 19.1%. Although a major distorting factor has to be contended with - it was in 1810 that the Bounty put in place a special, new, programme designed to raise the values of poor benefices[53] - it is clear that livings worth £150 or less did rather well during the postwar depression.[54]

For livings worth over £150 a year the conclusions are necessarily more tentative, but there is no evidence of calamitous falls during the postwar period. Figures presented earlier for rentals do not suggest such a collapse, nor does analysis of smaller benefices. The most probable general picture is one showing most benefice incomes holding steady, while a number lose, at any rate in the short term, some of the unexpectedly large gains made during the boom. The postwar depression, where it was severe, mainly took the form of a retreat from artificially high levels of prosperity. It did not drive clergy into penury. In describing it, apocalyptic pessimism is out of place; cautious pessimism, or even cautious optimism, is both more appropriate and more easily justified.

v. *Enclosure*

A major continuity in agrarian history during the Georgian era was the enclosure movement. Before 1750, enclosures were sometimes accomplished informally, through a local agreement; but after this date the passing of an act of Parliament was the usual procedure.[55] This change from informality to formality marks the effective start of the movement. Over the three-quarters of a century between the accession of George III and that of Victoria, the number of enclosures averaged about forty a year, reaching a peak between 1800 and 1820, when the average doubled to over eighty a year.[56] Their frequency then fell away sharply, soon reaching twenty a year.[57] By 1830, most of what was going to be enclosed in England had been.[58] The revolution was over, and about a quarter of the cultivable land, over six million acres, had been surrounded by the now-familiar hedges and ditches.

Enclosure served different purposes in different districts. The east and south-east - Norfolk, Suffolk, Essex, Kent - was the heart of the older, Tudor and Stuart movement, and in these counties the aim was to extend previous enclosures rather than create new ones. In much of the north and west, parts of the north midlands, and the south coast - counties like Durham, Lancashire and Cheshire, Shropshire and Staffordshire, Cornwall and Somerset, Surrey and Sussex - the Georgian movement made possible the cultivation of hitherto unused waste and commons. Finally, there was enclosure of open fields - the supersession of the ancient manorial system, with its 'strip' farming, by newly hedged and ditched fields. This was concentrated within a vast triangular wedge of land, with its apex at Middlesborough to the north, and its base running from Ipswich in the east to Portland Bill in the south-west. Enclosure without commutation was associated with the enlargement of previous enclosures, and with the fencing-in of waste and commons. Enclosure with commutation usually took place whenever a third category of land, the open field, was dealt with.

There were about 3,700 Enclosure Acts between 1760 and 1830.[59] In a total of around 10,500 parishes,[60] this implies that enclosure was experienced in 35% of all the places in England at this time. It is important to distinguish between cases where tithes were commuted at enclosure, and cases where they were not. Assuming a total of 3,700 Enclosure Acts, analysis suggests that enclosure with commutation occurred in 2,200 or so instances,[61] and that enclosure without commutation took place in the remaining 1,500. Enclosure without an accompanying commutation was completed in many districts; enclosure with commutation was geographically concentrated. On over 1,800 occasions in the total of 2,200 or so,[62] commutation was carried through in sixteen counties, all of them either wholly or partly within the triangle of countryside (Portland Bill-Ipswich-Middlesborough) already described.[63] It was the clergy of 'middle' England, of counties such as Lincolnshire, Leicestershire, Northamptonshire and Oxfordshire, who mainly benefited from commutation.

The agricultural advantages of enclosure without commutation were, from the 'progressive' farmer's point of view, numerous. The cultivation of hitherto fallow fields was an automatic result, and with it an increase in the production of cereals. Consolidation of holdings made for greater efficiency and higher crop yields; cattle, now fenced in, were saved from the ravages of a previous promiscuity and could be bred scientifically;[64] drainage schemes were easier to organise; improved systems of crop rotation could be introduced; waste was utilised; and the use of root crops, especially turnips and potatoes, became more widespread.[65]

While these improvements were going on, the clergy remained passive. When there was no commutation at enclosure, the system of tithe collection then in use was not altered. The more 'progressive' local farmers subsequently became the faster tithes rose and, of course, the opposite also holds. The history of enclosure without commutation is entangled with the agricultural history of the whole of England, and these threads have not yet been disentangled by historians. From the clergy's point of view, the financial benefits of enclosure without commutation were variable, with good gains in progressive parishes balanced by smaller gains elsewhere. This conclusion is tentative, but as local research becomes more systematic, greater precision will be possible.

Commutation of tithe, it has already been noted,[66] could take any one of three forms: it could be for land; tithe could be abolished in return for a cash settlement; or a corn rent, varying with the price of grain, could be substituted. Out of all the settlements made during the Georgian era, commutation for land accounted for about 85% or 90%, with the proportion rising still higher after 1810, to 95%. Cash agreements, always few, became less frequent when the Napoleonic boom began, and corn rents - the method agreed upon under the Commutation Act of 1836 - covered the rest.[67] The prevalence of commutation for land is made apparent by local figures: Yorkshire leads the field with a massive total of 354; Lincolnshire scores 266; Northamptonshire is next with 182; and Rutland, as small as can be, is still credited with 25.[68]

The clergy did well at commutation. As tithe-owners, they were in a position of privilege tinged with power. They could not be coerced into agreement. If they stood their ground, the enclosure had to be completed without commutation; they had the right to appoint an enclosure commissioner; and it was customary for them to be spared most of the costs that inevitably arose. They usually paid for the internal fencing of their own holdings, and for new farm buildings, if such were needed; but they avoided everything else: the expenses attendant upon the application to parliament and the drafting of a local act, solicitors' fees and payments to the commissioners, provision of external fencing and ditching, and the building of new bridges, roads and drains. Although enclosure was already expensive in the eighteenth century, the cost rose alarmingly during the wartime boom. A figure of under £1 an acre has been mentioned for the 1760s and 1770s; whereas, after 1790, £3 was 'not uncommon' and the average has been estimated at 34s.[69] To make a negligible contribution towards a sum as high as this was a considerable advantage.

Adoption of more sophisticated methods of commutation also benefited the clergy. The major issue, here, was to differentiate between arable and pasture. Before the mid 1770s it was normal practice to commute tithe for a straight proportion of the land to be allotted; after this date a higher proportion of arable was usually allotted than of pasture, often a fifth of the total as compared with an eighth or a ninth.[70] It is easy to see that this increasing sophistication benefited clergy in arable parishes, but less easy to see why it was adopted. The answer lies in the nature of tithe as a tax. Tithe in kind was set, theoretically, at 10% of the gross yield, an amount that did not take into account any of the costs of cultivation, which were inevitably much higher on labour intensive arable. Commutation for land turned the clergyman into a farmer, and he then had to meet all those labour and other costs which he had previously avoided. It was calculated by contemporaries that at least a fifth of the arable needed to be commuted in order to produce the equivalent of 10% of the gross yield, exclusive of costs; but the figure for pasture was set a lot lower, at only an eighth or a ninth. Hence the need for differentiation.

The exceptional conditions which prevailed during the Revolutionary and Napoleonic Wars improved the clergy's bargaining position. At this time the number of enclosures more than doubled from 40 a year to over 80, with a peak of 133 in 1812.[71] This is only one among several signs of farmers' over-confidence during these years. Whenever an enclosure was proposed, the clergyman's hand was strengthened; he could, in the last resort, successfully prevent any commutation. The desire to be rid of tithes was so strong, and speculative enthusiasm so great, that a number of extremely unwise schemes were carried through, whereby unnecessarily high proportions of land were allotted in lieu.[72]

Although the clergy, as a body, did well at commutation, some did much better than others. A lot depended upon skill in bargaining, and there was much to bargain about. When tithes were commuted for land, the planning of plots was a matter of some concern - several fields, unevenly distributed over a parish and far distant from the glebe, were less use than a consolidated group close by it or, even better, contiguous.

This was one issue that could be haggled over, and the fertility of adjacent fields was another. Because fertility varied, commissioners could not justifiably employ a rule of thumb; each act had to take local conditions into account. In cases where tithes were exchanged for a corn rent or cash equivalent, a special difficulty arose. The commissioners had to decide whether the rent or cash settlement should, or should not, take account of improved cultivation resulting from the proposed enclosure; and, if they decided that it should, they then had to calculate what this improved value might be expected to amount to - by no means an easy task. Finally, when assessing the bargaining muscle of individual incumbents, the social and political context of enclosure must be borne in mind. Enclosure awards were planned by big landowners, approved in parliament by big landowners, carried out by big landowners, and took into account the interests of big landowners. It follows that the wealthier clergy, closely connected to the gentry by the variously successful social cements of birth, marriage, and daily intercourse, were more likely to receive generous allotments than their poorer brethren who lacked these advantages.

Some enclosures were amicable, but others were contested. Where there was a contest, a local power struggle was initiated at one of two levels: parson could be set against squire, or parson and squire could be set against farmer. The outcome helped to determine how well clergy did at commutation. A good example of conflict between parson and squire is the enclosure at Oddington in Oxfordshire. The first shot was fired by the lord of the manor, John Sawyer. Writing to the clerk of the commissioners on 21 November 1790, he made it clear that he was not prepared to allow any corn rent substituted for tithe to take account of agricultural improvement resulting from the proposed enclosure. Sawyer's aim, seemingly, was to obtain the consent of the rector, Gilbert Parker, to an agreement detrimental to the rectoral interest; or, if such consent could not be had, to apply to parliament and see which side won. Consent was not forthcoming, so Sawyer applied to parliament. There he had the support of John White, MP, who piloted the local bill through the Commons. Neither was Parker alone; the living had for its patron a powerful collegiate body, Trinity College, Oxford. The college, in its correspondence with the clerk of the commissioners, insisted that the value of the tithes must be reckoned on their improved condition after enclosure. The college, moreover, had its way and a corn rent of £230 a year - far higher than Sawyer was initially prepared to accept - was finally agreed upon. John White was well aware of the pressure exerted by Trinity, and of its effectiveness. To the clerk of the commissioners, he wrote privately on 28 March 1791: 'I hope I shall never have any land in a parish where a college are patrons of a Rectory - that is between ourselves....' The clerical case was also argued in the House of Lords, where the Bishop of Bangor tried to get the corn rent more than doubled, to over £500 a year. This proved to be optimistic and the Bishop was forced to withdraw his plea when he realised that he was acting on false information regarding the size and fertility of the parish. Despite this unsuccessful episcopal intervention, the result was still a victory for Gilbert Parker.[73]

The award for Wigston in Leicestershire shows how the struggle for power at the second level - parson and squire versus farmer - could work itself out. The village stands just four miles south of Leicester. When it was enclosed in 1766, both the Duke of St Alban's (who held the great tithes) and the vicar (with the small) received very liberal allotments. Great tithes were exchanged for a farm of 291 acres, and small tithes for one of 88 acres. The total of 379 acres represented a little under a seventh of the available land, a smaller percentage than in a good number of enclosures elsewhere, but still sufficient to have the effect of enlarging the land-holdings of parson and squire, and correspondingly decreasing those of the farming community. Perquisites were also added. As was customary, the award stated that the allotments made to the Duke and the vicar were to be 'mounded and fenced round by ditches and quickset hedges guarded or fenced with good posts and double rails', and that these improvements were to be carried out at the expense of the other proprietors.[74] In the Georgian countryside, squire and parson, when linked in unity, were a force of formidable strength.

Commutation for land boosted the social status of the clergy. Many incumbents, hitherto socially undistinguished, now found that they were landowners, thus reviving the medieval tradition of the 'squarson' or parson-farmer. From this fountain of newly-won landed affluence, other benefits flowed. The magistracy, hedged about with property qualifications, was open to an increasing number of clergy; so, too, were the arms of more magistrates' daughters. The clergy became more affluent, more socially accepted, and more locally powerful. They also became more secular. Stripping themselves of the twin protections of poverty and professional dignity, they increasingly exposed themselves, at times of dearth, to that generalised anti-authoritarian anger which was a marked feature of the English (and European) countryside. In the dark winter of 1830-1, the incumbents whom the rabble mobbed, robbed, or trod to earth were, for the most part, rich.[75]

The financial advantages of commutation for land were considerable. This is clear from an important piece of research, which contrasts the size of glebes in counties of old enclosure with that of glebes in counties of new. The major finding is that the average glebe in the former was a shade over 44 acres, whereas in the latter it was more than two and a half times as large, just under 118 acres.[76] This makes the point with some force. Commutation for land could turn a benefice into a distinctly desirable property.

On the other hand, it would be wrong to assume that commutation for land was the only, or necessarily the surest, path towards a swift advance in benefice values. The falseness of this assumption has been exposed by work that has been done on the clergy in Derbyshire. In the forty or so years between 1772 and 1824, rectories where land had not been taken in lieu went up a little faster in value than those where it had, by, in fact, 257% as compared with 238%.[77] The reason for this surprising result is not traced to methods or procedures at commutation, but to clerical estate management. Apparently, prior to 1815, it was customary for Derbyshire incumbents to lease their commuted estates for periods of up to twenty-one years at fixed rents; it was their tenants, in other words, who cashed in on the Napoleonic boom, not themselves. It would be interesting to know whether clergy were equally unworldly elsewhere. If they were, the conventional view of the commutation movement will have to be radically reassessed.

To sum up: certain aspects of the enclosure movement are clear, but others are not. Just over two parishes in every ten experienced enclosure with commutation, nearly always for land; about three in twenty experienced enclosure without commutation. The clergy's gains from the latter are hard to assess accurately, for in these instances they participated in benefits coming from general agricultural improvement, but did not reap any direct rewards. Nevertheless enclosure, especially on arable land, brightened the whole agricultural spectrum - more (and fatter) cattle; more (and better cropped) corn; more turnips; more potatoes; more sheep; indeed, more of everything. Ten per cent of the gross agricultural product became, with enclosure, an increasingly attractive proposition. Commutation for land did much to solidify the clergy's place in hierarchies of rural power, but its financial benefits are less certain. It is true that commutation substantially improved the size of the average glebe, but increases in land-holdings are not the same as increases in permanent income. The commutation movement was at its most active while the Napoleonic boom was at its height, and under boom conditions skilled estate management is called for. Some clergy, certainly those in Derbyshire, lacked the requisite finesse. Their decision in favour of long leases, at low fixed rents and with high renewal charges, turned their livings into something like lotteries. Whatever the immediate benefits of this system when the lease was first made out, it was not a method of management well-suited to boom conditions. Short periods of tenure, and rising rentals, were then the requirement. The missing link in the history of the commutation movement is whether the methods of management adopted by the Derbyshire clergy represent normal clerical practice; if they did, then that movement was less of a financial blessing to the clergy than historians have hitherto believed.

vi. *Clerical Estate Management*
In deciding to lease out their commuted estates for long periods at low fixed rents, the Derbyshire clergy were pursuing policies traditionally adopted by the church's greatest landowners, the bishops and cathedral dignitaries. Stress must be placed upon the word 'traditionally'. By 1800, there were bishops and canons who had radically altered the management of their estates, making the policies of the Derbyshire clergy anachronistic. It is therefore necessary to give a sketch of traditional practice, and then to contrast this with how an 'advanced' bishop or canon would approach problems of estate management.

Each of the twenty-six bishoprics in England and Wales had attached to it a varying number of estates. Sometimes these were large, sometimes not; but, whatever their size, there is a number of excellent reasons for believing that management was open, in nearly every case, to considerable improvement. One reason is connected with methods of administration. Most early Georgian bishops left the management of their estates to their secretaries, an arrangement placing too much power into a single pair of hands. Surrogate lords of all they surveyed, episcopal secretaries of the early eighteenth century did not enjoy a high reputation for intellectual capacity, bureaucratic efficiency or, for that matter, plain honesty. The system of management was also open to criticism. Its major fault was its archaic inflexibility. Estates were usually leased out in one of two ways; either the lease ran for a specified number of years, often twenty-one, or it lasted for what was known as 'three lives' - that is, until the death of the longest lived of three persons mentioned in it.[78] Income came from annual rents, and from 'fines' exacted for lease renewals. Since rents were usually low and fines usually high, there tended to be a gentle annual trickle of cash flow that turned itself, occasionally, into a glittering cascade.

Possibilities of peculation - and also of careful long term management - are clear from study of the revenues of the see of Durham. These episcopal estates were certainly numerous - a rental roll of the early eighteenth century, itself incomplete, lists 1,694 tenants and properties. Management was poor. Between the Restoration and the end of the first quarter of the eighteenth century, successive prince bishops pursued an unashamedly nepotistic policy, leasing out to relatives much property on very long leases and with very favourable terms. Had this process continued with the momentum it had gathered, the episcopal estates, vast though they were, would have lost much of their value. Fortunately for later holders of the see, it did not. Recovery took several forms. On the financial side, there was a systematic effort to increase fines for lease renewals. Running side by side with this change was another; leases for lives were discouraged, with those for short terms of years taking their place. By 1770, the great bulk of episcopal property was leased for terms of only seven years. Then again, the nepotistic alienation of property became a thing of the past. There was, finally, an improvement on the administrative side; bishop's secretaries served longer, were less corrupt, and were correspondingly more efficient. One instance will suffice to indicate what all this could mean for episcopal revenue. In 1771, the fine for renewing the lease of the manor of Gateshead was £159, yet within only seventeen years the cost had almost trebled, to £470 14s 0d.[79] This is an extreme example of reform, but it does expose how great the opportunities for 'improvement' in this class of property could be.

There were, in all, twenty-eight chapters.[80] All except two - namely, the chapters at Westminster and Windsor - were part of a diocesan organisation. A further miscellaneous group of seven establishments - the collegiate church of Manchester, and the deaneries of Brecon, Heytesbury, Middleham, Ripon, Southwell and Wolverhampton - were not attached to dioceses. It is important to explain the way in which chapters differed from each other. Half of them were 'old', that is, they had a structure that had remained unaltered since medieval times; while the other half were 'new', with an organisation dating from the sixteenth century.

The tapestry of cathedral establishment looks like this. Each chapter was presided over by a dean. Beneath him was a varying number of canons and prebendaries. The structure of old foundations diverged from the new. In the former, though not in the latter, there were numerous non-residentiary prebends, virtual sinecures without easily detectable clerical duties; these totalled 290. Residentiary prebends and canons, found both in old and new foundations, were fewer; numbering 230. Next, there was a group of 39 posts - either chancellor, treasurer, precentor or sub-dean - usually held either by the dean or by one of the residentiary canons. Then there was a larger group of 194 minor offices, all of them held in their own right, usually by a cleric not otherwise part of the establishment. These minor offices were known by a multitude of names: minor canon, vicar, vicar-choral, priest-vicar, preacher, chaplain, lecturer, organist, gospeller, epistoller, usher, teacher, sacrist, librarian, subchanter. The grand total of all these offices - deans and canons, prebends and chancellors, sacrists and subchanters - was 780.

The revenues of non-residentiary prebendaries, all of them in old foundations, were derived from a personal estate or estates. Deans and residentiary canons in these foundations also had their own lands, but they drew most of their income from fixed annual 'stipends' and from the yearly 'dividend', in which they all had an equal share. New foundations differed from the old in two ways. Except at Durham and Ely, deans and canons lacked any personal revenues, and by way of a harsh denial of egalitarian principle, it was customary for deans to receive a double share of the general dividend. Chancellorships, sub-deaneries, and treasurerships in pre-Reformation foundations were similar to non-residentiary prebends, in that they had estates of their own; minor offices held in their own right were provided with stipends, which by 1830 were mostly in the range of £50-£70 a year. There were, as might be expected, some anomalies; at Christ Church, Oxford, half the rent of Christ Church meadow, let for £250 a year, went to the dean, with the canons getting a sixteenth each. Thirty posts, twenty-four of them non-residentiary, were permanently annexed to bishoprics, and it was customary for bishops to hold a number of others, most notably the opulent deaneries of Durham and St Paul's, and at least one of Durham's 'golden' prebends.

The income of the 290 non-residentiary prebends mostly came from fines for lease renewals. These fines could be easily raised, if the office holder adopted methods similar to those used by successive Bishops of Durham during the second half of the eighteenth century. Those deans, canons, and chancellors who had personal revenues could employ similar tactics. Worst placed were the holders of the 194 minor offices; their stipends were usually fixed and did not keep pace with inflation. Sometimes, the incomes of cathedral dignitaries took a decided turn for the better as a result of industrialisation and urban growth. The most conspicuous examples are the 'golden' prebends of Durham and the three residentiary canonries of St Paul's. Coal was conveniently found beneath land belonging to the chapter at Durham, and the canonries of St Paul's benefited from extensive property development, both of them impressive instances of Fortune's curious habit of smiling, freely and broadly, on the already fortunate.[81] By the 1830s a prebend at Durham was worth over

£2,000 a year, while a canonry at St Paul's was equally remunerative.

The canonries of St Paul's and the 'golden' prebends of Durham were special cases. What about the general mass of episcopal and capitular property? There is, here, the evidence of a survey of royal patronage carried out at the start of George III's reign, and also figures in the 1835 Report.[82] The six bishoprics of Canterbury, York, London, Oxford, Bristol, and Llandaff were worth, in aggregate, £16,500 a year in 1760, a sum which had grown to £49,312 a year - an increase of 199% - seventy years later. Over the same period the deaneries of Canterbury, York, St Paul's, and Christ Church, Oxford, together with the canonries of St Paul's and of Christ Church and the prebends of Canterbury, went up from £5,750 a year to £17,041, a rise of 196%. Among the bishoprics the steepest rise was at Oxford, which quintupled, while the smallest was at Llandaff, which just failed to double in value. Among capitular property the two poles were represented by the canonries of Christ Church (nearly a quadruple increase) and the deanery of Canterbury (slightly better than the rise at Llandaff).

For incumbents the problems of estate management were more socially sensitive. Canons and prebendaries did not reside on their estates; rectors and vicars were supposed always to do so. A financially undemanding parson was likely to be a popular parson; just as a financially demanding parson was equally likely to be an unpopular parson. The 'generous' rector reaped a ready reward: peace ungarnished with gold. Such was John Lettice, vicar of the hop-growing parish of Peasmarsh in Sussex from 1785 until his death, at the age of ninety-four, in 1832. He was, as the letter quoted at the start of this chapter suggests, fond of the music of sovereigns; but he was fonder of parochial harmony. When he went to Peasmarsh, he pledged himself not to raise his tithes. This was a brave decision, since the living, valued at £260 a year, was by no means rich. In reaching it, the new vicar of Peasmarsh doubtless bore in mind that tithes were a particularly delicate issue with hop-farmers, because their crop yields fluctuated wildly. Lettice's pledge was kept. During his life, he received many generous presents; and, after his death, 'every cottage poured forth its inmates to follow the mournful train to the grave'.[83]

Very different were the characteristic attitudes of a contemporary Suffolk parson. John Leroo became rector of Long Melford in 1789. His predecessor had taken his tithes in kind, and had been moderate in his exactions. Leroo did not take his tithes in kind, and was not moderate in his exactions. His first step was to persuade local farmers to sign a twelve-year agreement for cash compositions; this was astute, for Long Melford, previously worth £461 a year, was now valued at £532. There was little local farmers could do to prevent the rise; the law stated that compositions could be arranged, or renewed, on the death and resignation of incumbents. The new rector continued as he had begun. When the first agreement expired in 1800, another was made, but this time it ran for only six years, and was at a higher rate. Fresh agreements were signed in 1807, and again in 1811. Two years later, Leroo carried through yet another plan to increase his income by splitting up a large estate and subsequently letting it to several tenants at revalued tithes; a clever sleight of hand that immediately boosted the living by a further £311 a year. By this time Long Melford was worth £1,294 a year, and subsequently more or less held its value until Leroo's death in 1819. In thirty years, he had raised the value of the living from £460 a year to over £1,200.[84] These details provide a fascinating background to events in the winter of 1830-1 when labourers, supported by farmers, put forward demands for a substantial reduction in the incumbent's tithes.[85]

More is involved in this contrast between John Lettice and John Leroo than a mere comparison between the desire for popularity and a quest for rising income. Actions such as those at Long Melford threatened the basis of a paternalist moral economy, located in the countryside and rooted in local custom. It was this tradition which the labourers tried to tap in 1830, by demanding 'contributions' from wealthy persons as well as large reductions in rents and tithes. Local customs took many forms, both social and economic in their overtones; the giving of clothes, or fuel, to the poor in winter, a parish feast at harvest time, and the like. In this way, they gave expression to that corporate responsibility of the rich towards the poor which was one of the saving graces of pre-industrial society. It is essential not to romanticise at this point. Every rural society in the world's history - modern India as much as ancient Egypt - has lived in fear of the black vulture of famine. It is the constant reality of this threat which forms the essential context of the paternalist moral economy of Georgian England, pre-eminently of the old Poor Law. To the rich, village customs were part of their duties, and to the poor they were part of their rights.

As the clergy rose in wealth, and also in social position - the two were interactive - the demands of social expectation pressed down upon them ever more heavily. They lowered their tithes in times of distress, not only because they sought popularity but because the rural community, rich and poor alike, expected it of them. A clergyman with land of his own could more easily afford a substantial tithe reduction than a rector or vicar who was dependent upon his ecclesiastical income. This point was not missed by conservative clerical pamphleteers, many of whom penned eloquent eulogies on the economic benefits which an aristocratic clergy could confer upon a beleaguered countryside.[86]

Clergy viewed their glebes and benefice incomes in different ways. Some, following Burke, argued that ecclesiastical property was 'mixed and identified' with the mass of private property; others, following Coleridge, thought of their benefices as trusts.[87] The first group defended their own rights; the second defended the rights both of themselves and of their successors. To those who agreed with Coleridge, a predecessor's neglect was a threat not only to their own livelihood but to the benefice itself, considered as an historical entity with a continuous life of its own. Once ecclesiastical property came to be considered as a trust, the issue of its proper management was raised above the horizon of a petty selfishness into the ethereal blue of a pure duty, to church and to posterity.[88]

All those who copied John Leroo in managing their property on strictly capitalist lines, aiming to maximise profits, had first to break free from an economic and social system hallowed by centuries of observance. The same conflict between residual semi-feudalism and incipient rural capitalism also split the landowning class. It was, ultimately, a struggle between two conflicting social philosophies; crudely, 'communalist' feudalism versus 'individualist' capitalism. The Derbyshire clergy stood for the old order; John Leroo stood for the new. Incumbents, in deciding what policy of estate management to adopt, had to choose between these two opposed views.[89]

vii. *The Policies of Queen Anne's Bounty*

No study of rising clerical wealth in the Georgian era is complete without elucidation of the policies of Queen Anne's Bounty. This body, with its board of governors, was founded by that monarch in 1704.[90] Whether its foundation is seen as evidence of royal generosity or of royal penitence depends upon one's point of view. At the time of the Reformation the church lost the monastic lands, the monastic tithes, and the monastic advowsons - a fine catalogue of royal sin; into the bargain, the clergy continued to pay their taxes, but to King, not Pope. It was these clerical taxes - first-fruits and tenths - which the Crown returned to the church when it founded the Bounty.

Income from first-fruits and tenths produced around £17,000 a year in the first decade of the eighteenth century, and it was this annual sum that the governors of the Bounty had the duty to administer. Unfortunately, they took a long time to sort out and organise their affairs, and the first grant was not made until October, 1714. Thereafter, the Board's policies were guided by six leading principles. The first of these was that of augmenting the value of the thing, the benefice, not of subsidising the income of the person, the incumbent. By this means the Bounty opted for long term good, and avoided allegations of bribery and suspicious practices. The second rule echoed the deeply held contemporary belief in the sanctity of solid assets, alias landed property. Augmentations were to be laid out in the purchase of plots of land; they were not to be left to an incumbent's discretion, nor were they to be used to buy government stock.[91] Extra income would be low, about 5% of capital invested, but it would be steady. Thirdly, the amount of each grant would be the same, being pitched at a capital sum of £200 - evidence of fairness and even-handedness. The next rule was discriminatory - augmentations were to be given in the first instance only to livings worth under £10. The plan was to raise the values of livings systematically, starting with those worth under £10, before moving on to those worth under £20, and then, later, working slowly up the scale.

The other two rules modified the fourth. Livings under £10 were to be given priority, but the selection procedure was to be by lot, and other considerations - density of population, non-residence of the incumbent, and so on - were not to be taken into account. No matter how many times a living was drawn in the lottery, it was not to be barred from eligibility. This blunted the Bounty's effectiveness as an instrument of church reform. The eighteenth-century mind was attracted to the idea of a lottery and indeed, the ecclesiastical system was sometimes approvingly likened to one. The governors of the Bounty, in thus validating contemporary thought, showed themselves to be men of their age, besides turning their backs, at the same time, upon any attempt to deal with the vexed problem of pluralism. Finally, the Bounty was prepared to relax the £10 limit in cases where an equivalent benefaction was forthcoming from another source. In these circumstances the limit was set at £35 a year, raised to £50 in 1718. By this means, it was hoped to enlist the support of powerful laity in the cause of securing clerical decency and dignity.[92] The drawback was that a lay patron could tease a supplementary sum out of the Bounty by augmenting his own living.

How did these rules work in practice? Until the passing of the Mortmain Act of 1736 they worked rather well. During the first twenty-two years of its active life the Bounty received 921 private benefactions, meeting these with 903 of its own, and it also made 234 augmentations by lot.[93] Since few livings received more than a single grant, these figures imply that about 1,100 benefices, equivalent to fifty or so a year, were augmented. Augmentations were never for less than £200, a sum which, when eventually converted into land, raised the value of a living by about £10 a year. To raise, within twenty-two years, over 1,000 livings by at least £10 each, and most of them by about £20, was no mean achievement.

The Mortmain Act of 1736 stifled the Bounty's innovative efforts, and had the effect of making it, for at least half a century, cautious and conservative. What the Act did was to prohibit the Bounty from receiving benefactions from the dying; but even more important than this irritating restriction was the redirection of policy which now took place. The governors, losing their nerve, returned to the original purposes for which the Bounty's endowments were intended, as well as to the earliest agreed rules. Previously, some grants had been given towards the provision of parsonages, but these now gradually ceased altogether; and the limit of eligibility for livings augmented in support of private benefactions was reduced again to £35 a year, from the £50 level that had been settled upon in 1718.[94] The effect of these changes was that the Bounty came to spurn a good deal of outside help, and turned its attention instead towards the annual hazard, the lottery. Since four-fifths of its grants had previously been made to meet benefactions from other sources, the gains made by livings could not but reduce considerably. Such was the price that had to be paid for a policy of safety first.

It was a long time before the Bounty regained its self-confidence. The first forward movements were cautious. As had originally been envisaged, the limit of eligibility for the lottery was raised from £10 a year to £20 in 1747; ten years later that for livings augmented by supplementary sums from other sources went up by the same margin, from £35 to £45. In 1788, both were raised again; the limit for the lottery from £20 to £30, and that for the others from £45 to £50.[95] With regard to private benefactions, the Bounty was now back to where it had been sixty years earlier, while for the lottery it had advanced its augmentations from livings under £10 a year to those under £30. Both values, it must be added, were not up-to-date; the Bounty's work continued to be based upon surveys carried out during the first decade of the century, and eligibility for grants still had to be proved from these. This failure to modernise the valuations used by the Bounty became increasingly limiting, and magnified the selectivity implicit in the inescapable arbitrariness of the lottery. Some livings received several augmentations during the course of the eighteenth century; others, equally or even more deserving, received nothing.

It was only after 1800 that the Bounty shook off its somnolence. Revival began in earnest with an act of 1803, which released it from one of the restrictions imposed after the passing of the Mortmain Act. Henceforth, the Bounty could allow its augmentations to be used to provide parsonages instead of being laid out in the purchase of plots of land. According to the Bounty's official historian, augmentations used for this purpose soon became 'quite common'.[96] A few years later, in 1809, a new valuation of livings was at last completed, so the governors could now readily discriminate between livings genuinely in need of assistance and livings raised by general economic circumstances into a more comfortable affluence. With new certificates also went new policies. The qualifying limit for the lottery remained at £30, but that to meet other benefactions was raised immediately from £50 to £80. In 1810, the limit for private benefactions was raised again, this time to £120, and in 1820 it went up to £200. The limit for the lottery, meanwhile, only moved up from £30 to £50.[97] The lottery was becoming increasingly forgotten; by the mid 1830s, augmentations by lot had almost ceased.

Not only did the Bounty return to the lines of policy it had adopted prior to the Mortmain Act of 1736, it also produced three new initiatives. The first shows the growing concern, felt by a number of contemporary churchmen, to give priority to the financial needs of urban parishes. In 1810, the governors decided that whenever a living with 'laborious duty' was henceforth drawn in the lottery, it should be entitled to as many augmentations as were thought fit, at a stroke.[98] The next year, there was another departure. This new possibility had been opened up by an Act of 1777, known as Gilbert's Act, but had not previously been taken advantage of. The purpose of Gilbert's legislation was to facilitate clerical residence by increasing provision of suitable houses in which incumbents could live. To livings bringing in £50 a year or less, the Bounty was permitted to make interest-free loans, up to a maximum of £100, specifically for the purpose of helping to provide parsonages; livings over £50 became entitled to loans equivalent to two years' income, at only 4%. (For loans greater than two years' income the rate was fixed at 5%, and clergy who were non-resident for more than twenty weeks a year had to pay 10%). These loans were to be independent of the work of augmentation by lot and benefaction, and were also novel in that they enabled the Bounty to extend its activities to every living, irrespective of value. The governors, however, were reluctant to make use of these opportunities - in 1781, they 'postponed' consideration of them. This postponement was to last for thirty years, but after 1811, when the decision to implement Gilbert's Act was finally taken, the Board became enthusiastic. By 1826, as much as £224,525 19s 9d was loaned on mortgages in this way, and ten years later interest was running at about £10,000 a year,[99] a figure suggesting that the capital sum had by now passed the £250,000 mark.

66

Giving priority to urban parishes and offering mortgage facilities with which to provide parsonages were two initiatives; a sustained campaign to eliminate the most severe examples of poverty was the third. In 1822, a committee was formed to set about the task of raising every living to at least £50 a year. Two years later, 400 were raised to this sum, and most of these were given a little extra as well.[100] Such swift and decisive action by the Board is amazing, when contrasted with its inertia of only twenty years before.

These three advances across the frontier of new policy have, as their context, a profound change in the way in which the Bounty conducted its operations. One of the main features of the Board in the eighteenth century was its autonomous character. It administered income from tenths and first-fruits on its own, helped only by private benefactions which were increasingly rare after the Mortmain Act of 1736. In 1809, as already noted,[101] the Bounty began to receive external financial assistance, in the form of annual grants voted by parliament. These in no way interfered with the ordinary, day-to-day, work of augmentation; they were intended to be, and indeed were, separate and supplementary. Eleven such annual grants, all of £100,000 each, were made in the years between 1809 and 1820, making a grand total of £1,100,000. As soon as the first grant was received the Board set up a Parliamentary Grants Fund, alongside the older Royal Bounty Fund. Administration of this new fund was flexible and imaginative. Anxious to attract further outside support, the governors decided in 1810 to raise grants from it to £300, if met by benefactions of only £200 - the benefactions could be in cash, land or tithes, and could also take the form of a rent charge or annuity bringing in an income of £15 a year.[102] The next year, a policy favouring populous parishes was started. Very poor livings with a population of beweeen 1,000 and 2,000 were raised without delay to £80, and those with over 2,000 people were raised still higher to £100. Later, this principle was extended; livings with over 5,000 people being boosted to £150, those with over 4,000 being brought up to £140, and so on, down to those with over 1,000, all of which were increased to £100. By 1820, the Board was engaged in the task of raising livings with a population of only 300 to at least £100.[103] All of this was done without waiting for benefactions; the pressing financial needs of the more populous parishes, both in town and countryside, were simply too great.

The thrust of what has been called the 'third church reform movement', with the Bounty as its spearhead, was the elimination of clerical poverty. Encouraging benefactions to meet the Royal Bounty Fund helped to achieve this; so did the differential policy, adopted in 1810, allowing the poorest benefices to receive several simultaneous augmentations from the lottery. Flexible use of the Parliamentary Grants Fund was a very important factor; parishes in heavily populated areas were given extra assistance, and the special committee, appointed in 1822, ferreted out places which had been overlooked. All this activity, although not abolishing acute poverty, raised most of the smallest livings into marginal respectability. What happened was not unexpected: the number of livings bringing in less than £1 a week went sharply down, and the number bringing in between £2 and £3 a week went sharply up. There are, on this matter, statistics for 1810 and for 1830. In the former year, 1,061 benefices failed to beat the £1 a week mark; in the latter year only 297. The reduction works out at 72%. Figures for places worth between £100 and £150 a year look very different; here the rise was from 1,211 to 1,602, an increase of 32%.[104] In the context of the postwar depression - a period when its efforts could receive no help from advances in the agrarian economy - the Bounty undertook the most energetic campaign against clerical poverty ever to be mounted in Georgian Britain. To reduce the number of livings worth under £50 by almost three-quarters within twenty years was, in these particular circumstances, an exceptional achievement.

Despite its newly adventurous policy, the Bounty remained in many ways the same as it had always been - a thoroughly eighteenth-century institution, suspicious of sudden change and clinging closely to ideals of gradual improvement. Fresh developments, like the conscious attempt to meet, in the ecclesiastical sphere, the demands of an industrial society, together with the elimination of many of the worst examples of glaring poverty, the provision of parsonages, and so on, did not disturb the fundamental principles upon which the Bounty operated. The governors maintained their declared policy of making moderate augmentations, which were to be turned into long-term investments yielding a modest increase in benefice income; and they continued to augment the thing (the living), rather than the person (the incumbent). The lottery, undeniably the weakest link in the Board's system of management, was not so much abolished as allowed to decline quietly into senescence and inactivity.

The governors' attitude towards the lottery illustrates their greatest corporate weakness - lack, at times, of a sufficiently positive courage. The Board was criticised by political Radicals for its soft treatment of pluralistic and non-resident clergy, and this criticism was well aimed. Apart from Gilbert's Act, which required non-residents to pay 10% interest on mortgage loans to build parsonages rather than the normal 4% or 5%, the Bounty in no way penalised those clergy who did not constantly care for their parishes. Only once throughout the period, at the time of the first parliamentary grant, did it adopt a combative stance, and even then it soon became less pugnacious. When the rules for distributing the new grant were first drawn up, it was decided that interest on an augmentation would not be paid if the incumbent was either non-resident or held another living worth over £150 a year. Within a year, the Bounty had already begun to shift its ground; interest would now be paid unless directions to the contrary were given. Later, the governors gave in almost completely; pluralists were now to be paid interest, as were non-residents certified to be in need by their bishops.[105]

A further criticism of the Bounty is that it was not sufficiently selective. It was set up to help the very poor; and yet even in the earliest agreed rules it was established that the limit of eligibility set for the lottery should be appreciably lower than that to meet benefactions - £10 a year as against £35, with the gap being widened a further £15 in 1718. More seriously, the Bounty failed to update the original surveys of value, used to assess eligibility; it was not until 1809 that this important work was carried through. Throughout the eighteenth century a number of livings continued to receive augmentation, although their needs were no longer pressing. Some of the rules adopted in the early nineteenth century can be criticised along similar lines. Following the modifications to the Royal Bounty Fund that were adopted in 1820, livings up to a value of £200 a year qualified for augmentations to meet benefactions, but the limit for the lottery was now set at only a quarter as much. This meant that comparatively wealthy incumbents - men holding several livings in the range of, say, £120 to £180 a year - could legitimately obtain private benefactions for each of their benefices, backed on every occasion by a supplementary capital grant from the Bounty.

This leads on to another criticism. If a landowner happened to be the lay impropriator of a living augmented by lot, he could safely watch the Board raising the incumbent's pittance at no expense to himself, whilst still pocketing both great and small tithes. If he happened to be the patron of a living held by one of his relations - a happy position in which not a few landlords found themselves - he had but to make a benefaction in order to elicit further financial aid from the acquiescent governors. The fact that rights of private patronage were considered a species of property, disposable on the open market, gives a special twist to these objections. Since each and every augmentation increased the permanent value of a benefice, and hence its worth at point of sale, the Bounty was open to the charge that its work had the ultimate effect of increasing the wealth of private patrons as well as boosting the incomes of the beneficed clergy.

The irony of this was not lost upon some contemporaries. One man who saw to the heart of the matter was John Penn, a Norfolk incumbent with several small livings. In 1811, he wrote to his bishop, complaining about the policy of the Board. Penn, apparently, was suffering from gout. Life, he pointed out, is uncertain; his widow might soon want his meagre savings. How was he to raise the £200 required to elicit one of the new £300 grants offered by the Bounty? Would it not be better if the governors adopted a different plan, appropriating a given sum to each poor living and paying interest of 5% on it, but keeping the principal for itself?[106] In this way the patronage rights of wealthy laity would no longer rise in value at the church's expense, and incumbents of poor livings would be assured of an increased income. This letter anticipates in many respects the centralised organisation of the church's finances which has evolved since it was written.

On the credit side, and to set against these criticisms, is the Bounty's consistent policy of opting for long-term good rather than more glamorous short-term gains, and also the strengths of its philosophy of gradualism. It was pragmatic. It tried not to raise false hopes; it did not succumb under the pressure of the problems it faced; and it extended its activities to cover provision of parsonages. Even its much-criticised policy of deliberately encouraging private benefactions can be defended on the ground that it greatly increased the capital sum available for augmentation. The single best defence of the Bounty, however, is the sheer amount of quiet, continuing, good the governors achieved. Between 1713 and 1844, the Board laid out £3,401,600 in augmentations.[107] Even if compounding on the interest that this capital sum provided is not taken into account, it can readily be appreciated that the Bounty's financial support was worth a great deal to the clergy. Assuming a 5% return on capital employed, £3.4 million produces an income of £170,000 a year. Private benefactions, in the years between 1713 and 1844, totalled about £1,150,000.[108] The annual return on £1.15 million works out at £57,500. This amount, when aggregated with the compounding interest on the Bounty's own augmentations, was a very considerable benefit to the clergy, especially when it is remembered that the governors had started out with only their initial income of £17,000 a year. The stewardship of the Board, although not without blemish, was good; it served the church faithfully and well over a long period.

viii. *Benefice Incomes, 1700-1840.*
It is time, now, to give the argument perspective, by examining how benefice incomes fared between 1700 and 1840. There is no difficulty in achieving statistical exactness with regard to the situation at the end of the period: the value of every living in England and Wales appears in the pages of the massively detailed 1835 Report;[109] but arriving at an accurate valuation of livings in 1700 is a different matter. All that there is to go on are the two surveys which formed the basis of the Bounty's work, both of them commissioned by the Board in the first decade of the eighteenth century. The first of these, subsequently published as Ecton's *Liber Valorum*, gives the number of livings in each diocese worth £50 a year or less; while the other, unpublished, is rather broader, with a list of all livings not above £80 a year. Neither is complete, but they are the only surveys available.

In the first decade of the eighteenth century, the Bounty Board found 5,082 livings worth under £80 a year, a huge total bearing in mind that there were around 10,500 benefices at the time. The comparable figure in the 1835 Report is 1,173, a drop of 77%.[110] Diocesan statistics give an even better idea of change. At Bangor, in Wales, livings under £80 a year went down from 91 to 5; at Chichester the number fell from 288 to 23; at London the decrease was from 272 to 25; and at Exeter it was from 345 to 34.

The contrast for livings worth under £50 a year is starker still. According to Ecton, 3,826 livings were worth less than £1 a week,[111] and there was little numerical difference between the five classifications - under £10 a year, under £20 a year, and so on. By 1830, this total of 3,826 had fallen to 297, a very steep fall by any reckoning. General economic factors - agricultural advance, the Napoleonic boom, the enclosure movement, and so on - helped to achieve this; and a large contribution was also made by the Bounty. All through the eighteenth century, its efforts were solely concentrated upon assisting livings worth less than £50 a year; then, in the early nineteenth century, a series of special measures was put into effect. These have been discussed earlier.[112] Their effect was to bring about a much improved relative performance by the poorest livings. As has already been shown, livings worth under £50 a year numbered 1,061 in 1810,[113] a figure which has to be compared with the very much smaller total of 297 mentioned in the 1835 Report.

Difficult though it is to believe, these figures understate rather than overstate the contrast between 1700 and 1840. The Board's two initial surveys were tailored and trimmed to meet its own needs. There was no interest, at that time, in discovering benefice values as a statistical exercise; the Board's sole concern was to find out how many benefices qualified for augmentation. Because the first surveys were not comprehensive, they were not complete. Later, other poor livings had to be added to the list. The number of these additions is uncertain, but an example shows how numerous they may well have been. In 1735, the Bishop of Bath and Wells informed the Board of the existence of 7 vicarages or rectories, and of a further 43 perpetual curacies, all of them under £50 a year in value, none of which had been included in either of the first two surveys.[114] There were more than 3,826 livings which failed to reach £50 a year in 1710; and there were more than 5,082 which did not reach £80.

Comparisons between Ecton and the 1835 Report do not reveal the percentage rises achieved by poor livings. To do this, two samples were taken from a wide range of counties, five of them Welsh and four English. The first sample, restricted to vicarages and rectories appearing both in Ecton and in the 1835 Report, was drawn from 312 parishes; while the second, of perpetual curacies alone, came from 119. The vicarages and rectories did exceptionally well; there was an average value for these of £34 a year in the first decade of the eighteenth century, rising to an average of £191 a year by 1830, an increase of 462%. The perpetual curacies, partly because their initial values were lower, did even better; an average of a mere £14 a year in 1705 was turned into an average of £110 a year by 1830, a rise of 686%.[115] More than a fifth of the perpetual curacies achieved rises of a least twenty-fold.

The explanation for this spectacular performance is hidden, discreetly, in the Bounty Board's benefice files. It is clear from these that many of the poorest livings, especially the poorest perpetual curacies, were dependent upon augmentations for income, and augmentations increased out of all recognition, both in frequency and in size, once the Board launched itself on its new phase of activity in the first decade of the nineteenth century. A good example of this is the perpetual curacy of Marsden in Whalley, Lancashire.[116] Its fortunes began to change for the better in the 1780s, when it drew three prizes (1783, 1784, and 1789) in the lottery. It did even better, as from 1810, when the Board began its differential policy of favouring populous places. In that year the lottery augmented it by £200; in 1811 it did so again, but by £600; and in 1812, yet again, by £400. A benefaction of £300 in 1816 put a little icing on the cake. This perpetual curacy was by now worth £106, when as recently as 1810 it had been bringing in £43; in 1743 'the present clear improved yearly value' had been £1 16s 8d.

Sometimes, manna dropped from heaven overnight. This was what happened to the perpetual curacy of Witton in Great Budworth, Cheshire.[117] Until 1817 it did reasonably well out of the Board's funds - an augmentation from the lottery in 1812, and two others to meet benefactions in 1722 and 1770 - but it was when it received

£1,000 as a lump sum endowment that its situation really began to alter. From a value of £31 a year in 1770 it rose to £84 by 1817, and then doubled at a stroke.

The Bounty concentrated much of its energy upon places where the income was derisory and uncertain. At Ash Priors, in Somerset, the perpetual curate could rely, without benefaction, solely upon a stipend of £6 13s 4d paid 'since the memory of man'. Three augmentations from the lottery, and two to meet benefactions, raised it to £70 by 1830.[118] There was another fixed payment in lieu of tithes, this time of £8 14s 1d, at Hardham in Sussex.[119] Here, there were eight augmentations, all from the lottery, four of them after 1810. Ecton reckoned the living at £6 a year; it had crept up to £29 by 1812; and the Ecclesiastical Revenues Commission found it was worth £66. When the perpetual curate of Rainow in Prestbury, Cheshire, applied to the governors for a grant in 1811, he told them his income was only £26 a year - £16 from lands bought with the proceeds of three previous augmentations, £1 from surplice fees, and the remaining £9 as a 'seat wage', presumably a form of pew rent. The governors listened attentively. The perpetual curacy was endowed immediately with £1,400 from the lottery, and received another £400 the next year.[120] With the added help of a final benefaction in 1825, it managed to reach £99. Finally, back to the west country, and the perpetual curacy of Coleford in Newland, Gloucestershire.[121] From there, in 1804, the Revd Thomas Thomas wrote to the Board's Secretary, Richard Burn, informing the governors of his plight. Apparently, it was customary for the perpetual curate to receive the surplice fees and also the income from several sermons preached to local benefit societies, but a new vicar was withholding payment. Since the curacy was only worth £22 when last valued, in 1791, Thomas' anxiety can be appreciated. His letter ends on a sad, pleading, note: 'If therefore the Gentlemen who are the Trustees & Governors of the Queen's Bounty would have the goodness to grant another Lot to this Chapel, it would be doing the poor Curate thereof a real Act of Charity, & which would in some Measure compensate for my present Loss & Disappointment.' Nothing, unfortunately, was forthcoming, but on a later occasion, in 1819, the curacy attracted a lump sum of £1,200, raising it without delay to £56 a year.

For richer livings, there is nothing comparable to Ecton. On a nationwide scale, there is only the Bounty's unpublished survey, giving the number of parishes valued at £80 a year or less. The difficulty with this is that it excludes all the best benefices. Knowledge of some of these opulent vicarages and rectories was come by fortuitously. When the bishops were originally asked to supply information by the Bounty Board, a few also sent a miscellaneous batch of returns to do with other matters such as frequency of services, size of parishes, and so on.[122] Among these are two further documents, one sent by the Bishop of Exeter and the other by his brother of Lincoln, naming livings worth more than £50 a year and sometimes over £80. These are invaluable records. The Exeter list, from Devon and Cornwall, covers 85 parishes, of which 14 were over the £80 mark. The Lincoln figures, from Bedfordshire and Buckinghamshire, Hertfordshire and Huntingdonshire, Leicestershire and Lincolnshire, are a smaller sample of 32, with two above £80.

The rise for this sample of 117 livings is strong, though less so than for the poor vicarages and rectories analysed earlier. Five failed to double in value between 1710 and 1830, and a further eighteen notched up rises of between 100% and 200%. The rest all did better. West Allington, in Devon, went up from £80 to £685; and Parkham, also in Devon, improved from £100 to £635. Although strong rises were less frequent among the sample from Lincoln, two did exceptionally well. One of these was Lessingham, where the increase was from £118 to £924; the other was Sutterton, up from £78 to £885. For the sample as a whole, the average rise was 325%: 336% at Exeter, and 288% at Lincoln.

The conclusion that poor livings rose faster in value than the rich is unexpected, as is the conclusion that bishoprics and cathedral posts failed to outpace the richer benefices. Between 1760 and 1830, episcopal and capitular property rose in value by 200%.[123] In the preceding half-century, growth is unlikely to have been substantial. Rentals - a good guide to movements among ecclesiastical estates - were sluggish at this period, with most increases being below 15%.[124] A rise of 250% for episcopal and capitular property between 1700 and 1840 would seem to be the upper limit.

From these assorted pieces of evidence, it is possible to estimate the advance in benefice incomes between 1700 and 1840. Perpetual curacies did best, with a rise of 686%; below them are the poorer vicarages and rectories, which recorded an improvement of 462%; and at the bottom are the richer incumbencies, with an increase of 325%. Since most early eighteenth-century livings were of moderate value, and many of them were not even that - the incomplete survey, quoted earlier, lists 5,082 under £80 a year - these three sets of figures indicate an overall rise of at least 400%.

Clerical incomes are not, of course, the same thing as benefice incomes; the salient missing factors are the incidence of pluralism and the size of private means. Both of these will be discussed later.[125] Meanwhile, future findings can be anticipated, to the extent of stating that there was an increase in pluralism between 1700 and 1830. At the start of the period about one in six of the beneficed held more than one living, whereas by the end the figure was one in three. Growth in private means cannot be quantified, but was certainly substantial. The social standing of the clergy improved, and there was more opportunity to supplement benefice income from other sources, notably teaching. Taken in the round, the incomes of the clergy probably rose by at least 700% between the foundation of the Bounty and the reforming era of the 1830s.

What about inflation? Here, there are two main problems: a lack of statistical information, and interpreting such statistical information as there is. For the years after 1790, wholesale prices of domestic and imported commodities have been indexed.[126] If 1790 is taken as the starting-point, prices rose over the next half-century; if 1800 is chosen, they fell. It seems best to give variations over decades. For the 1790s, the index is never lower than 85.2, and manages to reach 136.6 by the decade's end. Between 1830 and 1839, in contrast, there is greater stability; the low of 82.5 was reached in October and November 1835, and the high of 107.2 in January 1839. The late-Georgian era was not, on this evidence, a period of serious long-term price inflation.

During the eighteenth century, there were two main trends. Until 1750 or 1760, price levels were generally stable, except in time of war; after the middle years of the century there was a tendency for prices to rise gently.[127] In view of this, and also taking into account the statistics for the years after 1790, it is reasonable to conclude that inflation probably did not much exceed 100% between 1700 and 1840.

The relevance of these figures for clerical life-style is a further problem. The index of wholesale prices is weighted, but this reflects the needs of the average family of the time. Most clerical families, clearly, were not average. Those who enjoyed the status of gentry lived at a level of luxury unknown to the labouring majority, and many of these luxuries, especially foreign commodities - coffee, tea, liquor (either smuggled or with duty paid) - rose much more steeply in price than essential articles. The reason for this is straightforward. Because international trade was primitive, undue pressure was exerted by demand upon supply. For incumbents, levels of inflation were higher than for most people - perhaps 200% between 1700 and 1840, as compared with only 100% or so. Yet even an inflation of 200% is less than a third as much as the likely increase in clerical incomes. The conclusion is inescapable: the beneficed clergy enjoyed a much higher standard of living in 1840 then they did in 1700.

Chapter 3 Notes

1. John Lettice to James Plumptre, 22 September 1825, C.U.L., Add. Mss.5866, f.35.

2. See, for instance, the judgment of E.L. Jones, 'Agriculture, 1700-80', in Floud and McCloskey, *op.cit.*, p.66: 'the agricultural growth of the eighteenth-century was, as it were, a part of the history of an expanding universe, not something that began with a 'big bang''.

3. Hobsbawm and Rudé, *Captain Swing*, pp. 258-9, 317-23; J.H.Clapham, *An Economic History of Modern Britain: The Early Railway Age 1820-1850*, pp. 139-42.

4. C.P.Hill, *British Economic and Social History, 1700-1964*, pp. 9-11.

5. Clapham, *op.cit*, p. 134.

6. R.Trow-Smith, *A History of British Livestock Husbandry, 1700-1900*, p. 202, 206-7.

7. Hill, *op.cit.*, p.50.

8. G.E. Mingay, *English Landed Society in the Eighteenth Century*, p.52.

9. *ibid.*, pp.54-5; see, also, G.E. Mingay, 'The Agricultural Depression, 1730-1750', *E.H.R.*, Second Series, VIII (1956), 323-8.

10. Lord Ernle, *English Farming*, pp. 195-7, 207, 209.

11. *ibid.*, pp. 220-1.

12. Clapham, *op.cit*, p.18.

13. The sources used in this section are: Best, *Temporal Pillars*, pp.64-65; Rosalind Mitchison, 'Pluralities and the Poorer Benefices in Eighteenth-Century England', *Historical Journal*, V (1962), 188-90; and Report of the Ecclesiastical Revenues Commission, *P.P.*, 1835, XXII, 111-1060.

14. See above, p. 34.

15. *P.P.*, 1835, XXII, 372-3. Further examples of litigious Georgian clergy are to be found

in W.B. Maynard, 'The Ecclesiastical Administration of the Archdeaconry of Durham, 1774-1856', pp. 134-50.

16. The best analysis of episcopal incomes is in *P.P.*, 1851, XLII, 93 ff. This source gives the annual net income of each see, using septennial averages and employing as a base the years 1829-35.

17. B.R.Mitchell and P.Deane, *Abstract of British Historical Statistics*, p. 399, note A. The National Debt stood at £244.72 million in 1793, and at £834.26 million in 1815 - see E.B.Schumpeter, 'English Prices and Public Finance, 1660-1822', *R.E.S.*, XX (February, 1938), Table VII,37.

18. A full list would have to include alcohol and beverages - wine, tea, cider, cocoa, hops and malt; domestic animals - dogs; miscellaneous household articles - candles, glass, paper; building materials - slates, bricks, stone and tiles; newspapers; houses; that old stand-by, tobacco; hair powder and hawkers; and many more (see Hill, *op.cit.*, pp.146-7).

19. P.K. O'Brien, 'Government Revenue, 1793-1815', p.9.

20. W.F.Galpin, *The Grain Supply of England during the Napoleonic Period*, pp.161-88. In March 1809, licences to trade with Britain were granted to French merchants.

21. See above, pp. 4-5.

22. S.Pollard, 'Investment, Consumption, and the Industrial Revolution', *E.H.R.*, Second Series, XI (1958-9), 217- 220.

23. According to A.D. Gayer, W.W. Rostow and A.J. Schwartz, *The Growth and Fluctuation of the British Economy, 1790-1850*, I, Table 39, 468, prices stood at 109.6 in January 1799, at 141.3 in January 1800, and at 181.1 in March 1801. This is a monthly, weighted, index of wholesale prices for domestic and imported commodities, using prices in the years 1821-5 as its base of 100. It is criticised in P. Deane and W.A. Cole, *British Economic Growth*, p.14.

24. The index cited above stands at 133.0 for January 1808, and at 175.3 for August, 1812. The figures for the latter month are six points lower than those for March 1801, a fact vividly illustrating the viciousness of the earlier inflation.

25. See the argument in, e.g., J.E.Williams, 'The British Standard of Living, 1750-1850', *E.H.R.*, Second Series, XIX (1966), 587.

26. Deane and Cole, *op.cit.*, Table XVII, p.65, states that domestic consumption of corn equalled 18,556,000 quarters in 1790, and 23,196,000 in 1810, a rise of 25%. These are rather hazardous figures, however. They are based in part upon an eighteenth-century source - Charles Smith, *Three Tracts on the Corn Trade and Corn Laws* (1766) - and also take it for granted that the relationship between consumption and population did not vary, whereas in times of scarcity it transparently did.

27. Gayer, Rostow and Schwartz, *op.cit.*, I, 503; Lord Ernle, *op.cit.*, p.269; Thomas Tooke, *A History of Prices,* I, 290, 373.

28. Schumpeter, *R.E.S.*, XX, Chart I, 23.

29. See below, Table I. The main technical inaccuracy in the returns is that land where tithes were commuted was not included. Since commutation was never as popular as it was between 1806 and 1812, the figures fail to take account of the fact that the area subject to tithe was shrinking sharply at this time. Small rises recorded for counties where the commutation movement was making particularly strong headway bear this out - there are five (Bedfordshire, Buckinghamshire, Huntingdonshire, Nottinghamshire, and Northamptonshire) where the range of increase is from a derisory 0.5% to a maximum of 11.9%.

30. *ibid.*

31. *P.P.*, 1814-15, V, 1098-9.

32. F.M.L.Thompson, *English Landed Society in the Nineteenth Century*, pp.218-20. The aggregate rentals of these ten estates went up from £38,272 10s 0d a year to £81,376.

33. W.R.Ward, 'The Tithe Question in England in the early Nineteenth Century', *J.E.H.*, XVI (1965),68.

34. Hill, *op.cit.*, p.236,270; A.J.P.Taylor, *English History, 1914-1945*, p. 465,511.

35. Gayer, Rostow and Schwartz, *op.cit.*, I, Table 39, 468.

36. G.E.Fussell and M. Compton, 'Agricultural Adjustments after the Napoleonic Wars', *E.H.*, IV (1939), 189.

37. E.L.Jones, *The Development of English Agriculture, 1815-1873*, pp.12-16; Fussell and Compton, *E.H.*,IV,188.

38. M.J.R. Healy and E.L.Jones, 'Wheat Yields in England, 1815-1859', *J.R.S.S.*, Series A, CXXV(1962), 574-9.

39. Fussell and Compton, *E.H.*, IV, 195; *P.P.*, 1821, IX, 68, 75 (evidence of John Lake). See also *P.P.*, 1833, V, 74 (evidence of Robert Hughes); and *ibid.*, 307 (evidence of William Taylor).

40. *P.P.*, 1833, V, 622 (evidence of George Smallpiece); *ibid.*, 475 (evidence of Charles Osborn).

41. Fussell and Compton, *E.H.*, IV, 201.

42. *P.P.*, 1836, VIII, Part II, 5.

43. *P.P.*, 1833, V,110-11 (evidence of Robert Wright); *P.P.*, 1821,IX, 92-3 (evidence of G.B.George); *ibid.*, 38-9 (evidence of R.C. Harvey).

44. Fussell and Compton, *E.H.*, IV, 198-9.

45. *P.P.*, 1833, V, 318,320-1 (evidence of William Blamire); *P.P.*, 1821, IX,64, (evidence of J.C.Curwen); *P.P.*,1837, V,319 (evidence of William Blamire).

46. Thompson, *op.cit.*, p.218.

47. H.G.Hunt, 'Agricultural Rent in South-East England, 1788-1825', *A.H.R.*, VII (1959), 98-108. Part of the reason for the recovery after 1815 was that the area of land under cultivation increased by a small amount (*ibid.*, 99-101).

48. *P.P.*, 1821, IX, 34 (evidence of R.C. Harvey).

49. R.J.Thompson, 'An Inquiry into the Rent of Agricultural Land in England and Wales during the Nineteenth Century,' *J.R.S.S.*, LXX(1907), Table I, 590, and Appendix A, 612.

50. Austin, *op.cit.*, Table XIV, p.170.

51. *P.P.*, 1818, XVIII, 361.

52. There were 3,503 livings with values of £150 or less that were returned by the bishops in 1815, and there were a further 858 benefices in the same category that had been earlier certified to the Bounty but which were omitted in the 1815 returns.

53. See below, pp. 66-68.

54. There are two further sets of returns detailing the number of poor benefices early in the century. The first of these (*P.P.*, 1809, IX,37) is defective, lacking certificates from four dioceses - Ely, St David's, Norwich, and Rochester. The second (*P.P.*, 1810, XIV, 92-3), with some minute variations, duplicates the first, but with the difference that the four non-cooperative bishops of the previous year had now been induced to change their ways. According to this second return, there were 3,998 livings bringing in £150 a year or less. It will be noted

that this total is 363 less than the aggregate of 4,361 to be found in the later source, published in 1818, that we used in our text. The discrepancy gives rise, in the mildly cynical mind, to the suspicion that one or more bishops may have absent-mindedly forgotten a few places here and there, when communicating with the Bounty in 1810. This calumny is, needless to say, wholly without foundation. However, in fairness it must be added that some returns, when compared with disclosures made a year earlier, do look a trifle odd. In London, the number of livings worth less than £150 a year seemingly went up by 50 from 79 to 129; at Norwich the increase was 60 (272 to 332); at York it was 54 (411 to 465). How this can have happened defies explanation. (For figures to do with clerical residence in these three dioceses at the same period, see below, pp.196-197.

55. Hill, *op.cit.*, p.12.

56. Estimates of the number of enclosures between 1760 and 1830 vary (see below, note 59). Between 1800 and 1809 there were 847, and between 1810 and 1819 there were 853 (G.R. Porter, *The Progress of the Nation*, I, 156).

57. Porter, *op.cit.*, gives the number of enclosures between 1820 and 1829 as only 205, less than a quarter of the annual average over the previous two decades.

58. Only in four English counties - Cambridgeshire (10.8%), Oxfordshire (9.8%), Westmorland (8.6%), and Buckinghamshire (6.0%) - was more than five per cent of the land enclosed between 1821 and 1870 (see E.C.K. Gonner, *Common Land and Inclosure*, Appendix D, pp. 279-81).

59. Ward, *J.E.H.*, XVI (1965), 70, gives a total of 3,128 between 1757 and 1835; but his figures are strongly criticised in Evans, *op.cit.*, p.111, n.10. A parliamentary return of 1836 - *P.P.*, 1836, VIII, Part II,505 - lists 3,828 Enclosure Acts over the same time-scale as that used by Ward, while another parliamentary return of the same year (*P.P.*, 1836, XLIV, 1-293) contains about a hundred less. We have followed this last source, because it is the most detailed. It is pointed out in P.W. Whitfield, 'Change and Continuity in the rural church: Norfolk 1760-1840', p.102 that the number of Acts of Parliament is not indicative of the real level of enclosure; many pieces of legislation were no more than ratifications of long-standing private agreements.

60. Parliamentary returns on clerical residence - for which, see below, Table, XVIII - usually give a figure between 10,450 and 10,600.

61. Ward, *op.cit.*, mentions a figure of 2,220.

62. *ibid.*, 71.

63. Wholly within this triangle were Northamptonshire, Nottinghamshire and Leicestershire, Buckinghamshire, Bedfordshire and Berkshire, Cambridgeshire and Oxfordshire, Huntingdonshire and Rutland; together with the greater part of three other counties - Lincolnshire, Warwickshire and Wiltshire; slightly over half of Derbyshire; and a large slice of both Yorkshire and Gloucestershire.

64. It would not be wise to make too much of this point. E.L. Jones, 'Agriculture, 1700-80', in Floud and McCloskey, *op.cit*, p.84 doubts whether suppression of indiscriminate breeding - 'the mating of everybody's son with nobody's daughter' - was a material advantage resulting from enclosure.

65. See, e.g., Hill, *op.cit.*, p.14.

66. See above, p. 40 .

67. Evans, *op.cit.*, p.95.

68. *J.E.H.*, XVI,71.

69. Evans, *op.cit.*, p.104.

70. *ibid*, p.99.

71. See above, p. 54 .

72. Evans, *op. cit.*, p.l0l.

73. D.McClatchey, *Oxfordshire Clergy*, pp.104-7.

74. W.G. Hoskins, *The Midland Peasant*, pp.250-4.

75. See above, pp.8-11.

76. Figures based upon Ward, *J.E.H.*, XVI, Tables II and III, 73. For seven counties of old enclosure - Devon and Cornwall, Norfolk and Suffolk, Cheshire and Lancashire, and Sussex - the total area of glebe was 79,245 acres among 1,793 parishes. For five counties of new enclosure - Yorkshire, Lincolnshire, Northamptonshire and Leicestershire, and Oxfordshire - there were 231,815 acres among 1,966.

77. Austin, *op.cit.*, p.192.

78. Best, *Temporal Pillars*, p.63, note l.

79. Edward Hughes, *North Country Life in the Eighteenth Century*, pp. 305-8, 323,326,328. Nepotism among eighteenth-century Bishops of Durham is discussed in J.C. Shuler, 'The Pastoral and Ecclesiastical Administration of the Diocese of Durham 1721-1771', pp.88-91, 98-100, 104-6, 108-11, 249-53. It is clearly an interesting topic.

80. Information on the structure and financial resources of cathedrals can be found in *P.P.*, 1835, XXII, 35-111, and *P.P.*, 1836, XXXVI, 21.

81. The mining interests of the church are discussed in C.W. Coolidge, 'The Finances of the Church of England 1830-1880', pp.69-74. He concludes (p.74) that 'the income from this source to the ecclesiastical corporations was truly impressive'.

82. E.N. Williams, The *Eighteenth-Century Constitution*, pp.348-50; and *P.P.*, 1835, XXII, 35-111. The figures quoted in the survey of royal patronage are all approximate.

83. *G.M.*, C11, Part II (November, 1832), 479.

84. M.S. notebooks at Long Melford, quoted in A. Tindal Hart, *The Eighteenth-Century Country Parson*, pp.104-8.

85. Hobsbawm and Rudé, *op.cit*, p.121.

86. See, e.g., A College Incumbent, *Ecclesiastical Taxation and Augmentation of Small Benefices*, p.14,19; and S.T. Bloomfield, *An Analytical View of the Principal Plans of Church Reform*, p.45.

87. The clearest statement of Coleridge's views on the nature of ecclesiastical property can be found in *On the Constitution of Church and State*, ed. John Barrell, pp. 33-92, esp. pp.39-47. *Church and State* was published in 1830.

88. See, e.g., Thomas Arnold, *Principles of Church Reform*, p.7., where he describes church property as 'set apart for ever for public purposes', and as 'saved out of the scramble of individual selfishness'. Coleridge's views are here very dominant.

89. A detailed discussion of leases for lives and for terms of years, including varying methods of calculating fines at lease renewal, can be found in Coolidge, *op.cit.*, pp.36-52.

90. See above, p. 2.

91. The prohibition on purchasing government stock with the proceeds from augmentations was lifted in 1831, but only for the Parliamentary Grants Fund, which had been set up in 1809 - Best, *op.cit.*, pp.221-2.

92. The best concise account of the Bounty's early years is in *ibid.*, pp.78-93.

93. Statistics from *ibid.*, Appendix IV, pp. 537-8.

94. *ibid.*, pp.108-9, 219. No augmentations to buy parsonages were permitted during the second half of the eighteenth century.

95. *ibid.*, p. 109.

96. 43 Geo. III c. 107; Best, *op.cit.*, p.205, 218-19.

97. *ibid.*, pp.230-1.

98. *ibid.*, p.213.

99. 17 Geo. III c.53; Best, *op.cit.*, pp. 217-18.

100. *ibid.*, p.214.

101. See above, p.17.

102. Best, *op.cit.*, p.220.

103. *ibid.*, pp. 213-14.

104. Figures for 1830 are derived from *P.P.*, 1835, XXII, 1053; those for 1810 are from *P.P.*, 1810, XIV, 92-3. The latter return, as already shown (see above, note 54), lacks the precision to be found in a further source - *P.P.*, 1818, XVIII, 361. This later parliamentary paper, however, does not classify livings into categories - under £10 a year, under £20 a year, and so on - and cannot therefore be used for present purposes.

105. Best, *op.cit.*, p.216.

106. Revd John Penn to Bishop of Norwich's secretary, 28 March 1811, N.R.O., NRN/l, Box 719.

107. According to Christopher Hodgson, *An Account*, Table, p.CCCLVI, augmentations out of the Royal Bounty Fund amounted during this period to £1,900,900 - £1,222,800 (64.3%) by lot, and £678,100 (35.7%) to meet benefactions. Support from the Parliamentary Grants Fund was a little less - a total of £1,500,700, of which £1,135,200 (75.6%) was by lot, and £365,500 (24.4%) was to meet monies from other sources. Interestingly, the net income of all incumbents and curates in the early 1830s was also £3.4 million (see below, p. 92).

108. From Hodgson, *op.cit.*, Table, p.CCCLIII-CCCLV, it can be calculated that private benefactions to meet grants from the Royal Bounty Fund totalled £903,858 between 1713 and 1844. Calculations for the Parliamentary Grants Fund are more problematical. Bounty grants from this fund, to meet benefactions, came to £365,500. As has been seen, it was the Board's practice to make £300 grants to meet £200 benefactions; thus, assuming a constant relation of 3 to 2 between grant and benefaction, private monies paid into the newer fund can be calculated at £243,667, making a total of £1,147,525.

109. For a description of the 1835 Report, see below, pp.89-91.

110. *P.P.*, 1835, XXII, 1053. A full comparison with the original certificates can be found in Table IV, below.

111. See J. Ecton, *A State of the Proceedings of the Corporation of the Governors of the Bounty of Queen Anne*, p. 249. According to this source, 1,216 benefices were then worth under £20 a year, 906 were between £20 and £30, 921 between £30 and £40, and 783 between £40 and £50. The original paper from which Ecton made these calculations is to be found in 'Bishops Returns of Poor Livings under £80 made in 1705', in Q.A.B., Box 1-3.

112. See above, pp. 66-68.

113. See above, p. 68.

114. 'Certificates of value of livings made in 1715 onward', Q.A.B., Bundles I and II.

115. See below, Table III and Table IV.

116. Q.A.B., F. 3197.
117. *ibid.*, F.5119.
118. F.151.
119. F. 2053.
120. F. 2305.
121. F. 1180.
122. 'Bishops Returns of Poor Livings under £80 made in 1705', Q.A.B., Box 1-3.
123. See above, p. 62.
124. See above, p. 46.
125. See below, pp. 81-85, 189-209.
126. For a description of this index, see above, note 23.
127. See, e.g. Schumpeter, *R.E.S.*, XX, 26.

4

Image and Reality

i. *Landowning and Farming*

'Opulent persons', admitted a bishop in the mid 1830s, 'not unfrequently enter into Orders'.[1] This is one reference, among many in the contemporary literature, to the clergy's improved social standing. It is not difficult to find others. Charles Girdlestone, vicar of Sedgley in Staffordshire, was sure that 'a great part of the beneficed clergy have some income to spend, out of property of their own'.[2] A correspondent of the *Norwich Mercury* went further. Speaking of the clergy in general terms, he thought it was 'sometimes' the case that a member of this 'order of gentry' lacked private means.[3] Too much should not be made of these comments. The vision of contemporaries was distorted on this matter. Because the social status of the clergy was rising, there was an understandable tendency to exaggerate the swiftness of the ascent. The facts do not support the contention that the clergy of late-Georgian England were mostly members of the ruling class; analysis of clerical social origins, developed in detail in a later chapter,[4] shows that only a fifth of all incumbents were related, either by blood or marriage, to the peerage and gentry.

Attempts by contemporaries to quantify social status in financial terms are rare. An effort was made by Bishop Phillpotts ('Henry of Exeter'), in the course of some correspondence with Peel on church reform. Peel was in favour of a radical redistribution of cathedral property, a 'violent' measure which Phillpotts considered unnecessary. 'In my own diocese', he wrote, 'the pecuniary means of the clergy, as a body, are, I have no doubt, at least two fold the amount of ecclesiastical income.'[5] Although lucidly put, the Bishop of Exeter's claim should not be accepted at face value; it must be borne in mind that he was, as always, arguing a case. To test the accuracy of Phillpotts' assertion, we gathered together a selection of biographical sources, combing them for evidence of private wealth. At first sight, it would seem that Phillpotts was right. We found rich hunting parsons, rich non-hunting parsons, and even, may it be said, rich Evangelical parsons. However, as will become apparent, the reliability of biography as a yardstick against which to judge this matter is severely open to question.

Benjamin Newton, rector of the Yorkshire living of Wath from 1814 until 1830,[6] is a good representative example of a hunting parson. He mixed with the best Yorkshire society, kept his own pack of greyhounds, coursed the hare, hunted the fox and shot partridge. Unfortunately for Newton, addiction to field-sports was, from time to time, productive of inconvenience - on one occasion, after a shoot, he had a thorn taken out of the the middle of that part of the body which resembles a 'large cushion of flesh', by his wife.[7] Newton's style of life was lavish. He regularly dined on venison, turtle and champagne, and occasionally paid about £100 for a pipe of port - yielding at least 93 dozen bottles - which he shared with one or two neighbouring gentry and clergy. As befitted his place in society, he married well - his wife's family had an interest in a company owning a coal-mine in the Forest of Dean, and his brother-in-law, John Fendall, was Governor of Java.[8] Newton farmed an extensive glebe at Wath, rented land, and owned a good deal of his own. On one occasion, he turned down an offer of £2,900 for 69 acres, including £800 for wood;[9] and he held at least 500 acres at Biddisham, nearby.[10] In 1818, he sold some canal shares for £60 each and bought £6,200 of other stock.[11] Newton was a very rich clergyman indeed.

Another 'squarson', Archer Clive, illustrates by his life the change in attitudes taking place among the clergy. Archer's father, a Whig MP and Herefordshire landowner, had gained the advowson of Solihull in Warwickshire as part of his wife's dowry. It was decided that Archer should succeed to the living. This he duly did in 1829 when the incumbent, 'Old Curtis', obligingly died.[12] Curtis had kept a pack of harriers, but the new rector dispensed with any such visible sign of identification with the way of life lived by gentry in the countryside. Although he sometimes hunted and shot with other leading members of Warwickshire society, Archer Clive felt uncomfortable about doing so.[13] Times were changing. In 1818 Benjamin Newton had visited a poor man in the last stages of consumption immediately before going coursing with a neighbouring incumbent. Twenty years later Archer Clive went to Lichfield races, but had to be secretive about the expedition, because many of his parishioners would 'think me little better than a Heathen if they heard of it'.[14] Because their scruples had to be respected, it was necessary to live two separate existences as squire and parson. Archer Clive did not find this easy. He was a conscientious parson - we see him installing a new heating system in the parish church, endowing a chapel of ease, attending Sunday schools regularly, and reading Psalms to the aged in the local workhouse[15] - but he was also a squire with estates that kept on growing. His wife Caroline, a minor novelist, was mistress of Olton Hall near Solihull. This, in fact, represented but a small part of her family's patrimony. Her elder brother Edmund, like Archer a clergyman, inherited a very large Warwickshire estate, worth fully £8,000 a year. He died young, and would have been succeeded by another clerical brother, had the latter not been indiscreet enough to fall down some stairs after a drinking bout, injuring himself fatally.[16] Lack of an obvious heir meant that prolonged litigation, in which Caroline and Archer Clive were heavily involved, followed Edmund's death. Meanwhile, some land in Ireland was bequeathed to Archer, as was the large family estate at Whitfield in Herefordshire. This last bequest sounded the death-knell for his clerical career. He sold the advowson of Solihull for £6,000 in 1847, and went to live at Whitfield, where he became a much-respected improving landowner.[17] The tension between social and pastoral functions had been resolved at last.

No such dilemma confronted that strange misanthrope, John Skinner, rector of Camerton in Somerset from 1800 until 1839. Rare for a Georgian clergyman, Skinner committed suicide, blowing out his brains with a shotgun.[18] The main theme in his life was social isolation. He complained that neighbouring clergy aped the manners and behaviour of those in a higher social sphere than themselves; while others hunted and shot, he visited archaeological sites and studied etymology. He strove to make his academic work into a 'shield and safeguard against the evils of life', and failed.[19] Persecuted by some of his parishioners,[20] laughed or sworn at by others,[21] insulted by both the squire's son and his own servants,[22] sometimes at war with his children and left to mourn a wife who died young, he was in the perilous position of being without a firm friend anywhere in the world.

Skinner was largely responsible for his difficulties. He was dictatorial,[23] judgmental,[24] reclusive and emotionally demanding. He was not, however, either uncaring or unjust. His parish might be a 'cross jade', but he was 'wedded' to it; he was determined to promote the welfare of its people, especially of the poor.[25] He became an overseer in 1811 for the express purpose of ensuring that the local coal company paid a proper contribution to the rates.[26] Further instances of his pastoral and social concern are ready to hand. He rebuked a fellow overseer for allowing a pauper to be left to rot in his own filth while maggots devoured him,[27] helped to pay the medical expenses of an injured collier and, in 1830, opposed an attempt by mine-owners to lower wages by three shillings a week.[28]

Skinner was also generous. About £1,200 was spent on renovating the glebe premises for use as a Sunday school. Once this had been done, Skinner paid the wages of a master - £11 a year - out of his own pocket.[29] Rather more money was spent on educating his children. Although despising social mimicry, he sent both his sons to Winchester; dancing and hand-writing masters were also employed, in order to equip them with the necessary social skills.[30] Unhappily, it is a moot point whether the expense and effort were worthwhile. Skinner's elder son, Owen, did go on to Trinity College, Oxford, but failed to complete his degree; while his younger son, Joseph, went to Sandhurst, from which he was unceremoniously dismissed.[31] A lot of money had been expended for rather a small return. In 1823 Skinner's education bill was running at slightly over £300 a year; and two years later it was running at slightly over £500 a year.[32] Since Camerton's value had dropped during the postwar depression from about £620 to around £500, the rector was required to draw on his capital.[33] This must have been considerable, but no indication of its nature or scope is given in the *Journal*.

Benjamin Philpot is an example of a clergyman in whom religious principles grew to maturity as his clerical career progressed: later in life he became a convinced Evangelical, although his first years of ministry gave no hint of this development.

Ordained in 1815, he lived until 1828 the life of a Suffolk squarson, shooting with avidity, promoting a cricket club at Southwold and having a half-share in a pack of harriers.[34] This he was able to do because he had inherited 'a nice little property with two farms' from his uncle in 1814.[35] On the same day as he became a landowner, he was elected fellow of Christ's College, Cambridge. He only kept his fellowship for two years. The advowson of Walpole in Suffolk had been included in his inheritance, and he moved there as soon as a 'suitable exchange' could be arranged with the 'sitting' incumbent.[36] The year of his move to Walpole was, also, the year of his first marriage, to a woman with a 'snug little fortune'. 'Snug' it may have been; easily lost it was also. Unwisely, Philpot agreed that his wife's money should go to the children of the marriage. There was only a single daughter, and she eloped with a young doctor taking - as a sensible precaution - her mother's fortune with her.[37] By now her mother was long since dead, while her father had taken as his second wife Charlotte, daughter of Jack Vachell, vicar of Littleport in Cambridgeshire.[38] Together with his second wife, Philpot migrated to the Isle of Man in 1828 to become rector of St George's, Douglas. Bishop Murray of Sodor and Man was anxious to 'enlist the services of gentlemen', feeling that local clergy lacked the requisite 'social and educational qualifications'.[39] The Suffolk squarson was to remain on the island for eleven years, during which time he forsook his former habits and adopted new ones. Symbolic of the change in his way of life is the selling of his inherited property.[40] Previously he had shot and hunted, wined and dined. Now he organised missionary and temperance meetings, and suppressed public houses.[41] By the time of his return to England in 1839, to become rector of Cressingham in Norfolk, Philpot was a very different man from the one who had left eleven years earlier.[42] He had resolved the tension between social and pastoral functions in a manner diametrically opposed to that chosen by Archer Clive.

John Skinner's *Journal* shows that contemporary sources are sometimes reticent about the clergy's private wealth. What a diarist could do, a biographer could do better. We have in mind the description of the early clerical career of John Lonsdale, Bishop of Lichfield from 1843 until 1867. Lonsdale, we are led to believe, married 'an heiress in a small way' called Elizabeth Steer. Her inheritance had descended from a former governor of Hull, who had been 'given' some unreclaimed land at the mouth of the Humber, known as Sunk Island, by Charles II. This 'small property' is described as having remained in the Steer family's possession until the mid 1830s.[43]

If Lonsdale's biographer had cared to read *Hansard's* account of a certain House of Commons debate in 1830, his sketch of the Bishop's family background would have been more accurate. Sunk Island did not belong to the Steer family, but to the Commissioners of Woods and Forests. In 1771, this body leased the property to members of the Steer family for thirty years, with the lessees paying a fine of £1,550 and £60 a year in rent. Since the value of the island was then £960 a year, the cost of the fine should have been more like £8,400. When the first lease expired, another thiry-year agreement was signed, this time with John Lonsdale and some co-partners. For the first year the rent was £700, for the second it was £2,000, and the annual sum was then settled at £3,000. The explanation for this sudden increase is that Lonsdale, like his predecessors, had been improving the property. Before 1800 the Steers had spent about £20,000 on land reclamation, and in 1802 Lonsdale had invested a further £10,000, expanding the cultivable area from 4,000 acres to 5,000. Together with his co-partners, he then let the island at a rack-rent of £10,000 a year, making a clear profit of £7,000 a year. Upon expiry in 1831, the lease was not renewed.[44]

From biography the labyrinthine complexity of clerical intermarriage - which did much to consolidate personal fortunes - also stands revealed. An excellent example is that of the links that bound the families of Stanley, Hare, and Heber. Edward Stanley, rector of Alderley in Cheshire and subsequently Bishop of Norwich,[45] married Catherine Leycester, daughter of the rector of Stoke-upon-Terne in Shropshire. By this union, the future bishop became related to the Hares; Catherine's sister, Maria, wedded the Revd Augustus Hare, whose more famous brother, Julius, sat at the feet of Coleridge and taught F.D. Maurice to think. One of the cousins of the Hare brothers married Reginald Heber, hymn writer, rector of Hodnet in Shropshire, and also, briefly, Bishop of Calcutta;[46] and it was at Hodnet rectory that Maria Leycester met Augustus Hare. These links were avowedly aristocratic. Edward Stanley was the younger son of the squire of Alderley Park; the remnants of the Hare estates were sold for £60,000 in 1806:[47] and the Hebers had extensive property at Hodnet, as well as land at Marton in Yorkshire.[48]

The private wealth of some clergy was so great that it bore little intelligible relation to the sums received in benefice income. If, like John Lonsdale, a cleric was able to sub-lease a large estate at a rack-rent of £10,000 a year, the income from a rectory or two was likely to seem paltry by comparison. Nevertheless, the information that has been gathered does not, in fact, prove the truth in Henry Phillpotts' claim that the private means of the body of beneficed clergy were at least twice the sum obtained by way of ecclesiastical income. The clergy so far mentioned are all special cases. They were wealthy men in their own right; and they also shared something else in common - they had all managed to pick a large plum out of the ecclesiastical pie. Hodnet was worth £1,884 a year; Solihull brought in £1,455; Wath produced £981; Herstmonceaux (held from 1832 by Julius Hare) was valued at £920; Stoke-upon-Terne at £878; Cressingham at £607; Alderley at £514; and Camerton at £481.[49] It is necessary, when discussing the less affluent majority, to fall back upon general considerations. Most Georgian rectors and vicars were not directly related to the peerage and gentry; and the median ecclesiastical income in 1830 was under £300 a year.[50] This sum was much less than Benjamin Newton, or even John Skinner, received; and, piling one relative disadvantage upon another, the social connections of most clergy were nothing like as good as those of the Hares and the Hebers. The truth is that there is no means of verifying the private wealth of the body of beneficed clergy. The views of Henry Phillpotts asserted as always with confidence and conviction, can claim only the status of interesting (but probably exaggerated) speculation.

Some clergy owned land, while others farmed it themselves. There were ancient restrictions on clergy leasing and renting land, but these had long ceased to be effective.[51] Early nineteenth-century legislation tacitly accepted the practice, but endeavoured to control and restrict it. Under an Act of 1803,[52] episcopal permission had to be obtained to farm land other than glebe, and the same was now to be true for plots allotted at enclosure, if these exceeded eighty acres. It is not known how many eighteenth-century incumbents evaded the earlier legislation, nor is it known how many took advantage of the relaxations permitted in the first decade of the nineteenth. One source of information about clerical farmers is the land tax returns, which have been analysed for Bedfordshire. The county was assessed in 1797, and then again in 1804; on the first occasion there were 34 parishes which made returns, and on the second there were 73, for a total of 107. Reflecting the fact that the commutation movement was well advanced in the county, there were 48 clerical proprietors; but for present purposes it is more interesting to note that clerical occupiers numbered 43.[53] Unfortunately, it is uncertain what the term 'occupier' means. According to a different source - diocesan records for Oxfordshire - it usually meant little. In this county, in the mid 1780s, there were 55 resident incumbents. Although sixteen of these were described, in contemporary visitation registers, as occupiers, it can be said with conviction that only two were, with a further five doubtful cases.[54] Another piece of evidence, again from Oxfordshire, suggests that few clergy applied for episcopal permission to farm land under the 1803 Act. In the Bishop of Oxford's Act Books, for 1812-30, there are records of only seven licences, two given to curates and five to incumbents.[55] Three of the latter had gone to a single clergyman, John Hyde, perpetual curate of Hailey.

A few clerical farmers, both rich and poor, achieved notoriety. One rich farmer who made the rogue's gallery was Joshua Waterhouse, at one time a Fellow of St Catharine's College, Cambridge. Waterhouse paid such poor wages to his labourers at Little Stukeley in Huntingdonshire that they all refused to work for him, so he looked after his large farm, worth about £400 a year, himself. Dressed in corduroy breeches, light grey stockings, and a coarse blue coat with metal buttons, he could often be seen driving his pigs to Huntingdon market. Waterhouse was eccentric. All the windows of his elegant rectory were boarded up to avoid tax. He lived in the kitchen, using the other rooms, whose floors were covered with Turkish carpets, as granaries.[56] William Sewell, vicar of Troutbeck in Westmorland, was eccentric in a different way. Tall and muscular, he settled disputes between his parishioners by force. He was also a keen sportsman, taking an active part in the local hunt. When his bishop, J.B. Sumner of Chester, unwisely visited Troutbeck in the shearing season, he found Sewell salving the cuts and sores of his neighbours' sheep in a cowshed. It was explained that the vicar normally cultivated no more than his own glebe, and that he only helped other farmers at busy periods.[57]

ii. *Teaching*

Private wealth was, for the clergy, the grand corinthian pillar supporting a life of ease. Other extra-ecclesiastical sources of income were significantly less convenient, in that they involved work; and work usually meant teaching. Of this, incumbents did a good deal. Indeed, in 1808, the Revd Sydney Smith, humourist, co-founder of the *Edinburgh Review* and confidant of Whig politicians, asserted with characteristic boldness that the 'whole concern' of education devolved upon the clergy.[58] This was a pardonable exaggeration. Clerical participation in teaching was so extensive that Coleridge wanted to unite the two professions, with the clergy in control. Both teacher and clergyman, he wrote, 'should be labourers in different compartments of the same field, workmen engaged in different stages of the same process, with such differences of rank, as might be suggested in the names pastor and sub-pastor, or as now exists between curate and rector, deacon and elder'[59]. At the upper end of the educational system, among the endowed grammar (or 'public') schools, the clerical stranglehold was almost complete. An example shows just how strong this stranglehold was. In 1832, the headmastership of Ipswich Grammar School fell vacant. The electors drew up a short-list of fifteen clerical candidates and these were eventually reduced to two.[60] A year later, in 1833, the Oxford and Cambridge University *Calendars* listed the headmasters of thirty-two well-known schools, all except one of whom were ordained.

Most teachers were clergy, but there were not many teachers. A lot of schools were in a decayed state; and even if the rot had not set in, it was still normal for classes to be exceptionally large, sometimes over a hundred. In 1818, an admittedly incomplete survey was published.[61] For three counties - Norfolk, Kent, and Sussex - the author of the survey obtained information from twenty-five schools. There were only twenty-eight masters and ushers at these, of whom twenty-two were clergy, fourteen of them beneficed. Since there were over nine hundred incumbents in the same three counties,[62] less than 2% of them were schoolmasters.

It quite frequently happened that a 'public' school, that is, one open to all, had been turned into a private establishment. Such was Berkhamstead School in Hertfordshire. A Chancery suit, begun against the headmaster in 1735, lasted until the 1830s. A receiver was appointed in 1752, but the school limped on. Thomas Dupré, headmaster from 1805, resided for ten years, teaching about six of his own pupils in the schoolroom. In 1815, he obtained the wealthy Lincolnshire living of Willoughby, subsequently having a licence not to reside, on the pretence of being at Berkhamstead but living, in fact, elsewhere. Between 1811 and 1832, revenue amounted to £15,645; the master's salary for the same period was £5,993. Parts of the school, the master's residence in particular, had been kept in good repair, but the usher's apartments were virtually uninhabitable, with many tiles missing from the roof. Not that the usher noticed. Successive holders of the office, including a certain Revd Michael Dupré, had been non-resident since the late eighteenth century. In 1832, a timely visit by the Charity Commissioners brought about much-needed reform - 'whilst our Report was in the press, the school was reopened, and Mr Dupré is now engaged in instructing seven free scholars in the schoolhouse'.[63]

Some clergy started schools of their own. Kensington Grammar School was founded in 1831 by a Sussex clergyman, J.H. Howlett, vicar of Hollington. George Millers, vicar of Runham and Stanford, kept a private school at Ely 'for many years'. William Jones of Broxbourne, whose diary has been published, made use of a converted barn, teaching mostly foreigners; in 1799, the roof fell in during the night, a cataclysmic event from which the school took some time to recover.[64] As this last example implies, many of these clerical schemes were tenuous and unsatisfactory. At an Epsom preparatory school, kept by the Revd E.C. James, the pupils were required to sleep in sheets made out of former pupils' towels sewn together. Once a term, as a special treat, the boys were drenched with Epsom salts instead of being given any breakfast.[65] Scarning School in Norfolk, which had once educated several famous men, had only about 50 boarders at the turn of the nineteenth century, and these lived in a row of squalid buildings. Fights with local boys were frequent. The master, the Revd Mr Priest, was a leading agriculturalist with two or three livings, but died insolvent.[66]

A less formal arrangement was to teach a few pupils at home. Not untypical was the experience of Henry Manning. When he first went to Harrow in 1822 he was behind in classics; during the holidays he therefore arose each day at five, read until eight, and then rode over to the neighbouring parish of Sundridge to study Latin and Greek with the curate there.[67] From time to time reference is made to private teaching in clerical biography. For the learned who had access to noble society, financial rewards could be great. A good example is the early career of C.J. Blomfield. Ordained in 1809, he soon obtained the rectory of Dunton in Buckinghamshire, where he went to reside, taking noble pupils at fees of up to £300 or £400 a year each, rates which few except former fellows of Trinity could successfully demand. 'At this time', according to his son, and biographer, Blomfield probably regarded ordination 'rather as affording means and leisure for literary pursuits, than as offering in its own peculiar duties that wide field of usefulness which ere long opened upon him.'[68]

The fees which Blomfield charged his private pupils were exceptionally high. Other clergy, lacking Blomfield's reputation, asked for less. Evidence on this matter is diffuse, and not always easy to come by. It was, it would seem, normal practice to use a sliding scale, with fees in inverse proportion to numbers taught. There are examples of this scale in operation, among schools in Kent and Sussex soon after the close of the Napoleonic Wars. At this time 'between twenty and thirty' boarders at Maidstone Grammar paid 40 guineas a year each; sixteen pupils at the Prebendal School, Chichester paid 60 guineas; and at Horsham School, where numbers did not exceed two, the rate was 200 guineas.[69] These fees, it must be remembered, were not shared out among many pairs of hands; as was pointed out earlier,[70] there were 25 endowed grammar schools in the three counties of Kent, Norfolk, and Sussex in the years around 1820, at which only 28 masters and ushers were teaching. Since the line dividing a grammar school from a strictly private establishment was, in a good many instances, exceedingly thin, the financial attractions of teaching do not need to be spelt out. In many cases a single pupil, or perhaps two, at least doubled a clergyman's income. A school such as that of William Jones at Broxbourne could easily bring in £500 a year.

'Clergy of more slender fortune' - wrote a clerical pamphleteer in the early 1830s - 'are, for the most part, enabled to bring up a family' on the proceeds from teaching.[71] As with many exaggerations, there is a grain of truth in this statement. A small minority of incumbents, probably less than 2%, taught in grammar schools. On the other hand, a good deal of private teaching was done by clergy. If a nobleman employed a private tutor, the odds were that the tutor was a clergyman. Some incumbents started their own schools, while others taught at home on an ad hoc basis. Fees were considerable, and could easily enough surpass benefice income. The preference for teaching as a career option is clear enough, and the financial attractions of teaching are also clear enough, but the number of clerical teachers is unknown.

iii. *The Evidence of the 1835 Report*

The great Report of the Ecclesiastical Revenues Commission was compiled just a few years before tithes were compulsorily commuted under the Act of 1836. The scope of the commissioners' work was comprehensive - they investigated the value of every bishopric, cathedral post and living in both England and Wales,[72] taking the precaution of averaging income over three years. It is less easy to assess whether the period chosen for the survey - from January 1829 until December 1831 - was representative of agrarian conditions in the late 1820s and early 1830s. The summer of 1829 was exceptionally wet, but that of 1830 was wetter, producing the most serious outbreak of sheep rot during the century, apart from 1879-80.[73] The price of wheat, which had not exceeded 70s a quarter since September 1821, reached a peak of 75s 11d in 1829; the next year it varied between 74s 11d and 55s 5d; and in 1831 it moved between 75s 1d and 59s 2d.[74] These then were years of high cereal prices and of low yields. There is also the fact of the Last Labourers Revolt, that wave of social unrest which swept across the southern counties during the winter of 1830-1.[75] All tithes, especially those in kind, became hard to collect, and many clergy made either 'solicited' or 'unsolicited' reductions in their compositions.[76] The commissioners were not especially impressed by these examples of clerical generosity. Clergy had to show that abatements had been made because crop values had fallen; sums given back to farmers to help alleviate distress, and arrears in payment for which clergy did not press, were not allowed to count.[77] In this way, the commissioners managed to minimise the distorting effects of rural unrest, and pre-empted the hostile criticism that they had accepted, as part of their computations, the sometimes artificially low sums received by clergy in the winter of 1830-1.

The Report is a monumental work containing page after page of fascinating detail about every nook and cranny of the church; starting with the bishoprics, going on to the cathedral chapters, and then dealing, in alphabetical order, with the dioceses.[78] Every rectory, vicarage, and perpetual curacy gets a mention. There are gross values, net values, and curate's stipends, where applicable; and also a list of other ecclesiastical appointments held by the office-holder or incumbent. It is all immensely valuable information, but it is the raw material of analysis, rather than the finished article. What is of paramount interest is to know the incomes of the beneficed clergy; and, when calculating these, there are no short-cuts to certainty. Truth lies at the end of a long and winding road. The historian has to work out the incomes of each incumbent separately, moving at a measured pace from diocese to diocese and from place to place. It is a slow and tortuous journey, but one well worth the effort. When travelling from St Asaph to York, via Exeter and St David's, we passed by a total of 7,490 beneficed clergy. The main finding was that the typical (or median) income of English incumbents was £275 a year; while in Wales, much poorer, the median was set much lower, at only £172 a year.[79] The difference was thus between an income of £5 10s 0d a week in England and £3 10s 0d a week in Wales.

Extravagantly wealthy incumbents were few and far between. Only 76 had incomes over £2,000 a year, all but sixteen of whom held some cathedral preferment - which sheds an interesting sidelight upon the contemporary movement for cathedral reform. Some well-known names appear on the list. Sydney Smith is there. His income, principally from a canonry at St Paul's, was £2,887 a year. Another famous name is that of the classicist, Thomas Gaisford, Dean of Christ Church, Oxford. Algernon Peyton, rector of Doddington, comes first with an income of £6,921 a year; second was Gerard Wellesley, Wellington's younger brother, and also a prebendary of Durham - his preferments brought in £5,170 a year. W.R. Hay, well-hated in Radical circles for his involvement in Peterloo, is included. So, too, are relatives of two notorious nepotistic Bishops: Pretyman-Tomline of Lincoln and Winchester and Sparke of Ely.[80] Both of Sparke's sons appear, together with their brother-in-law, Henry Fardell. So does G.J. Pretyman. But his brother, Richard, managed to escape notice by means of the tactic of not returning the value of all his livings.

Although extreme opulence was rare, meagre ecclesiastical incomes were common. There were 550 incumbents in Wales, of whom 141 (25.6%) earned £100 a year or less.[81] In England, the crowd gathered at the base of the ecclesiastical pyramid was smaller, but still far from negligible. There, the incomes of 1,081 beneficed clergy out of 6,940 (15.6%) failed to make three figures.[82] It is interesting, as well as instructive, to distinguish between rectors and vicars on the one hand, and perpetual curates on the other. No less than 645 of the poor English clergy, 60% of the total, held perpetual curacies. Although some perpetual curacies were endowed with tithes, they were mostly cursed with a fixed pension paid either by a clerical appropriator or - as was more likely - by a lay impropriator.[83] The large number of poor perpetual curates is a strong indictment of private patronage; an indictment which, moreover, can be pressed home still more vigorously, when it is brought to mind that the efforts of the Bounty, especially in the early nineteenth century, were concentrated upon raising the values of livings that were penurious.[84]

No rigid profile emerges locally, a fact made clear by comparisons between Norfolk and Kent.[85] Great wealth was more common in Kent, but affluence was more common in Norfolk. There were eight Norfolk clergy among 408 (1.9%) who broke the £2,000 a year barrier, while in Kent there were seven among 285 (2.5%). Many Kentish presentations were in the gift of the Archbishop of Canterbury, and two successive holders of this highest of ecclesiastical offices, Archbishops Moore and Manners-Sutton,[86] both cultivated the habit of favouring family and friends. Among the clergy of this county were James Croft, who married one of Manners-Sutton's many daughters, and two of Archbishop Moore's sons, Robert and George.[87] Robert Moore's income was £2,549; his brother's reached £3,592; and James Croft earned £3,362. The nepotistic exercise of archiepiscopal patronage helps to explain why exceptional opulence was more frequent among Kentish clergy than among those in Norfolk. But at lower levels of affluence, the balance was tilted the other way. There were 22 Kent clergy (7.7%) who earned between £700 and £1,000 a year, but in Norfolk the proportion was twice as high, 63 among 408 (15.5%). The typical Norfolk incumbent was wealthier than his Kentish counterpart.

Norfolk and Kent were two of the richest counties in England and Wales; Cumbria was among the poorest.[88] At £108 a year the median income was 60% lower than that in England as a whole. Only a quarter of all incumbents earned £192 a year or more, whereas in Kent only a quarter earned £216 or less. There were nine Lakeland clergy with more than £500, but fourteen with less than £50. These, indeed, were 'peasant' clergy, nearly half of whom lived off less than £100 a year. The gulf separating them from rich clergy was, from every viewpoint, unbridgeable. Their social origins were more obscure, their education less distinguished, their style of life more primitive, their incomes less attractive. They stand apart, and must receive, in any general review, special and separate treatment.

iv. *The Church and the Anti-clericals*
Satire and ridicule, rather than a careful examination of truth, were the order of the day in the contemporary Radical press. The church, it was contested, was part of 'Old Corruption', also variously known as 'The Thing' and 'This Babylon which is to fall'. The point was sometimes expressed pictorially. Corpulent 'Mistress Virago Church' of the *Church Examiner* was depicted as suckling a brood of bishops at her massive breasts; and at her feet lay a basket of choice fruit, and a rather bored-looking pig, also suckling her young. 'The Arms of the Church' - a cartoon caption in *Figaro in London* - included a shield, guarded by a devil symbolically dressed in lawn sleeves and carrying an episcopal crook.[89] Hanging from the end of the crook were bags marked £50,000 and £700,000.

The Georgian bench was wealthy, but could not match the opulence which *Figaro* implied. Inaccuracy, moreover, is not confined to anti-clerical captions. Estimates of the clergy's wealth made in Radical publications are vague, variable, and vacuous. They are also wrong. According to the 1835 Report, the net income of all incumbents and curates was £3.4 million a year.[90] Estimates made by anti-clericals were usually at least twice this sum, and frequently a good deal more. The *Church Examiner* came up with £8 or £9 million a year, a sum with which *Man* agreed.[91] *Punchinello*! regretted the fact that the 'well-fed cormorants' received £14 million a year, *Isis* reckoned the cost of 'religion' at £20 million a year, and a speaker at a meeting of the National Union of the Working Classes estimated the combined wealth of the English and Irish churches at £12 million a year, or '£24 a minute'.[92] R.M. Beverley, a prominent Dissenter, erred on the side of modesty with his guess of £7,596,000.[93] The *Black Book*, first published in 1820, reckoned that 'the 26 bishops, 700 dignitaries, and about 4,000 non-resident incumbents, principally belonging to the aristocracy, enjoy nearly the whole ecclesiastical revenues, amounting to betwixt 5 and £6,000,000, and averaging about £5,000 a year each'. £5,000 was doubtless a misprint for £1,000. This error was not allowed to stand in the way of further allegations. 'The Church', declared the *Extraordinary Black Book* of 1831, 'is a monstrous, overgrown CROESUS in the State'. This 'croesus' had certainly grown in size during the intervening decade; the church's wealth was now estimated at £9,459,565 a year.[94] Extravagant estimates in radical publications were occasionally questioned by readers. 'A Workman' wrote to the *Destructive*, asking for details of its claim that the church's annual revenue was nearly 'FIFTEEN MILLIONS'. In reply, the paper was forced to admit that this figure had been copied from the *Gauntlet*; and the editor, without any apparent sense of self-contradiction or embarrassment, then went on to state that the estimate made in the *Extraordinary Black Book* came 'as near the truth as any we have seen published'.[95] Much nearer, of course, was the 1835 Report.

A lack of concern for the truth among anti-clericals is also revealed, in another way. Publication of the 1835 Report should have come as a salutary shock to them but, if it did, most of them took pains to conceal the fact. Some even carried on repeating the same old tired lies as though nothing had happened. In 1849, long after the troubled political waters of the early 1830s had subsided, the author of the *Black Book* produced a new work, belligerently entitled *Unreformed Abuses in Church and State*. In this, he had the effrontery to reckon the clergy's annual income at £9,165,438, nearly all of it consumed by the bishops, cathedral dignitaries, and about 4,000 incumbents, most of them pluralistic and non-resident. The average income of these ecclesiastics was calculated at upwards of £2,000 a year each.[96] As one contemporary pamphleteer recognised, 'it is perhaps impossible to retire from the always bloody field of polemics, without some share of the disgrace and pain of defeat'.[97]

Anti-clerical propagandists should have fared better. Even without the help of the 1835 Report, it was still possible to estimate the church's wealth. A good method was outlined by a contemporary clerical pamphleteer, H.F. Stephenson, a little-known Evangelical. There were, he thought, 10,533 livings, whose total income was £2,750,000, making an average for each of £261 1s 8d,[98] only £24 less than the figure later given by the 1835 Report. How, it may be asked, did Stephenson compile such accurate statistics? The answer is simple: he was good at guesswork, and he made creative use of the parliamentary returns on property tax for 1806-12, analysed in the previous chapter.[99] Stephenson took the return for 1810, which reckoned the value of all tithes at £2,353,253;[100] and then added a little to this sum, thus arriving at his total of £2,750,000. If an obscure Evangelical parson could do so well, there can be little excuse for the gross ineptitude of the Radical press.

v. *A Place in Society*

Most churchmen agreed that the 1835 Report showed the clergy to be too poor. A median income of £275 a year for English incumbents was simply not enough. The sort of sum enjoyed by the typical Norfolk cleric of the period - £395 a year - was generally regarded as more acceptable. In his highly influential *Plan of Church Reform*, Lord Henley argued for a minimum incumbent's stipend of £400 a year; and he thought it would be 'one of the greatest blessings that could be bestowed upon the country' to have a clergyman with between £800 and £1,200 a year in every place whose population exceeded 1,500 or 2,000.[101] Since this particular pamphleteer was both an Evangelical and a noted church reformer, his views are telling. If, with such impeccable reforming credentials, Lord Henley failed to challenge conventional aristocratic notions, what was to be expected of the great mass of clergy, who were neither Evangelicals nor shared the noble lord's enthusiasm for reform?

On the evidence of the 1835 Report, the ecclesiastical incomes of a third of the beneficed clergy exceeded Lord Henley's suggested figure of £400 a year.[102] This happy band enjoyed a standard of living reserved for few. The best contemporary analysis of national income is an imperfect return of those paying income tax in 1801. Incomes would have risen appreciably between this date and 1830, but the return is still of some use. What it shows is that around 26,000 families in England, Scotland, and Wales had, in 1801, an income of £400 a year or more.[103] It is among this hallowed minority that the Hares and the Hebers are to be found.

Wealthy clergy lived comfortably enough, but they were not on a par with the wealthiest in the land. Even Algernon Peyton could not hold a candle to an earl. On one estimate, there were 300 titled families in the early nineteenth century, most of them with at least 10,000 acres and some with over 50,000.[104] Since, as a rough rule of thumb, rentals reached £1 an acre in the post Napoleonic era, the nobility were well out of reach of the rest of the population, including the clergy.

It is not easy to compare the financial standing of the clergy with that of other professions. One of the few professional groups to have received intensive study is the attorneys, and for them no nationwide estimate of earnings can be made due to lack of evidence, a situation which probably prevails elsewhere. Nonetheless, the account books of Christopher Wallis, an attorney at Helston in remote Cornwall, are still illuminating. The general run of his work was similar to that of other contemporary attorneys, and embraced much of what would now be done by an estate agent as well as a solicitor. Wallis was exceptional in two respects. He was unusually hard-working

- always awake by 6.30 a.m., he regularly put in a twelve-hour day, seven days a week - and he extended his activities beyond the boundaries of an attorney's work, to act as steward to the Cornish estates of Lord Arundell. This vigorous and aggressive man enjoyed a high, and strongly rising, income. The profit from his business as an attorney, supplemented by income as Lord Arundell's steward, was £560 in 1794; by 1800 it was £823; the next year it leaped to £1,800; and it then fluctuated over the next four years, between the two extremes of £1,610 and £2,130.[105] If a self-made Cornish attorney, in a profession with few graduates, could make over £1,500 a year, it is easy enough to understand that an aristocratic parson with only half as much would not consider himself unduly wealthy.

A third of the clergy in 1830 earned over £400 a year from their benefices, while a further third did not manage to make as much as £200 a year. The ecclesiastical incomes of most of these poor incumbents were in the range of £60-£180 a year, putting them on the same level as the emerging lower middle class - teachers, clerks, shopkeepers, and the like.[106] Even a low clerical income of £100 a year was well above what the labouring majority received. According to the income tax return for 1801, 175,000 families earned £2 a week or more. Allowing both for tax evasion and for subsequent increases in earnings, this number may have doubled during the next thirty years, to around 350,000. Even so, with the population now approaching 15 million, this figure represents only a fraction of those in England, Scotland and Wales. By 1830, the Algernon Peytons of this world could claim the status of middle gentry; an incumbent with £400 a year was approaching the outer fringes of the squirearchy; and poor clergy, about level with the lower middle class, were nevertheless among the richest ten or fifteen per cent of people in Britain.

vi. *An Adequate Income for a Gentleman?*

The Georgian parsonage was often the hub of the local community, the centre around which everything revolved. Much was expected of the rector or vicar, especially in places where there was not a resident squire. There was a myriad of ways in which an incumbent could help the poor - blankets in winter, a parish feast in summer, numerous little personal gifts and donations. Some clergy did what they could for their parishioners' ailments, with the help of a medicine box. Village schools were often run by clergy, and sometimes even built at their expense. In many places, moreover, vicars and rectors took a leading part in organising local poor law relief. In all of these ways, clergy had the power to influence profoundly the day-to-day lives of their parishioners. It must not be forgotten that the authority of the Georgian incumbent was, literally, magisterial. It was a society in which one in every four magistrates was a clergyman, and one in every six clergymen was a magistrate.[107] Clerical styles of life reflected this strong position in rural society. All clergy, even curates, kept at least one servant; they lived in spacious houses, expensive to heat and keep in repair; they entertained, travelled and bought books. They were gentlemen, fulfilling the demands made upon gentlemen. Such was their world.

It is possible to build up a detailed profile of clerical expenditure, by piecing together the minutiae recorded in account books. The relevant contrasts are given in records left by two very different clergymen, both of them bachelors.[108] James Plumptre, sometime Fellow of Clare College, Cambridge, and successively vicar of Hinxton in Cambridgeshire and of Great Gransden in the same county, was a meticulous recluse with a moderate income of £225 a year. In 1802, at the time he compiled his accounts, he was living at Hinxton with only a single servant, his housekeeper, Mrs Sutton. James Woodforde, perhaps the most famous rural clergyman of any generation, was less meticulous, less reclusive, somewhat richer, and master of a household of no less than seven. In 1799, he was rector of Weston Longeville in Norfolk, living there with his niece, Nancy, and a coterie of five living-in servants: his two farming men - Ben Leggatt and Briton - a cook, a maid and a boy.

Neither account book is entirely reliable. Plumptre reckoned his expenditure for the year at £204 14s 3d, leaving an unexplained shortfall of £20 6s 7d that vexed him; and Woodforde's accounts suggest that he spent £251 9s 4d, probably about £100 less than the actual figure.[109] Since both men lived within their means, the Hinxton accounts show what a reclusive incumbent could do with an income of £4 10s 0d a week at the turn of the nineteenth century, while those for Weston Longeville show what was possible for a larger household on £7 a week. In the 1830s, life would have been easier for both, especially for James Woodforde. It was in 1799 that the first great Napoleonic inflation began, and prices towards the end of that year were at least a third higher than they were in the 1830s.[110] 1802 was deflationary, but price levels were still at least 20% above those prevailing three decades later.[111]

Housekeeping expenses at Hinxton - food, fuel, Mrs Sutton's wages - came to £73 1s 8d, just under £1 10s 0d a week. This is a low sum, but then Plumptre's parsimony must be remembered. He was unmarried; there is no mention of any dinners in his accounts for this year; and he was content with only an occasional personal luxury, such as a gallon of currant wine, or a bottle of brandy. (For the latter, incidentally, he paid the modest sum of four shillings). Taking into account all the other expenses which must inevitably arise, it is clear enough from this that clergy earning £100 a year or less found making ends meet extremely difficult, particularly if they were married.

Woodforde, by now fifty-nine and gouty, no longer entertained on the lavish scale that had earlier been habitual. There are no menus for 1799 comparable to one for March 1795, at an entertainment in honour of his squire, John Custance and family. 'We gave them', he recorded wistfully, 'a couple of boiled Chicken and Pig's face, very good Peas Soup, a boiled Rump of Beef very fine, a prodigious fine, large and very fat Cock-Turkey roasted, Maccaroni, Batter Custard Pudding with Jelly, Apple Fritters, Tarts and Rasberry Puffs. Desert, baked Apples, nice Nonpareil, brandy Cherries and filberts. Wines, Port and Sherries, Malt Liquors, Strong Beer, bottled Porter, &c. After Coffee and Tea we got to Cards...'[112] Such things were now past. Only three dinners are recorded for 1799. On 1 May a local cleric, Mr Maynard, was entertained; in June, Mrs Bodham, the wife of another local clergyman, dined; and the same month Woodforde was host to his wine-seller, Mr Priest and family. There were two extended visits. At the end of March, Betty Burroughs, a local seamstress, stayed for two days while she altered some of Nancy's mourning attire; and on 25 September Nancy's brother, who lived in Somerset, rode unexpectedly into the yard. As is the way with relatives, he stayed somewhat longer; indeed, right through the autumn and well into January of the next year. Apart from these two visits, and three dinners, social life at Weston Longeville parsonage was domestic. Local gentry call sometimes, either morning or evening, for a glass of wine or a cup of tea, but that is all. Woodforde was, now, a moderate parson.

Out of around £170 he managed to pay the food bill for seven and the wages' bill for five, as well as meet the expense of fuel for the household.[113] These things could easily have cost more. The total was kept down because Woodforde practised self-sufficiency. He kept his own geese, chickens, pigs, ducks, cows and turkeys; he brewed his own beer and mead; his garden supplied much fruit, including grapes and figs; butter was homemade. A farm, moreover, was attached to the glebe, and this supplied wheat, oats and turnips. An extensive garden and a small farm - neither of which was enjoyed by James Plumptre at Hinxton - were effective ways of ekeing out a clerical income. Together, they probably reduced Parson Woodforde's food bill by between £50 and £70 a year.

The cheapness of most provisions also helped. Even when inflation was at its most hectic, beef cost only sevenpence a pound, veal the same, mutton a halfpenny more.[114] Woodforde took full advantage of low prices. The bill for meat came to £43 12s 6d, enough to buy over half a pound per capita per day for the whole household of seven. But fish for the year cost only 9s 8d, and flour came to no more than £6 0s 4d. Drink was, naturally, a considerable item in Woodforde's accounts. The bills for malt and hops amounted, on their own, to £21 18s 0d, well over three times what was spent on bread. (Wines and spirits, it should be noted, were listed under private expenses). Home-brewing was one of Woodforde's specialities; he personally concocted vast quantities of mead and cider, as well as beer. Some appeared at dinner for his guests, but most went to make up a part of his servants' diet.

High levels of rural unemployment kept down servants' wages. Woodforde's long-serving and faithful farming-man, Ben Leggatt, had been employed for nearly a quarter of a century. When Ben had begun working at the parsonage, in 1776, he had been paid £10 0s 0d a year;[115] and in 1799 he was still paid £10 0s 0d a year. Ben's assistant, Briton, was similarly treated. He had been employed for about half as long, since 1785, and his wages had remained at £8 0s 0d. Cooks could be had somewhat cheaper. Molly Salmon, admittedly rather poor at her job - on one occasion, she accidentally added eggs to some milk and rice prescribed as a post-innoculation diet[116] - earned £5 5s 0d in 1776, and in 1799 Woodforde's current cook received the same wage, as did his maid. At the bottom of the familial hierarchy was Woodforde's boy-servant; this post brought in £2 2s 0d a year. For the record, the total wages' bill was £30 12s 0d.

Clergy had to meet a variety of miscellaneous expenses - repairs, medicine, clothes, postage, and the upkeep of their gardens. Woodforde spent £54 4s 8d on these items, and Plumptre laid out £32 3s 7d. Expenditure on repairs was in each case similar, at around £6, but otherwise it was different. 'Physic', in Woodforde's large household, cost £16 18s 7d, but Plumptre's medicine bills were only £2 2s 6d. Woodforde dressed a little more elegantly, spending £20 4s 8d on clothes as against £12 13s 2d; he also laid out twice as much on his garden. The contrast in amounts spent on correspondence is interesting. Parson Woodforde lived within the social circle formed by neighbouring clergy and gentry; there are no references to bills for letters and parcels for this year. Plumptre, more isolated, tried to keep in regular contact with friends and acquaintances. He was worried by the amount he had spent on letters and parcels - £5 13s 11d was 'too much' for a single year - 'but I scarce know how to curtail my correspondents',[117] a reminder that even former dons can make amusing spelling errors.

Calls upon an incumbent's charity were many and varied, and James Plumptre tried to meet most of them. He gave subscriptions both to local causes, such as Hinxton Friendly Society, and to national ones, such as S.P.C.K.; a lame sailor had benefited by 3d, a penniless traveller by 1s; William Stubbins had been given 6d for learning the Lord's Prayer, and Rachel Bates had received 1s for teaching him; another sixpence had gone to a poor woman at Chesterford; rather more, 10s 6d, to an 'Irish Roman Catholic clergyman in distress'; blankets for the poor at Hinxton had cost £4 15s 6d, while his tenant there, Richard Scott, had received £1 1s 0d in acknowledgement 'of the pleasure I receive from his Industry in the care of his garden and good example in the parish'. At the start of the year he set aside £15 for this item, but had spent £22 13s 8d, considerably more. Plumptre did not begrudge the extra expenditure; on the contrary, he was prepared to spend more in the future - 'I will ... allow more for another year, and if necessary, restrain my expenses in other respects to enable me to do it'.[118] The total for the year, about 10% of Plumptre's net income, is impressive testimony to his willingness to make his purse available in the service of others.

Parson Woodforde was less generous, donating £13 8s 4d. An annual present for Nancy took up £10, and the remainder was divided among local causes and needs. Personal servants received 14s 6d; Weston Longeville Purse Club was given 10s 6d; valentines for children amounted to 6s 4d; the parish poor were given £1 5s 6d at Christmas; Woodforde's sailor was old rather than lame, and got 6d rather than 3d; in July a foreigner, accompanied by a man and a woman, came to beg for alms, and when Woodforde discovered that one of the men could talk Latin fluently he gave them 2s 6d to share; and Mrs Norton, a parishioner, received the same amount, firstly because she was bed-ridden, and secondly because her husband treated her badly, being both unruly and extremely averse to sleep.[119]

Both men spent around £36 on private expenses, but their pleasures were different. James Plumptre liked travel, James Woodforde liked wine. A single journey to Norwich, plus the expense of staying there, cost the large sum of £4 1s 7d according to Plumptre's accounts. Parson Woodforde did not go anywhere, not even on holiday, but he did enjoy himself at home, drinking both regularly and heavily. His wine bill for the year came to £24 0s 0d. Port, he grumbled, was now 33s a dozen - in 1774 it had been only 18s[120] - so his annual expenditure on wine would have bought nearly fifteen dozen bottles, equal to roughly half a bottle a day. He probably drank much more. Ten years earlier he complained to himself that he was drinking heavily, and he was consuming at that time nearly a bottle of port a day.[121] The explanation for the discrepancy between stated expenditure and probable consumption lies in bills paid to his farrier, Johnny Reeves. One for 'wine, etc' came to £3 18s 0d, and another for 'rum etc' amounted to slightly less, £3 15s 0d; two more, one for £2 19s 6d and the other for £2 3s 0d, were not specified. This makes a total of £12 15s 6d, a little over half the sum paid to his official wine-merchant. Most of this liquor, obtained through the agency of the local farrier, was smuggled. Parson Woodforde experienced no qualms in accepting smuggled port and brandy, much of it sold to him by a character who went by the name of Moonshine Buck.[122] Prices were low; in 1788, he paid 9s 6d a gallon for smuggled brandy, and even less, just over 5s 6d a gallon, for smuggled gin.[123] At these prices it was possible to kill yourself for two shillings, and £12 a year would have supplied well over half a pint of brandy or gin a day.

Reading was not one of Parson Woodforde's strong points. Literary references are sparse throughout the five volumes of the *Diary*,[124] and there are no bills for books among the acounts for 1799. A local cleric did buy on his behalf, 'by desire of' Nancy, Lavater's *Essays on Physiogonomy*, but there is no mention of Parson Woodforde paying for them.[125] Where Woodforde was parsimonious, Plumptre was self-indulgent. He acknowledged his inability to resist purchasing books as a fault, and yet his contrition was mixed with a strong element of self-justification. 'A love of buying books', he told himself, 'may become a *lust* as much as eating, drinking, or any other extravagance. I will therefore be more moderate another year, and endeavour to keep within bounds; 'tho I buy books now that I may have them to read, when my money will be wanted for other purposes'.[126] All in all, Plumptre spent £41 3s 8d on books - £34 7s 7d on those for himself, and £6 16s 1d on those to 'give away'.

These two sets of accounts give clerical poverty, as well as clerical wealth, an immediacy and a sharpness that would otherwise be lacking. Multifarious basic requirements - food, fuel, servants' wages, repairs, medicine, postage, upkeep of garden and glebe, clothes - cost James Plumptre £105 5s 3d; these same items at Weston Longeville amounted to over twice as much, £224 4s 8d. Allowing for imperfections in his account books, Plumptre probably spent around £120 on these items. In view of Woodforde's less accurate accounting, and also taking into consideration the proceeds from his garden and small farm, a realistic total at Weston Longeville would be about £320. In the less inflationary 1830s, James Plumptre would have been able to meet the same needs out of £100 or so, and James Woodforde could have managed on a third less, say £210. Such were the sums that a reclusive bachelor with a single servant, and a moderately hospitable incumbent with a household of seven, needed to have, if each was to pay his way in the world. Without a larger income, nothing was left for travel, books, wine or charity.

Spare income increased the sense of personal freedom, and added flexibility to life. This was a freedom to be deeply treasured, available to few in Georgian England. For incumbents with more than £300 a year, a large range of personal pleasures came within the ambit of possibility; and for the elite with over £500 a year, life was easy indeed.[127] A well-stocked cellar could be had cheaply; frequent travel was no longer ruled out; and a good library could be built up. Rich clergy were able to move within a wide social circle, they could entertain, and could indulge themselves in rural sports and pastimes; poor clergy were forced by their poverty into social isolation, unable to seek solace in either the spiritual delights of the brandy decanter or the animal delights of the chase. There were, in this sense, two cultures among the Georgian clergy. There had always been clerical poverty, and this was not eradicated; there had always been clerical opulence too, and this was not levelled. Between the two there was a gaping chasm.

vii. *On the Top of the Mountain*

History is full of symbolic actions and events, and the 1830s in England was an era in which such symbols lay thick on the ground. A first step towards adult suffrage was taken with the Reform Act of 1832, the old poor law was swept away by the Act of 1834, municipal corporations were reformed a year later. The church did not emerge unscathed from this passion for change. First Whigs, then Tories, then Whigs again, tried to tackle the thorny issue of tithes. It says much for the contemporary assessment of the urgency of this question that commutation bills were introduced in every year between 1833 and 1836; the fourth effort, by Lord John Russell, successfully reached the statute book. Pluralism was dealt with in 1838, and the unreformed cathedrals were tidied up two years later.

Many of the marks of the new age can be seen in Russell's Act of 1836,[128] which commuted all moduses, tithes in kind, and compositions for a form of corn rent. The Act tried to reach a compromise between landlord and parson, striving to meet the legitimate grievances of the one and to protect the legitimate interests of the other. Landlords complained that the parson was the sleeping partner in agriculture; every increase achieved in agricultural production, and every acre of land that was successfully reclaimed, led automatically to an increase in tithes. Now this passive role of the parson was to be abolished, and tithes would no longer rise as agricultural production rose. From the clergy's side there was a justifiable fear that commutation, coming as it did after several years of agrarian depression, would stabilise benefice incomes at low levels. When tithes were commuted, their value was to be averaged over a period of years in order to reduce the impact made by the depressed conditions of 1834 and 1835; and a way must be found to ensure that the pockets of the clergy benefited, at least to some extent, from future agricultural prosperity.

A 'fair' valuation of tithes was therefore considered to be a legitimate clerical interest; and this was duly safeguarded by the Act. When calculating the value of tithes in each place, the Act stipulated that an average was to be taken over the seven-year period prior to commutation, prior, that is, to 1836. This ensured that the depressed years of 1834 and 1835 were balanced by several others. A second legitimate clerical interest - that the clergy should not miss out entirely in any future agricultural boom - was protected by forging a link between the new tithe rent-charge and cereal prices. Once the average annual value of tithe over the years between 1829 and 1835 had been worked out, the resultant sum was to be split into three equal parts; and it was then calculated how many bushels of wheat, barley and oats each of these parts would buy. The quantities of these three cereals, when converted into cash, became the new tithe rent-charge.[129] The cereal equivalents of tithe were thus to be fixed, quantitatively, for all time; benefice incomes, therefore, would no longer rise in line with agricultural production, as they had in the past. On the other hand, under the Act, the prices of the three new cereal equivalents were to be determined on seven-year moving averages, using the years from 1829 to 1835 as a base. This meant that the clergy's future earnings were given a kind of 'inflation-proofing'. Official thinking went like this: Agricultural prosperity was just round the corner; this prosperity, when it arrived, would lift cereal prices; and higher cereal prices would gradually feed through to the rent-charge. The logic of such official thinking was impeccable. The only drawback was that the opposite scenario - severe agricultural depression dragging down cereal prices, and with these lower prices, also gradually feeding through to the rent-charge - was not considered.

Implementation of the Tithes Commutation Act was entrusted to three permanent commissioners, with their headquarters in London, helped by numerous assistant commissioners and surveyors, who brought to their task the advantage of local knowledge. The work of this bureaucracy, modelled on that of the poor law commission, was steady and methodical. It was also slow. 90% of all apportionments had been made by 1852, and most of the rest were completed by 1860, although a very few of the most intractable cases lingered on into the 1880s.[130] One reason for delay is that the tithe rent-charge was fixed compulsorily by commissioners in those cases where local parties could not reach voluntary agreement, and the commissioners' decision was sometimes challenged at law. A more serious source of frustration was that the legislature blocked the commission's plan for a comprehensive national tithe survey, so the work of commutation had to be done from old maps, often incomplete and erroneous. Then there were problems stemming from human error; there was, it would seem, widespread ignorance of the terms of the 1836 Act, and some of the local surveyors were, unhappily, insufficiently competent. Finally, as would be expected, there was a good deal of haggling at a local level, with tithe-owners arguing about ownership and tithe-payers arguing about boundaries.[131]

Commutation was much cheaper than enclosure.[132] The salaries and expenses of commissioners and assistant commissioners were met out of national taxation; no local Act of Parliament was required; new fences did not have to be put up, nor was there a need for new bridges and roads. Unlike enclosure, tithe-owners were not on principle exempted from their share of administrative costs; but it was held that they had no interest in apportionment of the rent-charge among tithe-payers, and should therefore be saved this expense. This was fortunate, since apportionment was by far the largest item in costs. As against enclosure, now more than £2 an acre, commutation was usually carried through for less than 4s, and was often cheaper still.

A good number of clergy received special treatment when commutation was carried through. Many assistant commissioners took the view that incumbents were unable to defend their interests as ably as lay impropriators, and therefore did the distasteful work on their behalf. In this, they were encouraged by the terms of the Act. Tithe rent-charge was to express the average value of tithes in the years 1829-35, not the average receipts. If clergy had taken less than tithes were worth, the commissioners were empowered by the Act to set matters right. The Act also allowed commissioners to use discretion. They normally did not exercise this in cases where voluntary agreement had been reached, preferring to accept the sum agreed between the parties, even if this differed from what they had calculated themselves, but they did use discretion in making compulsory settlements. The 1836 Act permitted a valuation to be raised or lowered by a maximum of 20% if, in the commissioners' judgment, it did not 'fairly represent' the sum that ought to be taken in calculating a permanent commutation.[133] Such adjustments were usually upward. In Staffordshire, only 9 rent-charges (6.0%) were fixed below the average for 1829-35; 50 (33.1%) were between 1% and 10% above; and a further 17 (11.3%) were higher by between 10% and 20%. More remarkably, 15 of these Staffordshire charges (9.9%) were fixed more than 20% above the average, and therefore exceeded the commissioners' official discretion.[134]

Tithes held up well in the years after 1836. As had been expected, there was a return to agricultural prosperity; and this had the desired effect of keeping the tithe rent-charge at a high level. There were, however, tight reins on any boom. There were now to be no more rearranged compositions, as by John Leroo at Long Melford; no more broken moduses, as at Cottenham; no more extensions of tithe rights over reclaimed land; no more gains at enclosure; and no more future improvements in benefice incomes from better crop rotation, better drainage, and better cereal yields. Tithe rent-charge, in fact, held steady for half a century. Using its value in 1836 as the base of £100, the average until 1885 was £102 11s 9d, with a high of £112 15s 6½d (in 1875) and a low of £89 15s 8½d (in 1855).[135]

Then catastrophe struck. In the 1880s, the pillar of English agricultural prosperity was shaken to pieces. As with all severe crises, the causes were many and the correct prescriptions far from clear. There were, in fact, three simultaneous waves of technological change. The Canadian prairies were opened up, the combine-harvester was introduced, and steam took the place of sail.[136] Competition was suddenly very powerful: the Canadian prairies took care of supply; the combine-harvester took care of costs; and steam navigation took care of transport. Among the casualties of this competition was the tithe rent-charge. In 1881 it stood at a little over £107; by 1887 it was down to under £87 10s 0d; and in 1901 it reached a low of £66 10s 9d.[137] The fall in twenty years was 38%.

Whereas the Tithes Commutation Act eventually made lesions in the trunk of the Church's economy, the Deans and Chapters Act[138] merely lopped a little deadwood from some of the branches. Cathedral establishments, most people admitted, lacked tidiness.[139] Residentiary canons varied in number from place to place; there were too many sinecure non-residentiary prebends; minor offices - vicars choral, ushers, and the like - were not standardised. The Act did not touch the minor offices, but it did reorganise the rest. The number of residentiary posts was to be reduced by 103; and all of the 290 non-resident prebends, together with the offices sometimes attached to them, were to be disendowed. The impact upon the incomes of the clergy cannot be calculated precisely, but the capitular property involved certainly brought in an income of at least £70,000-£80,000 a year.[140] The full force of the Act was not felt immediately; the rights of those with tenure were respected, a hallowed principle enshrined in several other pieces of contemporary legislation. Ultimately, the Deans and Chapters Act cut into the incomes of about 200 parochial clergy, each of them with earnings in excess of £500 a year, and also hit the pockets of about the same number of incumbents who were on less than £500 a year.[141]

Finally, pluralism. The first piece of legislation to deal effectively with this matter was the Pluralities Act of 1838.[142] This tightened regulations severely. The main restriction upon the future freedom of clerical action was the stipulation that no incumbent could henceforth hold more than two livings, and the requirement that the joint value must not be over £1,000 a year. The financial consequences of the new hard line against pluralism were, in the long term, considerable. In 1830, a third of all incumbents held a second living, a few had a third or a fourth, and a minute half-handful had a fifth; the ratio of livings to incumbents was, in fact, 1.4:1.[143] By 1879, this situation had been transformed completely. Livings now numbered 12,695, while incumbents amounted to around 11,940, producing a ratio of livings to incumbents of no more than 1.06:1.[144] It follows from these facts that, over the half-century from 1830 to 1880, the virtual elimination of pluralism reduced the earnings of the beneficed clergy by over 30%. This is, within any perspective, a substantial fall. Indeed, it was probably sufficiently serious to more than wipe out the gains which the clergy had made over the same period, both from augmentation of benefices, and from the consistent level of prosperity that was, at this time, the leading characteristic of English agriculture.

In view of subsequent legislative changes, the 1835 Report marks a watershed. The upward movement of clerical wealth which had been sustained with few setbacks during the previous century and a quarter, first levelled out, and then, much later, plummeted. Some beneficed clergy lost some of their income as a result of the Deans and Chapters Act. Worse still, pluralism was, for the first time, effectively restricted, by the Pluralities Act of 1838. Most seriously of all, tithes were set on a new footing by the Commutation Act of 1836. The initial effect of this piece of legislation was to ensure that the clergy did not gain as much as they would otherwise have done from the return of agricultural prosperity. The application of this gentle brake was as nothing compared with the eventual implications of the Act. The values of livings, having moved ahead steadily during the high Victorian years, collapsed dramatically in the 1880s as the tithe rent-charge went into a tail-spin. Some brief contrasts graphically illustrate what happened. When the Ecclesiastical Revenues Commission completed its survey, it discovered that 2,956 benefices were worth between £100 and £200 a year. Over the succeeding half-century, the number of livings in the same category fell modestly, because some were propelled by prosperity into higher ranges. By 1880, there were 2,597, 12% less than in 1830. This was not to last. Within only twelve years the total had passed the level reached on the eve of Victoria's reign by a handsome margin. In 1892, there were 4,173 benefices in the £100 to £200 a year range, 1,217 (41%) more than in 1830, and 1,576 (61%) more than in 1880.[145] The collapse in benefice values was incomparably more serious than anything experienced in the post Napoleonic depression. It is a fitting and necessary tail-piece to any analysis of the 1835 Report.

Chapter 4 Notes

1. J.H. Monk, *A Charge* (1835), p. 19. Monk was Bishop of Gloucester and an Ecclesiastical Commissioner.

2. Charles Girdlestone, *A Letter on Church Reform*, pp. 6-7.

3. *Norwich Mercury*, 25 December 1830.

4. See further, below, pp. 109-112.

5. *Correspondence between the Lord Bishop of Exeter and Members of the Commission of Ecclesiastical Enquiry*, p. 18.

6. For a brief outline of Newton's career, see C.P. Fendall and E.A. Crutchley, *The Diary of Benjamin Newton*, pp. vii-viii

7. *ibid.*, p. 233.

8. *ibid.*, pp. 5-6.

9. *ibid.*, p. 4.

10. *ibid.*, p. 66.

11. *ibid.*, p. 144.

12. Mary Clive, ed., *Caroline Clive*, pp. 27-8.

13. *ibid.*, pp. 28-30, 163.

14. Fendall and Crutchley, *op.cit.*, p. 261; Mary Clive, *op.cit.*, p. 77.

15. *ibid.*, pp. 28-32.

16. *ibid.*, pp. 9-17.

17. *ibid.*, p. 237, 274-5.

18. H. Coombs and A.N. Bax, *Journal of a Somerset Rector*, p. xi,xxii.

19. *ibid.*, p. 265, 89.

20. On one occasion a pot was tied to his dog's tail, and on another a mason's son wrote an

obscenity on the rectory gates (*ibid.*, p. 131, 141).

21. *ibid.*, p. 98, 113, 161.

22. *ibid.*, pp. 87-8, 107.

23. The rector demanded implicit obedience to his will. His three children, especially the eldest, Owen, refused to give it, so they were occasionally banished to their grandmother's (*ibid.*, p. 165, 182).

24. In 1822 he confided in his diary, 'I am more and more disgusted with the people around me', particularly with their drinking habits (*ibid.*, p. 30).

25. *ibid.*, p. 174.

26. *ibid.*, p. xx.

27. *ibid.*, p. 67.

28. *ibid.*, p. 69, 244-6.

29. *ibid.*, p. 38, 80.

30. *ibid.*, pp. 48-9, 79-80.

31. *ibid.*, p. 128.

32. *ibid.*, pp. 48-9, 100.

33. *ibid.*, p. 128, 148-9.

34. A.G. Bradley, *Our Centenarian Grandfather*, pp. 66-8. This biography was composed from manuscripts left by Philpot himself.

35. *ibid.*, p. 65.

36. *ibid.*, pp. 61-2, 66. Whilst a Fellow he loaned £2,000 to his college, which suggests that his 'nice little property' was, indeed, rather nice.

37. *ibid.*, pp. 66-7, 221.

38. *ibid.*, p. 113. Vachell's house was wrecked during the East Anglian bread riots of 1816 (see above, p. 8). His successor as vicar was one of the sons of Bishop Sparke of Ely (for whom, see above, p. 90).

39. *ibid.*, p. 128.

40. *ibid.*, p. 129.

41. *ibid.*, pp. 181-2, 200.

42. *ibid.*, p. 237.

43. E.B. Denison, ed., *The Life of John Lonsdale*, p. 8.

44. D.W. Harvey and Sir Edward Knatchbull, House of Commons, 30 March 1830, *Hansard*, Second Series, XXIII, 1070-1, 1081-3.

45. Edward Stanley, Bishop of Norwich, 1837-49.

46. Reginald Heber, Bishop of Calcutta, 1822-5.

47. A.J.C. Hare, *The Story of my Life.*, I, 1-13, 44-5.

48. George Smith, *Bishop Heber*, p. 7, and note.

49. *P.P.*, 1835, XXII, 157, 251, 287, 303, 509, 525, 527, 729.

50. In England, in 1830, the typical (or median) income of the beneficed clergy was £275 a year; in Wales at the same date the median was £172 a year (see below, Table V).

51. The Henrican Plurality Act - 21 Henry VIII c. 13.

52. 43 Geo III c. 84.

53. P.A. Bezodis, 'The English Parish Clergy', II, 296-7.

54. McClatchey, *Oxfordshire Clergy*, p. 118.

55. *ibid.*, p. 119.

56. *G.M.*, XCVII (September, 1827), 279-80. Waterhouse, unhappily, met an untimely end. A local man regularly stole things from the rectory, was as regularly caught by the rector, but was never brought before the magistrates. After one of these innumerable break-ins, Waterhouse decided to change his tactics, apprehending the man and threatening him with punishment. This was not a wise thing to do. The thief, angered by the rector's new-found illiberality, hit him over the head and thrust him in a convenient meal tub. Some local boys heard Waterhouse's screams, but assumed he was playing a joke, and left him to die. This tragic incident occurred in 1827.

57. P.H. Ditchfield, *The Old-Time Parson*, pp. 175-6; William Addison, *The English Country Parson*, p. 123; A. Tindal Hart and E. Carpenter, *The Nineteenth-century Country Parson*, pp. 60-1.

58. *E.R.*, XIII (October, 1808), 28.

59. Coleridge, *On the Constitution of Church and State*, p. 42.

60 *Bury and Norwich Post*, 21 March 1832. Growth of teaching as a lay profession was a later development in the nineteenth century - see, e.g. Alan Haig, *The Victorian Clergy*, p.52. He points out (*ibid.*) that headmasterships remained a clerical preserve into the new century.

61. Nicholas Carlisle, *A Concise Description of the endowed Grammar Schools in England and Wales*.

62. In the early 1830s the total was 907-408 in Norfolk, 285 in Kent, and 214 in Sussex.

63. House of Commons, 24 June 1835, *Hansard*, Third Series, XXVIII, 1127-1130; *P.P.*, 1833, XVIII, 289-303, esp. 300 note. I am indebted to my good friend, Christopher Coulter, for these references.

64. O.F. Christie, *The Diary of the Revd William Jones, 1777-1821*, p. 112, 124.

65. W.R.W. Stephens, *A Memoir of Richard Durnford*, p. 14.

66. Augustus Jessopp, *Random Roaming*, pp. 168-93.

67. E.S. Purcell, *Life of Henry Manning*, I, 12.

68. Blomfield, *A Memoir of C.J. Blomfield*, I, 11, 16, 21-2.

69. Carlisle, *op.cit.*, I, 588, II, 593, 602.

70. See above, p.87.

71. [A Non-beneficed Clergyman], *A Letter to his Grace the Archbishop of Canterbury on Church Reform*, p. 21 .

72. See above, p. 15.

73. Chambers and Mingay, *The Agricultural Revolution*, p.128.

74. *P.P.*, 1833, V, 21-2 (evidence of William Jacob).

75. See above, pp. 8-11.

76. For some examples from Kent and Sussex, see above, p. 11.

77. *P.P.*, 1835, XXII, 24.

78. Analytical problems are discussed in the Statistical Appendix, p.269.

79. Full figures are in Table VI and Table VII.

80. E.B. Sparke, Bishop of Ely, 1812-36; George Pretyman-Tomline, Bishop of Lincoln, 1787-1820, and of Winchester, 1820-27.

81. See below, Table VII.

82. See below, Table VI.

83. See above, pp. 35-6.

84. See above, pp. 66-8, 71-2.

85. See below, Table VIII.

86. John Moore, Archbishop of Canterbury, 1783-1805; Charles Manners-Sutton, also Archbishop, 1805-28.

87. In December 1830, George Moore was confronted outside his Wrotham mansion by a hostile crowd shouting 'bread or blood' - see *The Times*, 9 December 1830.

88. *P.P.*, 1835, XX11, 1052 gives the average net benefice income in the various dioceses. St David's comes last, with an average of £137 a year, followed by Sodor and Man at £157 and Carlisle at £175.

89. *Figaro in London*, 14 July 1832.

90. *P.P.*, 1835, XXII, 25.

91. *Church Examiner*, 11 August 1832; *Man*, 21 July 1833. £9 million was also quoted in *Slap at the Church*, 21 April 1832.

92. *Punchinello!* 3 February 1832; *Isis*, 4 August 1832; *Poor Man's Guardian*, 17 March 1832.

93. R.M. Beverley, *Letter to the Archbishop of York*, p. 38.

94. [J. Wade], *The Black Book*, p. 308; [J. Wade], *The Extraordinary Black Book*, p. 49.

95. *Destructive*, 7 September 1833.

96. [J. Wade], *Unreformed Abuses in Church and State*, pp. 212-3.

97. John Riland, *Ecclesiae decus et tutamen: The Extension, Security and Moral Influence of the United Church of England and Ireland*, p. 283.

98. H.F. Stephenson, *A Letter to Lord Henley*, p. 49.

99. See above, pp. 49-50.

100. See below, Table I.

101. Lord Henley, *A Plan of Church Reform*, p. 11, 22.

102. See below, Table V.

103. *P.P.*, 1852, IX, Appendix, Table I, 964. The total of those returning incomes above £60 a year was 320,759. These figures are for England, Scotland and Wales.

104. J.F.C. Harrison, *The Early Victorians, 1832-1851*, pp. 90-1.

105. R. Robson, *The Attorney in Eighteenth-Century England*, pp. 119-26, and Appendix III, pp. 162-5.

106. Harrison, *op.cit.*, pp. 103-5.

107. According to a return for 1831 (*P.P.*, 1831-2, XXXV, 231-72) there were 5,127 active rural JPs, of whom 1,321 (25.8%) were clergy. See also, below, Table XIV.

108. Full details are in Table IX, below.

109. Problems in compiling Woodforde's accounts are set out in Table IX. There is also the further difficulty, in making an estimate of his real level of expenditure, that he practised self-sufficiency.

110. For December 1798, Gayer, Rostow, and Schwartz's index of wholesale prices stands at 98.6, but for December of the next year it stands at 140.9 (*The Growth and Fluctuation of the British Economy*, 1, Table XL, 469.).

111. *ibid*. The figure for December 1801, according to this index, was 132.6; but for October 1802 it was 117.0.

112. J. Beresford, *The Diary of a Country Parson*, IV, 179, entry for 6 March 1795.

113. According to his accounts, Woodforde spent £146 17s 4½d; but he sometimes made omissions, as when Briton went to Norwich for 'many things' for the tithe audit.We have therefore added £25 to the stated sum.

114. Beresford, *op.cit.*, V, 301.
115. *ibid.*, I, 189.
116. *ibid.*, I, 190, 196.
117. C.U.L., Add. Mss. 5810, f. 40.
118. *ibid.*, f. 41.
119. Beresford, *Diary*, V, 164, 171, 186, 206.
120. *ibid.*, V, 99.
121. *ibid.*, III, 205.
122. See, e.g., *ibid.*, I, 197-8, 201, 282, 328.
123. *ibid.*, III, 30.
124. See, e.g., II, 39-40, 61, 175, 233, 311; V, 283.
125. *ibid.*, V, 219.
126. C.U.L., Add. Mss. 5820, f. 45. The italics are Plumptre's own.
127. Figures for clerical incomes are in Table V.
128. 6 and 7 William IV c. 71.
129. Best, *Temporal Pillars*, pp. 466-7; Evans, *The Contentious Tithe*, p. 130.
130. Evans, *op.cit.*, Appendix, p. 170.
131. *ibid.*, pp. 136-43, 148-9.
132. *ibid.*, p. 156.
133. *ibid.*, pp. 153-6.
134. *ibid.*, Table I, p. 154.
135. Venn, *Foundations*, p. 173.
136. Hill, *British Economic and Social History*, pp. 137-8.
137. Best, *op.cit.*, pp. 470-1.
138. 3 & 4 Vic. c. 113.
139. See above, pp. 60-62.
140. Twenty-eight prebends had separate estates attached to them, realising a varying income which cannot be reckoned accurately. Excluding these, the total annual value of the threatened posts was £64,639.
141. The Act axed 393 pieces of preferment, 103 residentiary posts and 290 non-residentiary. The great majority of these residentiary posts were worth at least £300 a year, but the 290 non-residentiary prebends cannot be classified as neatly.
142. See below, pp. 207-208.
143. See below, p. 201 .
144. According to parliamentary returns on clerical residence for 1879 (for which, see below, Table XVIII), there were 12,695 benefices. Of these, 11,186 had resident incumbents. Assuming that such pluralism as still existed was limited to the holding of a second living, we reach the conclusion that the remaining 1,509 livings were held by 754 clergy. Hence the calculation that beneficed clergy numbered 11,940.
145. 'Report of committee on the diminished incomes of the clergy', *Chronicle of Convocation*, XXIX (1893), Table III, p. 11 (figures for 1892); *ibid*, Table A, p. 12 (figures for 1880); *P.P.*, 1835, XXII, 1053 (figures for 1830). Some examples of spectacular falls in income, in the period 1875-89, are to be found in J.S. Leatherbarrow, 'The Rise and Decline of the Squarson (with special reference to the Diocese of Worcester)', p. 174.

The Clergyman as 'Squarson' and Magistrate

i. *Birth*

The door behind which the Georgian incumbent was born is, in the popular historical imagination, an oaken door. The clergy are thought to be, from the moment of birth, inevitably and ineluctably members of the ruling class. Clerical culture, according to this view, is uniformly the culture of the spacious manor house and of the elegant rectory. Jane Austen has done much to fix the appropriate images: the long gravel drive; the firs in front of the 'adequate' mansion; the clear, clean lines of the neatly balanced windows; a set of stables to one side, a further set of stables to the other side. It is the imagery of comfort and condescension.[1]

The clergy were predominantly rural men, few of them coming from the towns. A clerical parent may have been a 'Gent.' or an 'Esq.', or something even better, but he was not a manufacturer or an operative. Often a clergyman worked in the county in which he had been born. This in itself is a vital clue to one of the dominant characteristics of rural society at this period - it generated its own leaders and did not import them from outside. The clergy, then, were rural men leading rural lives; their attitudes were rural, their loves were rural, and even their hatreds were rural. They were part of the old, pre-industrial, society.

It is also undeniable that the social standing of the Georgian clergy was improving. A weight of evidence to support this contention has been collected by P.A. Bezodis. He studied three main areas - the counties of Sussex and Bedfordshire, and the archdeaconry of York - and painstakingly tracked the social origins of the clergy there, using the scattered and necessarily incomplete evidence of land-tax returns, visitation records, wills and college registers. His first conclusion is that an incumbent, at the beginning of the nineteenth century, was likely to be advanced in status over his early Georgian predecessor almost as decisively as that predecessor was likely to be advanced over an incumbent who was middle-aged at the outbreak of the Civil War. Secondly, in a brilliant phrase, he concludes that there was an 'easing and transfusing of a professional dignity into a status of genuine social emancipation'.[2] These arguments are soundly based: rising benefice income, the gradual disappearance of the fatal Jacobite taint, the triumph of a rational religion, and consolidating power in the localities of the magistracy, itself often clerically dominated, all worked the same effect. The clergy came increasingly to be seen as socially respectable, politically important, and doctrinally sound.

Jane Austen, writing in the first and second decades of the nineteenth century, would not have found it difficult to find examples of 'squarsons' - men from the ranks of the peerage and gentry. Most of them lived as gentlemen, doing the things gentlemen did. They rode to hounds, hunted the hare, shot pheasant and partridge, and took a major part in the social life of the countryside. The most secular-minded were extremely unpopular among the rising group of intensely energetic and deeply devout Evangelicals, who sometimes referred to them as the 'mighty Nimrods of the cloth'; they also managed to annoy a good many church reformers, since they formed a strong bulwark against the adoption of any of their 'plans'. It was the aristocratic clergy who gained most from private patronage, widespread pluralism, and so on; and it was they who had most to lose from change. Their interests were exceedingly well represented in Parliament and on the Bench, they wielded power and influence over their fellow clergy, and were the main target of contemporary anti-clerical satire. All were rich, and the good majority were pluralists.[3]

Although most incumbents were rural men, although their social status was improving, and although 'squarsons' had become numerous, it is important not to overstress the extent of change. The popular notion of the uniformly landed gentry background of the late-Georgian clergy is well wide of the mark. In the richest parts of England - counties such as Kent and Hampshire - the number of incumbents either born into, or subsequently married into, peerage or gentry might now reach a quarter of the total; but elsewhere the figure was unlikely to be much above 15%. Overall, it seems probable that about one late-Georgian incumbent in every five was a 'squarson'. Although a sizeable proportion this is a long way from numerical dominance.[4]

One reason why 'squarsons' were fewer than might be expected is to do with the conservatism of eighteenth-century society. Among the clergy, customary attitudes showed themselves by the preservation of the tradition of familial clerical service. This was a well-established tradition by the middle of the seventeenth century, and not entirely moribund by the middle of the twentieth. Certain families produce clergymen with great regularity, and there must be a few that have nurtured at least one clergyman in every generation since the Reformation. Patronage undoubtedly strengthened the tendency. Some Georgian bishops gained among contemporaries an illustrious reputation as nepotists, and quite a number of incumbents also had patronage rights, which they used on occasion to promote the interests of themselves, their sons and their clerical relations.

The number of clergy from non-gentry clerical backgrounds was high everywhere. In richer counties, the proportion in the 1830s was often around 20%. Reliance upon traditions of family service was even more marked in outlying districts. The main reasons for this are that the clergy there were less well-educated; there were fewer eligible squires' daughters; and livings were mostly much lower in value. Fewer clerical gentry meant more clergy from non-gentry clerical backgrounds: not 20% or so of the total, as in rich counties, but in some cases a figure as high as 30%.[5] Old ways were sustained and strengthened by local custom. It quite frequently happened that father and son obtained incumbencies in the same county. Among clergy active in Norfolk in the early 1830s, this was true in thirty instances; among those in both Kent and Sussex at the same period, it was true in five.

A further social fact is cross-fertilisation between professional groups, a phenomenon found in the sixteenth century as well as the twentieth. As part of this process, the English parsonage has produced more than its fair share of politicians, generals, and lawyers, as well as poets, writers and artists. Nor has the flow of ability been entirely in one direction. Those with professional parents formed, throughout the Georgian era, an important third element in the solid social core of the clergy. Blomfield's father was a Bury St Edmunds schoolmaster;[6] Richard Watson of Llandaff had a similar background;[7] Bishop Monk of Gloucester came from a military family;[8] Joseph Allen, Bishop, successively, of Bristol and of Ely, was the son of a Manchester banker.[9] A known professional background was a little less common than a clerical or aristocratic one - it might be true of around 15% of incumbents in a given area [10] - but a good many of the church's leaders nevertheless came from this group.

If 20% of the clergy were aristocratic, a further 20% came from non-gentry clerical households, and 15% had professional backgrounds, what about the remaining 45%?[11] A few, but only a few, are known to have had humble origins. In a sample of 532 alumni, reference was made to artisan or tradesman parentage on 23 occasions (4% of the whole).[12] There was considerable variety. The most improbable were a goldwire-drawer, and a barber-cum-wigmaker; while the most frequent were drapers (4 instances), followed by mercers (3), ironmongers (2) and brewers (also 2). The rest are a curious assortment: a butcher, a grocer and a seed-factor; a saddler, a skinner, and a tanner; a wood-stapler and a furrier; a cork-cutter and a comb-maker. It was a standard defence of the unreformed system that the church was a 'career open to talents'. Men from humble backgrounds became incumbents, and a number climbed even higher. A few reached the top of the profession. Bishop Kaye of Lincoln,[13] an eminent ecclesiastical historian, was the son of a Hammersmith linen-draper; the father of John Moore, Archbishop of Canterbury, 1783-1805, was a Gloucestershire grazier; Edward Maltby, Greek scholar and Bishop of Durham (1836-56), came from Presbyterian weaver stock. Such men were not numerous, but there were enough in every era to give some solidity to the conservative argument that the Church was an 'open' career.

A large wedge of about 40% still remains unaccounted for. Scarcely any of these were the sons of clergy or gentry - it simple was not possible, nor was it natural, for an eighteenth-century country gentleman to hide his light under a bushel in such a way. Most of these socially mysterious clergy came from commercial and trading backgrounds, from the professional classes, and from the lower ranks of rural society, small farmers, and the like.[14] This large group of obscure clergy, approaching half the total, makes it necessary to abandon any easy generalisation about the social composition of the late-Georgian clergy.

The contemporary record, particularly the anti-clerical record, paints an altogether different picture. The Georgian clergy may not have been a homogeneous social class, but this fact escaped the contemporary notice. What was conspicuous was what was seen. Closest to view, naturally enough, was the aristocratic clergyman - conspicuous by action and eloquence (or lack of it), by morality (or lack of it), and by social tact (or lack of it). The clergy's rising importance and prestige lent credence to the popular image. This image was nevertheless flawed; it reflected part of the truth, not the whole. The cartoon contrast of a rich aristocratic rector and his poor, socially undistinguished curate, was no more than it set out to be - a source of dry humour, touching almost incidentally an exposed social nerve. There were many aristrocratic incumbents, and there were many poor curates. However poor incumbents were also numerous, and it was even possible to find, from time to time, curates who were better off than the rectors or vicars by whom they were employed.[15] The unlikely combination of a church-woman, such as Jane Austen, and a vitriolic nonconformist pamphleteer, such as R.M. Beverley, unchallenged by precise research, has unfortunately held the stage. The parsons have all been seen as gentry, and the varieties of conflicting social experience have been, most unwisely, ignored.[16]

ii. *The functions of the magistracy.*

The 'squarsons', although fewer in number than popularly believed, nevertheless have importance. Of nothing is this truer than of the part this section of the clergy played, through membership of the local Bench, in upholding order in the countryside. There are, here, critical continuities: clergy who served as magistrates in the first half of the seventeenth century, and others who served in the second half of the nineteenth.[17]

We catch a glimpse of one type of clerical JP in the pages of the diary of that most kind-hearted and attractive of men, Francis Kilvert. On 22 May 1871, Kilvert paid a visit to Glascwm, some nine miles or so from his beloved Clyro in Radnorshire. He strolled through the village, and then went and knocked on the vicarage door. For a period, no one answered - the maid, who was 'quite a new servant', automatically went to the back door, where visitors from the village always came, and did not in fact know where the front door was. However, she was eventually directed to it and ushered Kilvert into the hall, where he came up against an elderly gentleman with a 'stout frame, ruddy face, white hair, stern long sweeping eyebrows and a merry odd twinkle in his eye'. He was facing the Revd Benjamin Marsden, clerical magistrate, vicar of Glascwm and curate of Colva and Rhulen.

'I am bishop here', announced the vicar; then, after fetching the church key, he added, 'come and see the Cathedral'. This introductory description turned out to be not inappropriate. Glascwm church was long, low and whitewashed; it had an immense chancel, an equally large belfry and a small nave. As the vicar explained, it was in a good state of repair because he had long foreseen the failure of compulsory church rates - abolished three years previously - and had therefore stripped the church and made the parish pay for a new roof. The parish was well managed in other ways. All the people came to church. Loyalty to the principles of Dissent was corresponding rare; there was only an endowed fortnightly Baptist sermon and meeting in a farmhouse. There was, also, only one public house in the village, recently opened. Marsden maintained control: whenever the customers made too much noise, it was his practice to put his head out of his bedroom window, 'holla to them' and 'they fly like the wind'.[18]

Benjamin Marsden was the 'patriarch of his parish'; he was a man 'before whom vice trembled and rebellion dared not show itself'.[19] But these words are not used of him; they appear as part of R.W.Church's portrait of the typical late-Georgian incumbent, in one of those passages - found with considerable ease in the literature of the Oxford Movement - showing how profoundly the clerical character had changed for the better in the years since Keble had preached his Assize Sermon. This is worthy of mention, because a central fact about Marsden is, precisely, that he was not a late-Georgian. Ordained in 1827, he spent his early years in the ministry serving various Welsh curacies before becoming vicar of Glascwm in 1851.[20] He reminds us, therefore, of the inevitable slowness of social change: a clerical figure believed to be typical of one age can easily be found in another.

The Revd Benjamin Marsden, clerical magistrate and vicar of Glascwm, has a further importance: he incarnates the truth in the adage that people become what they do. Traits of character, constantly called forth in the pursuit of a particular profession or occupation, come to have a precision of line that would, otherwise, not be there. This general truth is particularly applicable to those who exercise authority. Responsibility for maintaining law and order stamps a man in a way that few other daily tasks can match.[21] This is strikingly clear in the instance of the vicar of Glascwm. When he put his head out of the bedroom window and shouted, in order to quell disturbance at the public house, he acted with all the authority of the parish JP but without any of the dignity of the parish priest.

The depth of the psychological indenture brought about by the work - the extent of the formation of a distinctively magisterial character - depended upon the part that a clergyman played on the Bench. There were three circles of authority, three rings of power. The outer ring was, in reality, not a ring of power at all. It was made up of those, both laymen and clergy, who had been appointed to commissions but had never qualified themselves to act by taking out their *Dedimus Potestatem*. Throughout the Georgian period, and also beyond, this was common practice. It meant that being a rural magistrate was, in such instances, reduced to a matter of status; a man was able to say he had been placed in the commission and nothing more. For those in the inner ring, there was a taste of real power. Here were men who had taken out their *Dedimus*, and were thus qualified to act; but their participation in the magistracy was occasional rather than regular. Their services were called upon during times of disturbance, but they shouldered little of the burden of the day-to-day work. Finally, we reach the centre. Each county in the eighteenth century was probably much the same. There were a few men, typically numbering between five and ten, who were responsible for the great bulk of day-to-day administration. Around this hub the wheel turned.

In the exercise of magisterial authority the formal was mixed with the informal, in a blend of functions that was typical of the England of the eighteenth century. Quarter Sessions occupied centre-stage. Held, as the name implies, four times a year, these had a formalised court procedure, and a thick sheaf of business to get through. Serious crimes such as murder, arson, rape, and so on were heard at Assizes. Quarter Sessions coped with the rest. Petty Sessions, in contrast, were unstructured: there was no formal court procedure and no staff of permanent officials. Called by JPs in a locality, Petty Sessions could be held on a regular basis, monthly, say, or they might be organised whenever occasion demanded. The preferred meeting place was often an inn. Finally, there were what might be termed 'domestic sessions'. Here, informality reigned supreme. The magistrate, with or without a clerk, sat in his own parlour, dispensing justice to whoever came to see him. This was an onerous part of any active magistrate's duties; indeed, one contemporary observer reckoned that the 'principal share' of any JP's business was conducted in his own house.[22]

The range of this domestic magisterial work comes through clearly, in a description of the life of a conscientious JP around the turn of the nineteenth century. Every day that that most liberal of politicians, Samuel Whitbread, was at home at Southill Park in Bedfordshire, somewhere between two and ten local people visited him. Some came for advice, others to make complaints, and others, still, to answer complaints made about them. Some examples of the sort of cases that Whitbread had to deal with will give a sense of the variety of a justice's work. There was, for instance, a visit from George Wheatley. He was involved in a wage dispute with his employer, Abraham Woodard: Whitbread, sympathetic, awarded Wheatley 32s. Anne Horth also received a good hearing. She requested a warrant against the putative father of her illegitimate child, and the request was granted. Resolution of issues to do with poor law relief was a frequent requirement. We see Whitbread awarding an extra 2s a week to John Lincoln while his child was ill, and ordering the local overseer to supply linen to John Adams, as well as paying for his shoes to be mended. Then there were minor criminal cases - Robert Stevens, an army deserter, was summarily committed to Bedford goal. Finally, there were clarifications of law - William Saville, a farmer, was told that the poor did not have a right to glean without leave.[23] The work, undeniably, was both demanding and time-consuming.

The essence of the rural magistracy was this: there was breadth in function, and there was depth in power. In origin a judicial body, the Bench had steadily accrued to itself administrative, executive, and quasi-legislative responsibilities. By the end of the eighteenth century, magistrates were formulating local poor law policy; they were ordering the construction of, and subsequently supervising, houses of correction, prisons and mental hospitals; places of Dissenting worship were licensed by them; highways were maintained by them; there was supervision of weights and measures, and also of local markets; responsibility for keeping law and order rested, unless circumstances were exceptional, solely upon their shoulders; keepers of ale-houses applied to them for the renewal of their licences at the annual 'Brewster Sessions'; disputes between masters and apprentices were resolved by them; they appointed, and supervised, local constables; they enforced the increasingly severe Game Laws; their signatures were appended to numerous orders for the removal of paupers, and for the incarceration of lunatics; authorisations for use of boats on Sundays had to be dealt with; and there was a host of other matters that had to be attended to. The panoply of powers evident here is, by any yardstick, impressive. There are, moreover, two further points of great importance. The first of these concerns the nature of the interaction between the Bench and central government. It has been powerfully argued that the magistracy was in no way either slavish or dependent. The relationship with central authority was characterised by a high degree of interdependence: JPs often asked the advice of the Home Secretary, but they also often followed their own line on matters of policy.[24] The Home Office papers for the winter of 1830-1, when rural incendiarism was at its height, lead to the same conclusion. Secondly, in a society lacking a permanent police force, the ubiquity of the Bench gave it an authority that it would otherwise have lacked. For many of the people of England in the eighteenth century, contact with government was made through the magistracy.[25]

iii. *Clerical Recruitment*

The work of a rural JP was fine work, but it was not work obviously appropriate for a clergyman. The clerical JP was at once both judge and pastoral adviser, two fundamentally incompatible roles; he might be called upon to imprison a man for some offence on one day and then have the duty of consoling the same man's family the next. Tension and conflict were unavoidable, and came to cause unease among the clergy themselves. One leading churchman, also a clerical magistrate, expressed the difficulty with agreeable cogency, in a pamphlet written in 1830. The 'offices' of a clergyman and a JP, claimed W.L. Bowles, are 'so far distinct, that, except in cases of necessity, and for the good of the community, I would not wish to see a Minister preaching on Sunday, and sending a poacher to prison, or taking the examination of a frail parish damsel, on Monday'.[26] This was a neat point, neatly made.

The difficulty described by Bowles is so transparent, and also so serious, that it is pertinent to ask why clergy joined the magistracy in the first place. Part of the answer is to be sought in prevailing attitudes towards pastoral ministry. Those attitudes are typified by Parson Woodforde. His relation with the people of Weston Longeville was not, fundamentally, a pastoral relation, but a relation of a kindly country squire towards a 'family' of (usually uncomplaining) dependants.[27] Clerical participation in the rural magistracy can only be understood in the context of a particular view, strongly held among the Georgian clergy, of what the essence of being a clergyman was. That view was the more entrenched, in that it expressed beliefs about professionalism that were shared with the members of other occupational groups, the barristers and physicians, for instance. The central emphasis was upon attainment of status, not upon development of a set of professional skills. What the clergy, lawyers and doctors of eighteenth-century England wanted was a life of leisure and culture, a life without work, a life such as only gentlemen had; they were much less interested in being valued by society for the professional services they were able to offer, or for the specialist knowledge that they had managed, over many years, to acquire.[28] The prevalence of this notion of clerical professionalism is a recurrent theme in this book. It explains the formalism in attitudes towards 'doing duty'; and it also explains why clergy accepted appointments in commissions of the peace. For if a man was not a gentleman before he became a JP, he was certainly a gentleman afterwards. Membership of the magistracy carried gentry status with it. Meeting the requisite landed qualification only went a little of the way towards achieving this desirable state of affairs. As from 1733, a candidate for the Bench needed to have an income from land of over £100 a year.[29] This sum fell well short of defining the limits of gentility; a squire needed to have £500 a year, at the very least. What conferred high social status upon the magistracy was the nature of the work itself. 'It was', as has been rightly said, 'a matter of courtesy to refer to all country magistrates as being members of the landed gentry, as indeed in social terms they all were'.[30]

Put this way, it is easy enough to understand why the Georgian clergy, a rising social class, found inclusion in the magistracy attractive. The strength of the clergy's desire for appointment has, indeed, been generally acknowledged by historians; but, contrastingly, the point at which desire turned into satisfaction has been, from time to time, put to the question. Sidney and Beatrice Webb thought that there were very few clerical JPs before 1740 or 1750. There had, they point out, been some in the early part of the seventeenth century; but public opinion had then turned against the idea.[31] It was a long time, according to the Webbs, before the pendulum swung back again. After the Revolution of 1688, they argued, the practice of selecting clergy as JPs 'seems, for half a century, to have been for the most part abandoned'. It was not until the middle of the eighteenth century that clergy were recruited into the magistracy in significant numbers; and even then, the Webbs imply, their inclusion was viewed with reluctance. Clergy were now chosen, they assert, for negative reasons, not for positive: the number of JPs was rising because of pressure of work, and there was a lack of suitably qualified squires.[32] This account held sway for over half a century, but has now been decisively overturned. Innovative work has been done on the social composition of the commission of the peace for 1761; in that year, 1,038 clergy gained appointment.[33] In the light of this finding, it is most unlikely that the practice of including clergy in commissions was 'for the most part abandoned' until 1740 or 1750.

The process by which incumbents entered the magistracy in the early years of George III's reign has been analysed by Diana McClatchey, in her study of the Oxfordshire clergy. What holds for Oxfordshire probably holds for other areas also. There were, it would appear, four avenues to appointment. These are laid bare in the formation of the commission for Oxfordshire in 1769, the only year for which detailed information is available. The first, and surest, way for a cleric to enter the magistracy was through recommendation by the Crown. Lord North, as prime minister, wrote to the Duke of Marlborough, lord-lieutenant of Oxfordshire, 'suggesting' a number of names in February, 1769; on the list were ten clergy. Two other clergy appointed to the commission were also Lord North's nominees, making twelve in all. The prime minister of the day was not the lord-lieutenant's only correspondent. Letters of recommendation were also received from several local gentry. Proposals coming from this quarter were treated with the same courtesy as were Lord North's: all were accepted by the Duke of Marlborough, an act of magnanimity on his part that added a further eight clerical names to the list. Next, there is a letter from the Revd Theophilus Leigh, writing in his capacity as acting chairman of Quarter Sessions, and supporting the claims of a further two clergy; he also seems to have personally nominated two more. Finally, and virtually inevitably, there was the need to pay close attention to familial obligations. The back-stairs - to use an uncharitable term - were, in fact, employed by fewer clergy than might be expected. In 1769, only one Oxfordshire incumbent got himself on the commission by exploiting access to the Duke of Marlborough's patronage;[34] twenty-four others achieved the same result by different means.

Consideration of appointments to the Oxfordshire magistracy in 1769 offers fascinating insights into the workings of local government. The theoretical position was that the privilege of recommendation lay with the lord-lieutenant; at the same time, the Crown reserved the right to add names to the list and claimed, also, a power of veto.[35] What happened in practice, at any rate in Oxfordshire, was rather different. Members of the Bench co-opted clergy and gentry; and a large number of appointments was made by the Crown. The lord-lieutenant did not make many nominations on his own behalf, and he did not turn down any names that the other parties put forward. There was no need to employ the Crown's power of veto. What was happening was that central and local government were working together in harmony. There were, also, lessons for those clergy seeking admission to the magistracy. They needed to be on good terms with their neighbours among the clergy and squirearchy; and they were well advised not to say or do anything that might annoy anyone in Whitehall.

The position of the clergy within the rural magistracy, already strengthening by the seventh decade of the eighteenth century, became in subsequent decades even stronger. In 1836, 3,266 clergy were appointed to commissions.[36] This figure is to be contrasted with the finding that 1,038 clergy were appointed to commissions in 1761.[37] Clerical membership of the rural magistracy had trebled within three-quarters of a century. In some areas clerical JPs were rare before 1770 or so, but then became quite common. Cardiganshire is a good example. In the commission for 1775 there were 2 clergy and 97 laity; in that for 1816, clergy numbered 25 and laity amounted to 135.[38]

Obtaining appointment to a commission was one thing, taking out a *Dedimus Potestatem* was another. It is a severe weakness in most contemporary statistics dealing with the clerical magistracy that no distinction is made between qualified and non-qualified JPs. The magnitude of the difficulty is evident from comparison between two sets of parliamentary returns: one set, for 1831, shows there to have been 1,321 qualified clerical JPs, while another set for 1836 (quoted above) calculates the total figure for all clerical magistrates, both qualified and non-qualified, at 3,266.[39] It would therefore seem that, in the early 1830s, 40% of clergy appointed to commissions took out their *Dedimus*. Assuming the proportion was the same at the start of George III's reign, the tentative conclusion must be that qualified clerical JPs numbered 415 in 1761, rising to 1,321 in 1831.[40]

The situation in 1831 must be considered a broad context. Firstly, there is the need to examine the extent to which the body of beneficed clergy was now committed to magisterial work. It has frequently been asserted by other historians that, in 1831, one in every eight beneficed clergymen was also an active clerical JP.[41] This would be right, were it not for the fact that a minor error has always been made when arriving at this calculation: pluralism, for some mysterious reason, has not been entered in the ledger. The degree of clerical participation in the rural magistracy was, therefore, greater than is generally thought. In 1831, one in every six of the beneficed clergy combined the functions of local parish priest and local active parish magistrate.[42] This is an interesting statistic. Worthy of recall is the earlier analysis of the social standing of the late-Georgian clergy. Around 1830, a fifth of all incumbents were related, either by birth or marriage, to the peerage and gentry.[43] Active clerical JPs were almost as numerous. The similarity in numbers between clergy of high social standing and clergy who were active magistrates was not, it may be suggested, coincidental.

The geographical distribution of clerical JPs was far from even. In Sussex, successive Dukes of Richmond used their authority as lord-lieutenant of the county to exclude clergy from active membership of the Bench altogether.[44] Something similar seems to have happened in Derbyshire; there were not any active clerical JPs in this county either. Active lay justices in Sussex and Derbyshire in 1831 numbered 268.

It might be argued that clergy were excluded from the magistracy in Sussex because, being close to London, it had a plentiful supply of suitably qualified squires. This line of reasoning is not without force, but it is far from providing a sufficient explanation. Clerical magistrates were fairly sparse in some other counties within reasonable travelling distance of the metropolis, but not in others. Thus, the proportion was 9% in Middlesex, and 13% in Hampshire; but in Surrey it was 15%, and in Essex it was 30%, while in Norfolk, a stronghold of the squirearchy if ever there was one, the figure was an unreservedly staggering 40%.[45] There is, clearly, a need to take full account of the subtleties involved in processes of selection to the magistracy. Every locality had its own history, and its own way of doing things. Social interaction between clergy and gentry was in no way standardised. It is tempting to correlate the large number of clerical JPs in Norfolk with the high social standing of the clergy there.[46] Presumably, too, the system of co-option has strong and immediate relevance; once four or five clergy had been appointed to serve in a district, they might tend to select further magistrates from among the ranks of their own brethren, forming a clerical coterie. All of this helps to explain why the geographical distribution of clerical JPs was uneven.

More accurate is the contention that clergy were asked to join the Bench because of a dearth of qualified squires. This certainly seems to have been the case in some districts of Warwickshire and Oxfordshire, for instance.[47] The strength of the clerical magistracy in much of Wales, and also in Cumbria, prompts the same conclusion. In Carnarvonshire in 1831 clerical JPs made up more than half the Bench, a situation of numerical dominance for which there is no parallel elsewhere. In Breconshire, Denbighshire, Flintshire, and Merionethshire the proportion was a third or more. In Westmorland, there were 12 active clerical JPs in a complement of 30 (40%); and in Cumberland there were 15 among 54 (28%).[48]

The Georgian enclosure movement also affected the picture. This emerges from further, and more detailed, investigation of the commission of the peace for 1761. At the beginning of George III's reign, clergy accounted for 6.5% of the Bench in Bedfordshire, 9% in Warwickshire, 14.5% in Northamptonshire, 15% in Lincolnshire, and 18% in Cambridgeshire. These figures have to be compared with the general assessment that, for England and Wales as a whole, clergy made up 11% of all appointments in 1761. Thus, clerical representation was a little lower than the national average in Bedfordshire and Warwickshire, and a little higher in Northamptonshire, Lincolnshire and Cambridgeshire. Over the next eighty years, clergy consolidated their position in a manner that is particularly striking. Focusing attention solely upon magistrates who had qualified, clergy were 41% of the Bench in Bedfordshire in 1831, 36% in Warwickshire, 42% in Northamptonshire, 47% in Lincolnshire, and 45% in Cambridgeshire. Aggregating figures for these five counties, there were now 205 active lay justices (57%) and 153 active clerical justices (43%).[49] That the enclosure movement was good for the clergy's social standing, turning them into landowners and clearing the path to the magistracy, is readily apparent. That it was also good for their economic standing is, as already argued, more open to doubt.[50]

iv. *The Clerical contribution*

Analysis of clerical representation within the active rural magistracy gives, in many ways, a misleading impression of what had been achieved. The term 'activity', when applied to a Georgian magistrate, is capable of more than one interpretation. Most JPs played a modest role on the Bench; the burden of the work was borne on only a few shoulders.[51] The point needs to be strongly made that, among the few, the clergy were prominent. The first was also the most famous. Richard Burn (1709-85) was Chancellor of the diocese of Carlisle; he is described by Sidney and Beatrice Webb as the most active JP in Westmorland.[52] It is not, however, upon this that his fame rests. Burn's achievement was to write one of the most popular legal text-books of the eighteenth century. The first edition of *The Justice of the Peace and Parish Officer* came out in 1755. Others followed in quick succession. The tenth edition, expanded to four volumes, dates from 1766, and the fourteenth from 1780. Burn's death in 1785 in no way stemmed the flow. The nineteenth edition was produced in 1800, and the thirtieth, in five volumes, in 1869. There never was anything that compared with Burn. Magistrates, up and down the land, regarded *The Justice of the Peace* as required reading once they had been appointed.

It is not difficult to find examples of other Georgian clergy who rose to positions of authority on the Bench. Mention may be made of Henry Zouch, chairman of West Riding Quarter Sessions towards the close of the eighteenth century; of John Foley, joint chairman of Gloucestershire Quarter Sessions, 1796-1800; and of Samuel Partridge, chairman of Holland Quarter Sessions in Lincolnshire in 1809.[53] It was the unhappy fate of a fourth clerical JP, W.R. Hay, to achieve a status of clouded infamy. Called to the Bar early in life, Hay switched careers, becoming a cleric, though not entirely forsaking the law. Hay came to play a dominant role within the Lancashire magistracy. Around the turn of the nineteenth century, his fellow magistrates found that the problems posed by Salford Hundred - which included Manchester and a number of industrial centres in south-east Lancashire - were growing beyond their control. They therefore decided to appoint a salaried chairman. The necessary parliamentary proceedings were conducted on the Bench's behalf by Hay, who was, moreover, chosen as the first occupant of the newly created post. Hay was salaried chairman of Salford Hundred sessions from 1805 until 1823. The opprobrium attaching to his name stems from the part that he, along with another clerical magistrate, C.W.Ethelston, is alleged to have played in summoning the yeomanry, and reading the Riot Act, on that most inauspicious occasion, 'Peterloo'.[54] To injury was added insult. In the aftermath of Peterloo, Hay, with monstrous celerity, received as his 'reward', Rochdale, which was one of the finest and juiciest plums to be found anywhere in the ecclesiastical pie.[55] The selection of W.R. Hay as vicar of Rochdale was, arguably, one of the most tactless actions perpetrated in Georgian Britain.

A systematic study of the clerical magistracy has yet to be written. Its lack represents a sad gap in the historical canon however; modern research on Gloucester-shire and Oxfordshire has helped to rectify the omission. In both these counties, clerical representation on the active Bench was either at, or close to, the national average. Gloucestershire and Oxfordshire are, in this sense, typical of the country as a whole.[56] What is interesting about the research is its congruity. When it comes to day-to-day business, there was - in Gloucestershire as in Oxfordshire - a rising level of clerical activity. Between 1775 and 1800, 22 JPs attended three or more Gloucestershire Quarter Sessions annually; among the twenty-two were eight clergy. There were, also, 16 JPs who attended twice: eleven were laymen and five were clergymen.[57] After 1800, it would seem, clerical participation increased. There is, dating from 1824, a private letter written by Lord Redesdale, one of Gloucestershire's leading landed magnates. 'That unbought magistracy', Lord Redesdale wrote, 'consists in many parts of the clergy. In this county the business could not be done without them; indeed they do nearly *the whole*'.[58] Clergy also did 'nearly the whole' in Oxfordshire. In 1780, 83% of convictions were signed by clerical magistrates; in

1800 the figure was 75%; in 1820 it was 87%; and in 1830 it was still 72%.[59]

Nor were Gloucestershire and Oxfordshire exceptional. There is, from other areas, evidence in support of the contention that clergy played an important role in day-to-day county administration. In October 1799, a Quarter Sessions was called for the West Riding; on the Bench were two laymen and four clergymen. In the East Riding, in July 1821, ten clergy went to Quarter Sessions and only six laity. In Breconshire a meeting of Quarter Sessions, held in October 1826, was attended by eight lay justices and by ten clerical. When the Buckinghamshire magistracy met in Quarter Sessions, also in 1826, an observer noted twenty-one laymen and seventeen clergymen on the bench.[60] It is impossible to be aware of facts such as these without feeling that historians have been seriously remiss in not paying more attention to the magisterial role of the Georgian clergy.

Several reasons can be advanced to explain the growing influence exerted by the clergy within the magistracy. That influence is to be seen, in the first instance, as a consequence of the alliance between squire and parson in the Georgian countryside. The clergy were a rising social class closely identified, both in sentiment and in interest, with the gentry. Placed in this perspective, growth in the influence of the clergy within the magistracy looks like, and indeed is, a natural development. Pragmatic considerations also played a part. The workload of the Bench was getting heavier; a higher premium was being put upon magisterial competence; and there were a lot of clergymen who had the required skills. The clergy, in short, were both good at, and qualified for, magisterial work. There are clear and straightforward reasons why this was so. They were learned men, the great majority having a university education. They were dispersed throughout the country, frequently living in districts where there were no resident squires. They were often knowledgeable about the local rural economy. Finally - an important point - they were not a notably peripatetic social class.[61] A further reason has been put forward by Anthony Russell.[62] He argues that more clergy were put into commissions because a powerful resident incumbent, backed by a supportive squire, was perceived to be an effective bastion against the introduction of egalitarian principles imported from France. Although hard to verify, this line of reasoning has great *prima facie* merit. The French Revolution gave a sharp and effective fillip to the ideology of order, and it also had the effect of firmly cementing the 'alliance' between church and state. The role of the clergy, in binding together the bundle of sticks that was society, was thought to be crucial.[63] An obvious way of helping to achieve this was by recruiting incumbents to the magistracy.

v. *Retreat*

The year 1831 is a landmark in the history of the clerical magistracy: the first parliamentary return, giving information about the number of clerical JPs who had qualified, was placed before parliament. Thereafter, the extent of clerical involvement was carefully monitored. There is a return summarising the number of clergy appointed to commissions in 1831-4;[64] we know, in 1840, 'The Names, Addresses, and

Residencies of Justices of the Peace, Ministers of the Established Church, now in the Commission of the Peace in the several counties of England and Wales';[65] and there are, also, further returns detailing clerical appointments to commissions in 1836-42 and in 1843-63.[66] Usually, in early nineteenth-century England, publication of parliamentary returns is an accurate indicator of a growing public concern. The issue of the clerical magistracy is no exception to this general rule. In the 1830s and early 1840s opposition to the inclusion of clergy in commissions began to mount. Interestingly, distaste at the conjunction of the magisterial and priestly offices was felt both by government and by the clergy themselves. The pendulum of public opinion, which had swung against the clerical magistracy in the seventeenth century, was swinging against it once again.

Lord John Russell's tenure of the Home Office from 1835 until 1839 seems, in many ways, to mark the tide's turn. Russell, evidently, was not pleased by the complexion of the Bench; it was, he felt, too Tory and too clerical.[67] What he wanted to see were more Whigs and more Dissenters. He set about the task of adjusting the balance of representation by introducing, occasionally and discreetly, what amounted to innovations in procedures of selection. He added names to lists of proposed appointments, that were then submitted to lord-lieutenants for approval; and, in cases where the expected nod was not forthcoming, still went ahead with his nominations, submitting the names to the commissioners of the Great Seal, who duly acted upon his recommendations.[68]

This shift in policy, in so far as it affected clerical recruitment to the magistracy, found support. The Warwickshire Bench is an example. The chairman of Quarter Sessions, Sir J.E. Eardley Wilmot, told the House of Commons in 1837 that he had 'long contended' that clergy ought not to be put in commissions; what prevented him from supporting an absolute prohibition was the extreme difficulty of filling the Bench, 'in many counties', without them.[69] The Earl of Warwick, lord-lieutenant of the county, concurred. He had, he told the House of Lords in 1839, been in his present position for seventeen years. During this time, he had placed twelve clergy in commissions; six in his first year in office, and the other six at various times over the remaining sixteen. In the latest commission, for 1839, only one cleric had been appointed.[70] The Earl remained lord-lieutenant until his death in 1853; and, after 1840, 'hardly any more clergy' were made magistrates in Warwickshire.[71]

The clergy were able to read the writing on the wall. Not only that, others watched them doing so. One such was John Wright, a witness before the poor law commission in 1834. Wright was an experienced magistrate who lived near Thetford in Norfolk, a county where the proliferation of clerical JPs has already been noted. In his evidence to the commissioners, he deprecated the practice, particularly prevalent in 'recent years', of 'greatly increasing' the membership of the Bench. He was especially harsh, in this respect, about the clergy; there seemed to be, he said, a policy of 'adding to the commission of the peace the names of almost every clergyman in a county'. This was, for a resident of Norfolk, an entirely pardonable exaggeration. In

1836, 135 clergy - just under a third of the beneficed body - were placed in the Norfolk commission.[72] 135 clerical magistrates in one county seems a lot; it seems even more when it is remembered that some incumbents would not have been able to meet the requirement of landed income in excess of £100 a year, while others would have been living in districts of the county where there was already a full complement. Wright was certain that things had been taken too far, and he believed that the clergy were beginning to agree with him. He was convinced that the 'exercise of political power has materially diminished the influence the clergy ought to have in their respective parishes'. Of this, he went on, 'many [of the clergy] are now aware, and find the ministerial more influential than the magisterial character'.[73] The pastor was beginning to triumph over the judge.

The change in public mood was sensed by the church's leaders, of whom Blomfield and Phillpotts are representative examples. Earlier in their careers, both men had been enthusiastic supporters of the clerical magistracy, a fact which is not surprising in view of the mutual unregeneracy of their past. Blomfield had become an incumbent in 1810, when he was no more than twenty-four; and, within a year, a second living had been added to the first. It was not long before he was recruited to the Bench. In 1813, we find him writing to a friend that he was 'now a Commissioner of the Turnpikes (there's for you) and a Justice of the Peace; and the county business will never get on without me ... I shall, moreover, probably be a Commissioner of the Property Tax - all of which offices will a little interfere with Greek'.[74] Blomfield coped easily with the inconveniences that his new duties imposed upon him; he used to ride to Petty Sessions in yellow overalls, in order to protect himself from the mud of the Buckinghamshire lanes.[75] The early career of Henry Phillpotts was virtually identical to that of Blomfield: a first living in 1804 at the age of twenty-six, and a second living in 1805 at the age of twenty-seven. He resided at neither. Conscious that this turn of events might seem a trifle strange, Phillpotts's biographer steps forward with an explanation, not requiring elaboration - 'his good fortune in being allowed as a young man to hold two benefices without residing at either must be explained by his connection by marriage with Lord Chancellor Eldon'.[76] It must, indeed. Within two years, Phillpotts had exchanged his first living, Kilmersdon near Bath, for Bishop Middleham in Durham. The future bishop was still a pluralist, but he was now a resident one, not a non-resident. He was also something else, a clerical JP; it was, wrote his biographer, 'apparently' at Bishop Middleham that Phillpotts 'acquired the reputation of being a zealous though not always popular magistrate'.[77] Neither with Blomfield nor with Phillpotts was the young man father to the bishop. Blomfield was consecrated to Chester in 1824, moving to London in 1828. As a bishop, he 'disapproved' of the 'union' of priestly and magisterial functions; these 'secular duties', in Blomfield's view, 'would be likely to interfere too much with the spiritual'.[78] The Bishop of Exeter did not agree with his brother of London about much, but the clerical magistracy was a topic where their minds could meet without acrimony. This is evident from a speech delivered by Phillpotts to the House of Lords in 1844. In reflective mood, the Bishop of Exeter looked back to his ministry at Bishop Middleham, nearly forty years earlier; 'it was his own fortune', he said, 'at one time to be the Minister of a populous parish in the county of Durham, and it was his misfortune to be obliged to act as a magistrate, in consequence of the paucity of country gentlemen'.[79]

There is no need to overstretch the intellectual nerve-fibres in order to understand why there was a strong body of respectable ecclesiastical opinion which, in the 1830s and early 1840s, was beginning to doubt the efficacy of clergy engaging in active membership of the Bench. Being a clerical JP under a Tory government was one thing, being a clerical JP under a zealous and reforming Whig administration - thought in some ecclesiastical circles to be about to 'despoil' the church - was something rather different. The sense of turmoil is evident in the diary of a contemporary Cotswold parson, who voiced the inner thoughts of many of his clerical brethren. Francis Witts was a sensible and hard-working senior clergyman: he had been rector of Upper Slaughter since 1808 and was a well-established member of the Gloucestershire Bench. On a visit to Cheltenham in 1833, he was pleased to hear that the Tory candidate - a 'very steady, upright, grave man' - had been elected chairman of Quarter Sessions. This was certainly a turn for the better. Things, recently, had been going less well. When last at Quarter Sessions, the rector of Upper Slaughter had not enjoyed himself: a 'most unjustifiable attack on the clerical magistrates was made by that hot headed, ill conditioned veteran Whig, Colonel Kingscote'. As a result of this experience, he more than doubted 'the wisdom in the present excited state of the country of a clergyman appearing at the Quarter Sessions; the contention between Whig and Tory runs high'.[80] There was change in the political context, and there was also change in the work itself. In the winter of 1830-1, labourers joined forces with farmers in many parishes in order to bring about reductions in tithe; and, during that same winter, a number of clerical magistrates found themselves thrust to the forefront, having to quell disturbance.[81] In the restless countryside of the 1830s, the advantages in being a magistrate were not always immediately apparent.

Pragmatic considerations had, on this occasion, a close affinity with the fruits of spiritual insight. There had always been clergy who had considered the magisterial role unsuitable for one whose master's Kingdom was not of this world. Of the truth of this, Evangelicals in particular were easily convinced. William Jones's sentiments were shared by many clergy with similar religious views. One day in October 1816 Jones left (with the 'greatest reluctance') his 'cell' at Broxbourne, in order to mingle for a while with the magistrates in the justices' room at Cheshunt. It was not an agreeable experience. 'There they were', he noted in his diary, 'crowded, & "bothered" with Acts of Parliament, complaints of rates, &c, &c.' This led him to ruminate on the magistracy in general. 'Many clergymen', he reflected, 'are Magistrates, - but the office seems to me unsuitable for any Minister of the Gospel; it must consume much of his time, & create many enemies. O! how glad I was to quit the room, & breathe the free, open air!'[82] Charles Simeon's opinions were not dissimilar. By far the ablest strategic thinker among the early Evangelicals, Simeon was unable to see that membership of the magistracy was advantageous, from the clergy's point of view: an incumbent would either become damagingly secular in his concerns or, if this tendency was resisted, he would experience needless friction with others on the Bench. 'Unless in very peculiar cases', he declared, 'I disapprove of Clergymen being Magistrates; they must necessarily displease one party [to a dispute] and are likely to be ensnared into secular habits by their brother justices, or else to be hated and doubly opposed by them'.[83]

The pastoral logic in Simeon's remarks came to have increasing appeal. There was, as we pointed out in Chapter One, a consensus regarding pastoral practice between Evangelicals on the one hand, and high churchmen and Tractarians on the other: the man who magnified his priestly office did not wish to magnify other offices.[84] Through the 1830s and 1840s, more and more clergy were repudiating the ideal of the 'squarson'; there were, now, theological preoccupations. There was, also, peer group pressure. Other clergy wanted to know how many services an incumbent had, whether he supported parochial clubs, and how the village school was doing. There was less talk of Quarter Sessions, and still less talk regarding the likely whereabouts of the partridge and the hare. This alteration in fundamental attitudes only slowly affected the majority - it was a long time before the leaven lightened the dough - but there was, certainly, a discernible change among the generality of clergy by mid-century.

The combination of expediency and changing pastoral practice put a permanent brake against the further development of the clerical magistracy. As from the early 1830s, patterns of recruitment started to alter markedly. Between January 1831 and August 1834, there were 2,007 appointments to the Bench: 333 of these (17%) were clergy and 1,674 (83%) were laity.[85] The new trend is even clearer in statistics for appointments between 1836 and 1842: 401 clergy (13%) and 2,689 laity (87%). After 1842, returns were not compiled on a regular basis, but it is nonetheless evident that the pace of social change quickened in the 1840s and 1850s. Clerical appointments averaged 67 a year over the six-year period 1836-42, but over the longer twenty-year period between 1843 and 1863 the average fell to 42 a year.[86] Lord John Russell gave a sharp spin to a wheel that was already turning; and others have kept it spinning ever since.

Chapter 5 Notes

1. The social status of the English episcopate, 1660-1836, is analysed in N. Ravitch, *Sword and mitre*, pp.118-32, esp. Table VI, p.120. See, also, R.B. McDowell, 'The Anglican Episcopate, 1780-1945', *Theology*, L (June, 1947), 202-9; and Soloway, *Prelates and People*, pp 6-16.

2. Bezodis, *The English Parish Clergy*, I, 147, 165.

3. In the three counties of Norfolk, Kent and Sussex, there were 116 incumbents with gentry or peerage backgrounds in the early 1830s. Among these, only 45(38.8%) were not pluralists.

4. See Table X.

5. *ibid.* There are important continuities here. In the diocese of Oxford in 1680, 19% of incumbents were the sons of clergy; in 1760 the figure was also 19%. In the archdeaconry of Hereford the figures were, respectively, 23% in 1680 and 23% in 1759; while, in the archdeaconry of Salop, 25% of the beneficed clergy came from clerical households in 1680 and, once again, 25% in 1759; see Marshall, 'The Administration of the Dioceses of Hereford and Oxford,' p.98.

6. C.J. Blomfield, Bishop of Chester, 1824-8, and of London, 1828-56.

7. Richard Watson, Bishop of Llandaff, 1782-1816.

8. J.H. Monk, Bishop of Gloucester, 1830-56.

9. Joseph Allen, Bishop of Bristol, 1834-6, and of Ely, 1836-45.

10. See Table X.

11. Haig, *The Victorian Clergy*, Table 2.3, p.36 analyses a large Cambridge Honours sample in the period 1841-3. His findings are mostly similar to our own. Unknown parentage, for example, accounted for 44.3% of the students that were included; and 21.0% came from clerical households. However, there is one major difference: only 10.3% of Haig's sample are described as aristocrats. His definition of what constitutes high social status is narrower than our own. Haig restricts himself to parentage; we take into account, also, marriage into the landowning class. Secondly, Haig counts as aristocrats only those whose fathers were either peers or had pedigree appearing in nineteenth-century editions of Burke's *Landed Gentry*. We adopt a broader approach to evidence of high social status - the list of reference books we have used is to be found in the Bibliography.

12. *ibid.*

13. John Kaye, Bishop of Bristol, 1820-7, and of Lincoln, 1827-53.

14. Problems of social identification are discussed in Haig, *op.cit.*, pp.35-7.

15. See below, pp. 234-8

16. Interestingly, a similar conclusion is reached by Esther Moir in her study of the Gloucestershire clergy in the last quarter of the eighteenth century. At that time, she notes, the clergy of the county had no real social 'unity or cohesion'; Esther Moir, *Local Government in Gloucestershire*, p.26.

17. In this section, we concentrate solely upon the rural magistracy. The clergy made a major contribution to local government in the countryside; but in the towns the part they played was much more modest. For the record, it is worth noting that Kitson Clark calculates that, in 1831, there were 97 active clerical JPs in the various boroughs of England and Wales, a figure which compares with 1,264 active lay JPs in the same year; G.S.R. Kitson Clark, *Churchmen and the Condition of England, 1832-1885*, p.146; see, also, *P.P.*, 1831-2, XXXV, 231-72.

18. William Plomer, ed., *Kilvert's Diary*, I, 343-7.

19. R.W. Church, *The Oxford Movement. Twelve Years, 1833-1845*, p.3.

20. *Crockford* (1870), p.469.

21. The psychological and moral dimensions of magisterial work were not generally recognised by contemporaries. An exception is Thomas Gisborne, *An Enquiry into the Duties of Men*, I, 426, 'Every situation and employment in life influences, by a variety of moral causes, the views, manners, tempers, and dispositions of those who are placed in it. The Justice of the Peace can plead no exemption from this general rule... He is liable to become dictatorial, brow-beating, consequential, and ill-humoured; domineering in his inclinations, dogmatical in his opinions, and arbitrary in his decisions'.

22. *ibid.*

23. Godber, *History of Bedfordshire*, p.432.

24. E.A.L. Moir, 'Local Government in Gloucestershire 1775-1800', pp.231-68. See, especially, her statement (p.251), 'it seems clear that a relationship existed [between central and local authority] which might be called personal and informal, in which the magistrates turned to the government for help and advice, and were equally prepared to criticise and amend government actions when they thought necessary'.

25. Hence, of course, the importance of clerical participation in magisterial work. We are reminded, forcefully, of a point made with power and clarity in Clark, *English Society*, p.277, 'The ubiquitous agency of the State was the Church, quartering the land not into a few hundred constituencies but into ten thousand parishes, impinging on the daily concerns of the great majority, supporting its black-coated army of a clerical intelligentsia, bidding for a monopoly of education, piety and political acceptability.'

26. W.L. Bowles, *A Word on Cathedral-Oratorios, and Clergy-Magistrates*, p.32. Bowles was vicar of Bremhill, Wiltshire, 1804-50; he was also a canon of Salisbury. We see, in him, Coleridge's clerisy in action: Bowles was, at once, a poet, antiquary, historian, and pamphleteer.

27. See above, p. 95, and also below, pp. 151-2.

28. Philip Elliott, *The Sociology of the Professions*, p.14ff. Note, particularly, his statement (p.15), 'professionals [in pre-industrial England] were an appendage to the high-status groups in society'. See, also, Heeney, *A Different Kind of Gentleman*, pp.4-5; and Anthony Russell, *The Clerical Profession*, pp.16-27, 47-9.

29. 5 Geo.II c.18. The requirement of landed income in excess of £100 a year was reaffirmed by 18 Geo.II c.20. To press home the point, this Act also required all JPs to subscribe to an oath stipulating their means.

30. Thompson, *English Landed Society in the nineteenth century*, p.111.

31. S. and B. Webb, *English Local Government from the Revolution to the Municipal Corporations Act: The Parish and the County*, p. 350.

32. *ibid.*, pp. 350-1.

33. Eric J. Evans, 'Some reasons for the growth of English rural anti-clericalism, c.1750 - c.1830', *Past and Present*, LXVI (1975), 101 and note 78.

34. McClatchey, *Oxfordshire Clergy*, pp.184-6. See also Moir, *Local Government*, pp.41-3. Moir stresses the importance of political allegiance and hereditary influences.

35. There is, being eighteenth-century England, an exception to this procedure - in Lancashire, appointments were made by the Chancellor of the Duchy of Lancaster.

36. See below, Table XIV.

37. See above, p.116.

38. S. and B. Webb., *op.cit.*, p.351, note 1. Jacob, 'Clergy and Society in Norfolk', p.429 has compiled some fascinating statistics. In Norfolk, in 1762, only two out of 192 JPs were clergy. In 1787, twenty new JPs qualified; seven were clergy. The next year the figure was nine among twelve; in 1789 it was eleven among fifteen; and in 1790 it was nine among eighteen.

39. See below, Table XIV.

40. Apart from lack of statistics to do with qualified JPs, there is also the further difficulty that there was a good deal of double counting. Evans, *Past and Present* , LXVI, 101 refers to this. See, also Moir, *Local Government*, p.72.

41. See, e.g., Gilbert, *Religion and Society in Industrial England*, p.81; and also Russell, *op.cit.*, p.159.

42. Difficulties in calculating the number of beneficed clergy at this period are outlined in the Statistical Appendix, p.269.

43. See above, pp.109-12. See also below, Table X.

44. *The Times*, 29 November 1816. See, also, Henry Brougham, House of Commons, 7 February 1828, *Hansard*, Second Series, XVIII, 163, 'There are some Lord Lieutenants, I know, who make it a rule never to appoint a clergyman to the magistracy'.

45. See below, Table XIV. The figures for one other Home county - Kent - are decidedly odd. In 1831, the relevant parliamentary return (*P.P.*, 1831-2, XXXV, 231-72) states that there were 2 active clerical JPs and 145 active lay JPs. However, another return for 1840 (*P.P.*, 1840, XLI, 351-94) states that there were, in that year, 38 active clerical justices in the county. It looks as if the return for 1831 is wrong. Such a discrepancy between parliamentary returns is not to be found for any other county.

46. See below, Table X.

47. R. Quinault and J.Stevenson, eds., *Popular protest and public order*, p.187; McClatchey, *op.cit.*, p.181.

48. See below, Table XIV.

49. Evans, *Past and Present*, LXVI, 101, 104, and note 87; see also below, Table XIV.

50. See above, pp.58-59.

51. See above, pp.113-4.

52. S. and B. Webb, *op.cit.*, p.354.

53. Moir, 'Local Government in Gloucestershire', p.159, note; S. and B. Webb, *op.cit.*, p.351, note 2, p.357.

54. We use the word 'alleged' because the sources, as is usual on such occasions, dispute with each other vigorously over the detail of what went on. There is, for instance, no unanimity over whether, or not, the Riot Act was read, let alone by whom. The views of the protagonists are set out in Donald Read, *Peterloo*, and in Robert Walmsley, *Peterloo: the case reopened*.

55. S. and B. Webb, *op.cit.*, pp.353-4; Read, *op.cit.* pp.75-6. Walmsley, *op.cit.*, p.133, note 1 points out that Rochdale was in the gift of the Archbishop of Canterbury, not the Crown, and that it was given to Hay to redeem a promise made two years before. This in no way detracts from the tactlessness of the decision to promote him.

56. In Oxfordshire in 1831 there were 18 active clerical JPs in a Bench of 71; clergy were, thus, 25% of the total, a figure in line with the average throughout the country. In Gloucestershire in the same year there were 176 active magistrates, of whom 49 (28%) were clergy.

57. Moir, *Local Government*, p.45.

58. Lord Redesdale to Lord Colchester, 18 September 1824, in Lord Colchester, ed., *The Diary and Correspondence of Charles Abbot, Lord Colchester*, III, 340, quoted in Moir, *Local Government*, p.53. Italics in text. Lord Redesdale had a country seat at Batsford Park near Moreton-in-the-Marsh. His sentiments were shared by a contemporary Gloucestershire parson, Francis Witts, rector of Upper Slaughter from 1808 until his death in 1854. According to a diary entry for 6 July 1827, Witts thought it was 'most desirable ... that the younger squires should engage in the county business and not leave all to the clergy, as is too often the case, while their attention is absorbed in fox hunting, racing, London amusements, or the gay frivolities of Cheltenham, Brighton, etc', see David Verey, ed., *The Diary of a Cotswold Parson*, p.72. Witts was conscientious in everything, including the keeping of his diary: he left, in all, some ninety volumes. I understand from my friend Francis Witts (the rector's great-great-grandson) that it is planned, in due course, to publish the massive script in its entirety.

59. McClatchey, *op.cit.*, Table, p.191.

60. S. and B. Webb, *op.cit.*, p. 384, note 2. The Webbs also state that, in 1831, clergy made up more than half the acting justices in eight counties - Cornwall, Hereford, Lincoln, Norfolk, Somerset, Brecon, Denbigh, and Glamorgan (*ibid.*, quoted in R. Quinault and J.Stevenson, *op.cit.*, p.186). This is wrong. In 1831, clergy constituted the majority of acting magistrates only in Cardiganshire (see below, Table XIV).

61. See below, p.150.

62. Russell, *op.cit.*, p.151. This author also suggests (*ibid.*) that changes in the social composition of the landed class assisted growth in the clerical magistracy. There was, he argues, an influx of mercantile families, a development which had the effect of reducing the number of laity who were regarded as qualified to serve. This is a speculative point, yet to be proved. Certainly, it does not hold for Gloucestershire. In this county, notes Moir, 'the new commercial and industrial forces and the new men they brought with them were quickly assimilated to the old' (*Local Government*, p.160).

63. See above, p.16.

64. *P.P.*, 1834, XLVIII, 217-34.

65. *P.P.*, 1840, XLI, 351-94.

66. *P.P.*, 1842, XXXIII, 445-70; *P.P.*, 1863, XLVIII, 259-79.

67. E. Halevy, *A History of the English People, 1830-1841*, p.221, note 2; L. Strachey and R. Fulford, eds., *The Greville Memoirs, 1814-1860*, IV,156-7.

68. See House of Lords, 9 February 1836, *Hansard*, Third Series, XXXI, 178-82; House of Lords, 5 July 1838, *Hansard*, Third Series, XLIII, 1268-82. Russell's encroachment upon the prerogative of the Lord Chancellor was, it must be emphasized, very gradual.

69. House of Commons, 10 February 1837, *Hansard*, Third Series, XXXVI,420; Quinault and Stevenson, *op.cit.*, p.188.

70. House of Lords, 2 August 1839, *Hansard*, Third Series, XLIX, 1139-40; Quinault and Stevenson, *op.cit.*, p.188.

71. *ibid.*

72. See below, Table XIV.

73. First Report of the Poor Law Commissioners, Appendix C, *P.P.*, 1834, XXXVII,375.

74. Blomfield, *A Memoir of C.J. Blomfield*, I, 38-9.

75. *ibid.*, I, 38.

76. G.C.B. Davies, *Henry Phillpotts, Bishop of Exeter, 1778-1869*, p.17.

77. *ibid.*, pp.17-18.

78. Blomfield, *op.cit.*, I, 39.

79. House of Lords, 14 June 1844, *Hansard*, Third Series, LXXV, 879.

80. Entry for 16 October 1833, in *The Diary of a Cotswold Parson*, p.93. 'Not a single voice was raised by a solitary layman' in support of the clergy, Witts complained.

81. See above, pp.9-11.

82. Christie, *The Diary of the Revd William Jones*, p.258; quoted in Russell, *op.cit.*, p. 153.

83. A.W. Brown, *Recollections of the conversation parties of the Revd Charles Simeon*, p.129; Russell, *op.cit.*, p.153.

84. See above, p.23.

85. See below, Table XIV.

86. *ibid.* In 1836, as many as 3,266 clergy were appointed to county commissions (see below, Table XIV.) By 1861, the figure had fallen to 1,357: 1,183 in England and 174 in Wales (*P.P.*, 1861, LI, 665). Twelve years later, in 1873, there was a further modest reduction to 1,187: 1,043 English and 144 Welsh (*P.P.*, 1873, LIV, 33-57). Finally, there are figures for 1887 (*P.P.*, 1888, LXXXII, 193-406) analysed in Carl H.E. Zangerl, 'The Social Composition of the County Magistracy in England and Wales, 1831-1887', *J.B.S.*, XI (November, 1971), Table 2, 118. Zangerl calculates that, according to this last set of parliamentary returns, there were 687 clerical appointees to county commissions in 1887: 602 in England and 85 in Wales.

6

Problems of Church Reform

The Church, as she is at present regulated, we are bold to say, is the Mother and Propagatrix of alienation. *Critical Review* (1815).

A step-mother's neglect is naturally requited by something of a step-mother's unpopularity. Thomas Arnold (1832).

i. *Education*

Clergy shared a common culture, based upon a common education. Education, like the culture, was provided by the English grammar school or by the private tutor, frequently himself a clergyman, and then by Oxford and Cambridge universities. A private tutor was, in many ways, preferable to a grammar school. Although there were centres of creative life - Shrewsbury under Samuel Butler, and also, rather later, Rugby under Arnold - the endowed grammar (or 'public') schools had not as yet begun to ride that surge of popularity which was destined to carry them triumphantly through the Victorian era. There were good reasons for the contemporary scepticism. Many were places of violence, brutality and inefficiency. The nadir was reached in 1818, known as the 'year of revolutions'. The set-piece display was a famous riot at Winchester, during the course of which insurgent scholars barricaded themselves in a tower and had to be lured out by a false offer of peace. There was also trouble elsewhere - a minor revolt at Eton; disturbances at Charterhouse; placards threatening the headmaster of Shrewsbury with violence.[1]

When tempers had cooled sufficiently for lessons to restart it was to the classics, interspersed with a grounding in the principles of mathematics, that pupils applied themselves. This fundamentally Renaissance ideal of culture also inspired those, like Arnold, who anticipated the future. Religious instruction, as one or two examples will suffice to show, was neglected. At Eton, where the notorious Revd Dr Keate held sway for many years, there was only a 'prose' every Sunday after lunch, presided over by Dr Keate himself. Sometimes he read aloud a short discourse on abstract morality, taken from a collection of eighteenth-century sermons; and sometimes he read a passage from the works of a 'pagan' writer - Epictetus, for example. The lesson was short; immediately afterwards, he gave the fifth and sixth forms the subject of their

Latin theme for the ensuing week. At Harrow around 1820, the only religious instruction consisted of the Headmaster, Dr George Butler, reading Paley's *Evidences* with the sixth form for half an hour on Sundays in his library.[2]

Not all future clergymen enjoyed the dubious benefits of a Georgian grammar school education, but most of them did attend one or other of the two ancient universities. Reliable statistics on this matter are first available for the decade 1834–43. Among those ordained during these years, a little over 80% had been to Oxford or Cambridge; of the remainder, 4% were from Trinity College, Dublin, a further 3% or so had been educated at the freshly opened university at Durham, and the residual 10% were 'literates', lacking a university education at all.[3] Figures for the eighteenth century are not readily available. A sharp distinction, at this period, has to be made between clergy in rich dioceses (particularly those within easy reach of Oxford and Cambridge) and clergy in poor. There are, by way of illustration of this truth, figures for the diocese of Norwich (dominated by Cambridge men) and also for St David's. At Norwich, between 1637 and 1800, there were 4,212 clergy. Of these 4,131 - in other words, virtually all of them - had signed college registers; and 60 held degrees from elsewhere, leaving a derisory total of 21 literates.[4] What was exceptionally rare in Norwich was exceedingly common in St David's; indeed, the one was the converse of the other. In south Wales, 762 men were ordained between 1750 and 1800; and, of these, only 45 (5.9%) had degrees. It would seem, moreover, that the proportion of graduate clergy in St David's fell during the course of the eighteenth century; up until 1750 about one-third of those who were ordained had degrees.[5] This statistic suggests the startling conclusion that more clergy were graduates in 1700 than in 1800. Startling as it may be, it is probably not erroneous. As will shortly be seen, aggregate figures for admissions to Oxford and Cambridge declined sharply during the second half of the eighteenth century.[6] This implies that the number of Oxbridge-trained ordinands declined too. The shortfall was certainly accommodated in one way, and probably in two. Firstly, there was, during the course of the eighteenth century, a sizeable increase in the incidence of pluralism among the beneficed clergy: or, to put the matter another way, a sizeable decrease in the number of rectors and vicars.[7] Secondly, it was probably the case, as the evidence from St David's suggests, that the fall-off in Oxbridge ordinands was counterbalanced, at least in part, by a rise in literates. Hence the conclusion that the proportion of graduate clergy was higher in 1700 than in 1800. A change in this regard, however, is unlikely to have been very substantial, because it was largely confined to outlying districts where the proportion of literates was already high. The typical English incumbent, whether in the mid-nineteenth century or the mid-seventeenth, was an Oxbridge man.

As at the grammar schools, university curriculums were mainly classical and mathematical in emphasis, with the theological element severely restricted in scope. Theology, moreover, largely meant studying the works of the influential English theologian, William Paley. Paley was capable of humour - a quality not to be found in the works of many of his numerous imitators - but his piety was rationalistic and provoked little deep questioning concerning the fundamental matters of faith. Theological papers, whether in college or in university examinations, did not do much to excite thought. Perusing those set at Cambridge in the 1820s, the main impression is of the universally descriptive and declaratory tone of the questions - 'Give Paley's arguments for the existence of God', 'State Paley's major principles of morality', and the like. Dissent - even comment - was not asked for, nor was it expected.

A 'liberal', and largely non-theological, university education found many defenders, even among the clergy. An influential statement of its underlying philosophy was made by Pusey, in a pamphlet in 1833. True education, he contended, was dialectical rather than didactic; its aim was not the imparting of knowledge, but the formation of 'habits and powers of thinking'.[8] There were two main practical results of such a view: theology was slow to develop as a separate discipline at university, and scholarly clergy were more likely to produce editions of Greek texts than they were to write works of Christian devotion. Even where clerical influence upon the universities was at its strongest, the value of a 'liberal' education was highly regarded. At Durham, despite endowment by Bishop and Chapter and the direct influence of both upon curriculum development, courses in theology were not introduced until 1846, fourteen years after the initial foundation.[9]

Throughout the Georgian era, the eclectic tradition of clerical learning, already well established, remained firm. Both the quality and the range are impressive. Butler and Berkeley in philosophy; Sterne in literature; Malthus in political economy; Crabbe in poetry; Jethro Tull in agriculture; Gilbert White in natural history; Stephen Hales in chemistry; Burn in law. The flow of talent was still far from stagnant among those rising to eminence in the 1820s and 1830s. Blomfield, Monk and Maltby, all of them destined for the late-Georgian Bench, were three of the foremost classical scholars of the age; Whately did original work in political economy; William Buckland was a leading geologist and mineralogist; and Arnold an authority on ancient history. Study of the clergy's contribution to culture shows why Coleridge chose them as the nucleus of his learned class or 'clerisy'.[10] There were many academics among the cathedral dignitaries; and one in six of the parish clergy had been, at some time, a don.[11] Theologically, however, the clergy was not well educated. Few, except professional scholars like Pusey or Connop Thirlwall, read any of the works on Biblical criticism which came out of the German universities in the early nineteenth century. All left university after taking several examinations in Paley, and having attended a course of twelve lectures by one of the Divinity professors.

The fragmentary quality of theological education at university would have mattered less, if there had been a number of good theological colleges. Unfortunately, there were not. In 1800 there were none at all, and twenty-five years later there were only two. Both catered solely for the needs of 'literates'. A start was made in 1816 with the foundation of St Bees College by Bishop Law of Chester, and his example was followed six years later by Thomas Burgess of St David's, who was responsible for launching Lampeter.[12] Plans to turn the unreformed cathedrals into theological colleges came to nothing.[13] Introduction of ordination training for graduates had to wait upon a series of initiatives. First was Chichester (1839), followed the next year by Wells,[14] and then a longer gap before Cuddesdon (1854). Although earlier there had been a certain amount of informal teaching - at Cambridge the great Evangelical, Charles Simeon, held fortnightly 'conversation parties' for ordinands [15] - little enough was organised on a formal basis. The Georgian clergyman did not enter Orders as a trained man.

ii. *The Clergy as a Profession*

In 1812 George Crabbe, poet and clergyman, informed Sir Walter Scott that he had 'two sons, both in Orders, partly from a promise to Mrs Crabbe's family that I would bring them up precisely alike, and partly because I did not know what else to do with them'.[16] Crabbe was not alone in his perplexity. The difficulty was that alternative professions developed slowly. Only a few professional bodies - the solicitors and the barristers are the best examples - were established before 1800. It was the new towns, requiring as they did the development of effective local government, better town planning, and more sophisticated financial institutions, that created the need for civil servants, engineers and bankers. There are many examples of the amorphous state of professions in the Georgian period. The civil engineers did not form a society until 1771, and later set up an institute in 1818, which was incorporated ten years later. The mechanical engineers were even slower to organise themselves, not forming an efficient professional organisation until 1847. Medicine and dentistry were also set on a firm footing in the 1840s and 1850s: the Pharmaceutical Society dates from 1841, and the College of Dentists from 1857, just one year before the medical profession was organised under the 1858 Medical Act.[17]

Professions were undeveloped because, among other things, the educational system did little to encourage growth. Before the foundation of Durham in 1832, there were only the two ancient universities in England - a paucity of choice which compares most unfavourably with that available in the majority of contemporary Continental states, and is also somewhat paltry when compared with what was provided in Scotland. A main function - one is tempted to say *the* main function - of both Oxford and Cambridge was to give future clergy a 'gentleman's education', in classics and mathematics. Some colleges, like Emmanuel at Cambridge for example, were pseudo-seminaries, it being rare for a graduate from them not to enter Orders. The close relationship between the church and the two ancient universities is a matter of great importance. We have seen how it was that, in the decade 1834-43, over 80% of the church's manpower was recruited from among the ranks of Oxford and Cambridge matriculants. It was suggested that the proportion in 1700 may have been rather more, and in 1800 somewhat less.[18] So intimate was the connection between gown and church that the health of the one vitally affected the health of the other.

Oxford and Cambridge in the Georgian era were not static institutions. The number of admissions, a measure of their vitality, was reasonable up until 1730, took a decided turn for the worse in the period from 1740s through until the 1760s, stabilised during the rest of the eighteenth century, and then increased massively during the late Georgian era. At Oxford the most vigorous period during the eighteenth century was between 1710 and 1719: admissions then averaged 321 a year.[19] Across at Cambridge the high-point was reached even earlier, between 1700 and 1709, when the level of admissions was 249 a year.[20] Aggregating the figures for the two universities, admissions averaged 546 a year during the first three decades of the century. Numbers then began to fall. At Oxford, admissions in the decade 1730-9 averaged 271 a year; in 1740-9 only 221; and in 1750-9 no more than 182, the low-point of the century. At Cambridge the critical decade was the fourth, when numbers fell away to 163 a year; in 1720-9 the figure had been 225 a year. No strong recovery was set in train at any time before 1800. What this means is that, decade after decade, the figure for aggregate admissions was a far cry from the buoyancy experienced early in the century. Up until 1730, as noted, the average was 546 a year; but over the period 1730-99 the average was 382 a year, a decline of 30%.[21]

Soon after the new century dawned, the two ancient universities awoke from slumber. The decisive decade was the second, when aggregate admissions amounted to 619 a year, significantly higher than the level achieved in 1700-29. The post-war surge was carried even further in the 1820s - aggregate admissions reached 850 a year, a staggering 37% improvement on the previous decade, itself a record. After movement came stability. Numbers remained broadly unchanged from the 1830s until the 1850s, and the volume of entrants recorded in the 1820s was not surpassed until the 1860s, when a fresh phase of growth was entered upon.[22]

It is the final piece in the jigsaw that is the major surprise. Whether numbers were going up, or whether they were going down, the proportion of students subsequently taking Orders remained the same. A random sample of 500 Cambridge matriculants between 1752 and 1799 has been analysed; it was found that 252 (50.4% of the sample) later became ordained.[23] Of those who entered Cambridge in the year 1800, 51% took Orders; and of those entering in 1830, the same was true of 50%.[24] Meanwhile, across at Oxford, the ratio of matriculations to subsequent ordinations, in the decade spanning 1834 and 1843, was once again close to 2:1.[25] Here is a social reality that has to be reckoned with. The expansion of the two ancient universities in the early nineteenth century was great, and it was also sustained; yet figures for Oxbridge-trained ordinands kept decorously in step throughout the period. By the 1830s, the arithmetic was becoming puzzling. The number of incumbents, at the start of the decade, was in the region of 7,500;[26] while, between 1834 and 1843, ordinations averaged 535 a year.[27] The obvious conclusion is the correct one. The influx into the ranks of the clergy carried profound, and potentially explosive, consequences.

The first, wholly unavoidable, result was that the age profile of the clergy became radically altered. It simply was not possible for young men to flock into the profession in such numbers without making the clergy, over time, a much younger - and more vigorous - body. As the clergy became younger, they became more receptive to novel ideas. It is worth noting, in passing, that this long-term shift in the pattern of clerical demography was one of the reasons for the success of the two great Victorian religious movements, based at Clapham and at Oxford. It must be stressed, however, that a surplus of clerical recruitment over natural wastage created conflict and tension; the ordinands of the 1820s and 1830s did not rise either quickly or easily into positions of power within the church.[28] Death is the courtesy that the old pay to the young. The incumbents of Georgian England were not, in this regard, well-mannered; they clung on to life, and they clung on to their parishes.[29] This response may have been ignoble, but it was human.

As clerical numbers grew, competition for benefices grew also, an unpalatable development from a curate's point of view. Nor did life become any easier for the newly ordained. Difficulty stemmed from lack of structure to clerical employment. Curates were taken on and paid by incumbents; arrangements were often informal; and episcopal intervention was, in a good many instances, at best haphazard and infrequent. In these circumstances, the flood of ordinands that characterised the late-Georgian period had the unfortunate effect of strengthening petty rectoral tyranny. If Noodle did not like the terms he was offered, it was always possible to turn to Foodle. The beneficed clergy had always tended to treat their employees as an inferior race, and the great increase in clerical numbers reinforced this attitude. To have several young men all clamouring for a curacy was a situation which an unscrupulous incumbent could exploit to the full. The curate's lot had not been a happy one during the eighteenth century. The intensification of competition for employment added desperation and sadness to traditional weakness.[30]

The church in Georgian England had to cope with violent oscillations in its manpower. The difficulty was not that the numbers entering the clerical profession fluctuated over years, or even decades; rather it was the case that availability of manpower fell away, and then surged, during a working lifetime. I have compiled figures, necessarily approximate but nonetheless highly illuminating, which deal with this. It appears, that, during the first three decades of the eighteenth century, ordinands averaged around 320 a year.[31] Numbers then started to decline. The nadir was reached in the period from the 1740s until the 1760s. The average figure for ordinands, in these three decades, is calculated at 245 a year,[32] 23% less than the rate of entry during the first three decades of the century. In the 1770s and 1780s numbers rose a little, and then steadied. This was scant preparation for the transformation that took place soon after 1800. Ordination numbers in the second decade of the nineteenth century were about 40% above the level in the first;[33] in the 1820s, moreover, there was a further increase of close on 40%. The annual average had by now reached 530,[34] well over double the figure in the 1740s, 1750s and 1760s, and two-thirds more than that of the first three decades of the eighteenth century. Violent change on a scale such as this could have been accommodated had parochial structure been fluid, but it was not. There were about 10,500 livings in 1700, and there were also about 10,500 livings in 1830. The effects of oscillating ordination numbers were not in these circumstances trivial. The prolonged famine of the mid-eighteenth century made for an increase in pluralism among the beneficed clergy;[35] there simply were not enough clergy to go round. In contrast, the feast of the early nineteenth helped to create the opposite effect; it was now increasingly the case that, whenever a vacancy occurred, patrons had to deal with the claims of numerous curates, all desiring promotion.[36] I have already indicated that the beneficed clergy resisted this pressure for change as well as they could, striving to hold on, if they were pluralists, to all of their parishes. But with time, inevitably, this feat became difficult. A church recruiting ordinands at a rate of 530 a year was very different to a church where ordinands were running at no more than 245 a year.

It is remarkable that, with the great increase in the size of the two ancient universities in the early nineteenth century, the proportion of matriculants subsequently becoming ordained held steady and did not fall. Inertia is the most likely explanation. Continued preference for a clerical career was part of a general rigidity of choice and was, for this reason, the harder to change. Few graduates would have been likely to find even a minor role in any of those novels of romance and adventure so popular towards the end of the Georgian period. There was, instead, a striking preference for established career patterns, and a corresponding failure to meet the challenges which a new society presented. Of the 143 men who matriculated at Cambridge in 1800, there were 113 who subsequently took degrees. Among these alumni were to be found 73 clergy, 12 lawyers and 3 landed gentry. Thirty years later, career choices were similar. There were 405 matriculants at Cambridge in 1830, 307 of whom completed their courses. These alumni, like their predecessors of 1800, did not look beyond the three traditional choices of the Church, the Law, and the Land: there were 203 clergy, 38 lawyers and 18 landed gentry among the total of 307. Altogether, 84% of alumni opted for one of these three choices; while, in 1800, 78% had done the same.[37] It is possible to sift through the records of literally hundreds of graduates without finding a single banker, manufacturer, or civil engineer.

The incumbents of Georgian England were taught by clergy at school.[38] They attended universities where they were supervised by clerical dons.[39] They mixed with friends who were mostly destined to lead clerical lives. It is therefore not surprising that they ended up as clergymen themselves. It was possible to move through the prevailing system and still develop a meaningful sense of vocation, but the cultural milieu of a 'liberal' education did little to encourage this, and nor, for that matter, did reading the rationalising works of Paley. Ordination was for many prospective clergy a conditioned reflex rather than a conscious decision of active intelligence and will. Tradition decreed that a son, often a younger son, should take Orders;[40] and tradition was adhered to, even in the midst of a changing society.

iii. *Becoming Ordained*

In 1822 the Hon George Spencer, the youngest son of George John, the second Earl, and a brother of Lord Althorp, the future Whig Chancellor of the Exchequer, was seeking Orders in the diocese of Peterborough. He therefore wrote to the diocesan examiner, the Revd T.S. Hughes, asking what books to read in preparation for his ordination examinations. The reply was inimitable. It was, Hughes assured him, 'impossible that I could ever entertain any idea of subjecting a gentleman with whose talents and good qualities I am so well acquainted as I am with yours, to any examination except one as a matter of form, for which a verse in the Greek Testament, and an Article of the Church of England returned into Latin, will be amply sufficient'.[41] The diocesan examiner was as good as his word. Spencer was duly ordained in December of the same year.

Informality in ordination examinations mirrors contemporary practice. Stories of candidates being examined on the cricket field, or during a leisurely shave,[42] find parallels in other professions, in, for example, an account of an eighteenth-century attorney being quizzed over breakfast and muffins.[43] The competitive examination was not suited to the social structure of eighteenth-century England; it was not until 1802 that the first Honours List was introduced, at Oxford. In their lack of zest for formalised competition, the Georgian clergy were truly men of their age.

The church's ordination discipline was lax in the eighteenth century, and it continued to be so throughout most of the nineteenth. Many bishops saw little point in being strict. If a candidate possessed a degree and a Title for Orders, and was willing to subscribe to the Thirty-nine Articles, it was extremely difficult in practice, if not in theory, to refuse him. Some diocesans imposed doctrinal tests - Herbert Marsh of Peterborough and Henry Phillpotts of Exeter being especially noted for their dislike of Evangelical principles[44] - but those who suffered under such a policy could usually obtain a Title elsewhere. Ordination examinations were not standardised until the 1880s and, before the formation of the Central Advisory Council of Training for the Ministry, in 1912, the church lacked a centralised selection procedure.[45] Personal laxity must be judged within the context of failure to implement administrative reform.

iv. *Finding a Living*

The Revd Hon George Spencer was a fortunate clergyman. He was fortunate in his birth, and in his ordination examination, and fortunate in his subsequent career. After he was ordained in December 1822, he served as curate at a most suitable spot, Great Brington, conveniently placed within easy walking distance of his family's seat at Althorp. Two years later a further piece of luck came his way; the rector of Great Brington tactfully resigned, and the youngest son of the second Earl duly found himself incumbent of the family living.[46] His career conforms to one of the classic models for the Georgian clergy - three simple steps of ordination at twenty-three or so, curacy in a family living 'kept warm' by an obliging incumbent and, thirdly, almost immediate preferment to that same living. What could be easier? What indeed!

The career structure of the Georgian clergy has not received the attention it deserves. It has a double significance: it forms part of that dim region in the awesome continent of necessary church reform, and it reveals what the effects of the contemporary system of ecclesiastical patronage could be. It is known that patronage fostered pluralism, but the evils of patronage went deeper than this. It not only ensured that the wealthy grew wealthier while the poor became poorer; it also meant that opportunities for career advancement were cut off. What is particularly interesting - and it is this which has not received the attention it deserves - is to observe the effects of the oscillations in clerical numbers that took place during the Georgian period. The clergy's career structure was under stress. It remains to be discovered where the cracks appeared.

The Georgian church was, in many major respects, an aristocratic church. Lay influence, epitomised by the legislative power of parliament in the ecclesiastical sphere, permeated the establishment. Advowsons, with rights of presentation attached, descended through landed families along with hereditary estates - or, if this was not the case, a suitable living could always be purchased on the open market. A fifth of all incumbents were related, either by birth or marriage, to the gentry. The Bench was closely allied with the peerage, and there were plenty of rectors and vicars who, like sad Mr Collins, feared their patron more than they feared their bishop. It was an essential part of this aristocratically controlled system that a curacy should be a smooth stepping-stone to something better. Often enough it was. Of those ordained soon after the turn of the nineteenth century, 20% obtained a first incumbency within five years of ordination, many of them within one year or at most two.[47] Such ease of preferment is one of the best indications of aristocratic control. As might be expected, the great forward surge in ordinands that began towards the close of the Napoleonic Wars made quick promotion more difficult. Among those 'entering the church' in the mid 1820s, only 15% gained incumbencies in five years or less, a significantly lower proportion than had previously been the case. The old style of effortless promotion for the few did not, subsequently, return.[48]

At the opposite pole to the clerical elite were those who remained curates all their lives. There was nothing new about the difficulty in obtaining an incumbency. Writers in the eighteenth century frequently compared the church to a lottery[49] - an apt, but inexact, analogy, since the luckless many who kept receiving 'blanks' knew that the 'tickets' were not fairly drawn; bishops could give winning numbers to their sons and relatives, and the aristocracy could buy them. Complaints that the clerical profession was overcrowded were made often enough, even when numbers were still manageable.[50] A pertinent example for present purposes is the career of W.B.Stevens. He certainly started well: assistant master of Repton School in 1778, at the age of twenty-two, and headmaster the next year, following the death of the previous occupant, the Revd Dr Prior. But then things started to go wrong. He failed in love, and he began to fail in his career. Hating teaching, he sought a living that would give him 'independence'; but he sought for many years in vain. His patron, Sir Robert Burdett, promised him Great Dalby, but then let him down. In the 1790s, Stevens strove for promotion in earnest, making over twenty applications for livings. In 1798, he eventually gained two small Warwickshire incumbencies; but then, sadly, within two years he was dead from a stroke, at the age of forty-five. Stevens's failure is particularly instructive because he had direct access to powerful patronage through several avenues. He had gained, at the age of twenty, a reputation as a minor poet; he counted as friend the influential banker, Thomas Coutts; he had been headmaster of Repton since he was twenty-three; and - an added bonus - he had been elected perpetual fellow and lecturer in moral philosophy at Magdalen College, Oxford, in 1795. The lesson for other clergy, less distinguished, does not need to be spelt out.[51]

There were clergy in the eighteenth century who were never beneficed, and the same was true in the early nineteenth. 20% of those ordained around 1805 met one of three fates : they either remained as assistant or stipendiary curates throughout their careers; they might do no better than gain a perpetual curacy, usually lacking both social status and financial value; or, in a few cases, they vanished into obscurity later in life. This proportion, similar to that of clergy becoming beneficed within five years, is exceptionally high, bearing in mind that university expansion had not yet begun. It might be expected that, as competition for employment mounted, a higher proportion of the clergy would have spent their lives unbeneficed, but this turns out not to have been the case. 20% of those ordained around 1805 experienced ill-fortune in their clerical careers; the same is true of 20% of those ordained around 1815, 20% of those ordained around 1825 and, also, 20% of those ordained around 1835.[52]

The size and stability of the group of clergy doomed to career-failure has an importance which it is hard to understate. The clergy, after all, formed the core of the educated class. 80% of them, or thereabouts, had been to either Oxford or Cambridge;[53] and yet it was these men who filed, one by one, into the distant recesses of obscure rural curacies, remaining there for twenty, thirty or maybe forty years. That so many of the clergy accepted their fate, becoming country curates and remaining for the whole of their lives as country curates, is eloquent of the nature of Georgian society. There was a lack of career opportunity, and this could mask personal ambition.

A fifth of the clergy in late-Georgian England could look forward to nothing better than being curates all their lives, and a further quarter, for one reason or another, were also never beneficed. Early death or emigration consistently claimed between 8% and 10% of each years's crop of ordinands. If both these fates were avoided, there remained a third alternative, perhaps equally undesirable: to become a teacher in one guise or another. There was a shift here. Early in the nineteenth century a tenth of those becoming ordained subsequently entered professional academic life, but a young don of the 1840s was much less likely to be a clergyman. By this time, only 2% or 3% of the clergy - scarcely a quarter as many as before - were becoming Fellows of Colleges.[54] The number of fellowships was, clearly, failing to keep pace with the rise in clerical numbers. The universities' loss was the schools' gain. As the grammar schools were reformed and grew in size, demand for teachers rose and the supply that met this demand was largely clerical. Of those matriculating at Cambridge in 1800, only one became a schoolmaster; but among the entrants for 1830, this was true of seventeen.[55] This is a significant development; but, in the context of the clergy's career structure as a whole, all that it did was to compensate for the simultaneous decline in the number of clerical academics. The four categories mentioned above - early death, emigration, entrance into academic life or into school-teaching - consistently released from competition for benefice appointment somewhere between a fifth and a quarter of the clergy throughout the early nineteenth century.

Since a fifth of the clergy were relegated to the status of genuinely perpetual curate, while a quarter found some safe haven protected from the chilly blasts of competition, there was a vigorous thinning out of the clergy's ranks: only 55% of those who were ordained found a benefice. Some scaled the ladder of preferment easily, but others found the going difficult. If a curate was not quickly successful, his chances of advancement became increasingly slim. Numerically speaking, the group of clergy beneficed within five years was as large as the group beneficed in over five years but within fifteen. The first group, in other words, was twice as concentrated as the second. The third and final group - comprising those who took more than fifteen years to find a first benefice - was only a little smaller.

In summary, out of every hundred men ordained in late-Georgian England, twenty sought in vain all their lives for a benefice, while a further twenty-five either died young, emigrated, or went into teaching. Among the remaining fifty-five, twenty found a benefice in five years or less, twenty took somewhere between six and fifteen years to do the same, and for the final fifteen finding a benefice took longer.

This does not resolve the problem of how the influx into the clergy was accommodated. This could have been achieved in several ways. As more men flowed into the clerical profession, more might have flowed out - either through early death, or emigration, or by opting for some other career. An opening of safety valves in this fashion would have been an effective, though not elegant, solution, but it did not occur; year after year such escape routes were used by a similar proportion of clergy. An alternative method of accommodation, involving less personal pain, would have been the opening up of new opportunities for advancement. This seems especially pertinent to the plight of the late-Georgian clergy. After all, urban development was creating career opportunities in plenty; these, however, were not taken advantage of, and new urban incumbencies were not formed on any scale until after 1840. The third possibility is that incumbents might have retired, or died, earlier: intensification of pressure at one end of the profession being relieved by a lessening of pressure at the other. This is an attractive answer to so perverse a problem. It suffers only from the drawback of being almost certainly false. Towards the close of the period, in the 1830s, there were so many clergymen in their fifties and sixties that the probability is of a rising trend in life expectancy, not a decline.[56] Fourthly, the ecclesiastical system could have been like an enormous piece of blotting paper, exhibiting an extraordinary capacity to absorb an ever-increasing number of clergy, by means of the simple expedient of requiring a higher proportion of them to spend their lives vegetating in rural curacies. Once again, this sounds plausible but was not, however, the case. Massed against it is the fact that a fifth of those ordained around 1805 were never beneficed, and neither were a fifth of those ordained around 1835. This leaves a fifth possibility, that did indeed take place: quick promotion was achieved by fewer clergy, and, following on from this, finding a second living became even more difficult than finding a first. This is discussed in a later chapter, dealing with pluralism and non-residence.[57]

v. *Town or Countryside ?*

Once a Georgian curate did finally find a living, the odds were that it was situated in the countryside. Emphasis upon urban ministry was a major development of the Victorian era; a man who was ordained in 1720, or even in 1820, did not expect to obtain an incumbency in the city. One reason for this is that the typical Georgian town was more like a densely populated village than its modern counterpart, with its surrounding suburban sprawl. It is instructive in this connection to study contemporary ordnance survey maps. The lack of surburban growth is apparent everywhere. Birmingham, as late as 1834, was still a relatively compact square, despite the doubling of its population during the first three decades of the nineteenth century from 74,000 to 147,000.[58] Only to the north-west, through Bilston to web-shaped Wolverhampton, was there any continuous housing development. Elsewhere in the vicinity, places were fairly well nucleated. A survey of central Lancashire, completed between 1842 and 1844, shows the area to have had an urban geography similar to that of the midlands ten years earlier. Despite its population of over 25,000, Wigan resembles a child's version of a capital 'H'; and Preston was shaped like many an inland port, its houses and factories huddled together on a double bend in the river Ribble.[59] Even London confirms the lack of suburban development. Somewhat earlier, in 1822, Oxford Street marked its effective northern boundary. At this date St John's Wood was under the plough, while Hampstead and Highgate were villages, separated by the Vale of Heath. To the west, it is true, the line between town and countryside was less distinct, but even in this area housing was mainly restricted to main roads and soon became less dense - the population of Hammersmith in 1821 was a little under 9,000; of Fulham about 6,500; of Twickenham just over 4,000; and of Teddington only about 850.[60] A late-Georgian vicar of Twickenham would have considered himself a rural man.

Not only were towns small in size, they were also, in a great many instances, single parishes. The crucial determining factor is age. Most old corporate towns - Bristol, Cambridge, Leicester, Oxford, Nottingham, Northampton, Norwich - were already divided; many newly emerging industrial centres - Bolton, Sheffield, Stockport, Leeds - were not. To accidents of historical geography were added the forces of clerical vested interest: urban incumbents resisted change because they stood to lose a large slice of their income from surplice fees, paid for conducting baptisms, marriages and funerals; in 1834, twenty-seven London clergy received over £200 a year from this source.[61] Nor did the legislative situation help; at the close of the Napoleonic Wars, a separate Act of Parliament was required to subdivide each parish.

Something was done to make parochial subdivision easier by the Church Building Act of 1818, and other laws, along similar lines, were passed in the 1820s and 1830s, but these were all piecemeal. The first effective legislation in this field was Peel's District Churches Act of 1843.[62] In 1840 the parish of Leeds was conterminous with the city of Leeds, and the same was true of Wigan and Preston. Until these monolithic units were broken up, urban incumbents were inevitably few.

vi. *The Parochial System*

Paradoxically, one of the major weaknesses of the Georgian church was its commitment to what it considered one of its greatest strengths: the preservation of the parochial system. Childerley might be a decayed community [63] - a few houses, a ruined chapel, and a population of 54; it might be tiny, only 1,000 acres or so; it might be isolated, at the end of a cart-track off the Madingley Road, somewhere between Cambridge and Huntingdon; and it might be poverty-stricken, with a benefice income of only £20 a year; but - and this was the difficulty - Childerley was also a parish, and, according to classic pastoral theory, every parish must have its own resident incumbent.

The beneficed clergy were rural men, and a good many of them were also isolated men. Loneliness is a common theme in clerical biography and diaries, especially among the less wealthy who lacked an easy entrance into county society. This, unhappily, was one of the costs which had to be paid for the preservation of the principle of Establishment. In contrast with the peripatetic trend in the nonconformist ministry, the Anglican clergy worked in their own parishes, and their own parishes only. A few of the early Evangelicals - John Berridge, Henry Venn of Huddersfield - favoured itinerancy, but their acknowledged Cambridge leader, Charles Simeon, was severely critical, and the practice gradually became less common among them.[64] Simeon was upholding what he saw as a fundamental principle of Establishment - the maintenance of a constant relation between one pastor and one flock. For him, it was a spiritual matter. It was his influence that did much to prevent a split within the Evangelical movement on the itinerancy issue.

A more usual defence of the inherited parochial system was, broadly, utilitarian. Those who defended the *status quo* were not utilitarians in the strictly philosophical sense of that term; as often as not, they were content to say that a resident clergyman 'had many opportunities for usefulness', was a 'permanent benefit to the countryside', or such like. The nearest most churchmen came to being philosophical utilitarians was in echoing either the arguments, or the phraseology, of Warburton's *Alliance of Church and State* (1736). Warburton had been brutally frank. Society would fall apart without the cement that only religion could give; realising this, the state habitually made an alliance with the church holding the allegiance of the majority of its citizens; the Anglican church was, in England, the church of the majority; there was thus an alliance between it and the state; and, under the terms of that compact, it was the clergy's task in every parish to uphold the civil power. For Warburton, a resident clergyman was as much the embodiment of a political necessity as he was the fulfilment of a spiritual need. Similar thoughts, less bluntly expressed, are common enough coin in Georgian sermon and pamphlet.

The practice demanded by theory was a daunting prospect. In Norfolk alone there were 625 parishes, mostly with small populations.[65] Even in counties which have since become heavily industrialised, a similar patchwork of rural parishes is discernible. Warwickshire is one example. Here, among 198 parishes surveyed in 1830, three-quarters had populations of under a thousand. There were 13 parishes with less than 100 inhabitants, and the total with less than 500 people was 104 (52.5%).[66] No one, it seems, ever seriously pondered the advisability of placing clergy in sparsely populated rural parishes. The theory of Establishment, when looked at in the cold light of day, made scarcely any pastoral sense at all. This dilemma was resolved in the mid-twentieth century with a return, in the countryside, to considerable local pluralism without any Georgian-style increase in stipends.

Pastoral care of a rural parish of 400 or 500 people posed, for the clergy, spiritual and psychological problems diametrically opposite to those that a vast urban incumbency presented. Men need, by and large, a challenging environment to bring out the best in them, and the environment for pastoral ministry in the countryside of Georgian England was not, except in periods of acute social tension, normally such. Temptations to laziness were compounded by the nature of much clerical work. Several items of the staple clerical diet, notably, taking baptisms, marriages, and funerals, must inevitably lack calories when the population of a clergyman's parish is low.[67] To the inherent temptations, eighteenth-century convention added others. Regularly to preach one's own sermons had about it something of the flavour of 'enthusiasm'; it was thought more fitting to purchase a collection by a well-known divine, and rely most of the time on them instead.[68] Church services were not frequent, and quarterly Holy Communion was the norm.[69] It would also seem that, in too many parishes, pastoral visits of a general character - to see Mrs Jones, not Mrs Jones dying - were not numerous.[70] There existed a vacuum, at the heart of much rural clerical life; some filled it with hunting, others with teaching, many with reading, the majority with miscellaneous leisure pursuits. The pastoral ideal of the Georgian church - a resident clergyman in every parish - was arguably a major reason for a good deal of spiritual neglect, and for a lot of unnecessary clerical apathy.

vii. *Poverty of Livings*

The parochial system also made little economic sense. There were two main problems: there was the problem of livings that were poverty-stricken, and there was the problem of extreme regional variations in benefice values. The first problem, of the overall incidence of clerical poverty, needs to be put in perspective. A radical transformation took place in the years between 1700 and 1830. Concerning this transformation the figures are quite clear: a total of over 3,800 livings worth under £50 a year was reduced, during the course of a century and a quarter, to only 300 or so.[71] After 1830, modesty needed to be turned into respectability, not, usually, an arduous task; but despite the great advances that had been made, a genuine difficulty remained. The broad contemporary view, which took account of the special financial demands made upon the clergy, set £150 a year as a reasonable lower limit for an incumbent's income. If this is accepted - and the earlier analysis of the account books of James Plumptre and Parson Woodforde has provided solid grounds for doing so - then it must be concluded that 3,500 livings, a third of the total, did not in 1830 meet this requirement.[72] A lot had been done, but there was much still to do.

The second problem, that of regional differences, also became less acute. Poor perpetual curacies, many of them clustered in mountainous or otherwise inaccessible districts, rose faster in value than poor rectories and vicarages; and poor rectories and vicarages outstripped the wealthier livings.[73] Regional variations were not, however, eliminated. At the time the Ecclesiastical Revenues Commission compiled its Report, the median value of benefices in Kent, one of the richest counties, was £257 a year; while in Cumbria - among the poorest - the median was £102 a year.[74] A degree of pluralism was justified in every region, solely on the ground of the poverty of livings, and ought to have been the norm in a few, where most benefices were not worth enough to maintain an incumbent in reasonable comfort.

It is not difficult to test the hypothesis that poverty was the root of pluralism. All that needs to be done is to discover how many poor livings were held in conjunction with another or others, and then to compare these findings with the situation for rich. A large sample of 1,215 benefices was taken from three counties, all of them areas where wealthy livings jostled against poor. Results for each of the three counties were similar. As at the end of 1833, a higher proportion of livings below median value were held in plurality than of livings above, but the contrast was never particularly marked. In one of the three, 70% of livings below the median were held pluralistically, as against 60% of those above, a margin of 10%.[75] In the other two counties, the margin was smaller - in one of them it was 7% (58% against 51%), and in the other it was 5% (61% against 56%).[76] The argument that pluralism was largely caused by poverty has little to be said for it: only a few more poor livings were held with another or others than was the case among rich.

Nor is it true that pluralism was most widely practised where it was most easily justified. The opposite, indeed, is nearer the truth: pluralism was least widely practised where it was most easily justified. When considering Cumbria, with a median value of only £102 a year for livings, even the most ardent Radical politician would have found it difficult to resist the logic of the argument in favour of compensatory pluralism; and yet it was in Cumbria that this form of pluralism was found especially infrequently. Of livings under the median, only a quarter were held with another or others, and the remaining three-quarters were not. But livings above the median, curiously, divide along lines similar to those for rich counties - 55% in plurality, 45% not.[77] It is facts such as these that cast a long shadow over that system of patronage which so dominated the Georgian church.

viii. *A House to Live in?*

To My Successor
If you chance for to find
A new house to thy mind,
And built without thy cost;
Be good to the poor
As God gives thee store
And then my labour's not lost.

George Herbert

Another potent problem of church reform was the issue of clerical accommodation. This was, in one respect, all too simple. Around 1830, there still were nearly 2,900 parishes without any residence-house at all.[78] History was largely to blame for this situation. The deficiency can usually be traced a long way back in time, to one of the many monastic appropriations made in the Middle Ages. Whenever a church was appropriated, the parsonage, if there was one, went with the tithe; and this building was then either used by the appropriating monastery for its own purposes or it was let out to a layman - only rarely did it happen that the parsonage was used to provide permanent accommodation for the clergy serving the parish. Efforts were made to improve matters, especially during the fifteenth century, but on the eve of the Reformation there remained nevertheless a large number of parishes without parsonages.[79] The same continued to be true afterwards. With the dissolution of the monasteries, rectorial and vicarial tithes were impropriated - sometimes by cathedral chapters, but more often by laymen. A *stipendarius*, later known as a perpetual curate, was employed to serve the church, and he usually had to find his own accommodation.[80]

The Georgian church did not exercise any corporate responsibility for the upkeep of its buildings, whether churches, chapels, or residence-houses. In this, it acted in harmony with other English institutions. Foreigners lamented - just as Englishmen praised - the lack of centralised administration. The Poor Law was organised locally; education was in the hands of grammar schools and private tutors; the professions were only just beginning to organise themselves. The ecclesiastical, as so often in Georgian England, reflects the secular. If a parsonage needed to be built, it was the personal responsibility of the incumbent or patron of the living to do so.

The picture is complicated by the Bounty's intermittent involvement in the financing of building plans. The major changes in policy are already familiar.[81] Until the mid 1730s, the Board's attitude towards augmentations sought for the purpose of providing parsonages vacillated; some requests were granted, others were refused. But after the passing of the Mortmain Act of 1736, the Board's attitude hardened. No augmentations for the purpose of purchasing parsonages were made during the second half of the eighteeenth century. Then, in 1803, removal of the shackles of the Mortmain Act changed the situation, and augmentations out of the Royal Bounty Fund to provide parsonages soon became fairly frequent. A little later, in 1811, the governors mounted a new initiative, putting into operation powers granted them under Gilbert's Act of 1777. This Act empowered the Bounty to make loans, specifically for the purposes of building, rebuilding, and repairing parsonages, to every living in England and Wales, irrespective of value. By 1824, over 500 of these loans had been arranged; and two years later the capital sum set aside for this part of the Board's work had reached £225,000.

Despite the Bounty's efforts, little enough was achieved during the early nineteenth century. According to official returns, parishes without parsonages increased in number by 250 in the short period between 1818 and 1833.[82] Although discrepancies in data account for the decline - there were 337 fewer parishes in the earlier survey - it is clear that no significant gains were made in the years after Waterloo. If the situation was static then, the period of the Bounty's greatest activity in this field, the historian is hard-pressed to find reasons why there should have been any substantial improvement during the previous century, when, of course, the Bounty intervened much less.

Lack of a parsonage was one problem; inadequate accommodation was another. This second obstacle to reform was less formidable than the first, but was still of weighty proportions; the comparable figures for 1833 are 2,900 parishes without a parsonage at all, as against 1,700 places where the residence was described by the incumbent as 'unfit'. Fifteen years earlier, 'unfit' residences numbered 450 or so more.[83] This is where the mortgages arranged by the Bounty come in; most of them, it seems, were used to rebuild and repair residence-houses. The statistical congruence is impressive. Between 1818 and 1833 the number of unfit parsonages decreased by thirty a year; and between 1811 and 1824 the Bounty made 503 loans on mortgage, equivalent to thirty-nine a year.[84] This implies that the initiative in improving parsonages came largely from the Bounty, representing central authority, and scarcely at all from clergy and patrons acting on their own behalf. This conclusion is strengthened by another piece of evidence. What, one wonders, happened to those 'quite common' augmentations out of the Royal Bounty Fund which were also used to provide, or improve, parsonages? It seems that clergy, like their benefactors and patrons, relied on mortgage facilities provided by the Bounty; there was precious little individual initiative in this direction.

The state of parsonages officially described as 'unfit' was very variable. At one extreme were residences whose unfitness was blatantly apparent - decay, neglect, or a combination of both, had rendered them uninhabitable; next came parsonages which, although structurally sound, were unsuitable for married clergy with families; then there were houses which some well-to-do incumbents, anxious to imitate the gracious living of the gentry, considered insufficiently commodious, and lastly came a number built upon such a palatial scale that upkeep had become prohibitively expensive.

Examples of all four types can be found dotted around the country. At Rushall in Norfolk the parsonage was a thatched cottage, so poorly built that the incumbent complained it was 'in danger of being blown down every high wind'.[85] An excellent example of the second type - a solid, but nonetheless outmoded, structure - was the parsonage at West Dean, a tiny village almost hidden by hills in Sussex's delectable Cuckmere valley. Two major features were that it was built of flint, and that its small windows, few in number, were dressed with sandstone. Downstairs, there were just two main rooms, the one rather small (16' x 8') and the other much larger (17' x 15' 9"). The floor of the smaller was raised up some four feet, suggesting that it may once have been the dais of a medieval hall. The site sloped from north to south, allowing a cellar, partially above ground-level, to be built under the smaller room. A circular staircase led to two upper chambers, both open to the roof.[86] The building was certainly no later than the fourteenth century, and may well have been in existence as early as the twelfth.

The parsonage at Sharncut in Wiltshire, once described by Cobbett as a 'good solid house' and earlier vilified by its incumbent as 'only a cottage',[87] introduces the third type of situation: places where accommodation may or may not have been adequate. Quite often, in these instances, it is hard to distinquish between cases where incumbents were being realistically factual and cases where they were being snobbish. The difficulty is that there are no clear criteria either of adequacy or of ostentation. All that there is to go on are official returns, and the comments in these are tantalisingly short. Sometimes they purport to be straightforwardly descriptive, as when an incumbent describes his residence as a 'cottage'; and sometimes they have strong undertones of social disapproval, evident in such epithets as a 'mere cottage', 'a mere paltry cottage', and even 'a mere labourer's cottage'. Comment could be ruthlessly condescending - 'a most mean and sordid building', said the rector of Thrigby in Norfolk of his parsonage; and it could be pompous - the residence at Strethall in Essex was 'deficient in the most needful accommodations'.[88] It is not known how many incumbents claimed their parsonages were unfit simply as an excuse for non-residence, and how many, in describing them as cottages or mere cottages, voiced a genuine grievance.

Fewer ambiguities surround the fourth category of parsonage. There were in some places residence-houses built upon so grand a scale that even a comparatively incidental item, such as payment of window tax, was a financial burden. It was of such a parsonage that the incumbent of Gotham in Nottinghamshire complained to Archbishop Herring at his visitation in 1743. There were, he commented bitterly, 'six score windows'; the house had '8 Stair Cases, & not one good one'; and - a final touch - there were 'an hundred Doors made of Sawn Boards on ye Premises'.[89] No rector could be expected to live in such a derelict mansion.

The law, or rather the limitations of law, was a major reason for the haphazard state of many parsonages. Repair, enlargement, and upkeep were all left to individual initiative, or lack of it. An incumbent could choose to live in the parsonage himself, or he could knock it down and build another; he could rent it out, or he could leave it untenanted; he could not sell it - that, to use the appropriate legal jargon, would prejudice his successor's 'interest' in it; but otherwise he was free to use it as he pleased. Only when he either resigned or died did his own interest in it cease and then either he or his heirs became liable for dilapidations, payable to his successor in the benefice. Here, again, responsibility was personal. Outgoing and incoming incumbents (or their representatives) appointed their own surveyors, made their own estimates, tried to reach agreement, and then, if all else failed, had to seek legal redress. If the outgoing incumbent was a spendthrift, and if his heirs were impoverished, then the new incumbent had to manage as best he could. The form taken by the law on dilapidations also operated to the new incumbent's and, ultimately, the church's disadvantage. Precedent, confirmed in 1829 by the judgment in *Wise v Metcalfe*, decreed that an incumbent must repair, restore and rebuild his benefice buildings, but only when necessary; he did not have to make improvements, nor need he decorate the interior, and it was found that he was legally entitled to any fixtures and fittings he had himself added.[90]

Law was not the only factor; lack of centralised administration was another. To place responsibility for repair and upkeep in the hands of incumbents was a recipe for chaos. Clergy did not own their parsonages, they only had an 'interest' in them. From a financial point of view they were encouraged to make improvements only in those rare instances where successive incumbents came from the same family, so that the residence-house would come to be regarded as virtually the family's own.[91] Elsewhere, which in this context means almost everywhere, there were no financial incentives to improvement at all.

Then, of course, there was poverty. Livings varied greatly in value, and clerical incomes covered a wide range: incumbents with sparse financial resources lacked the means to provide, or to improve, a parsonage, and, because litigation was expensive, poor clergy could not afford to start actions for recovery of dilapidations. In the meantime the residence-house continued to deteriorate further. Such was the downward-spiral of poverty, decay and neglect.

Non-residence, especially if it was caused by pluralism, gave this spiral an extra twist. A parsonage was particularly likely to deteriorate if a neighbouring incumbent agreed to serve the living. Some curates were allowed to live in the official residence-house, but others had to find their own accommodation.[92] There are many instances of places where non-residence led, gradually, to the complete decay of the parsonage, its rebuilding. On the other side, there were incumbents who gave the unfitness of the residence-house as the excuse, albeit weak, for not residing. In this way, non-residence and neglect reinforced each other. If fewer parsonages had been 'unfit', more clergy would have resided; and if more clergy had resided, fewer parsonages would have been 'unfit'. The relation between non-residence and decay of the parsonage was one of mutual causality.

Social structure is also important. Georgian England was, by and large, a stable and hierarchial society, neither excessively mobile nor noticeably fissile. Clergy, once they settled in place, tended to remain there, often for life. With age, they developed a vested interest in not moving, as retirement brought with it a double financial penalty: loss of benefice income unrelieved by any compensating pension, and liability for dilapidations. Many incumbents remained in a single place for long periods, sometimes for more than half a century. Some guidelines are given by the situation in an averagely wealthy county - Sussex - at the end of 1833.[93] In 126 cases among 279 benefices (45% of the total), there had not been a vacancy since the end of the Napoleonic Wars, nearly twenty years earlier. Pride of place belongs to three clergymen: S. Bale, an ardent bibliophile, had been at Withyam since 1778; W. Kinleside at East Angmering since 1775; and James Capper at Wilmington since 1779. These three are the most spectacular examples among the thirteen incumbents who had held a Sussex living since before the outbreak of the French Revolution; and in a further twenty-nine instances no vacancy had occurred since the end of the eighteenth century.

A good many incumbents embraced architectural expectations that were too grandiose. They wanted a mansion; and, if they could not afford that, they did not set about rebuilding at all.[94] The activities of Sydney Smith are an extreme example, but they do graphically illustrate what was a general tendency.[95] In 1809, he was required by his diocesan, Vernon Harcourt of York, to reside and do duty in his Yorkshire living of Foston. No rector had been resident since the reign of Charles II, and the parsonage was consequently in a sad state of disrepair, so Sydney Smith hired a house at Heslington, twelve miles away, preparing meanwhile to rebuild at Foston. He was one of the first clergy to take advantage of Gilbert's Act of 1777, borrowing £1,600 from the Bounty, which he repaid at a rate of £130 a year. An architect was employed in 1813, and then promptly dismissed when his plans were found to involve too much expense. With characteristic daring, the rector of Foston now took upon himself the dual roles of architect and clerk of works. He soon encountered difficulties, principally with building materials - 150,000 of his own bricks were burnt and then found to be useless. An oxen-train, used for transportation, also proved a failure; so he hired a team of horses, which fortunately turned out to be more effective. Despite these problems, building was completed in about a year. Other improvements were made at the same time. An approach road was built; stables and farm buildings were added; and the garden and extensive glebe, both of which were in a poor state, were tidied up. The whole project, Sydney Smith told Lord Eldon in 1820, cost over £4,000, with the incumbent's own contribution being in the region of £2,500.[95] With this sum, it was possible to build an extremely spacious parsonage. Some time afterwards, there is mention of a 'cavalcade' of house-guests - comprising a family of four and several other people, accompanied by three men-servants, two maids and five horses - approaching up the newly laid drive.[96]

The situation which had developed seems to defy remedy. In fact, it did not. The forces of reform were, admittedly, less numerous than the forces of reaction, but what they lacked in number they more than made up for in strength. To counterbalance the negatives mentioned above there were two positives. Both were powerful on their own; and, yoked together as they were, they ought to have been irresistible. A change in social habits created the desire for improvement, and a change in the value of livings created the means with which to fulfil the desire: it could well be asked what else was required. Benefice incomes rose by at least 400% between 1700 and 1840, and showed the inflation rate a clean pair of heels.[97] Many newly wealthy incumbents, who found themselves with medieval parsonages, were encouraged by their own standards of respectability to translate their affluence into bricks and mortar. Also relevant, here, is the change in the style of life that occurred during the early centuries of modern England. A Georgian incumbent would scarcely have recognised as fit for human habitation the cottage which his celibate priestly predecessor of medieval times had lived in and no doubt regarded as perfectly adequate. A few fairly spacious parsonages had been built in the fourteenth and fifteenth centuries, but most were small, probably with no more than four rooms and possibly with only two. Compare this with an average new Georgian rectory - drawing-room and dining-room, four or five principal bedrooms, two or three servants' rooms, some stables, an outhouse - and the reality of social change becomes immediately apparent.[98] A Georgian incumbent, especially if he was a magistrate, was not satisfied with a medieval cottage. Professional respect, as well as social position, made him wish for something better.

The clergy may have wished for something better, but most of them did little enough about it, at any rate when it came to providing, or improving, the official parsonage. A number, doubtless, built houses of their own, letting out the parsonage meanwhile; others were hamstrung by lack of sufficient financial resources. Yet it still remains necessary to place, side by side, the paradoxical facts that livings were rising faster in value than they had ever risen before, and that the social status of the clergy was rising faster than it had ever risen before, yet the number of parishes lacking a parsonage altogether, and of parishes with residence-houses in varying stages of 'unfitness', remained alarmingly high.

ix. *Doing Duty*

It has always been an attractive disadvantage of the clerical life that the minimum requirement of work is pitched too low. Taking Sunday services, catechising the young, preparing candidates for confirmation, visiting the sick and elderly, and being responsible for what sociologists felicitously call 'rites of passage', namely baptisms, marriages and funerals: the list is not long, nor are these duties necessarily time-consuming. The problem always has existed, and probably always will, but it applies with particular force to the Georgian clergy. In one of those towns which were still single parishes, these routine requirements were an overwhelming burden; but in the great majority of benefices, they were light. The temptation was for a cleric to look after more than one parish, and this temptation, it must be added, was one which many in the profession were unable to resist.

The slow rhythm of parochial life is evident from Parson Woodforde's *Diary*. He was benign, he was tolerant, and he had broad human sympathies; but he does not appear to have made many pastoral visits, and the reader of the *Diary* is forcefully struck by his distance, emotionally speaking, from the poor. Barriers were even erected within his own household. He did not enjoy a 'like for like' relationship with anyone, not even with his faithful farm-servant, Ben Leggatt. When Ben, after twenty years' service, suddenly and unexpectedly found himself in love, it was altogether characteristic for Woodforde to find out what was happening at second-hand. Relations with the parish of Weston are best described as kindly but formal - Woodforde pays for his men-servants to be taught to read; he makes a generous subscription during a period of harsh weather; he 'orders' Ben Leggatt to sit up all night with a labourer in the throes of smallpox; he does not himself teach his servants to read, nor does he relieve the problems of unemployment by taking on extra labour, nor put himself to the trouble of nocturnal visits during times of severe illness.[99]

These are valuable hints about pastoral practice. Weston was a small place with a population of only 350, easy enough to look after and to care for. Parson Woodforde was, throughout his incumbency, nearly always resident. One of the few references in the *Diary* to a long period away, a holiday visit to Somerset relations, is buried among the entries for the summer of 1795. 'Duty' was done by a clerical friend, Mr Maynard. Woodforde was away for nineteen Sundays, paying his temporary curate £10 0s 0d,[100] not a princely sum to serve a living worth over £250 a year. Another local incumbent, Thomas Jeans - a man of some social pretension and married to a woman of still more social pretension[101] - took such logic a step further, by permanently forsaking his rectory at Witchingham in favour of the more socially exhilarating metropolis. Substitutes willing to do duty were found easily enough. Jeans left rural Norfolk sometime in 1796, and did not return until the summer of 1801. His visit was brief but necessary. The acting curate, the Revd Mr Beevor, was at the time temporarily indisposed, 'holidaying' in the King's Bench prison on a charge of challenging an army officer to a duel.[102]

The Revd Mr Beevor was not a normal curate, but a neighbouring incumbent - the rector of West Barsham, in fact - fulfilling a curate's duties; so was Mr Maynard. Together, they introduce two major aspects of what might aptly be described as the co-operative neighbouring incumbent syndrome. Mr Beevor assisted permanently, Mr Maynard only temporarily. Each could claim they were doing little more than extending normal clerical practice; incumbents, especially if they were pluralists, quite often lived outside their parishes and rode over to take services on Sunday. In doing the same, neighbouring clergy were following well-established precedent. The problem is to discover how many beneficed clergy were prepared to co-operate with each other in this way.

A lot were. Decisive on this point are some statistics for Devon in 1779. In the diocesan returns for that year, a total of 390 places were included.[103] Of these, 65 (16.7%) were permanently looked after by neighbouring rectors of vicars. This is a large figure, and it would have risen appreciably during the summer months when temporary arrangements, not indicated in diocesan returns, were doubtless made from time to time. One living in every six in late eighteenth-century Devon was permanently served by a neighbouring incumbent acting as curate.

This is a high proportion, and yet in remote districts it could be higher. A good example is a pair of isolated coastal deaneries - those of Waxham and of Repps, in north-east Norfolk.[104] Church life might be expected to be lethargic in an area such as this. The values of livings were low, villages were few and thinly populated, and the only place of any substance was North Walsham. Catfield was surrounded by swamp and marsh; and Happisburgh, as late as the 1880s, still boasted only a single shop - the road to North Walsham, seven miles away, consisted mainly of shingle.[105] Coastal erosion was a constant threat. Sometime between 1775 and 1826, the chancel and much of the nave of the church at Mundesley became ruinous, and they remained dilapidated until 1903. Repair work was carried out more swiftly at Sidestrand; there the church tower fell down in 1841, but was roughly rebuilt seven years later.[106] At Eccles, however, repair work was never carried out at all. The ruined church tower, according to an observer in the 1880s, could be seen 'standing up from the beach like a solitary tooth'.[107]

If there is an expectation of lethargy, this expectation is not disappointed. At the turn of the nineteenth century, almost a third of the parishes in the two deaneries were looked after by neighbouring incumbents: in 1794, the figure was 21 in a total of 72 places with churches. Such a state of affairs can only be appreciated in its full enormity when compared with the derisory figure of eight parishes enjoying at the same period the presence of a resident incumbent doing duty. A visitor, travelling through this part of Norfolk at the turn of the nineteenth century, was three times as likely to find a church service being taken by a neighbouring incumbent as by a resident rector or vicar.

Such arrangements were popular because they were cheap, a matter of giving another incumbent some pocket-money rather than of having to provide for a curate, with or without a family. In the returns for 1794, sums of money paid to 'co-operative' incumbents were mentioned on eight occasions; the lowest payment was £10 10s 0d a year, the highest £30, and the rest were all between £18 and £25. Twelve years later the tariff had risen somewhat, but was still set very low. Two cases of £20 stipends occur; a further nine were for £30 or less; and at Hickling £40 a year was agreed. None of these twenty-one payments is high.

The year 1806, when 23 incumbents served other incumbents' churches, marks the nadir. At each of the next three visitations, there was a sharp decline. In 1813 the number was 17, by 1820 it had been reduced to 11, and by 1834 it was down to 8. There were now as few incumbent-curates as there had been resident rectors or vicars forty years before.

The timing of the initial decline was not a coincidence. The year 1813 also saw the passing of the Stipendiary Curates Act,[108] a decisive and, in many ways, radical piece of legislation. The provisions of concern here are those laying down a scale of stipends to be paid to curates who were also incumbents. These were now fixed at a minimum of £50 a year, or the whole value of a benefice if it was worth a smaller sum than this amount. It can readily be seen that the new scale threatened the pockets of those clergy in Waxham and Repps who employed other incumbents as curates; in 1806 only one neighbouring incumbent whose stipend is known was paid over £30 and even he received no more than £40. Now, every stipend had to be raised.

Such evidence as there is, suggests that the new regulations were complied with. Four stipends are mentioned in the returns for 1820, and a further three in those for 1834. Only one was for less that the legal minimum of £50 - John Hepworth paid £40 at Hanworth. He may have felt justified in his liberal interpretation of the law. Hanworth was only part of a parish, Gunton was the other, so he paid only part of a stipend. The other six payments were all for £50 or more, and one (given in special circumstances) was for £110. One of the aims of the 1813 Act had been to eliminate incumbent-curates by making non-residence, without accompanying duty, less profitable. In this part of rural Norfolk, at any rate, the Act was successful.

Legislation gave reform an initial boost, and a rise in the number of resident incumbents doing their own duty helped to further it. Until 1820 there was no sign at all of renewed life: 8 residents in 1794; 7 in 1806; 7 again in 1813; and then 9. This makes the subsequent improvement - there were 17 resident incumbents in 1834 - the more impressive. It would be useful to know how many residents there were in the late 1820s, before the crisis in Church and State set in, but the returns for 1827 have not, unfortunately, survived. After 1820, reform from within did give impetus to the earlier reform from without, but the starting date for internal change remains unknown.

The action, *in tandem*, of legislation and self-reform, reduced the number of incumbent-curates; and yet this abuse was not eliminated. In 1834, there were still eight of them scattered about the two deaneries. Visitation returns contain vital clues to their survival, and it is interesting that, although special factors usually account for the preservation of custom, there were parishes where, in certain circumstances, the employment of a neighbouring incumbent could occur for the first time in nearly half a century. Abuse might be old, but it could be new.

At one or other of the five visitations held between 1794 and 1834, 44 of the 72 places with churches (61.1% of the sample) were described as having a neighbouring incumbent acting as curate; and yet only at Bassingham was this true on each occasion. The parish had become, with time, a special case. The vicar in 1834 was Thomas Arden, and the incumbent acting as curate was his father, F. E. Arden. (It was here that the stipend of £110 was paid).[109] At Barningham North the custom was a remnant from an earlier age, and the acting curate was uncertain as to the whereabouts of the incumbent, who had held the living, without residing, since the turn of the century. There might have been an incumbent acting as curate earlier, but the returns, the least communicative in the two deaneries, are silent on the point. At Catfield, disruption had been brought about by a change of incumbent; the new vicar informed Bishop Bathurst that he was 'about to reside'. Paston and Witton illustrate what could be called the continuity principle. They were served as a pair by Stephen Cook, formerly *bona fide* curate but now also vicar of Oulton. He had gained an incumbency and forgotten to relinquish his two curacies. Stalham and Westwick exemplify a different principle, that of reciprocity. Benjamin Cubitt, vicar of Stalham, served Westwick; Edward Wymer, rector of Westwick, served Stalham. (Westwick, incidentally, was similar to Catfield, in that the employment of a neighbouring incumbent was novel there). Finally, there was Sidestrand, which had as rector Edward Edwards, headmaster of Huntingdon Grammar School. In his absence, services were taken by John Cubitt, probably Benjamin's brother or, at any rate, a near relation.

This is a good selection of differing situations, and clearly illustrates some of the intractable problems which reformers found themselves up against. Sheer neglect, as at Barningham North, was one such; others were the force of familial arrangements (Bassingham); difficulties posed by interregnums (Catfield); unwillingness on the part of newly promoted incumbents to give up curacies (Paston and Witton); the fact that some beneficed clergy found it mutually convenient to serve each other's livings (Stalham and Westwick); and, finally, the strong tradition which allowed clerical schoolmasters to hold, primarily for purposes of recreation, a rural living. These are some of the reasons why incumbent-curates were numerous towards the end of the eighteenth century, and why, later, they sometimes proved exceptionally difficult to remove.

x. *Winter and Spring*
The visitation returns of Waxham and Repps are important in another way - as an interesting insight into the neglected subject of religious observance in the Georgian countryside.[110] What they reveal is a surprisingly vigorous spiritual revival. Services, especially celebrations of Holy Communion, were becoming more frequent; congregations were growing; catechising was on the increase; and schools were springing up everywhere. Although an unquantifiable amount of this improvement can be put down to the sheer slovenliness of some of the early returns, the greater forthrightness and conscientiousness of the post-Napoleonic clergy is, in itself, indicative of the changing mood.

The touchstone of the revival rests in the greater frequency of church services. In 1794 there was only one place - North Walsham - where double duty was customary each Sunday; elsewhere single duty, at most, was performed. The profile of the two deaneries at this time reveals double duty at one place, single duty at 47, and less frequent services at the remaining 24.[111] The incumbent of Thorpe Market complained that the church needed to be rebuilt; while at Horsey gatherings for worship were held fortnightly, 'the sea permitting'. The norms of 1794 were the rarities of 1834. During the intervening forty years, the number of places with services less often than once a week had dropped from 24 to 2, both of them small villages. North Walsham's splendid isolation, as the only place with double duty, had also ended. Now, there was Evensong every week at Neatishead, with Matins there on alternate Sunday mornings; services were twice weekly at eight new places (just introduced at Hickling); and they were as thrice weekly at Gimingham, where the Evangelical curate, William Andrew, has achieved immortality in the pages of Owen Chadwick's delightful *Victorian Miniature*. Congregations were large in many places - at Cromer, mention was made of 300 to 400 as a minimum and of 1,000 or more as a maximum. It is a sign of changing times that these big congregations in no way satisfied the zealous Evangelical vicar, William Sharpe.[112]

With regard to Holy Communion the position in 1794 was depressingly uniform: celebrations were never more than quarterly, and the number of communicants was, with few exceptions, abysmal.[113] Less than ten was the norm. At Waxham there had not been a celebration for seven years, because it was not possible to form a congregation at all. Only at five places were there more than fifteen communicants, and even at North Walsham, where numbers were higher than anywhere else, the total was little more than forty. These facts were recorded without embellishment; the comment from Stalham, where the incumbent was 'sorry to observe the small number of communicants', finds no echo in the other returns. By 1834, communicant numbers had risen out of all recognition. Twenty parishes returned figures of over 30, seven of these topped 50, and North Walsham had been overtaken by Cromer, where the average was between 80 and 150. At the opposite pole to Cromer were Brunstead and Swafield, both of which recorded only six. Forty years earlier such a figure would have been typical, but now it was archaic.

The catechetical work of the clergy had also grown considerably.[114] In 1794, regular classes were held at only seven places, and at the remaining sixty-five they were, at best, occasional. On this subject some of the clergy were prepared to be more forthcoming. Comment could be defensive - 'at present there are no children capable, the Poor can neither read nor write' (Horning); it could reveal frustration - 'the poor cannot be prevailed upon to attend' (Paston and Swafield); and it could be pert - 'it is not usual to catechise in small country churches nor do any attend for that purpose' (Bradfield). Rather later, in 1834, there was less need for clerical defensiveness. Regular catechetical instruction was now part of parish life at fifteen places: twice as many.

It was in the provision of schools that the greatest strides had been made. Here, one suspects, late eighteenth-century visitation queries are more defective than they are in other respects, but this only partially explains the change that had taken place. Officially, there were eight schools (five day schools and three Sunday schools) in the two deaneries in 1794. Cromer alone was accorded two places of learning, a Sunday school and a Free school. It is easy enough to see that these returns are inaccurate - there must have been more than a single school at North Walsham - but it is harder to get at the truth. The contrast with 1834 takes the breath away; instead of eight schools in seven parishes, the figure is at least 124 schools in 54 parishes. (The latter calculation, incidentally, does not include 'several schools' at North Walsham). The balance was tilted strongly towards day schools - there were 88 of these, as against 36 Sunday schools. Most parishes had at least two schools, and there were a few with as many, or even more, than the 1794 returns had given for both deaneries - '12 or 13' at Cromer, 9 at Sheringham, 7 at Worstead. Nowhere else in this work is there as stark a contrast.

All of this is relevant to the increase in resident incumbents in these two deaneries after 1820, and to the concurrent decline in incumbent-curates. Under the unreformed system, clergy trotted about the countryside on Sundays and services were organised to suit their convenience. Many incumbents had a formal relationship with their parishioners, being content to take Sunday services and so on; and it was a natural next step to conclude that it did not much matter whether duty was done by the incumbent or by a clerical neighbour. Local custom buttressed this attitude. It was normal practice in country churches to alternate between Matins and Evensong; some places had only two services or less a month; and parishes were grouped: one place worshipping in the morning whilst the next worshipped later in the day. It is easy to see how this made it possible for clergy to trot about, and equally easy to see how the flowering of church life made it harder for them to do so. The incumbent who took two services every week, who catechised regularly, and who kept a close eye on the village school was, by necessity, resident. Looking after three, four, or even five parishes was, for him, a physical impossibility.

The strength of this revival in coastal Norfolk between the 1790s and 1830s does not square with the conventional view, which holds that most late-Georgian rural parishes were inert and moribund. It is not possible to explain this revival away by arguing that the clergy of the two deaneries were cajoled into action by an energetic and thrusting diocesan. The Bishop of Norwich for most of the period was Henry Bathurst. He was a man of many good qualities, but not even his greatest admirer would wish to claim that he had as much as half an ounce of administrative ability, let alone admistrative zeal.[115] There is, of course, no disputing the argument that generalising on the basis of experience at Waxham and Repps is impossible: 72 parishes is, after all, a tiny sample in a total of over 10,500. On the other hand, there is the important factor of remoteness. If change had reached the wind-swept coastlands of Norfolk, an area as poor as it was isolated, it must be reasonable to infer that a good number of parishes in other secluded areas were also beginning to show signs of life.[116] If secluded areas were coming alive, the probability is that in more thriving districts, where communications were better, things were moving ahead at least as well. More work, it is clear, needs to be done in this field. The Georgian parish, unknown and unstudied, must step out of the historical shadow into the historical light.

xi. *Administration, Discipline, Law*

An incumbent may have failed to reside and do duty in his living for any one of a number of good reasons, such as poverty of the benefice and lack of a decent parsonage. What of the situation however where, from sheer obstinacy, he refused to do so? and what could be done to remove those who, by the immorality of their lives, brought church and clergy into contempt? The answer was, unfortunately, all too little.

The Bounty was virtually powerless. Some patrons managed, by sheer force of character or prestige of social position, to do something; but action was left largely to the bishops, armed with the rusted weapons of Canon Law and parliamentary legislation.

Much has been written by other historians, notably Norman Sykes, on the subject of episcopal administration. He stresses, correctly, the many obstacles that lay in the way of the bishops doing better. Towering over all the others is the unwieldy shape of diocesan geography. Although there were 136 dioceses in eighteenth-century France, in England and Wales the number at the same period was only 26.[117] If these English dioceses had been roughly equal in size, effective administration might have been possible, but such reflections are purely academic. Rochester covered less than a hundred parishes, Carlisle only 130; while, at the other end of the scale, there was Lincoln, with over 1,250, Norwich with nearly 1,100, and York with about 825.[118]

Nothing radical was done before 1840 to remedy this situation. Boundaries remained unaltered until 1836, when a partial reorganisation was carried through. What was wanted was a large number of new dioceses, and many suffragan bishops. What was immediately granted was one new diocese - Ripon - and no suffragan bishops. Ripon appeared, and Bristol disappeared; some small dioceses like Ely, Gloucester, Oxford, Peterborough, and Worcester, became larger; some large dioceses - Lincoln, Norwich, and York - became smaller. This was, however, all. Rochester was extended a decade later, and Manchester formed in 1848,[119] but a thorough-going reformation did not start in earnest until the late 1870s and early 1880s.

Diocesan geography was one factor, poor communication was another. Much abuse has been heaped, over the years, upon the eighteenth-century road. Horses, whole coaches even, disappearing into the jaws of enormous, water-filled, pot-holes; stories abound of seas of mud, broken axles, and runaway carriages; of highways indistinguishable from fields; of lightning attacks by the likes of 'Dick Turpin': all of it good material for situation comedy and semi-fictional romance. More recent judgment has sobered these accounts a little. The numerous private turnpike trusts did achieve something, and journey times between the major cities were reduced appreciably; there was also the beginning of a tentative technology. However, these advances, commendable though they were, did not reach out with any effectiveness into the countryside; and it was through the countryside that the bishops had to travel. Moving about from place to place was a slow and laborious process, and took up a good deal of a bishop's time.

The metropolis was, anyway, more important to him. Bishops had always had political functions, but their presence at Westminster became, under Walpole and the Pelhams, a necessary requirement. Bishops were political appointees, and the Bench was expected to vote with the Administration. A bishop's annual routine was one of residence in London during the 'parliamentary year' - roughly October until May or June - and then the summer was spent in his diocese.[120] Many incumbents if they wanted to see their bishop had to come up to town. London also held cultural attractions and was, in every sense, the centre of a bishop's universe - 'Out of Town', lamented one prominent ecclesiastic, 'is so far out of the world'.[121]

Bishops, it should be no surprise to learn, were more often chosen for political loyalty than for any administrative ability. One instance of the ineptitude which could follow concerns Hoadly, the Whig pamphleteer, promoted to Bangor, the most mountainous diocese, in 1715. The new bishop could not ride, was lame, and could walk only with the help of a stick.[122] As with other professions, like the law or the armed services, everything depended upon seniority.[123] Some men were not promoted to the Bench until they were already past retirement age, as with learned George Bull, who was seventy when he went to the remote and large diocese of St David's, in 1705.[124] Not only were bishops promoted late in life, they did not retire. From an administrative point of view, this was a sure recipe for disaster. To give but two examples: Vernon-Harcourt became Archbishop of York in 1808, when he was fifty-one, and he remained there until his death in 1847, at the age of ninety. He might have held the reins of power even longer had he not been standing on a wooden bridge in his park at Bishopthorpe when it collapsed, the subsequent paralysis somewhat hastening his death.[125] The second is Bathurst of Norwich who was promoted to this, the second largest diocese, in 1805, at the late age of sixty-one, and remained until 1837, dying in office when he was ninety-three. The failure of bishops to resign was a problem which literally refused to go away. In 1868 there were four bishops, at Winchester, Exeter, Bath and Wells, and Salisbury, none of whom was fit for work.[126]

Finally, there was money. Although in 1830 there were three sees worth over £15,000 a year, there were nine that did not bring in £3,000.[127] Work and remuneration were in no way related to one another - Durham, for example, was relatively small but inordinately wealthy, while Norwich was inordinately large but relatively poor. Translations were encouraged, being regarded as the appropriate reward for political services rendered; ambitious men moved rapidly through the poorer dioceses, on their way to 'something better'.[128] Episcopal administration was difficult enough as it was; lack of continuity made it much more so.

This, then, is a rough sketch of a typical Georgian prelate. (i) Promoted to the Bench late in life, (ii) he lingered on in office until he reached the portals of death itself. (iii) If his see was poor, he tried to obtain a translation from it as quickly as possible; (iv) if it was large, he had no suffragan bishop to help him. (v) Most of his time was spent in London; he only visited his diocese in summer, occasionally touring the countryside. (vi) These episcopal visitations were not a pleasant part of his duties; travelling about was slow and tedious. (vii) Finally, it was almost certainly the case that he had not been promoted for such administrative capacities as he possessed. They are seven excellent reasons why the Georgian bishop faced an uphill task.

The inefficiencies of the Georgian church were real enough, and many of its structures were ramshackle, yet it was possible for a man with drive and stubbornness to bring about changes from within. No study yet exists of the administrative reforms of the 'new breed' of bishop, who emerged after the Napoleonic Wars. Most of them

- Blomfield of London, Monk of Gloucester, and Kaye of Lincoln - were church reformers, though their 'plans' varied; Phillpotts of Exeter, on the other hand, was conspicuously not. All four were elevated to the Bench between Peterloo and the Reform Bill - Kaye to Bristol in 1820, Blomfield to Chester in 1824, Monk to Gloucester in 1830, and Phillpotts to Exeter the same year.[129] They all accepted the tenets of conventional morality - whatever their differences of opinion, Blomfield and Phillpotts agreed that it was a clerical parent's duty to 'provide' for his sons; and yet they were determined, as far as was humanly possible, to make the inherited system of episcopal administration work. The contrast between their style of episcopal government and that of the older generation of prelates - men like Bathurst and Harcourt - is discussed briefly in a later chapter.[130]

Bishops, in unguarded moments, sometimes admitted how independently-minded some of the clery were. One such moment occurred when William Cleaver, Bishop of Chester towards the end of the eighteenth century,[131] wrote privately to Lord Grenville, the Foreign Secretary. Cleaver, apparently, had tried to insist upon an incumbent residing, only to receive the inimitable reply: 'Upon my honour I did not know that a bishop had anything to do with me until upon receipt of your letter, I looked into Burn'.[132] (This is a reference to Burn's *Ecclesiastical Law*). One reason for this lack of contact was that the bishop's functions, as politician and scholar, separated him from his clergy. Another was the formality of relationships within the ecclesiastical hierarchy - bishops and incumbents did not meet on social occasions, but only at the infrequent formal visitations. They were simply unknown to each other. Then, from the clergy's side, there was a dislike of what was seen as unnecessary, official, 'interference'. Bishops, it was argued, lived mostly in London, knew little of local conditions, and were not therefore in a good position to assess situations. Further reasons for friction between bishops and clergy were legal in origin. The disciplinary bishop had somehow to breach the dyke of the parson's freehold, which gave security of life-tenure in a living. Secondly, the interlacing of ecclesiastical and secular jurisdictions meant that incumbents could counter disciplinary actions brought in church courts with petitions filed in the civil courts. Lastly, the bishop had to meet the costs of litigation out of his own pocket, and this, not unnaturally, tended to dissuade all except the most determined and conscientious (as well as wealthy) from taking action.

It was mainly over the issue of clerical residence that incumbents and bishops clashed. The Bench in this matter had to apply the law, as laid down by Canon and by parliament. The relevant regulations were outdated, ineffective, and arbitrary. Throughout the eighteenth century the only restraints were imposed by an ancient Plurality Act of 1529,[133] and by the 41st Canon of 1604.[134] Both were too liberal towards 'exceptional cases', were emasculated by vagueness, and had been rendered innocuous by two centuries of clerical non-compliance. In 1803, a new Residence Act was passed.[135] Although an advance on what had gone before, this was not an inspiring piece of legislation. Its tone is clear from the speech of its proposer, Sir William Scott. He evidently accepted the view, rich in cliché, that the church desperately needed 'prizes' in order to 'attract' the nobility. 'On all accounts, religious, moral and political', said Sir William, 'it was anxiously to be wished that the families of our gentry should continue to supply a large proportion of our clergy'.[136] This was a shorthand way of saying that nothing should be done by parliament to curb pluralism, because such action would offend the aristocracy. Radical change was not contemplated by ecclesiastical authority until the 1830s, and the first legislative instrument with any sharpness to it was the 1838 Pluralities Act.[137] It will be no surprise to learn that the Act was the brainchild of Blomfield, Monk, and Kaye.

xii. Senescence

There is one final problem of church reform: the problem of illness and old age. It has about it an unavoidable element of arbitrariness. There are, notoriously, some men who, despite all apparent effort to the contrary - poor diet, excess of alcohol, lack of exercise - manage to live well into the years when ripeness is all; just as there are others, much less fortunate, who die young, sometimes without obvious cause. The English clergy have always tended towards longevity, and those of the Georgian period are no exception to this general rule. The historian has to reckon with a remarkable fact. Although the incumbents of eighteenth and early nineteenth-century England lived in a society where epidemics were rife, sanitation primitive, surgery more likely to kill than cure, and medicine at best haphazard, a great number of them survived into late middle age. This emerges from detailed study of the age profiles of clergy active in the early 1830s, a period when the great influx of ordinands was beginning to make itself felt. Surprising though it may seem, despite the recent increase in young clergy, half of all those who held benefices were found, in the survey, to be over fifty.[138] This top-heavy age distribution in part reflects the prevalent career structure, which had the effect of unduly delaying promotion for many of those deserving it; but it is also witness to the major advantage in the style of life characteristic of the clergy at this period. The best recipe for longevity is to live a rhythmic, easy and unstrenuous life: a lesson which the Georgian incumbent found no difficulty in taking seriously to heart.

Although many of the clergy were elderly, few were very old. In a sample of over eight hundred, there was only one nonagenarian.[139] This was the Revd P. Candler, who had become rector of the Norfolk living of Lammas way back in 1764, and was still there seventy years later. There were eleven octogenarians, and rather more - as many as sixty - septuagenarians. Although less than 10% of the sample had passed seventy, 40% were in their fifties and sixties, which is graphic evidence of the success medicine had had in prolonging the lives of those ready for retirement.

The fact that half the beneficed clergy were over fifty prompts the question as to how many of them were unfit for work. The obvious place to turn to for information on this matter is diocesan records. Under the Residence Act of 1803,[140] an incumbent had to justify each instance of non-residence to his bishop. This novel intrusion into the clergy's private affairs produced a large spate of correspondence, and many bundles of forms; however the mass of material which has accumulated in county record offices is neither reliable nor informative. The documents filed under the 1803 Residence Act are quasi-legal: the bishop acted as judge, while the incumbent stood in the dock. No more than a cursory acquaintance with litigation is needed to appreciate that the evidence given by defendants is not always accurate; to preserve one's own liberty it can seem but a small thing to tell a little lie. Nor is this the only interpretative problem. Under the 1803 Act, ill-health was not the sole justification for a licence or exemption from residence; incumbents could also qualify on other grounds - 'residence in another living', for instance. A good number of those applying for licences or exemptions for reasons other than ill-health may have been unfit for work. As if this were not enough, there is the further difficulty that some ill incumbents resided in their benefices while employing an assistant curate to do duty for them. These resident clergy are not to be found in records to do with the 1803 Act.

Lacking detailed information, it is necessary to apply common sense to the problem. The paucity of clergy in their seventies and eighties is confirmation of the truth in the Biblical insight that three-score years and ten is the natural span of life. A man holding Nature at bay has little energy for anything else. On this ground, it is hard to escape the conclusion that regular performance of duty was impossible for most clergy over seventy. The same probably holds for a sizeable proportion of those over sixty. Incumbents in their fifties come in a different category. Some doubtless suffered bouts of occasional ill health, times when they began to feel their age, became aware of damp and cold, or found the routine of work a burden; a smaller number faced more serious problems, and were unfit all the time. By the same token, a few clergy under fifty were so ill that they could not reasonably be expected to carry out their duties.

These observations cannot be quantified in more than a rough and ready way. A figure of 10% for incumbents incapable of work marks the probable lower limit, since this would only include those who had passed their seventieth birthdays, plus a minute proportion of those who were younger. The upper limit could have been as high as 20%, but was probably not above 15%. The latter is still a formidably high figure. Among 7,500 incumbents,[141] it would mean that 1,125 were incapacitated. The problem of clerical old age, and consequent illness, was something no Georgian bishop could safely ignore. That they all did so, and did nothing whatever to rectify the situation, is more eloquent of the Georgian Bench than it is of the scope of the difficulty which the bishops faced.[142]

xiii. Knots

It is possible to make a *prima facie* justification for the failure of incumbents to reside, for almost every living in England and Wales. All that needs to be done is to make four assumptions, all reasonable enough. Residence, it can be claimed, could not be expected of the clergy on these counts: if there was not a parsonage; if the official accommodation was 'unfit'; if the benefice income was less than £150 a year; and if an incumbent was not fit for work. The first three of these assumptions can be quantified. At the end of 1833, they together justified non-residence from over 8,100 livings.[143] Benefices held by incapacitated clergy cannot be dealt with as neatly. The best guess is that these numbered between 1,050 and 1,575,[144] taking the total of justifiable instances of non-residence to within a range of 9,150 to 9,650. Since there were only 10,550 livings, the plight of the church looks desperate indeed, and it would seem a miracle that there were resident incumbents anywhere.

The situation was, in fact, less serious than these statistics suggest. Analysis of non-residence requires considerable refinement; as the earlier discussion of the spiral of neglect and decay has already indicated, there was much overlapping. Three-quarters of the livings without parsonages were to be found in places where the benefice income did not reach £150 a year; and the same is true of 40% of benefices with 'unfit' accommodation.[145] About half the livings with incapacitated clergy either did not bring in £150 a year or had something wrong with the parsonage.[146] The central problem of church reform can now be restated. At the end of 1833 there were, in round figures, 3,500 livings worth less than £150 a year; about 650 parishes worth over £150 a year were without parsonages; another 1,050 of these wealthier livings did not have 'fit' accommodation;[147] and there were, probably, between 525 and 785 places where the benefice income was reasonable and the parsonage was 'fit', but the incumbent was not.[148] These four categories come to 5,725-5,985, approaching six livings in every ten. To this total a single fine adjustment has to be made. A good number of the 'unfit' parsonages in the wealthier livings - perhaps as many as half - were not dilapidated. Allowing for these, justifiable failures of residence come down to a range of 5,225-5,475.

By no means all of these parishes, around half the total, had non-residents. There were poor clergy who resided and did duty in their parishes; there were incumbents who did not live in the official parsonage; there were the old and infirm who nevertheless carried on, until separated from their people by death. None of this is denied; on the contrary, it is most vigorously affirmed. What is denied is that the argument is in any way undermined. The Georgian church reform movement was, in the one thing that mattered, a failure. There were issues, poverty of benefices is an example, where much was achieved between 1700 and 1840; there were issues, the state of parsonages pre-eminently, where little was achieved; and there were issues, such as the plight of elderly clergy - where nothing ever could be achieved, because the issue was not seen to be an issue at all. But these individual successes and failures are, ultimately, beside the point. The rationale, of reform in the eyes of churchmen themselves, was the provision of a resident beneficed clergyman in every parish thoughout the land. This is what reform was about; it is also where the movement for reform conspicuously failed. The efforts made, though sometimes prodigious, were not prodigious enough. In 1833, it was true of half the benefices in England that they either did not meet the minimum requirement, agreed among contemporaries, for an incumbent's income - a requirement pitched at £150 a year - or that they did not provide fit accommodation for a clergyman to serve the parish, or that they were held by an incumbent who was not fit enough to work. The causes of failure are open to argument, but the fact of failure is not open to denial.

Chapter 6 Notes

1. Stephens, *Life and Letters of W.F. Hook*, I, 24-26; H.C. Maxwell Lyte, *A History of Eton College, 1440-1875*, pp.374-5; S. Butler, *The Life and Letters of Dr Samuel Butler*, I, 156, 158. For an alternative view of Georgian grammar schools, see Clark, *English Society*, pp.102-3.

2. Maxwell Lyte, *op.cit.*, p.370; P.M. Thornton, *Harrow School and its Surroundings*, p.242.

3. The source used here is *Chronicle of Convocation*, III, Appendix B, p.28. This, however, contains an error. It estimates ordinands in the period 1834-43 at 5,350: 2,076 from Oxford; 2,307 from Cambridge; 219 from Dublin; 83 from Durham; and 565 'literates'. The difficulty with this is that the sub-totals add up to 100 less than the aggregate figure. Haig, *The Victorian Clergy*, Table 2.2, p.32 argues that the number from Durham should be 183, not 83. Haig's argument makes sense.

4. E.H. Carter, *The Norwich Subscription Books*, p.47 and Table, p.55.

5. D.T.W. Price, *A history of Saint David's University College Lampeter*, p.5.

6. See below, p.135.

7. See below, pp.189-94.

8. E.B. Pusey, *Remarks on the Prospective and Past Benefits of Cathedral Institutions*, p.13. See also a pamphlet of 1834, 'what the grindstone is to the axe, that education ought to be to the mind' (*Letter to R.M. Beverley, Esq; By An Undergraduate*, p.21).

9. W.O. Chadwick, *The Founding of Cuddesdon*, p.6. On the origins of the University of Durham, see C.E. Whiting, *The University of Durham, 1832-1932*, p.33; and also Charles Thorp, *A Charge*, p.27, note.

10. Coleridge, *On the Constitution of Church and State*, p.36.

11. In a sample of 1,075 incumbents from four areas - Norfolk, Kent, Sussex, and Cumbria - the number of former dons was 175 (16.3%). In some other parts of the country, clerical academics were doubtless thinner on the ground.

12. Chadwick, *Cuddesdon*, p.2. On St Bees, see T. Park, *St Bees College, 1816-1895: a short history*; and on Lampeter, see Price, *op.cit.*

13. See, e.g., Pusey, *op.cit.*, pp.60-61; S. Butler, *Thoughts on Church Dignities*, p.10; and *Suggestions on Clerical Education: by a Late Fellow of Balliol*, pp.21-6.

14. On Wells, see E.L. Elwes, *The History of Wells Theological College*.

15. Smyth, *Simeon and Church Order*, p.98, 100.

16. *The Life and poetical Works of George Crabbe*, p.58.

17. G.S.R. Kitson Clark, *The Making of Victorian England*, p.261; A.M. Carr-Saunders and P.A. Wilson, *The Professions*, pp.109,133,155,157,178,299.

18. See above, p.132.

19. L. Stone, *The university in society*, Appendix IV, Table 1A, p.91.

20. *ibid.*, Appendix IV, Table 1B, p.92.

21. Calculations based on *ibid.*, Appendix IV, Table 1A, p.91 and Table 1B, p.92. Until the middle of the eighteenth century there are gaps in some college registers; figures for early decades are not, therefore, exact.

22. *ibid.*, Appendix IV, Table 1A, p.91 and Table 1B, p.92.

23. H. Jenkins and D.C. Jones, 'Social class of Cambridge University Alumni of the 18th and 19th centuries', *British Journal of Sociology*, I (1950), 99.

24. See below, Table XII.

25. According to Haig, *op.cit.*, Table 2.1, p.30 there were 3,840 admissions to Oxford between 1830 and 1839, while, between 1834 and 1843, there were 2,076 former Oxford students (54.1% of the figure for admissions in 1830-9) who became ordained. On the same basis, Cambridge ordinands were 54.0% of Cambridge matriculants at this period.

26. See above, p.90.

27. See also below, p.137.

28. See further on pluralism, below, pp.194-203.

29. See below, pp.161-2.

30. There is, in this connection, interesting correspondence between James Plumptre and his clerical cousin, John Lettice of Peasmarsh in Sussex. Lettice told Plumptre, in a letter of 6 December 1820, that 'I have been these two months unable from one ... circumstance or another to suit both myself & the Vicar of Rye with a successor [as curate] among Thirteen applicants'. Four disliked the accommodation that was offered; a further candidate lived too far away, and was therefore not known to local clergy; and some of the potential employees aroused Lettice's wrath - one had an 'Irish accent', another was 'all but a fast one; & getting loose'. The choice finally fell upon a young clerk, seeking to escape from the unhealthy environs of Romney Marsh. Lettice, as it turned out, could have done rather better. The new curate was consumptive, required constant medical supervision from the time of his arrival, and left within a year - C.U.L., Add. Mss. 5866, f.17,18,22.

31. In this, and subsequent, calculations, the method used is as follows. Average figures for Oxford and Cambridge matriculants are first derived from Stone, *op.cit.*, Appendix IV, Table 1A, p.91 and Table 1B, p.92. It is assumed that, on a constant basis, 50% of all Georgian matriculants later became ordained. Finally, the proportion of Oxbridge-trained ordinands is surmised - for the period 1700-29 a figure of 85% was thought likely. Ordinations would, of course, have lagged matriculations by five years or so, but this factor does not bring about material distortion, except in periods of rapid university expansion.

32. At this period the proportion of Oxbridge-trained ordinands is calculated at 70%.

33. In the first decade of the nineteenth century the average annual figure for aggregate admissions was 416, but between 1810 and 1819 the aggregate averaged 619, higher by 49%. Assuming that Oxbridge-trained ordinands were 80% of the total in the second decade as compared with 75% in the first, ordinations work out at an annual average of 387, 40% above the level of 277 achieved between 1800 and 1809. This calculation does not take into account the fact that, during a period of rapid university expansion, there will have been a time-lag of four or five years between rises in matriculations and rises in ordinations.

34. Assuming that 80% of all ordinands in the 1820s were Oxbridge-trained, the average annual figure for ordinations will have been 531, 37% higher than in the previous decade. Once again, time-lag effects have not been taken account of.

35. See below, pp.189-94.

36. See below, p.200.

37. See below, Table XI.

38. See above, pp. 37-9.

39. A.J. Engel, *From clergyman to don*, Appendix I, p.286 analyses a sample of men appointed

to college offices at Oxford in the period 1813-30; 92% were in Holy Orders.

40. Some figures on this matter, detailing the career choices of Cambridge alumni in the period 1841-3 to 1871-3, are to be found in Haig, *op.cit.*, Table 2.6, p.42. He shows that, in the mid-Victorian era, a clergyman was at least twice as likely to be a younger son as the eldest one. The same, we suspect, would hold of alumni in the period 1741-3 to 1771-3.

41. Fr Pius, *Life of Father Ignatius of St Paul*, p.99.

42. See, e.g., Blomfield, *A Memoir of C.J. Blomfield*, I, 57-9.

43. Robson, *The Attorney in Eighteenth-Century England*, Appendix II, p.159. This incident took place in 1775.

44. Herbert Marsh, an avid controversialist, Bishop of Llandaff, 1816-19, and of Peterborough, 1819-39; Henry Phillpotts, an even more avid controversialist, Bishop of Exeter, 1830-69.

45. F.W.B. Bullock, *The History of Ridley Hall, Cambridge*, II, 4.

46. Pius, *op.cit.*, pp.105, 122-3. Later, as Father Ignatius, Spencer became a well-known Passionist monk.

47. See below, Table XIII.

48. *ibid.*

49. Sykes, *Church and State*, p.189.

50. *ibid* pp. 201, 203-4.

51. G. Galbraith, ed., *The Journal of the Revd W.B. Stevens*, p.xi, xiii, xvi-xviii, xx-xxii, 485,487.

52. See below, Table XIII.

53. See above, p. 132.

54. See below, Table XIII.

55. See below, Table XIII.

56. See below, pp.161-2.

57. See below, pp.189-209.

58. The census for 1801 (*P.P.*, 1801-2, VII, 375) gives the population of Birmingham as 73,670; that for 1831 (*P.P.*, 1833, XXXVII, 678) arrives at a figure of 146,986.

59. Wigan, in 1841, contained 25,517 people (*P.P.*, 1843, XXIII, 141); and Preston, in the same year, 50,131 (*P.P.*, 1843, XXIII, 137).

60. The figures in the 1821 census were: 8,809 for Hammersmith; 6,492 for Fulham; 4,206 for Twickenham; and 863 for Teddington (*P.P.*, 1822, XV, 190-2).

61. See above, p.34 ; see also *Hansard*, Third Series, LVII, 1067-8; and Chadwick, *The Victorian Church*, I, 327.

62. The most important pieces of legislation in this field are the Church Building Act of 1818 (58 Geo. III c.45) and Peel's Act (6 & 7 Vic. c.37). Other laws include 59 Geo. III c.134; 3 Geo.IV c.42; and 1 & 2 Will.IV c.38.

63. See above, pp.33-4.

64. Smyth, *op.cit.*, pp.256-7.

65. Statistics from *P.P.*, 1835, XXII, 708-99.

66. Statistics from *ibid.*, 484-535. The full figures were: 104 parishes with fewer than 500 people; 45 with between 500 and 1,000; 23 with 1,000 to 2,000; 13 with 2,000 to 5,000; and the same number with more.

67. See also, below, pp. 151-5

68. Note, in this connection, an admonitory diary entry dated 10 May 1830, made by Francis Witts, 'By many among our Country clergy the composition of original sermons is far too much

neglected; disuse begets distrust of one's own powers, and a disinclination to the labour' - *The Diary of a Cotswold Parson*, p.87.

69. See also, below, pp. 155-7.

70. See, also, W.M. Jacob, 'A Practice of a very hurtful tendency', *Studies in Church History*, xvi (1979), 316, 'although many of the manner books insist on the duty of a clergyman to visit his flock, this does not seem to have happened to any considerable extent'.

71. According to Ecton (see above, pp. 70-1) there were 3,826 livings worth under £50 a year in the first decade of the eighteenth century, but this source understates the true number. In 1830, the total for benefices in the same category was 297 (see above, p. 71).

72. According to the Ecclesiastical Revenues Commission, the figure for livings worth under £150 a year was 3,528 (see above, p. 54).

73. See above, p. 71.

74. Statistics from *P.P.*, 1835, XXII, 111-1,057.

75. This was Norfolk. The full figures are: 88 livings under median value (30.6%) not held in plurality, and 200 (69.4%) in plurality; among livings above the median, 116 (40.4%) not in plurality, and 171 (59.6%) in plurality.

76. The margin was 7% in Kent. Here 76 livings (42.0%) under the median were not held in plurality, and 105 (58.0%) were; above the median, 88 (48.9%) not in plurality, and 92 (51.1%) in plurality. It was in Sussex that the margin was 5%. Here 54 livings (38.6%) under the median were not held in plurality, and 86 (61.4%) were held in plurality; and, above the median, 61 (43.9%) not in plurality, as against 78 (56.1%) in so. The median was £257 a year in Kent, £249 in Norfolk, and £212 in Sussex.

77. The full figures for Cumbria were: 75 livings under the median (73.5%) not in plurality, as compared with only 27 (26.5%); and, above the median, 46 (45.1%) not in plurality, but 56 (54.9%) in so.

78. *P.P.*, 1835, XXII, 1060. The figure given is 2,878.

79. Savidge, *The Parsonage of England*, pp.8-10.

80. Guy, 'Perpetual curacies in Eighteenth-Century South Wales', *Studies in Church History*, XVI (1979), 329-30 points out that there were forty-two perpetual curacies in the diocese of Llandaff in the early years of the eighteenth century. Forty-one of these had no parsonage at all; the exception was Peterston Wentloog - there the glebe house was in ruins.

81. See above, pp. 65-70.

82. *P.P.*, 1818, XVIII, 359; *P.P.*, 1835, 1060. The figure in 1818 was 2,626.

83. *ibid.* The figure was 2,183 in the earlier return, and 1,728 in the later.

84. See also, above, pp. 66-7.

85. *P.P.*, 1818, XVIII, 296.

86. Savidge, *op.cit.*, pp.30-1.

87. William Cobbett, *Rural Rides*, p.366; *P.P.*, 1818, XVIII, 325.

88. *P.P.*, 1818, XVIII, 297,285. These answers, it is interesting to relate, were similar to some of the responses that Wake and Gibson received from the Lincolnshire clergy in the first two decades of the eighteenth century ; see R.E.G. Cole, ed., *Speculum*, pp.xv-xvi.

89. S.L. Ollard and P.C. Walker, *Archbishop Herring's Visitation Returns*, IV,59, quoted in Savidge, *op.cit.*, p.88.

90. *ibid.*, p.159.

91. One example of such a family is the Crawleys. They achieved the feat at two places - Stow

and Heyford - both in Northants (see H.I. Longden, *Northamptonshire and Rutland Clergy from 1500*, III, 287-93). The same author refers to two other similar families, the Ishams and the Knightleys (VII, 209-27; VIII, 129-39).

92. See below, p.224.

93. The sources used here are: *P.P.*, 1835, XXII,111-1052; *Clerical Guide*, 1829 and 1836; Venn, *Alumni*; Foster, *Alumni*; and the *Gentleman's Magazine*.

94. See, for instance, McClatchey, *Oxfordshire Clergy*, p.23.

95. Nowell C. Smith, *The Letters of Sydney Smith*, I,160,214,268,362,418; Savidge, *op.cit.*, p.85,87; and Pearson, *The Smith of Smiths*, pp.163-6. Much of this material is most amusing. Further examples of grandiose Georgian parsonages, this time from the diocese of Worcester, are to be found in Leatherbarrow, 'The Rise and Decline of the Squarson', pp. 184-92.

96. Unhappily, the fruits of Sydney's endeavours can no longer be seen; the parsonage at Foston was burnt down to its walls in 1962 - Savidge, *op.cit*, p.87.

97. See above, p. 73.

98. Savidge, *op.cit.*, pp.13-48,151.

99. *Diary*, I, 181,191-4; v, 261,337,397.

100. *ibid.*, III, 217-18; IV, 245.

101. *ibid.*, II, 340; IV, 138,303,310.

102. *ibid.*, V, 313; Venn, *Alumni*, Part II, I, 215.

103. Arthur Warne, *Church and Society in Eighteenth-Century Devon*, pp.38-9,42. In the diocese of Worcester, in 1782, the situation was worse; among 212 parishes, there were 49 (23%) where duty was done by beneficed clergy who did not hold the cure - see Mary Ransome, *The State of the Bishopric of Worcester*, p.14. Things were little different in Oxfordshire. In this county, in 1778, among 165 parishes there were 40 (24%) where duty was done by neighbouring incumbents - McClatchey, *op.cit.*, Table, p.31.

104. Details of the Norwich diocesan records are in the Bibliography.

105. Walter Rye, *A History of Norfolk*, p.245.

106. C.M. Hoare, *A Short History of the Parish of Mundesley*, pp.29-30,52.

107. Rye, *op.cit.*, p.244.

108. 53 Geo.III c.149. See also, below, pp.222-41.

109. For further information on the Ardens, see below, pp.181-2.

110. There is a mass of information on this topic in Mather, 'Georgian Churchmanship Reconsidered', *J.E.H.*, XXXVI (1985), 255-83.

111. Judged against a national yardstick, frequency of services in the two deaneries was very low indeed - see Mather, *op.cit.*, Table, 267.

112. There is evidence that things were also improving elsewhere in the first three decades of the nineteenth century. Diana McClatchey found that this was the case in Oxfordshire (see *Oxfordshire Clergy*, pp.80-2); and Mather (*op.cit.*, 269) has detected a 'favourable trend' in Essex and Hertfordshire, in the archdeaconry of Chichester, and in the two south Lancashire deaneries of Manchester and Warrington.

113. In a nationwide context, frequency of Holy Communion in the Georgian period is analysed in Mather, *op.cit.*, Table, 271.

114. On catechising, see Russell, *The Clerical Profession*, pp.130-41; also Mather, *op.cit.*, 279-81.

115. See also, below, pp.196-7. Bathurst was Bishop of Norwich, 1805-37.

116. In support of this contention, see the evidence referred to in note 112, above.

117. Sykes, *Church and State*, pp.186-7.

118. See Table XIX.

119. *ibid*. It had been intended to set up Manchester in 1836, but the plan ran into difficulties. Establishment of the new diocese depended on the union of Bangor and St Asaph; and this could not occur until one or other of these bishops either died, resigned, or was translated. This event was postponed until 1846. Opposition to the union of the two dioceses then revived, but the decision to set up Manchester on its own was nonetheless taken in 1848.

120. Sykes, *op.cit.*, p.94.

121. White Kennet, dean of Peterborough, to Bishop Wake of Lincoln in 1712, quoted in Sykes, *op.cit.*, p.93.

122. *ibid.*, p.136.

123. See *ibid.*, p.147 for comparisons of the church with the army.

124. *ibid*, p.136.

125. Chadwick, *The Victorian Church*, I, 237.

126. P.T. Marsh, *The Victorian Church in Decline*, p.96.

127. See Best, *Temporal Pillars*, Appendix VI, p.545.

128. There was nothing new about the administrative problems that stemmed from frequent translations. Between 1600 and 1635, seventy bishops were consecrated; thirty-three of these were subsequently translated to other sees. Between 1800 and 1835, on the other hand, there were forty-one consecrations. Among these new bishops, there were twenty-seven who were translated at least once, always to a see with higher value ; Coolidge, 'The Finances of the Church of England', pp.31-2.

129. Kaye's efforts to curb the activities of non-resident, negligent, and immoral clergy are described in R. Foskett, 'John Kaye and the Diocese of Lincoln', pp.108-36.

130. See below, pp.205-6.

131. Cleaver's career - Bishop of Chester (1787), of Bangor (1800), and of St Asaph (1806) - is a neat illustration of the harm done by frequent translations.

132. *H.M.C.: Report of the Manuscripts of J.B. Fortescue*, VI,21. There is a lot of interesting information in this volume to do with plans of church reform at the turn of the nineteenth century.

133. 21 Henry VIII c.13.

134. *The Constitutions and Canons Ecclesiastical*, p.19.

135. 43 Geo.III c.84. For further information on the 1803 Residence Act, see below, p.194.

136. Sir William Scott, House of Commons, 7 April 1802, *Hansard*, XXXVI, 490.

137. 1 and 2 Vic. c.106.

138. If, which Heaven forbid, the reader is minded to challenge the claim that the Georgian clergy's longevity is remarkable and worthy of wonder, it need only be pointed out that, over the succeeding century and a half, very little change occurred in this regard. This emerges from a study of the Anglican clergy, published in 1977, by Stewart Ranson, Alan Bryman, and Bob Hinings. The three authors found that, in the mid 1970s, 57% of those in Orders were under fifty - the median age would seem to have been a shade over forty-six (see S. Ranson, A. Bryman and B. Hinings, *Clergy, ministers and priest*, Table, p.24). Although these statistics are not fully comparable with my own - Ranson, Bryman and Hinings include non-beneficed clergy in their sample, whereas I do not - the distortion is not too serious, because many curates took a long time to find a first benefice in the Georgian era. It would, indeed, be doubtful whether the age profile of any occupational grouping - in any community, and in any part of the world - changed

as little as that of the Anglican beneficed clergy over the century and a half between 1830 and 1980.

139. See Table XV. There are, also, some interesting statistics about the situation in Devon a little earlier, in 1821. In that year, apparently, more than a third of the beneficed clergy in the county had been in Orders for at least thirty-one years - see Michael Cook, *The Diocese of Exeter in 1821*, II, xii.

140. See further, below, p. 194.

141. See above, p. 90.

142. It must, in fairness, be added, that the failure to introduce an effective pension scheme for clergy is also a charge that can be levelled against the Victorian Bench. Nothing was done about the matter until the passing of the Incumbents' Resignation Acts of 1871 and 1887. These pieces of legislation had crippling defects. Pensions were restricted to beneficed clergy; more seriously, the chosen method of funding left more than a little to be desired - incumbents were to be paid pensions out of the proceeds of the livings they had earlier held. A satisfactory pension scheme for the English clergy was not introduced until the Clergy Pensions Measure of 1926 (Peter C. Hammond, *The Parson and the Victorian Parish*, pp.41-2; Best, *op.cit.*, pp.505-6,511; Haig, *op.cit.*, pp. 319-29).

143. As at the end of 1833, there were 2,878 parishes without a parsonage at all, and there were 1,728 places where the parsonage was unfit (see above, p.147). In addition, according to the 1835 Report, there were 3,528 benefices where the income did not reach £150 a year. The sum of these three categories is 8,134.

144. It has already been argued (see above, p.162) that the total number of incapacitated clergy was probably between 750 and 1,125. In a later section (see below, p.201), it is shown that the ratio of livings to incumbents was 1.4:1. The figure of 1,050-1,575 is arrived at by applying this multiplier to the probable number of incumbents who were unfit for work.

145. In the three counties of Kent, Norfolk and Sussex, there were 325 benefices which did not bring in £150 a year. Among these, 205 (63.1%) lacked parsonages altogether, and 62 (19.1%) did not have 'fit' accommodation. This large sample, it is assumed, is typical of England and Wales as a whole; of the total of 3,528 livings worth under £150 a year, 2,222 (63%) did not have a parsonage and 670 (19%) had 'unfit' accommodation. Since the total number of parishes without parsonages was 2,878, it follows by deduction that there were 656 places where the benefice income was over £150 a year and where there was not a parsonage. Similarly, the total number of places with unfit accommodation was 1,728; 670 of these officially dilapidated parsonages were to be found in benefices worth under £150 a year, and the remainder - a total of 1,058 - were in livings which brought in a larger amount.

146. There were 3,528 livings worth under £150 a year. Among livings worth over £150 a year, it is calculated that 656 did not have parsonages and 1,058 had 'unfit' accommodation. These three categories add up to 5,242. Since the total number of livings was around 10,500, it follows that half either brought in less than £150 a year, or had something wrong with the parsonage. It is assumed that a similar situation pertained among livings in the possession of incapacitated clergy.

147. See above, note 145.

148. Livings held by ill clergy, it is argued, numbered between 1,050 and 1,575 (see above, note 144). Around half of these were worth over £150 a year, and also had 'fit' parsonages (see above, note 146). Hence the figure of 525 to 785.

7

The Patrons

i. *Distribution*

Patronage, in the politics of the eighteenth century, was power. In certain instances the influence wielded by a patron could be described, in an exaggerated phrase, as a form of crypto-feudalism. The medieval tenant-in-chief had his band of retainers, to all intents and purposes a private army; the Georgian politician had his lackeys and his fags, men moulded by his will. This, however, was exceptional; loyalty was not usually synonymous with servility. Patronage, in normal circumstances, was expected to act as a kind of glue, whose function was to hold together the numerous interests and factions which shared, in so many instances, the common characterisic of being threatened with imminent fragmentation. The hope was that an appointment to a post here, or a post there, might be used to broaden an allegiance or to strengthen ties of family and friendship; but things, needless to say, did not always work out as planned. A patron's fondly cherished hopes were often dashed to the ground, as some protégé was encouraged by the bestowal of a little gift to seek another little gift from someone else. The important thing is that patronage was accepted as axiomatic: that the assumptions upon which it rested - that ties of financial interest should be also ties of party and that the forms taken by patronage were a wholly appropriate exercise of influence - were not questioned.

Patronage was sacrosanct among the political community, and it was equally sacrosanct within the ecclesiastical establishment. Erastianism was triumphant. The right of royal appointment to bishoprics was not challenged; nor, equally, was there strong opposition to lay patronage. What was natural to the state, went the argument, was natural within the church. When churchmen grumbled, they grumbled about abuses, and about what were seen as betrayals of natural justice. Foremost among abuses was simony; and foremost among betrayals of natural justice was the failure of lay patrons to pay adequate stipends to those perpetual curates serving the very parishes from which they drew a large portion of their wealth.[1] If there was any crypto-feudalism in the Georgian church, it was embodied in the relationship between the powerful lay patron and the powerless perpetual curate.

The strength of lay patronage was that it derived its ultimate sanction from lay endowment. The right to appoint was given to a layman because he had supplied the means to make appointment possible; in a sense, the power which patronage brought with it was justly earned. This relationship between endowment and appointment was already established in medieval times. Usually, a patron gained possession of the advowson, which was the right to choose, in perpetuity, the incumbent of a place; he could also hold a number of presentations, which was the right to fill a stated number of successive vacancies. Split ownership, both of an advowson and of a next presentation, was possible. The monasteries, forward in the work of endowment, held many advowsons; and most of these, together with the monastic tithes and the monastic lands, passed at the Reformation to laity. The lay patron had been a medieval figure; but, as from the sixteenth century, he became dominant.

The principle that gifts of endowment conferred rights of patronage was not confined to individuals; it applied equally to public bodies. One group of these, namely Oxford and Cambridge colleges,regarded the possession of a scattering of rectories and vicarages as necessary to their proper functioning. Virtually all dons were clergymen;[2] and it was argued that some means had to be found of removing from college life those who were considered unsatisfactory, as well as of 'providing' for dons who wished to marry; appointment to a college living met both requirements admirably. In other cases, ecclesiastical patronage was used as an instrument of power, not as a vehicle of policy. It was the Crown, the grammar schools, and the municipal corporations who found themselves in the happy position of being able to do this. The Crown and the schools held on to their advowsons throughout the eighteenth and early nineteenth centuries, but the rights of municipalities were ended by the Corporations Act of 1835.

The laity and corporate bodies did not monopolise ecclesiastical patronage; rights of appointment belonged also to bishoprics and chapters. As from the middle of the nineteenth century, the Bench began to extend its influence by encroaching upon other forms of patronage; but there is no hint of this in the eighteenth century. On the contrary, as the Whigs in general - and the Duke of Newcastle in particular - refined the processes of control and worked to grasp the minutiae of individual interest and concern, appointments to bishoprics and to the wealthier cathedral posts came to be more and more part of day-to-day political management.[3] Since more bishops now owed their promotion to their political dependability, the administration of the day, through these same bishops, strengthened its indirect hold over many of the vicarages and rectories that made up the parochial system.

The chapters and the bishops had a share in ecclesiastical patronage, as had the parochial clergy. Sometimes, as with bishoprics and capitular bodies, rights belonged to the office rather than the person. In some parishes, especially some urban parishes, appointment lay with whoever happened to hold a nearby vicarage or rectory. Usually, there were long-standing historical reasons for this. Other clergy held patronage in their own right. Being a clergyman was no bar to owning, or inheriting, an advowson or next presentation. This liberal view of things was taken a stage further: a cleric who owned an advowson was permitted, under ecclesiastical law, to appoint himself.[4] Quirkish though it may seem, an incumbent was not permitted to appoint himself if he held only the next presentation, without the perpetual advowson.[5]

A comprehensive survey of ecclesiastical patronage, covering over 10,700 advowsons and next presentations in England and Wales, was completed in 1830.[6] In broad outline, the situation which the survey describes was similar a century and a quarter earlier, when this study begins.[7] Private patrons were by far the largest group: they held 48% of all advowsons. Next, somewhat surprisingly, come the capitular and parochial clergy with 24%, half as many as the laity. The neat pattern of distribution does not end here. The capitular and parochial clergy held 24% of all advowsons, and the next group - their ecclesiastical superiors, the bishops - had 12%. The bishops were followed by the Crown, with 9%; and colleges, schools, corporations and a miscellaneous group of 'other' patrons brought up the rear, with the remaining 7%. The hierarchy of power is thus clear-cut. Laity with half of all advowsons; capitular and parochial clergy with a quarter; bishops with an eighth; the Crown with a little under a tenth; and the rest divided among schools, colleges and corporations. Such was the situation in 1830, on the eve of the Victorian era.

What held nationally did not always hold regionally. Ecclesiastical patronage was itself an outcrop of the historical deposit of local power and influence. Where a landowner was dominant, the probability was that he held more advowsons than his neighbours. Where manors were thick on the ground, laymen tended to hold a higher proportion of advowsons than elsewhere. Incumbents had 10% of all advowsons in some counties, but in others the figure was 20%.[8] Laymen could have half, they could have much more, or they could have less than a tenth.[9] In Devon, in 1782, the Bishop of Exeter had the right to present to 17 places, the Dean and Chapter of Exeter had 40 presentations, the Crown could muster 38, and private patrons held 254; most of the remainder were in the gift of university colleges and extradiocesan capitular bodies.[10] If the bishops were weak in Devon, they were far from weak in Kent. Here power, and the abuse of power, lay with the Archbishop of Canterbury. There were 361 parishes in the county, of which 130 (36.0%) were held by the Bench, with the great majority being in the gift of the Primate. Only 100 Kentish benefices (27.7% of the total) were held by laymen.[11]

Distribution of patronage rights, as between the different categories of patron, was not fixed in any rigid and immutable mould. The Crown sometimes ceded advowsons to laymen, and laymen sometimes ceded them to clergymen. Change took place in several ways: Crown patronage was given as a reward for political or other services; family history played a part, particularly when estates, with advowsons attached, descended to clergy; thirdly, and most pertinent, patronage rights could change hands in the market place. Advowsons were treated like other types of property, and thus could be, and sometimes were, either auctioned or sold privately. Lay patrons were able to accumulate handfuls of livings in this way, subsequently filling them, as they fell vacant, with their sons, relatives and clerical friends.

This fluidity was, nevertheless, peripheral. Although the lineal extinction of a family, or sheer financial necessity, could bring about a sudden shift, this did not happen frequently. The decision to dispose of a living was not taken lightly. Always, on such occasions, there lurked in the shadowed corners of a patron's mind nagging doubts, feelings about his duty to 'provide' for sons and sons-in-law. It was nepotistic considerations like these which also kept ecclesiastical patronage close-knit. Aristocrats presented aristocrats, related by ties or other blood, marriage, or friendship; bishops presented family and friends, as did Lord Chancellors; Oxford and Cambridge colleges filled their livings from among the members of their own high table fellowship. The clergy were more transparently self-seeking, presenting themselves. Nepotism was the link that joined together every interest. It was the source of a common psychological attitude, and of a common practice.[12]

ii. *Laymen*

Aristocratic influence was not all bad. The benefactions made to the Royal Bounty Fund and the Parliamentary Grants Fund came from 'those who counted'; and it was 'those who counted' who gave strong support, throughout the nineteenth century, to the church's educational effort. On the darker side, the wealthy lay impropriator was an anomaly that no twist of logic could justify. A situation that permitted the impropriator to take all the tithes of a parish, only paying in return a minimal sum to a perpetual curate, was inevitably a source of irritation. Laud attacked the evil, as did Burnet, but nothing was done about it. In the early nineteenth century, complaints were still being made on this score, but the rights of wealthy laity, protected in parliament by wealthy laity, were left undisturbed.

It is unwise however to generalise about the exercise of lay patronage. The contention that aristocracy and gentry were always a recruiting sergeant for pluralism does not hold. Some lay patrons encouraged pluralism to thrive, while others stifled it. What determined the practice of patronage was not whether a patron happened to be a bishop or an earl, but the number of livings he had in his gift. It was the accumulation of advowsons which led to an increase in pluralism. Patrons with five or ten livings were more pluralistic in their practice than those with only two or three, but the decisive contrast is between these groups and those with only one. What counts in any given district is not the distribution of patronage rights among the categories of patron, both lay and ecclesiastical, but the extent to which power had been concentrated in a few hands.

Norfolk vividly illustrates these truths. Private patronage was strong there because the local squirearchy was strong, and there was a pyramid of power, topped by a group of laymen with five advowsons or more. The most powerful were the most famous. Eleven families had five advowsons or more in their gift, and at least one member who had made, at some period, a weighty contribution to national political life. The Walpoles jostle the Townshends and Howards, names redolent of England's history. There could scarcely be a better example of aristocratic patronage at work.

Around 1830, two Norfolk private patrons held five presentations each. One of these was Sir Jacob Astley, who later took the title of Lord Hastings. The pick of his patronage had gone to the Revd H.N. Astley, third son of Sir Edward, the fourth Baronet; he had two livings, bringing in an income of £1,145 a year. Two more livings were held by the Revd Augustus Dashwood, another close relative: he was Sir Jacob's brother-in-law, having married his sister, Hester. As befitted a son-in-law rather than a son, the income of the Revd Augustus Dashwood, at £807 a year, was less than that of H.N. Astley. The final living had gone to Sir Jacob's chaplain, Caleb Elwin. He held, in all, four livings, including two sinecure rectories. It was said of him that he spent the 'greater portion' of his life at Melton Constable, Sir Jacob's 'princely mansion'.

The other family with five presentations were the Marshams of Stratton Strawless. Prominent in Norfolk society since at least the reign of Henry I, the family was now led by Robert (1783-1855), sometime High Sheriff of Norfolk. Two of the best livings in this family's patronage had, as their incumbent, Robert's son, Edward, who also held a third, for an income of £1,060 a year. The best living of all, Haynford, was not held nepotistically at this time, although it was to achieve this dubious distinction a little later, in 1836, when it was offered to Robert's son-in-law, W.A.W. Keppel, a younger son of Frederick Keppel of Lexham Hall. Keppel had been ordained in 1828. Soon afterwards, he had been presented by the Marshams to another Norfolk benefice, Brampton. It was this living he forsook in 1836 for Haynford.

Horatio Walpole (1783-1858), Earl of Orford, and sometime MP for King's Lynn, was patron of six livings, one of which, Itteringham, was held nepotistically. Its incumbent, Robert Walpole, classical scholar and traveller, was a grandson of Horatio, first Baron Walpole. Up until 1828 Robert also held Tivetshall, easily the best living in the family's patronage, but in that year he exchanged it for the equally rich metropolitan benefice of Christ Church, Marylebone. Tivetshall was now held by John White, the son of a Nottingham butcher. The other four livings had all gone to pluralists. Two - Alby and North Barsham - had been given to the same incumbent, the Revd Horatio Dowsing. Wolterton had as its rector a certain Stephen Allen, who was reputed to have lost a fortune in early life through extravagance.

The Wyndhams had estates in Yorkshire, the west country, and Kent, besides Norfolk. Their Norfolk stronghold was Felbrigg Hall. Patronage in 1830 was in the hands of Admiral William Wyndham, who, like Horatio Walpole, had the right to present incumbents to six livings, all except one of which were held by pluralists. The best two, Aylmerton and Felbrigg, had gone to the Revd Cremer Cremer, whose brother-in-law was a certain George Thomas Wyndham; George Thomas was the son-in-law of Admiral William. The small perpetual curacy of Sistead, along with another poor living, Ingworth, was held by the Revd Paul Johnson.

An other interest with six livings was the Hammonds, a family of lesser gentry who find no place in any of the standard textbooks on pedigree. Their two best livings, Great Bircham and Harpley - both previously held by the Walpoles - had gone to the same incumbent, W. Pratt; another cleric, the Revd George Coldham, had also been given a brace, being rector of both Gaytonthorpe and East Walton.

Bernard Edward, twelfth Duke of Norfolk, was head of a family unique among the English nobility for the frequency of its apostasy. The durability of the religious reversionary interest is, in every way, remarkable. Only one of the first thirteen dukes adopted his father's faith for life.[13] Bernard Edward's father had been a Protestant, so he himself was a Roman Catholic. The twelfth Duke held the title from 1815 until 1842, having inherited it from his Protestant cousin, Charles (1786-1815). The attitude of the Protestant duke towards the selection of suitable clergy to fill the family's seven livings was unconventional; and this trait was shared by his Roman Catholic successor. Only one incumbent, Thomas Sworde, held two livings in the Norfolk's patronage, both rather contemptible, being valued at £50 and £55 respectively. As with the Hammonds, two livings were held by non-pluralists, and there was no nepotism. In its practice of ecclesiastical patronage the house of Howard stands in splendid isolation, at a distance from others among Norfolk's powerful peerage and gentry.

Three interests are recorded as having eight benefices in their patronage. One of these - the Townshends - would have had nine, if the rectory of Stiffkey had been returned to the Ecclesiastical Revenues Commission. The rector of Stiffkey at this time was the Revd and Hon Frederick Townshend (1767-1836), a younger son of the first marquess. He failed to make any return, because he was insane. His mental instability can be traced back to a mysterious incident in the mid 1790s, soon after he had been presented to Stiffkey. Lord Frederick had driven up to London with his younger brother, Lord Charles, the latter hot from an electoral triumph at Yarmouth. As the post-chaise had driven into Oxford Street, Lord Charles had been found, shot dead, with a bullet in the brain. His death was never satisfactorily explained, and Lord Frederick failed to recover his mental composure after this event.

The other act of nepotism perpetrated by the Townshends was more prosaic; the pluralistic incumbent of Helhoughton was the Revd Arthur Loftus, who had married a daughter of the first marquess. Two clergymen had each received a pair of livings. One of these was Richard Phayre, incumbent of St Mary Coslany at Norwich, and also of Rainham. Ordained in 1831, he had been presented to both livings the following year, and they brought him in a good annual income of £721. The other pluralist was Thomas Bland, incumbent of Toftrees and Rudham; his income was £531 a year.

The Lombes were rising gentry. The name is met with in mid sixteenth-century Norfolk, but it was not until the eighteenth century that the family began to make its mark, partly as a result of marriage into the Marshams. Patronage was in the hands of Sir Edward Lombe. Sir Edward was in full agreement with fashionable nepotistic principle. Two livings - Scarning and Bawdeswell - had gone to the Revd P.D. Duval Aufrere, a relative by marriage; Eccles by the Sea was held by Edward Evans, a relative by blood; and a small perpetual curacy, Bylaugh, had been given to the Revd Henry Evans, great-nephew of Sir John Lombe, the aristocrat from whom Sir Edward had inherited his baronetcy in 1817. At Lyng the incumbent was Henry Anson, a younger son of the previous patron. He had been presented by his father, and was still there in 1833. All four of these clergymen were pluralists. Two more livings, Sparham and Foxley, had been given by Sir Edward to the Revd James Stoughton, lord of the manor of Sparham. Lombe patronage was worth £905 a year to him. Only Swanton Morley was not held in plurality, and this, curiously enough, was the best living in the family's patronage, being valued at £920 a year.

The other family with eight livings was that of Wodehouse, represented by John, created Baron Wodehouse of Kimberley in 1797. His third son, the Hon and Revd Armine, held three livings - Barnham Broome, West Lexham and Litcham - all in the family's gift, the only instance in which a powerful Norfolk patron was solely responsible for creating a triple pluralist. Armine's brother, the Hon and Revd William, was even more fortunate. He had received a pair of benefices from his father; and he also had another living in Cornwall. Armine's income was £928 a year, while his brother's was £1,192. Nepotism may have prompted a further choice of incumbent - at Bacton was the Revd G.L.W. Fauquier, the third initial standing, as it happens, for Wodehouse. This accounts for six of the eight advowsons in the family's patronage. The others, Crowthorpe and Rundall - neither of them opulent - had gone to the Revd J.J. Browne, master of Hingham Grammar School.

In 1822 Coke of Holkham married, as his second wife, Lady Anne Keppel, third daughter of William Charles, fourth Earl of Albermarle. Only one living among the nine in Coke's gift was worth more than £500 a year. This was Tittleshall, valued at £871. Installed there, as from 1826, was the Revd E.S. Keppel, fourth son of Coke's father-in-law. Keppel had received a further benefice from his father, making a total income of £1,377 a year. Coke could also claim some connection with the Revd W.H. Langton of St Mary's, Warham, the second best piece of preferment in his patronage. Langton was impropriator of Longford in Derbyshire: Coke was patron of Longford in Derbyshire. Two small perpetual curacies, Longham and Wendling, had gone to the Revd James Hoste, who held them along with two others. The other five livings had been given to different clergy, three of them pluralists and two of them not.

Sir Habord Habord, third Baron Suffield, was active and energetic in the county. Besides being chairman of Quarter Sessions, he established Norfolk Cricket Club and promoted allotments for the the labourers on his estates. He was the most powerful lay patron, holding eleven presentations, most of them to livings of moderate value. The Suffields were not as yet a clerical family - the first member to become ordained was one of the third Baron's eight sons, and he did not take orders until the 1850s. The third Baron was therefore deprived of the opportunity to become a nepotist, but he did not allow this consideration to prevent him from promoting pluralism. The best living in his gift, Blickling, had gone to the Revd J.D. Churchill, who held three others; and there are two instances of a pair being given to the same incumbent. Altogether, eight of the eleven were held by pluralists, and only three were not. It only remains to add that among his many accomplishments, Sir Habord Habord was to gain a reputation as an ardent church reformer , frequently delivering eloquent speeches in the House of Lords against every form of ecclesiastical abuse.[14]

Of the eighty benefices over which these eleven families held sway, only thirteen (16%) were not held in plurality. Twenty-four (30%) had been given to relatives by blood or marriage; in one instance a patron - Baron Wodehouse - had presented the same incumbent (his son) to three livings; and in eighteen instances these Norfolk laymen had presented the same incumbent to two livings. Only three patrons out of eleven were not nepotistic. One of the three was the Hammonds, whose lack of established social standing has already received comment; another was Baron Suffield, whose family lacked at this time any members in Orders; the third was the Duke of Norfolk.[15]

Norfolk patrons with between two advowsons and four promoted pluralism only marginally less than those with five or more. Three laymen held four livings each, seven had three, and thirty-four each had two. This makes 44 patrons for 101 livings, and seventy-nine of these (78.2%) were held in plurality. The difference between the practice of this group and the practice of the most powerful laity - who promoted pluralism in 67 instances out of 80 (84%) - is not material.

When rights of patronage were well distributed, a radically different situation pertained. Private patrons in Norfolk holding only a single advowson numbered 107, and these laymen fostered as much pluralism as was found throughout England and Wales as a whole; their practice was typical, while that of the Walpoles and Townshends was not. In England and Wales, in 1830, 52% of all parishes were held with another or others;[16] and for livings in Norfolk where the lay patron held only a single benefice in the county the percentage was also 52%. Norfolk private patrons with more than one advowson presented pluralists in eight instances out of ten, and the weakest patrons in Norfolk presented pluralists in five cases out of ten.

It would, however, be wrong to conclude that diffusion of patronage rights was an avenue to reform which was not beset by any obstacles: there was nothing to prevent several squires - each with a single piece of bounty to bestow - from rewarding the same incumbent, albeit at decent intervals. Whether they acted in this way, or whether they did not, depended upon the posture they adopted towards ecclesiastical patronage. It seems that the peerage, when holding sparse patronage rights, established pluralism more frequently than gentry in the same situation. This no doubt reflects their better social connections, as well as the higher financial expectations they would assume clergy under their patronage to have. In Kent, as already noticed,[17] the laity held only 100 presentations; and these, moreover, were shared among 77 individuals, with no private patron possessing more than three. Despite these facts it still was true that, in 62 instances, livings in lay hands in the county were held with another or others. The typical Kentish private patron was more pluralistic than average, despite diffusion of power. Part of the explanation lies in the fact that 17 out of the 77 were peers, a high figure.

If a private patron wanted to become really powerful, he was advised to concentrate his energies as far away as possible from London. Rich livings were fewer, but this was compensated for by lack of competition from other landowners. The success of the Lowthers illustrates what could be achieved. Of 82 livings in lay hands in Cumberland and Westmorland, this family owned 31. In Norfolk, huge though it was, the maximum accumulation was eleven; in Sussex, the Earl of Egremont - famous for his patronage of Turner - had fifteen; and in Kent, no private patron had more than three.

Analysis of the Lowthers' practice emphasises a different point. Livings in the family's gift were divided into two categories - 'good' and 'bad'. Each was treated according to different principles, the 'good' being reserved for pluralists and the 'bad' being given to non-pluralists. Twenty Lowther benefices were above the median Cumbrian value of £102 a year, and sixteen of these had pluralistic incumbents; but among the eleven others that were worth under the median, pluralists held only two.

Regional idiosyncracy is a reccurring theme in this book. The typical constantly proves elusive, and the facts stubbornly refuse to fit any tidy formula. Private patronage confirms this more fully than is usual. Historians are, today, sensitive to the subtle tones of locality. There is a wary and just reticence, a retreat from the easy generalisation of the past. Somerset is not Surrey, and Durham is not Derbyshire. Reality, nevertheless, still wears the robes of shock. How could it be that there were 21 private patrons with four advowsons or more in one rich county (Norfolk) and none at all in another (Kent)? Why were private patrons dominant in Devon? How was it that concentrations of patronage-power could make so much difference to levels of pluralism in some areas,[18] while its diffusion elsewhere[19] seems to have made so little? These are questions in search of answers.

iii. *Bishops*

A bishop viewed his rights of presentation in much the same way as did a peer. This is not to say that his concern was solely to feather his own nest, or to add a little down to that of one of his friends. It was more subtle, more complex than that. Patronage was seen as a matter of meeting, wherever possible, legitimate interests and demands, among which those of family and friends, although featuring prominently, by no means enjoyed a monopoly. Clerical acquaintances, men of literary or theological talent, even former college tutors, could all exert a pull of some force or other. Prelates were usually reticent about discussing the demands made upon them; but Walter King, Bishop of Rochester from 1809 to 1827, did on occasion write very frankly - perhaps too frankly - to Earl Fitzwilliam Five clergy, apparently, had some claim upon the bishop's generosity:

Mr Venables my nephew, has a small Vicarage in Somersetshire; and I must take the first opportunity for procuring for him by exchange, or otherwise, some additional Preferment.

Mr Davies my curate at Burnham. He is soon to marry a near Relation of mine, and I have long promised him the first Living of moderate value that I may have in my Gift.

Mr Buckland formerly my College Tutor, now my Chaplain; In addition to a valuable Sinecure

The Chancellor has just given him a good Living in my Neighbourhood. They are worth together 12 or 1300 a year. I am therefore no longer anxious about him, but he may hold another Living, & he has nephews in orders, and he will expect to have the disposal of something as opportunities may offer.

Mr Etherington. About Twenty five years ago came out of Yorkshire, a poor self taught Scholar, and found his way to Mr Burke. I recieved him from Mr Burke; We got him into orders and he has ever since been a Fag of mine at Gray's Inn and on other occasions....

Dr Winstanley the Principal of St Alban's Hall Oxford. He was unsuccessful in a Competition with me, for a Fellowship, soon after we entered at College .... I was engaged with him in the early part of my life in several literary projects, and pursuits....

These I believe are all the personal claims there are upon me.[20]

Bishops, being powerful, tended to promote pluralism. Of few is this more true than of two successive Archbishops of Canterbury, Archbishop Moore (1783-1805) and Archbishop Manners-Sutton (1805-28). Two of Archbishop Moore's sons, and one of Archbishop Manners-Sutton's many sons-in-law, have been noticed already, in the earlier discussion of incumbents earning £2,000 a year or more.[21] These three clergymen are typical of the exercise of patronage by the two prelates. In the early 1830s, there were 25 Kentish benefices where incumbents had been presented by Archbishop Moore, and 17 of these were held in plurality. His successor had filled 66 livings in the county, two-thirds of which were in the hands of pluralists. Altogether, Archbishops Moore and Manners-Sutton had presented pluralists in 61 instances out of 91 (67%), a higher proportion than among Kentish livings with private patrons.

Viewing things in wider perspective, it is difficult to see much distinction between the practice of the Bench and the practice of the wealthy laity. Among 597 livings held by laymen, pluralists were found to be ensconced in 380 (63.7%). The sample of episcopal presentations is smaller, from 247 parishes: among these, pluralists held 155 (62.8%).[22] Such evidence shows, with clarity and power, how ineffective the leadership of the Georgian church could be.

iv. *Incumbents*

Incumbents, like minor gentry, did not normally accumulate rights of patronage to a significant degree. Sometimes a rector inherited an advowson or two, but a large holding - four livings, or more - was rare. Lack of power is one reason why incumbents generally did little to foster pluralism. The other is that their patronage rights were often official rather than personal. It could happen that the presentation to a small perpetual curacy lay, *ex officio*, in the incumbent of a nearby benefice. Because rectors and vicars rarely owned substantial patronage on their own account, and because a proportion of the livings in their possession was held in an official capacity, their practice contrasts sharply with that of their ecclesiastical superiors, the bishops. In many counties, indeed, the difference was distinctly embarrassing. A good example is Cumbria, where bishops, in the early 1830s, had presented to 22 livings, of which 15 were held in plurality, while incumbents had presented to 42, of which only seven were held in plurality. The situation was less embarrassing in Sussex: here there were 41 episcopal presentees, of whom 29 (71%) held another living, and 49 incumbents presented by clergy, including 26 pluralists (53% of the total).[23]

The purity of clerical practice did, however, become a trifle sullied whenever incumbents seized the opportunity to present themselves. In Norfolk, at the end of 1833, there were 408 beneficed clergy, of whom 44 (10.8%) had managed this.[24] One cleric was patron and incumbent of three livings, and two more were patrons and incumbents of a pair of livings each. Careful cultivation of self-interest went hand in hand with promotion of pluralism. Altogether, 73 livings in the county had clerical patrons, of which 44 (60.3%) were held with another or others. Interestingly, 54 Norfolk livings were in the gift of bishops, and 32 of these (59.3%) were held in plurality.

v. *The Market in Advowsons*

Investment in ecclesiastical patronage held speculative attractions. Livings could not be bought or sold while they were vacant; purchasers therefore had to wait for 'sitting' incumbents either to resign or to die before they could name the clergyman of their choice. Because of this unavoidable element of risk, advowsons sold cheaply - usually for about five, or at most, seven times, the annual value of the living; they thus offered a cheap way of cashing in on any improvement in benefice values. Differing clerical attitudes towards estate management are also important. Livings with weak-charactered, old, or naturally benevolent incumbents did not yield their full potential; but the rate of return could be dramatically improved if a new patron installed a strong-willed relative as rector or vicar. Nor were there any effective legal constraints upon speculators; even after the passing of the 1838 Pluralities Act, there was still no limit at all upon the number of advowsons that could be owned by a patron. The Napoleonic boom in agriculture was a further incentive to speculation - agricultural production rose steeply; income from tithes rose steeply; and the values of advowsons also rose steeply. The final factor was advertising. Advowsons were marketed in much the same way as other kinds of private property: recreational facilities were extolled, as were the scenic delights of the surrounding countryside. This treatment of them doubtless did something to encourage acquisitiveness. Instructive in this connection is an advertisement in *The Times*, which runs:

North of Cornwall. To be sold by Private Contract, the next Presentation to the valuable Donative or Rectory of the Parish of North Tamerton, in the County of Cornwall, after the decease or resignation of the present incumbent, who is upwards of 53 years of age. The above donative comprises the great and small tithes of the parish, and is tenable with anything. North Tamerton lies on both banks of the River Tamar, is about 8 miles from Launceston, 4 miles from Holsworthy, and 8 miles from Stratton. The Bude canal passes through the parish of North Tamerton, greatly for the advantage and improvement thereof.[25]

Speculation, by its very nature, creates both winners and losers. The history of Long Melford in Suffolk amply shows how profitable it could be. Some aspects of the story of this parish have been described already.[26] It has been shown how John Leroo - vicar from 1789 until his death in 1819 - transformed benefice income by means of a series of financial ploys; terms for compositions were regularly renegotiated with farmers, and a large estate was expertly broken up. When Leroo entered the living it was bringing in £460 a year, and by the time of his death the value had reached over £1,200 a year. Interesting in themselves, these facts take on new meaning when a salient addition is made to the account. Leroo was not only rector of Long Melford, he was also patron of Long Melford: he had, in fact, purchased the advowson for the undemanding sum of £2,600 in 1783. He thus both presented himself and looked after himself. Each of his financial stratagems achieved two things: it added to income and it added to capital. During his life-time, income flows were realised but capital gains were not. Very soon after Leroo's death, however, the living was sold again, this time for £15,000. The profit of £12,400 was equivalent to an annual return of £344 (13.2%) on capital invested.

One clergyman's gain was another clergyman's loss. Leroo was succeeded by a caretaker incumbent in his eighties. His main function was to die, a simple action he resolutely refused to perform. The purchaser, the Revd W. Spurdon of North Walsham, was faced with a difficult decision. Should he hold on to the living, hoping for an agricultural revival, or sell and accept a loss on the bargain? The dilemma was resolved in 1823, when he sold it for £12,000, thus losing £3,000. The octogenarian, meanwhile, became a nonagenarian, and did not die until 1829.[27] Although a chastening experience for Mr Spurdon, it would be unwise to generalise upon the basis of it. Speculation in one form or another holds a deep seductive charm for human beings, and those whom the serpent has beguiled are not easily discomforted by the misfortunes of others.

Public bodies also at times had an ecclesiastical flutter, and the sums involved could be large. A good example of this occurred in 1817, when the Commissioners of Woods and Forests bought the wealthy living of Marylebone from the Duke of Portland for £40,000. As this deal indicates, the Duke's patronage was extensive. He had the right to nominate the rector, possessed four chapels within the parish - drawing the pew rents from each, and appointing their chaplains - and also appointed the chaplain of a fifth chapel. He was, moreover, financially astute. The commissioners later discovered that they had made a bad bargain. In 1830, it was revealed to the House of Commons that the upkeep of the chapels was costing £10,000 a year, while pew rents were only bringing in £8,000.[28]

The requirements of Oxford and Cambridge colleges were, as already indicated,[29] domestic. For each fellowship, they wanted at least one living. In this way, stagnation could be avoided. There would be vacancies in college livings for Fellows wanting to marry, or seeking a move into rural clerical life, while the college could ease out into the countryside any don who was considered unsuitable. A spate of buying by colleges apparently preceded the Mortmain Act of 1736,[30] and there seems to have been a revival of interest in the early nineteenth century.[31] Things did not always work out as the college anticipated, although it is to be hoped that the outcome was rarely as disastrous as it was for Oriel College, Oxford. About 1824, Oriel 'found itself in possession of £4,000, to do what it liked with'. The college looked around for a living; and, after some searching, eventually chose Twerton, 'an agricultural suburb' of Bath 'pleasantly situated on the banks of the Avon'. Twerton seemed to offer an excellent buying opportunity; the incumbent, Spencer Madan, might be young but he was also known to be dying. Unfortunately for Oriel, its dons were left to ruminate, over their port, on the implications of the linguistic distinction between 'known to be' and 'is'. As if this was not enough, worse was to follow; the college was informed that the new Great Western railway was to run over, or rather through, Twerton parsonage. Compensation of £4,000 was offered, with which a new parsonage was built at the extremity of the parish. However between this new building and the banks of the Avon lay the Great Western railway. As the years passed, industrial growth attracted people to Twerton, but changing social habits meant that fewer of the 'right sort of people' were attracted to Bath. When eventually the living fell vacant, which happened in 1852, the college had to persuade a luckless Fellow to take charge of what had by then become a growing manufacturing town.[32]

In some districts, the effect of an open market in advowsons was to concentrate private patronage in fewer and fewer hands. This did not happen everywhere; there were counties where lay patronage rights remained well distributed throughout the late eighteenth and early nineteenth centuries,[33] despite the encouragement to speculation given by the Napoleonic boom in agriculture. It can be stated, as a general rule, that where a large number of lay patrons held three advowsons or more, an acquisitive spirit of accumulation was at work. This spirit was certainly active in Norfolk. Between 1780 and 1830, patrons in the county with a single living each fell in number by 24, from 131 to 107; while, over the same period, patrons with between two livings and four increased by 5, from 39 to 44; and those with more than four swelled their ranks by 2, from 9 to 11.[34]

Interestingly, the majority of gains were made by families, such as the Lombes, who could not claim a long pedigree. Bereft of ecclesiastical patronage in 1780, they had gathered eight advowsons by 1830. Other names which managed to establish themselves are even less well-known: the Hammonds, with six gains for a total of seven; the Reynolds family, with four gains; the Bignolds, and the Musketts, with three each. A further eighteen minor gentry - none of them found among Norfolk private patrons in 1780 - had, by 1830, obtained a pair of livings each.

As is usual among the peerage and gentry, whether in the sixteenth and seventeenth centuries or in other periods, some families were doing well while others were doing badly. The Dukes of Norfolk increased their ecclesiastical patronage from one living to seven, and the Marquess of Cholmondeley made three gains, all from the Walpoles, to raise his holding to four. Somewhat lower down the social scale, Sir Thomas Smyth gained three benefices from the Wyndhams; and another knight, Sir Thomas Hare, made one gain fewer. The Suffields lost two advowsons but acquired five; and net gains of two were recorded by the Marshams, the Cokes, and the Wodehouses. Losses, however, were more frequent and more catastrophic. The Walpoles lost nine of their fifteen; the Wyndhams and the Earls of Suffolk each lost three; the Townshends and the Bacons each lost two. All of these did at least keep something, but there were four instances where aristocratic holdings of three livings or more disappeared completely. 'New' families, like the Lombes, Hammonds, and so on, made sixty gains; established peerage and gentry made a net total of nineteen losses.

Extinction of the male line was a major cause of aristocratic disaster. The history of the L'Estrange family shows what could happen. After the failure of the baronetcy, six of their eight advowsons descended to two Norfolk families, the Astleys and the Stylemans. The subsequent history of one of the eight livings - the rich rectory of Whissonsett - was tortuous. After coming into the possession of Sir Edward Astley, it was sold immediately to the Revd Richard Eaton of Elsing Hall for £1,700. By 1797, it had passed to another clergyman, the Revd John Crofts, and he, like John Leroo, subsequently presented himself.[35] Another L'Estrange advowson, Gressenhall, was also sold. The purchaser later presented his own son, and then sold the living to King's College, Cambridge, who expected an early vacancy. This college, like Oriel in its transaction over Twerton, was destined to undergo a long period of disappointment. The Revd Dennis Hill, a keen sportsman and avid bowls player, more celebrated for his port than for his divinity, was rector of Gressenhall for nearly seventy years, from 1807 until 1873.[36] A third living, that of Stanfield, was sold at about the same time as Whissonsett and Gressenhall, and followed a similar pattern. After changing hands frequently, it was bought - just as Whissonsett had been - by a clergyman. There was, however, a vital difference: the Revd W. Newcome, unlike John Leroo and John Crofts, did not present himself; the incumbent in 1833 was a certain Revd James Royle.[37]

The patronage of the Ansons fared almost as badly. Of the eight advowsons held in the late eighteenth century, only one remained in 1830. Extinction of the male line was not to blame in this instance. The family was led in the 1830s by Thomas William (1795-1854), created Earl of Lichfield in 1831. Instead of a sudden collapse, there was, in the case of the Ansons, a gradual disintegration, as livings were sold off to lesser gentry. With the Hase family, inheritance was the determining factor. Edward Hase of Sall was the brother of Sir John Lombe. Sir John's nephew, another Edward, on the death of one uncle inherited a baronetcy, and on the death of the other the Hase estates, together with four advowsons. In the case of the Earl of Buckingham's patronage, marriage is the explanation for decline. The daughter of the second Earl married the second Baron Suffield, and three advowsons were given to the new Lady Suffield as a marriage portion. Deaths, dowries, and disposals were the main reasons for the loss of aristocratic patronage.

There was a movement in Norfolk away from the peerage and established gentry towards new, previously unknown, families; and also a movement away from laity to clergy. Between 1780 and 1830, sixty-one livings were transferred from laity to clergy, or *vice versa*, and clergy made a net gain of twenty-one.[38] Purchase was, probably, a frequent method of exchange; the difficulty is to come by evidence of transactions. Two instances - the success of the Revd John Crofts at Whissonsett, and the buying of Stanfield by the Revd W. Newcome - have already been noted.[39] For the record, there is a third: the purchase of Bassingham from the Ansons by the Revd F.E. Arden. (He, incidentally, kept things in the family by presenting his son, Thomas).[40] These pieces of evidence are like nuggets of gold, rarely found; the historian usually has to make do with more homely dross, in the shape of proof of exchange without knowledge of its method. The Walpoles, for instance, ceded a pair of livings to a pluralistic incumbent, Benjamin Cubitt; he, in typical fashion, duly presented himself to one of the two, Stalham. The Bacons lost two advowsons, one of which went to the Revd Edward Frank, related through his paternal grandmother. This was Shelton; and the rector of Shelton in the early 1830s was the Revd Edward Frank. Benjamin Barker did even better than Edward Frank; from the Townshends he gained the wealthy advowson of Shipdam, to which he duly presented himself, and he also acquired All Saints, Rockland, again presenting himself. In the 1830s, he was one of the richest clergymen in England, with an income of £2,037 a year. The Revd C.H. Townshend (1798-1868) was less self-seeking than either of these. A minor poet, and friend of Southey, he undertook no 'active' clerical duties; although patron of West Walton, a wealthy living previously in the Marquess of Townshend's gift, he did not present himself, choosing instead his uncle, the Revd Atwell Lake.

This shift in power in Norfolk away from the laity and towards the clergy helps to explain the contrast, noted earlier, between the practice of the Norfolk clergy and the practice of the clergy in Cumbria. This contrast, it will be remembered, was stark: 17% of Cumbrian livings owned by clergy were held in plurality in the early 1830s, while in Norfolk the comparable figure was 60%.[41] The thread of logic is short and strong: an incumbent who inherited or purchased a living was likely to present himself, and incumbents who presented themselves were likely to be pluralists. The facts, moreover, fully support these contentions. Between 1780 and 1830, the Norfolk clergy gained, either by inheritance or by purchase, a net total of 21 livings from the laity;[42] at the end of 1833, there were 44 incumbents in the county who had presented themselves;[43] and, in the same year, 60% of Norfolk livings with clerical owners were held in plurality.[44] The causal links are simple and direct, and they are also established.

vi. *Resignation Bonds*

No discussion of ecclesiastical patronage is complete without elucidation of the convenient practice of exacting resignation bonds. These bound a presentee in a stated sum - often thousands of pounds - to vacate a living, after being given notice by the patron. Their use goes back until at least the sixteenth century, and they signal, in a striking way, the power wielded by important laity over clergy.

One of the main functions of resignation bonds was to lubricate the wheels of the advowson market. Since livings could not be sold while they were vacant, their value rose as incumbents became progressively more aged or ailing. On the other hand, because of the ban on purchases during interregnums, prospective buyers intending to install a relative or friend were well advised to act while the person for whom the living was being bought was still young, preferably not even old enough to be ordained. In such instances the living, once it had been purchased, needed to be 'kept warm' until the person for whom it was intended came of age. If the existing occupant died or resigned in the meantime, the living, far from keeping its natural heat, threatened to freeze overnight. In this emergency, the patron had three options: he could fill the living with a caretaker incumbent, preferably in his seventies or eighties; he could select a clerical friend, making a gentleman's agreement with him to vacate when asked; or he could be more legalistic, insisting that the new incumbent should sign a resignation bond.

These were the normal circumstances under which a bond was used, but it could also have more sinister undertones. A powerful patron might use a bond as a means of securing a hold upon a cleric, thus running the affairs of a parish to his own advantage. It was against this use that Bishop Gibson of London, always a zealous defender of the rights of the clergy, inveighed. Bonds, he complained in 1724, were a method of 'enslaving (incumbents) during Life to the Will and Pleasure of Patrons, and particularly of tempting them to submit to all the most unreasonable Agreements and Compositions for Tithes, which can be proposed'.[45] That clergy could be found who were willing to sign these bonds, and to accept their implied conditions, is witness to the power of many Georgian patrons and to the impotent poverty of many Georgian incumbents.[46]

Such manipulation of resignation bonds was clearly malevolent, but it would be wrong to conclude that they were always an evil. Their use was defended on two grounds. The first was pragmatic. Many eighteenth-century landowners considered that they were being altruistic in purchasing livings for relatives and sons; and they went on to argue that resignation bonds were a perfectly permissible method of forwarding such generosity. They felt that they were acting in good faith, and they believed that they were being sensible. The law dictated that livings could not be bought during a vacancy; it followed that the prudent patron would purchase a benefice, intended for a near relation, well before the prospective incumbent had come of age; the sitting incumbent might die or resign in the meantime; if a living was left for more than six months without a presentee, the right of patronage reverted to the bishop; an elderly caretaker incumbent might develop the awkward habit of refusing to die; therefore, if an 'inconvenient' vacancy arose after purchase, it seemed logical to appoint a temporary rector, imposing upon him, in return for his enjoyment of the fruits of the benefice, a binding agreement to limit his freehold by accepting the patron's right to give notice to quit. Both sides to the bargain stood to gain - patrons secured livings for their relations, and temporary incumbents secured a welcome extra source of income. The temporary incumbent would become, in effect, the deputy of the man for whom the living was eventually intended, and the employment of deputies was conventional behaviour in Georgian England. Central government sanctioned it, and local government sanctioned it; so, in a way, did the official ecclesiastical hierarchy, by its acceptance of the widespread practice of curates serving parishes whose incumbents were non-resident. This defence of resignation bonds was practical, as well as highly conservative, and had wide appeal.

The second defence was ethical. Bonds themselves, it was argued, were morally neutral, but they could be made to serve a variety of moral purposes. By inserting tough conditional clauses, a patron could insist upon fulfilment of pastorally desirable goals - constant residence, an increase in church services, the promise to build a school. Ends justify means, and power can be used to promote good equally with evil. Laymen rarely advanced such arguments, but there were bishops who were courageous enough to pursue this line of thought. An example is Burnet, but he encountered hostility on this account from other members of the late seventeenth-century Bench, and his actions in this regard were, in any case, already anachronistic.[47] Reform in human society rarely comes about through redirection of highly questionable practices into channels for good, and the history of resignation bonds does not disprove this general rule.

Change came in another way, through the imposition of limitations upon use. Nothing was done for the greater part of the eighteenth century, until hostilities were opened by Robert Lowth, Bishop of London. Lowth discovered that an incumbent had signed what was in effect an open bond, containing an agreement to resign without specifying a person to resign in favour of, and refused to institute. The result, *Bishop of London v. Ffytche,*, was a case, started in 1780, which lasted for three years. Lowth lost in the Court of Common Pleas, and in the King's Bench division; but he won, though only by the slenderest of margins, in the House of Lords. The final vote was nineteen to eighteen in his favour, the majority being made up of eighteen Bishops plus Lord Chancellor Thurlow. This looks like collusion, and it probably was.[48] The case established the illegality of general resignation bonds, but bonds to resign in favour of a specified person remained within the perimeter of the law.

Half a century later, under an Act of 1828, all resignation bonds were made illegal,[49] except in cases where both the presentee and the prospective incumbent were related, either by blood or by marriage, to the patron. For a number of decades after this no further legislative action was taken, and the use of a bond to keep a family living 'warm' remained legal throughout the high Victorian years - its scope severely restricted but the principle protected. This, moreover, was only the official and formal position. The probability is that a number of agreements continued to be made in defiance of law. In the nature of the case, examples are hard to find, but a biographical source did reveal one. Five years after the passing of the 1828 Act, that eloquent Radical politician, Lord Suffield, wanted to present Richard Durnford (a future Bishop of Chichester) to the wealthy Lancashire living of Middleton. However, in the carefully guarded phrasing of Durnford's biographer, 'there were reasons which made it difficult for Mr Durnford at once to take charge of his cure', so another cleric was engaged to hold it for two years until these difficulties had been resolved.[50] Just a year earlier, Lord Suffield had been unable to 'refrain' from quoting to the House of Lords a newspaper advertisement relating to the sale of the advowson of a living worth £650 a year, one of whose main attractions was that 'the church is gone to sea'[51] - a reference to the encroachment of the sea over the land upon which the church had formerly stood. The spectacle of the patron of Middleton pouring scorn upon the sale of an advowson has about it a rich glimmer of irony. It is an interesting commentary upon the state of transitional England that a Radical politician, together with a future bishop, should have been parties to an agreement in clear breach of the spirit of a recently enacted law.

Chapter 7 Notes

1. See above, pp. 90-1.

2. See above, p. 164, note 11.

3. For a sympathetic account of Newcastle's ecclesiastical activities, see C.R. Hirshberg, 'The Government and Church Patronage', *J.B.S.*, XX (1980), 127-39. Hirshberg concludes (137-8) that 'the Duke of Newcastle's success in controlling the placing of church personnel was not nearly as complete or as contrary to the wishes of top clergymen as contemporaries thought.'

4. An example is the Evangelical Cornelius Bayley (1754-1812). He built St James, Manchester, kept the advowson and nominated himself to the living in 1788 - Balda, 'Spheres of Influence', p.24.

5. To buy a next presentation was considered to be equivalent to purchasing office; but there was no objection to the acquisition of an advowson, since this was a perpetual trust.

6. *P.P.*, 1835, XXII, 1058. According to this return, there were 10,708 advowsons and next presentations. Of these, 5,096 (47.6%) were held by laity; the capitular and parochial clergy had 2,638 (24.6%); bishops came next with 1,248 (11.7%); the Crown had 952 (8.9%); and colleges, schools and corporations brought up the tail, with 774 (7.2%). A slightly variant analysis can be found in *P.P.*, 1836, XL, 5. Different treatment of split ownerships probably accounts for the differences between the two returns.

7. Although there are no figures for 1700, there is comprehensive detail in Browne Willis, *A Survey of the cathedrals* (3 vols., 1742). This has been analysed by Hirshberg, *op.cit.*, 111-14, esp. Table, 112-13. According to Hirshberg, the parish by parish information collected by Willis shows, when aggregated, that laity held 53.4% of all advowsons, that bishops, chapters, and the parochial clergy had 26.1%, the Crown came third with 9.6%, and all other classes of patron could muster between them no more than 10.9%. Not much changed by 1830, except that ecclesiastics had made gains from both laity and the miscellaneous group of patrons.

8. In Norfolk, clergy held 73 advowsons among 575 (12.7%); while in Cumberland and Westmorland the figure was 42 among 204 (20.6%). For further details, see below, Table XVI.

9. According to Hirshberg, *op.cit.*, Table, 112-13, laity held 68.4% of all advowsons in the diocese of Peterborough in 1742 (their highest penetration), and only 7.1% in Bangor (their lowest),

10. Warne, *Church and Society*, p. 31.

11. See below, Table XVI.

12. On nepotism, see Maynard, 'Ecclesiastical Administration of the Archdeaconry of Durham', pp. 43, 50-78.

13. Bossy, *The English Catholic Community, 1570-1850*, pp. 150-1.

14. See, e.g., House of Lords, 27 March 1832, *Hansard*, Third Series, XI, 931-3.

15. The sources used in the analysis of Norfolk private patronage were: G.E. Cockayne, *The Complete Baronetage*, and *The Complete Peerage*; Sir Bernard and John Burke, *A Genealogical and Heraldic History of the Peerage*, and *A Genealogical and Heraldic History of the Extinct and Dormant Baronetcies of England*; Joseph Foster, *The Baronetage and Knightage of the British Empire*; *The Peerage of the British Empire*; and *The Royal Lineage of our Noble and Gentle Families*; F. Blomefield and Charles Parkin, *An Essay towards a Topographical History of the County of Norfolk*; G.A. Carthew, *The Hundred of Launditch and Deanery of Brisley*; and F.A. Crisp and J.J. Howard, editors, *Visitation of England and Wales*.

16. See below, p.212, notes 66 and 67.

17. See above, p.173.

18. Norfolk is an example here.

19. An instance is Kent.

20. Walter King to Earl Fitzwilliam, n.d., endorsed by Fitzwilliam, 'BP of Rochester - Patronage and his intentions', Wentworth Woodhouse Muniments, Sheffield University Library, F33/18, quoted in A.D. Harvey, *Britain in the early nineteenth century*, p.67. King was an editor of Burke's works.

21. See above, p.91.

22. See below, Table XVI.

23. See below, Table XVI.

24. There was nothing unusual about the practice of the Norfolk clergy in this regard. The patron-incumbent was a frequent figure in the Georgian countryside, and he was also a frequent figure in the Victorian countryside. Indeed, it has been calculated that, as late as 1878, 'perhaps one living in ... eighteen was in the hands of a patron-incumbent' - M.J.D. Roberts, 'Private Patronage and the Church of England, 1800-1900', *J.E.H.*, XXXII (1981), 206.

25. *The Times*, 7 October 1823. Desmond Bowen, *The idea of the Victorian Church*, p.12 makes this comment: 'reading the *Ecclesiastical Gazette* where 'next presentations' were advertised with the notation 'incumbent is in his 65th year', makes the reader wonder whether the advertisement was a joke'. The whole point, of course, is that it was not.

26. See above, pp. 62-63.

27. Mss. notebooks at Long Melford, Suffolk, quoted in Hart, *The Eighteenth-Century Country Parson*, pp. 104-8.

28. *P.P.*, 1817, XV, 127-31; *Hansard*, Second Series, XXIII, 1076.

29. See above, p.172.

30. Best, *Temporal Pillars*, p. 102, note 2.

31. Colleges were encouraged by the clergy to buy. There is an entry in Francis Witts' diary, dated 4 July 1838: 'Wrote to Wadham College to furnish them with the particulars of the vicarage at Painswick, the advowson of which is now on sale, in case they should be disposed to become the purchasers' (*The Diary of a Cotswold Parson*, p.150). The Fellows of Wadham were not disposed.

32. T. Mozley, *Reminiscences*, I, 90, 93. The Librarian of Oriel College was unable to find any

trace of this transaction in college records.

33. Examples would be Kent and Sussex.

34. See below, Table XVII.

35. Carthew, *op.cit.*, II, 513, III, 449.

36. *ibid.*, III, 212.

37. *ibid.*, III, 394-5.

38. This fluidity might seem exceptional; in fact, it was not. Sales of advowsons occurred frequently, even in mid-Victorian England. Thus we find, as late as 1877, Frederick Martin complaining that 'in recent years, the sales of benefices amounted, at a rough estimate, to upwards of five hundred per annum, at which rate the whole of the livings in private patronage may be calculated to "change hands" about every ten years' - Frederick Martin, *The Property and Revenues of the English Church Establishment*, p.85. Further information on sales of advowsons in the Victorian era is to be found in Haig, *The Victorian Clergy*, pp.258-262.

39. See above, notes 35 and 37.

40. See above, p. 154.

41. See above, pp.177-8, 180-1.

42. See above, p. 181, 185.

43. See above, p. 177, 181.

44. See above, p. 178.

45. Quoted in Best, *op.cit.*, p.58.

46. An example is Sir John Ingilby, patron of Ripley in Yorkshire; in 1759, he forced the incumbent to agree never to raise the tithes (Evans, *The Contentious Tithe*, p.29).

47. Best, *op.cit.*, pp. 56-7.

48. *ibid*, p.57.

49. 9 Geo. IV c. 94.

50. Stephens, *A Memoir of Richard Durnford*, pp. 68-9.

51. House of Lords, 2 April 1832, *Hansard*, Third Series, XI, 1168.

8

A World of Pluralities

i. *Waxing*

The present omission of Parochial Duty is a great want of Policy in the conduct of the clergy, and threatens the Established Church with the greatest danger

Samuel Horsley (1796).[1]

It is one of the gentler ironies of history that the Augustan intellect, with its easy confidence in its own rationality and its corresponding contempt for the insights of every earlier age, should have permitted the regrowth - in the ecclesiastical sphere - of corruptions and decadences which, although they had luxuriated three or more centuries before, had already been cut down once by the sharpened sickles of Reformation and Renaissance reform. These reflections apply with particular force to what was arguably the major task of church reform - we refer to the reduction of pluralism. To achieve betterment here was also to achieve betterment elsewhere. An incumbent with one living in Surrey, and another in Suffolk, was inevitably non-resident; and a parish with a non-resident incumbent was in an invidious position when it came to ensuring both that there were enough church services and that there was sufficient provision of parochial activities.[2] Much of what has gone before in this book, the discussion of rising clerical wealth, the policies of Queen Anne's Bounty, the social status of incumbents, and so on, takes on a new immediacy, and a new meaning, when placed in the context of the performance of clerical duty.

There was no shortage of plans for reform in the eighteenth century; the difficulty was to implement them. Reformers said more or less the same things, proposed more or less the same remedies, and achieved more or less the same result: almost nothing. Burnet wanted to reduce pluralism, as did Secker; later in the century, Beilby Porteus[3] had similar aims; but the clergy did not cooperate, and nor, for that matter, did a lot of the bishops. Most plans of reform came to nothing: cumbersome diocesan geography remained the same; parish boundaries, both in town and country-side, remained the same; cathedral establishments remained the same; and the tithe system remained the same. There was no sustained effort to increase the number of parsonages. The laws regarding pluralism and non-residence were not altered. Episcopal control over the clergy was firmer in theory than it was in practice. Inactivity was extolled in a motto: *state super vias antiquas*.

The study of plurality among the eighteenth-century clergy, particularly in the first half of the period, is a neglected area of history. There are two main reasons for this. To begin with, there is a lack of nationwide data. Queen Anne's Bounty, in the first decade of the century, carried out its two surveys of benefice values;[4] but the governors never followed these up with a third, much-needed, investigation into the clergy. The omission was put right by the Ecclesiastical Revenues Commission; but its report, with its fine detail, did not come out until 1835. The second reason for neglect has to do with the nature of the diocesan record archive. This makes up with massiveness what it lacks in completeness. Having studied the unwieldy records of the diocese of Norwich covering the period between the 1790s and 1830s, one finds that a continuous series of visitation returns is available only for the two deaneries of Waxham and Repps, which represent well under a tenth of the full complement of parishes. Such neglect is, as on most occasions, the mother of ignorance. Plurality among the eighteenth-century clergy has remained a mystery in two vital respects: it is not known how much pluralism there was, and it is unclear whether this 'practice of a very hurtful tendency',[5] as it has been graphically called, was on the wax or on the wane.

Some progress has been made towards resolving these issues. A search of the records of Queen Anne's Bounty, now included with those of the Church Commissioners in London, has brought to light some invaluable documents,[6] comprising lists of parishes, together with the names of serving incumbents, submitted by bishops to the Bounty when the assessment of benefice values was made in 1705. The lists are far from complete, but they are sufficiently so to enable us to assess with reasonable accuracy the level of pluralism in the first decade of the eighteenth century. For the situation later in the century, analysis is not dependent upon any further act of serendipity. A good deal of modern research, much of it unpublished, has been done on the diocesan archive for the later eighteenth century. It is a comparatively simple task to collate and present the results.

When considering the returns made by bishops to the Bounty in 1705, I chose, as a matter of obvious policy, a sample which reflected geographical diversity. Four areas were studied: clergy from the diocese of Salisbury in the south; Exeter in the west; Peterborough in central England; and Carlisle in the north, and two main conclusions were reached. There was little plurality in early eighteenth-century England. Secondly, such pluralism as did exist was evenly distributed. All in all, I managed to trace the whereabouts of 445 incumbents; 72 (16%) were pluralists, and the remaining 373 (84%) were not. Among the small band of 72, moreover, was only a single incumbent with a third living. Nowhere was it the case that the 'practice of a very hurtful tendency' was rife. In the sample from Salisbury, 23% of clergy were pluralists; in Carlisle 19%; in Peterborough 17%; and in Exeter 14%.[7]

These figures are not wholly accurate. Some clergy included in the sample doubtless held livings in places which have been excluded, but the understatement of the incidence of plurality is unlikely to be serious. Pluralism in the Georgian era was largely localised; even in 1840, when there was much more plurality among the beneficed clergy than there had been in 1700, it was rare for an incumbent to hold livings in more than one diocese. One is forced back upon a fundamental insight, as clear as it is simple. It is impossible to study the returns made by bishops in 1705 without being struck by the plight of the beneficed clergy; the overwhelming impression is of poverty, and of non-plurality. This shows up in the dry bones of the statistical record, and is also clothed in the living flesh of specific comment. There were pluralists in 1705 who were pluralists only in name. The best example we came across was the perpetual curate of Woodbury in Devon. 'The incumbent', said his archdeacon, 'has another living to wit Sidmouth, but he receives no benefit from it, giving the profits of it to the widow of the last Incumbent who had the next Presentation after her Husband'. Such generosity was less likely a century later. The comment made of the vicar of Hennock, another living in Devon, sums up these returns much better than any of our words can: 'the incumbent', runs the entry, 'has but that bare smal liveing'.[8]

When looking at how things stood later in the century, a different procedure is required. The best method is to begin by studying non-residence, because more research has been done on this topic than on the closely connected subject of plurality. For the 1770s and early 1780s, figures are available for six counties: Derbyshire, Devon, Norfolk, Oxfordshire, Wiltshire, and Worcestershire. Interestingly, there is considerable regional variation. Best is Devon where, in 1779, 59% of parishes had resident incumbents.[9] At the opposite pole is Norfolk; here, in 1784, visitation returns were made by 579 parishes, of which only 128 - a mere 22% of the total - had residents.[10] Derbyshire in 1772 was a little worse than Devon in 1779: 52% of parishes had resident beneficed clergy.[11] Oxfordshire, Wiltshire and Worcestershire occupied the middle ground between Devon and Norfolk. In Wiltshire, in 1783, 39% of parishes were served by resident incumbents;[12] in Worcestershire a year earlier the figure was 39%;[13] and in Oxfordshire in 1778 the figure was also 39%:[14] a remarkable congruity. For the sample as a whole, parishes with residents amounted to 38%. Throughout England and Wales, the frequency of residence is unlikely to have been much different from this figure - the body of research summarised here covers 1,673 parishes, equivalent to around 16% of the total,[15] and constitutes a cross-section large enough substantially to even out the distortions due to regional disparity.

Having studied non-residence among the beneficed clergy of the 1770s and early 1780s, it is possible to tackle the issue of the extent of plurality at the same period. Most fruitful is an oblique analytical method. It is necessary to draw out, and use, future findings. In 1831, at the start of the era of reform, 44% of the parishes in England and Wales had residents[16] while, in the same year, 33% of the beneficed clergy were pluralists.[17] This suggests, other things being equal, that the clergy of 1780, marginally more non-resident than those of half a century later, were also marginally more pluralistic - say, an incidence of 36% as compared with 33%. This estimate is approximate. The difficulty is that a range of factors, apart from plurality, contributed towards the high levels of non-residence that characterised the later Georgian era. A lot of clergy had either dilapidated or 'unfit' parsonages; some of these rectors and vicars lived close by their parishes, and kept to the spirit, if not the letter, of the law. Other incumbents were aged, infirm, or sick; and there were also those who, for reasons that they kept to themselves, found Cheltenham or Brighton more amenable places in which to live than their benefices. All of this complicates the picture, but it remains true that pluralism was, by a good distance, the major cause of non-residence. The two things were, so to speak, natural correlates. In the absence of counter-evidence, it is best to take a neutral stance towards the other factors in the complex equation, assuming that they were no more, and no less, influential in 1830 than in 1780. Hence the conclusion that the beneficed clergy of the later eighteenth century were fractionally more pluralistic than their counterparts of the early nineteenth.[18]

At the heart of this discussion are two convictions. Pluralism, it is being argued, was much more prevalent towards the end of the eighteenth century than it had been towards the end of the seventeenth. Secondly, there was no nationwide trend; rates of increase varied considerably from place to place. Both convictions are supported by local evidence. Fullest statistics are for Sussex. In 1670. there were 232 clergy for 287 benefices; in 1734, 202 for 281; and in 1785 only 180 for 282.[19] Within one hundred and fifteen years, the number of clergy in Sussex had dropped by fifty-two, a fall approaching 25%. Clergy in the dioceses of Oxford and Hereford were also getting a taste for pluralistic habit. In Oxford, in 1680, there were nine pluralists, each with a pair of livings; by 1760, the number of pluralists had more than doubled to twenty-two, and these held forty-eight benefices. It was a similar story at Hereford, with 31 pluralists in 1680, and 61 in 1759.[20] Elsewhere, however, pluralism was less rife. A good example is the archdeaconry of York, which comprised most of the West Riding except the area north of the river Nidd. A visitation of 1734 was attended by 173 beneficed clergy representing 186 parishes; and by 1790 the number of incumbents serving the same number of parishes had been reduced by sixteen, to 157.[21] This points up well the relevant differences. In the archdeaconry of York, in 1790, parishes were a little under 20% more numerous than clergy; in Sussex, five years earlier, approaching 60% more.

The discovery that the clergy were holding more and more livings says much about the Georgian church. If poverty had been the main reason for pluralism, the rising clerical wealth that characterised the eighteenth century would gradually have reduced it. The plea of poverty assiduously used by eighteenth-century clergy was often no more than a convenient alibi. The cloth was tailored to fit the times. Incumbents in the age of Anne argued that £20 a year, or maybe £40, was not sufficient, even for a journeyman parson; those who lived in the middle of George III's reign used the same argument, adjusting meanwhile the level of a necessary subsistence, which was now set at £80 a year or £100. Later, the level was to rise again, touching £150 and even more. Lord Henley argued, in 1832, for a minimum of £400 a year.[22]

Two things which helped pluralism to flourish were the way the system of patronage worked and the lack of sound legal safeguards. In areas where private patrons had great ecclesiastical power, there were many clergy who held benefices in plurality; one need look no further than Norfolk to prove this point.[23] Secondly, parliament always had the power, at a single stroke of the pen, to put a stop to pluralism. All that was needed was a law with teeth. The difficulty, of course, was that parliament represented, and embodied, the interests of powerful lay patrons. The imposition of legal curbs upon pluralism amounted to the passing of a self-denying ordinance; and this was something which eighteenth-century parliaments were not prepared to contemplate.

The beneficed clergy could not be in two places at once; while pluralism was rife, non-residence would be rife. This is self-evident, as is the fact that an incumbent had to have somewhere to live. Provision of parsonages is crucial to any debate on clerical residence. The record is not one of which the eighteenth-century church could be proud. Queen Anne's Bounty, in its earliest years, allowed some augmentations to be spent on residence-houses; but it then drew in its horns, and did not allow any grants to be used for this purpose during the second half of the eighteenth century. Soon after 1800, the policy of subsidising provision of clerical accommodation was recommenced by the Bounty with a zeal which made its earlier efforts appear hesitant and ineffectual. But although the Board was now straining every nerve and sinew, the problem remained intractable.[24] As at the end of 1833, there were 2,878 places without residence-houses; while, among parishes which did have clerical accommodation of some kind, there were 1,728 parsonages which were officially described as 'unfit'. It is unlikely that things were any better in 1750.[25]

The practice of patronage, weak-kneed laws regarding pluralism, and the scarcity of parsonages, were three major reasons for widespread non-residence among the eighteenth-century clergy. A fourth cause of pastoral neglect was poor ecclesiastical administration. Few, and mostly vast, dioceses; an aged (and politically orientated) prelacy; slow and laborious travel; reliance upon the handwritten letter; an obdurate assertion of the parson's freehold; frequent episcopal translations; aristocratic permeation of the Bench; a largely rural and dispersed clergy. This was the reality, and the administrative consequences were neither unexpected nor trivial. The shepherd did not always know all his sheep by name, and was frequently unsure where some of them were to be found. This did not greatly worry the sheep - they, after all, were able to graze on pasture of their own choosing - but it should have worried the shepherd.

The tragedy of the eighteenth-century church is that reform became at once both more feasible and less likely. The values of livings grew, and yet the laws against pluralism became more outmoded; aristocratic bishops were unwilling to discipline aristocratic incumbents; the Bounty's effort to provide more parsonages petered out. With every surge forward in benefice values, stricter laws on clerical residence became both more justifiable and more than ever necessary; but, on the other hand, with every surge forward in benefice values, the church also became more attractive to the aristocracy; and as the church became more attractive to the aristocracy, so the likelihood of radical reform receded. This is, admittedly, a dismal picture, but it fits the facts.

ii. *Full Moon*

Around the turn of the nineteenth century, parliament decided that something had to be done about clerical residence. The main fruit of thought on this topic was Sir William Scott's Residence Act of 1803, mentioned earlier.[26] Scott's Act had two main aims. Firstly, it sought to legalise and to regularise non-residence. Henceforth, each and every incumbent who wished not to reside was required to obtain, from his bishop, either an exemption or a licence permitting this course of action. Although these licences and exemptions could be obtained for vague and sometimes unsatisfactory reasons - a state of unspecified 'ill-health' was, for instance, one such, while 'residence on another living' was another - the important point is that, without episcopal permission, non-residence became illegal. Bishops could revoke these licences and exemptions and, what is more, they could sequester the profits of a living whenever the reason given for non-residence was deemed inadequate. Secondly, the migratory habits of the clergy were now to be monitored. Bishops were to find out how many parishes did not have resident incumbents, and were then to send the figures to the Privy Council, where they would be collated prior to presentation as parliamentary returns. This was a bold move, and became bolder, as statistical sophistications were added. The first of these was introduced in 1809. Before this date, episcopal efforts were concentrated upon discovering parishes with non-residents. Henceforward their lordships had to adjust themselves to making a new style of return, which distinguished between parishes with residents and those with non-residents. The following year, another refinement was added: non-residents were now to be divided into those who performed Sunday duty in their parishes and those who did not. No major changes in disclosure were made after 1810.

A number of bishops were not overwhelmingly pleased with their new duties. This emerges from detailed study of the relevant Privy Council registers,[27] which show that the Council quite quickly became impatient with the dilatoriness of several diocesans - notably the Bishops of Bangor, Ely, Hereford, Norwich, and St David's - in making the returns required under the 1803 Act. A particularly fine example of episcopal intransigence was Richard Hurd, the scholarly Bishop of Worcester. He admitted in 1807 that he had 'ceased enforcing the laws against non-residence because they caused his clergy such inconvenience'.[28] In Hurd's defence, it has to be said that, at eighty-eight, he was a trifle elderly even for a Georgian cleric. The next year, Hurd was dead.

Although now armed with legal powers of sequestration, the bishops failed to cope, in an effective way, with spectacular cases of pluralism and non-residence. In 1821, in the diocese of Exeter, the incumbent of Dittisham lived at Penang and the parson of Honeychurch was resident in Brazil.[29] Both continued to enjoy the emoluments attaching to ecclesiatical office. The same holds of the Revd Francis Egerton, fellow of All Soul's, prebendary of Durham, and rector of the Shropshire livings of Whitchurch and Middle, each of which was comfortably endowed and, also, in the gift of his family. He went to live in France in 1802,[30] and remained there, dying in the year of Roman Catholic emancipation.

Sequestration was justified, in the case of Egerton, on grounds more substantial than permanent exile. He should, indeed, never have become a clergyman at all. Preaching presented difficulties. His teeth, unhappily, did not fit properly together - the lower set protruded over the upper, which had the effect of making speech difficult as well as giving him a disagreeably startling appearance.[31] As if this was not enough, he also suffered from semi-paralysis of the tongue.[32] These problems in no way exhaust the legitimate grounds for disqualification. To Egerton's physical quirks were added mental ones: he was thoroughly unstable, a constant sufferer from sudden and violent oscillations in mood. Finally, it could also be argued that his conception of what constituted sexual morality did not quite match what was required in a clergyman; he had, in all, five illegitimate daughters.[33]

Egerton was inordinately ugly, mentally unstable, and sexually over-active; he was also exceptionally rich. In 1823, he succeeded to the fabulously wealthy Bridgewater estates, becoming the eighth - and last - Earl. His income, scarcely paltry, was now enhanced to the tune of a further £40,000 or so a year,[34] which allowed the exile free rein to indulge his eccentricities. He had earlier, in 1814, purchased the Hôtel de Noailles, one of the finest private houses in Paris which commanded a central position in la rue St Honore.[35] The erstwhile rector of Whitchurch and Middle enjoyed shooting. Unfortunately, his physical disabilities precluded participation in this most aristocratic of sports; Egerton , nothing daunted, arranged for rabbits and pheasants to be let loose in his garden.[36] Bewildered passers-by listened to the inexplicable sound of gun-fire, as Egerton, supported by two lackeys, set about depopulating the assortment of game brought in for the day. Anything that failed to escape - and, given the circumstances, little did - was served up that evening, with all due ceremony, at dinner. Egerton liked shooting at rabbits and hares, and he also liked the company of numerous cats and dogs, which roamed his house. Towards two of the dogs Egerton developed an especial affection. As a mark of favour, they were often allowed to dine with him; but they did so on his terms, which included dressing them up as though they were human, in the livery of his servants, with napkins around their necks. What the dogs thought of such treatment is, unfortunately, not recorded.[37]

The fact that the Privy Council had to cajole several bishops into action, and the failure to deal with the likes of the incumbents of Dittisham, Honeychurch and Whitchurch, does not bode well. It would seem that, despite Parliament's new-found concern over the problems of pluralism and non-residence, little was done to improve matters. Hitherto, this failure has not been recognised. Historians have not offered a definitive interpretation of the parliamentary returns, tracking the residence of the beneficed clergy, that were produced between the passing of Sir William Scott's Act in 1803 and the onset, nearly thirty years later, of the era of parliamentary reform. There has been, from time to time, a ritual wringing of hands over how bad things were,[38] but this does not take us very far. What has been wanted has been a careful dissection of the available evidence, with the analytical eye moving steadily from diocese to diocese; but this is not hitherto what has been done, which is a pity, for an important discovery has always been within grasp. A number of returns, it soon becomes clear, are inaccurate or misleading. Once these erroneous figures are identified and removed, the failure of the late-Georgian Bench to do much about pluralism and non-residence becomes apparent.

The first four sets of returns, from 1805 until 1808, are neither useful nor informative.[39] Although the bishops had only to search out parishes with non-residents, the task was too much for some of them. Lincoln, for instance, returned 565 non-residents in 1805 and 1,169 in 1807; figures for Norwich are 351 in 1806 and 813 in 1808. The returns for the period from 1805 to 1808 are clearly unusable.

As from 1809, when residents were first distinguished from non-residents, the statistical ground is firmer but by no means certain. There are two main sources of difficulty. Returns for one diocese - St David's in Wales - are arbitrary and unreliable. In 1810 this diocese did not make a return at all; in 1811, 57 parishes are recorded as having residents; two years later residents almost doubled, to 108; and then, within a year, there was a further decline, to 86.[40] Nowhere else, fortunately, were there fluctuations as wild. The second source of difficulty is more subtle. For a period after the introduction of the fully sophisticated form of return, which distinguished between non-residents doing duty and those not doing duty, certain bishops made what were, in effect, false returns. What they did was to return as resident a number of non-residents doing duty. These errors were made in 1810 and 1811, and were subsequently corrected in 1813. Norwich furnishes the clearest example of what was happening. In 1809, that most liberal of bishops, Henry Bathurst, informed parliament that there were 353 residents in his diocese. Aware that this figure was rather low - Norwich, after all, contained nearly 1,100 parishes - he thought it worthwhile to append a short note to his return. 'Besides the 353 residents, there is a very large majority of the Non-Residents, who perform their duty, and are therefore virtually resident. This circumstance has not been accurately stated in the Return, but shall be rectified in future'. In 1810, and also in 1811, Bathurst set about the task of rectification. Residents in the former year were stated as 460, a rise of 107 within only twelve months; while, by the latter year, the total had increased by a further nineteen, to 479. Then comes the *volte face*. According to the official return, there were 335 parishes with residents in 1813, eighteen fewer than had been the case four years earlier. A year later there was a further reduction of seventeen, to 318. Returns for 1813 and 1814 agree with those for 1809, as do those for 1827. In the late 1820s, Bishop Bathurst reckoned that there were 360 residents in the diocese of Norwich, just seven more than he had returned in 1809.[41] This prompts a simple question. Why did the number of residents leap in 1810 and 1811? The question is simple, as is the answer. In these two years, 'virtual' residents were treated as though they were resident; Bishop Bathurst's process of 'rectification' was, in fact, synonymous with misclassification.

If the Bishop of Norwich enjoyed a distinguished reputation for administrative incompetence, so did Edward Vernon-Harcourt, Archbishop of the Northern Province. He went to York in 1808, and did not find this an easy diocese to grapple with. In 1809, according to Harcourt, there were only 152 residents for almost 900 parishes. Comment was required, and comment was duly made. 'There appear to be a very considerable number of clergy without any notice of their Residence or Non-Residence', he noted somewhat ingenuously; 'this circumstance arises from the Archbishop's having recently taken possession of his See, and therefore not having had time to make sufficient enquiry to ascertain the real state of residence within his Diocese. As the Archbishop proposes to hold a visitation of his Diocese in the course of the present year, he will be enabled to make a full and correct Return for the year 1810'. Full it may have been, correct it was not. As with Bathurst, Vernon-Harcourt's returns for 1810 and 1811 equated 'virtual' residence with actual residence. In 1810, 461 residents were returned, more than three times as many as a year earlier; and in 1811 the total crept up still further, reaching 483. As at Norwich, there was a greater degree of realism in 1813. Residents, now, numbered 341. Fourteen years later, in 1827, there were 364.[42]

Henry Bathurst and Edward Vernon-Harcourt were not the only bishops who misclassified non-residents in returns made for 1810 and 1811; the Bishops of London and Hereford did the same. It is the errors of these four prelates, compounded by the fluctuations at St David's, which have misled historians. The true situation with regard to clerical residence in the second and third decades of the nineteenth century emerges if the returns for St David's, and also for the four aberrant dioceses, are set aside. The relevant figures are best presented in a simple Table:

Digest of Parliamentary Returns on Clerical Residence, 1810-1827,
excluding the Dioceses of St David's, Hereford, London, Norwich and York.

Year	Parishes with Residents	Parishes with non-Residents doing duty
1810	3,003	433
1811	2,989	732
1813	2,996	1,052
1814	2,740	1,288
1827	3,193	1,032

It will not escape notice that non-residents doing duty rise sharply in 1814 only to fall away by 1827, while residents over the same period decline and then recover. A switch in classifications from resident to non-resident doing duty is the obvious, as it is also the correct, explanation. This clears away the final piece of statistical debris.

The other returns present a lucid and coherent picture. Towards the close of the Napoleonic Wars, the state of the church was static; the figures for residents in 1810, 1811 and 1813 are astonishingly similar, showing fractional variations either side of 3,000. Subsequently, there was a slight improvement, with about 200 more residents by 1827.

Even this advance was sporadic and irregular. In two dioceses, Worcester is one, Bath and Wells the other, the number of parishes with resident incumbents did not alter between 1813 and 1827; in nine the difference in either direction was five or less; and in a further four it was ten or less. Considerable improvement had, in fact, come about in only four dioceses. Two of these - St Asaph and Llandaff - were Welsh; the rise, for the pair, was 53. Then there was Lincoln, where the number of residents rose by 61, from 442 to 503. Finally, there was Chester; this diocese was comfortably ahead of Lincoln, posting an increase of 84, from 299 to 383.[43]

What, then, was the situation with regard to clerical residence in late-Georgian England? Sifting through the evidence, two sets of parliamentary returns stand out from the rest in terms of their accuracy and reliability. These are, respectively, the figures for 1813 and 1827. In both, unlike those of 1810 and 1811, 'virtual' residence was not sometimes confused with actual residence; nor, as in 1814, was there extensive misclassification of residents as non-residents doing duty. Even the figures for the most chaotic diocese of all, St David's, are reasonably coherent - parishes with residents amount to 108 in 1813, and to 131 in 1827. It is feasible, therefore, to compare these two sets of returns in their entirety, and to glimpse in the process an accurate picture of what the church was like in the decades prior to the era of reform. The picture is gloomy: the state of the church was neither healthy nor was it showing substantial improvement. In 1813, a total of 10,558 parishes throughout England and Wales made returns; and, of these, only 4,183 (40%) had residents. Fourteen years later, returns were made by 10,533 parishes, of which 4,413 (42%) had residents.[44] These findings give added significance to the earlier analysis of non-residence in the 1770s and early 1780s. At that period, it was discovered, 38% or so of parishes had residents,[45] 2% less than in 1813 and 4% less than in 1827. The developing pattern thus shows a very large increase in plurality and non-residence during the first three-quarters of the eighteenth century, followed by a marginal improvement in the half-century spanning the years 1780 to 1830.

As only four benefices in ten in late-Georgian England had resident incumbents, it is pertinent to ask about the other six. Three in twenty were served by the rector or vicar of the parish who, for one reason or another, lived elsewhere.[46] This category, of being non-resident but doing duty, is decidedly inexact. It might mean, in Bishop Bathurst's fine phrase, that an incumbent was 'virtually resident'; that is to say, he lived just outside his parish, and was, to all intents and purposes, a permanent resident; or it could mean that an incumbent was virtually non-resident, living at a considerable distance (maybe even ten or twelve miles away), and simply riding over on Sundays to take services. Where virtual residence ended, and virtual non-residence began, is a nice point for debate. The rest of the parishes in England and Wales - equivalent to 45% of the total - were not looked after by their own incumbent; services in these were taken either by a curate or by a neighbouring incumbent acting as curate. Parishes with non-residents not doing duty slightly outnumbered parishes with residents.

There was, also, considerable regional variation. Among scattered rural communities, figures for residence fell well short of the national norm. Examples are the deaneries of Waxham and Repps, discussed earlier. In this part of rural Norfolk there were, in 1820, only nine residents among 72 parishes.[47] The situation was better in South Lindsey - part of Lincolnshire - but was still scandalous. As in Waxham and Repps, nature was inhospitable. There was a lot of water in early nineteenth-century Lincolnshire; and water was never popular with the clergy, overlaid as it was with the fear of dankness and ague.[48] South Lindsey was, indeed, excessively rural. The area lacked industry, and boasted only three market towns of any substance: Market Rasen, Gainsborough, and Louth.[49] These three places exercised, over the clergy, a degree of attraction bordering upon the magnetic. Thus we find, in 1827, a local archdeacon complaining to Bishop Kaye that there were 'ten or twelve clergymen residing in the town of Louth far from their flocks whom they visit only on Sunday'.[50] This helps to explain why the category 'non-resident but doing duty' was well represented in South Lindsey. In 1830, among 215 parishes, there were 50 (23% of the sample) where duty was done by incumbents who lived elsewhere. Residents, indeed, numbered only a few more: there were 54 (25%). In a further 30 instances (14% of the total) parishes were looked after by resident curates. This leaves 81 places (38%) unaccounted for. Services in these were taken either by neighbouring incumbents or by curates who, like a lot of rectors and vicars, chose to live somewhere else.[51]

The combined strength of the many obstacles standing in the way of reform was formidable. A rural clergy, living a life of independent leisure; lax laws with regard to pluralism and non-residence; a top-heavy age structure among incumbents, with half being over fifty;[52] an average parochial population of no more than 500 in most counties;[53] numerous parishes without parsonages at all, or others with only 'unfit' accommodation; a complex system of patronage, many of whose aspects encouraged nepotism - given all these, the ideal of an incumbent resident in every place was unlikely to be realised. Nor was it. It is important to recall at this point the discussion which concluded Chapter Six.[54] Leaving aside situations where the logic of effective pastoral ministry favoured a degree of localised pluralism, four possible reasons for justifiable non-residence were identified. These were, in order, (i) lack of a parsonage altogether, (ii) 'unfit' accommodation, (iii) a benefice income below £150 a year, and (iv) infirmity or poor health. These four categories, we argued, applied to between 5,225 and 5,475 livings - half the total. This discussion can now be compared with what was actually the case.

Two main points must be made. First, the extent of non-residence, at six livings out of ten, exceeded what was justifiable. Second, one of the four justifications mentioned above - namely, a benefice income below £150 a year - bore little relation to reality. The rich English clergy were as non-resident and pluralistic as the poor Welsh.[55] Raising benefice incomes did not, by itself, ensure that standards of clerical duty improved. What was needed, in this regard, was the imposition of legal curbs, either preventing the clergy from holding several livings or placing a wealth limit upon allowable pluralism. No effort in this direction was made before 1830. The number of parsonages did not increase, nor was a clerical pension scheme introduced. In these circumstances, it is not surprising that clerical residence failed to improve.

Lurking in the background was, however, a hidden 'engine of reform'. The fuel for this was supplied by a lot of ageing and frustrated curates. Although they worked and sweated hard, they did not get very far. During the middle decades of the eighteenth century, the annual number of ordinations was around 245.[56] There was, after 1770, a modest rise; ordinations, at the end of the eighteenth century, were running at around 270 a year.[57] Stability was broken at the close of the Napoleonic Wars. Figures for ordinations increased extremely rapidly, soon reaching over 500 a year.[58] Between 1834 and 1843 the average was 535 a year.[59] Incumbents, in the early 1830s, totalled 7,500;[60] the ratio between the annual number of newly ordained curates and the full complement of beneficed clergy was, thus, 1:14. Chronic indigestion on this scale was not eased by the obliging habit of early death among the clergy. In 1833, the median age of Norfolk incumbents was 52, while in Sussex the figure was 47.[61] The frequency at which clergy resigned their livings in the 1820s and 1830s was probably no more than half the frequency of ordinations. The imbalance between recruitment and natural wastage had become critical. In the years after 1815, increasing pressure was put upon the already beneficed to share their good fortune with those who, although deserving recognition, remained without it. This pressure was resisted. Those who were 'in' did not divide the spoils with those who were, often permanently, 'out'.

Overcrowding of the profession did not bring about improvement, nor did the Evangelical revival. Evangelical effort was prodigious - philanthropy, prayer and proselytising, all conducted with vigour; and to this was added flair, as well as a touch of the grand manner: tracts were written with a speed and profusion not seen since the Civil War, Bibles were distributed by the ton, numerous public meetings were held. Many Evangelicals were bitter about clerical laxity, scorned wealth, and were appalled by episcopal maladministration. Yet, despite zeal and energy, the Evangelical movement failed to mount an internal revolution within the church. The leaven was unable to lighten the dough.

Most Evangelical leaders wished to work within the inherited social and political system; attacks upon aristocratic society, and aristocratic privilege, were carefully avoided. The way to influence, it was argued, lay along the path of conformity. A corollary of this position was that the clergy were well-advised to work within the inherited ecclesiastical system. Simeon created his Trust,[62] which bought advowsons and installed 'godly' men. Other leading Evangelicals considered that it was permissible to become pluralists in order to employ Evangelical curates. Alternatively, an incumbent might, like Cadogan of Reading, find himself with two livings at the time of his conversion. In this particular case, he kept both with a view to promoting godliness. All his clerical life, Cadogan remained vicar of St Giles, Reading, as well as rector of St Luke's, Chelsea. He was presented to St Giles in 1774, at the distinctly unripe age of twenty-three, and gained St Luke's from his father, Lord Cadogan, the following year.[63] Conversion meant that godly preaching on a godly Sabbath was now possible at two places. Attitudes consistent with preservation of the unreformed system are to be found among other influential Evangelical clergy. One of the early Evangelical bishops, C.R. Sumner - promoted to Llandaff in 1826 - was particularly old-fashioned.[64] He had earlier been private chaplain to George IV - not an obvious choice of preferment for an Evangelical clergyman - as well as Librarian to the King, Chaplain to the Household at Carlton House, and Historiographer to the Crown. After his move to Winchester in 1827, he stoutly resisted every attempt by the Ecclesiastical Commissioners to trim his extensive extra-diocesan patronage. He was also, when occasion required, a nepotist.[65] The reforming credentials of aristocratic Evangelicals were sometimes less than perfect.

Although the state of the church, considered as an institution, bordered upon the abysmal, the situation was not as desperate from the personal side. Most clergymen were not pluralists, and a majority also resided in one or other of their livings. The picture is clearest in the early 1830s. At this time two-thirds of English clergy held only a single living, while less than 6% held three or more. There were six incumbents with five benefices each, the upper limit.[66] Figures for Wales are similar; two-thirds with one living, 7% with three or more, and only a single incumbent with the maximum of four.[67] Although only four benefices in ten had resident incumbents, six incumbents in ten did reside in a parish where they held the cure of souls. Of the remainder, rather less than three in twenty did duty whilst living elsewhere, and the others neither did duty nor resided.[68] If any improvement was to come, the easiest way was by persuading - or requiring - these lax clergy to mend their ways. The late-Georgian bishop held the key to change in his hand.

The clergy was less pluralistic than historians have thought, and it was also less pluralistic than contemporaries thought. Even after publication of the 1835 Report, a great deal of nonsense continued to be spoken and written on this matter. Earlier, incredible claims were made. The best instance of absurdity occurred in a semi-official publication, the *Clerical Guide*. Its first edition came out in 1817, with a second five years later. The list of clergy in the first edition is not reliable, but that in the second is ridiculous. According to the *Clerical Guide* for 1822, the most profligate of all parsons was John Jones, credited with no less than thirty-four livings. Most of these were dispersed throughout Wales, although some were in London, Liverpool and Oxfordshire. A number of other Welsh clergy, it would seem, were also avaricious. There was David Williams with fifteen benefices, and John Williams, also with fifteen; Thomas Williams was credited with nineteen; William Williams had twenty-four. The Welsh clergy, according to the *Clerical Guide* for 1822, was clearly an endangered species.

John Jones's clerical career, although exciting, was short. By the time the next edition of the *Clerical Guide* was published in 1829, he had, so to speak, spawned a host of relations, all bearing his name and all holding his livings. David Williams - not to mention John Williams, Thomas Williams and William Williams - had achieved the same, not inconsiderable, feat. In fact, of course, John Jones, like these members of the Williams family, existed only in the minds of the proprietors of the *Clerical Guide* for 1822. Faced with the task of discriminating between individual Welsh clergy called John Jones, they had conflated them all into a single - and mythical - individual. This error had not been perpetrated in the first edition of the *Guide* in 1817, nor was it repeated subsequently. The editors of the 1829 edition of the *Guide* permitted themselves the self-indulgence of making a delicate allusion to the gross incompetence of their predecessors. 'The Proprietors', ran its advertisement, 'have to offer their best acknowledgements to the numerous gentlemen who have furnished them with information of the changes and alterations that have taken place since the publication of the Second Edition; and they trust in consequence of these communications the names of the *Incumbents* and *Patrons* of *Benefices* will be found more correctly described in the present, than in the two former Editions'. This remark deserves to be treasured by all connoisseurs of understatement.

The error made in the 1822 edition was a blunder of the first magnitude. Had the mythical John Jones existed, his income would have been £5,456 a year,[69] no mean sum for a Welsh clergyman. No contemporary bishop commented upon the original mistake, nor upon its subsequent correction. More remarkably, no ecclesiastical spokesman ever countered the use that was made of it. John Jones was the kind of encouraging cleric that a hostile anti-clerical did not meet every day. The anonymous author of the *Black Book* was pleased to get acquainted. This publication made great play of the fact that its quarrel was with the practice, not the theory, of the church. 'We prefer an established worship, not less as a means of maintaining a rational piety, than as a counterpoise to fanaticism';[70] or again, on a more grudging note, 'to the Church of England, in the *abstract*, we have no particular objection'.[71] For someone claiming to be pragmatic in attitude, this anti-clerical author was extraordinarily careless about fact. The *Black Book* of 1820, the *Supplement to the Black Book* of 1823, and the *Extraordinary Black Book* of 1831 kept on repeating the charge of aristocratic indolence among the clergy, supporting it with lists of pluralists. When the *Supplement* of 1823 reached 'Jones, Revd John', it duly noted down all the thirty-four livings mentioned in the *Clerical Guide* for 1822; and then, by way of good measure, it added sardonically: 'we believe he is also an Archdeacon, Chaplain of Christ's Church, Oxford, and Head of Exeter College. How he manages to discharge his multifarious duties at so many and distant places it is impossible to conceive'.[72] Indeed, it is. The treatment meted out to John Jones was the same as that meted out to 'D. Williams' 'J. Williams', 'T. Williams' and 'W. Williams'; the preferments listed in the *Clerical Guide* for 1822 were painstakingly copied into the *Supplement to the Black Book* for 1823. This is lamentable enough; but there is worse to come. When the *Extraordinary*

Black Book was put together in 1831, the list of pluralists was derived, without either addition or subtraction, from the *Clerical Guide* for 1829. Thus multi-pluralist after multi-pluralist - including John Jones, D. Williams, J. Williams, T. Williams, and W. Williams - melted away with the sun. The apparent transformation of the church between 1823 and 1831 received no comment from Wade, just as it received no comment from anyone else. Wade's *Supplement* was not rebutted, nor was the contrast with the *Extraordinary Black Book* exposed. Passion for truth was a scarce commodity in the contemporary 'great debate'.[73]

iii. *Waning*

There was, throughout much of the early nineteenth century, a growing restlessness and insecurity. Church and clergy never seemed to be far from scenes of agitation. Peterloo is one of the clearest examples. A part in the events of that day was played by two clerical justices, one of whom, W.R. Hay, felt the strength of popular wrath, just as he was also pleased to receive the favour of official recognition.[74] Or again, it was the robust support of the Tory cause by a group of Durham clergy that gave rise, in 1822, to a notable skirmish in polemical warfare. Known as the 'Durham Case', this was the first occasion during the post-war period when a local dispute had, as one of its consequences, the publication of a spate of pamphlets on church reform.[75]

Between repeal of the Test and Corporation Acts in 1828 and consideration of the Irish Bishoprics Bill in 1833, the church found itself assailed from all quarters. Wealthy incumbents were mobbed during the rural unrest of the winter of 1830-1;[76] it was difficult to be a bishop after episcopal votes held up the Reform Bill in October, 1831; Joseph Hume and Henry Brougham were hot against nepotism in Parliament; erring clergy were mercilessly hounded in *Slap at the Church* and the *Episcopal Gazette*.[77] Public statements by churchmen were rich in gloom; and the previous trickle of pamphlets on church reform turned into a flood. The watershed was reached in 1832 and 1833, when fears of Whig 'spoliation' were at their height and the radical press was at the peak of its confidence.[78] It is this highly charged atmosphere which formed the inescapable context of ecclesiastical affairs.

Despite the prevailing ecclesiastical panic, leading churchmen did not come either quickly or easily to the conclusion that pluralism and non-residence were unmitigated evils, and that they should, without more ado, be rooted out. Indeed, far from it. Even among noted church reformers - as among, also, their lordships, the bishops - there was a clear perception of the merits of the unreformed system, and an equal unease at the prospect of reform being taken too far and too fast. Pluralism and non-residence were defended on four main grounds. The first defence - a staunch old stand-by, if ever there was one - was the social argument. The poor, it was claimed, stood to benefit more from the bountiful ministrations of a rich pluralist than from the necessarily more constrained care of a poor non-pluralist. This was the line taken by Henry Phillpotts, newly raised by Wellington to the see of Exeter. He told the clergy, at his primary visitation in 1833, that 'it is often found far more advantageous to the people, to the poor especially, that there be one incumbent of two livings, who is thus placed in easy, or moderately opulent, circumstances, than two separate incumbents, each with a straightened income'.[79] This kind of appeal had been made before, and would be made again. Its major defect lay in the thrust of its own logic: the argument, if true, seemed to suggest that plurality was preferable to non-plurality.

Casuistry was also employed in the cause of upholding pluralism. Having more than one living may have been an evil, but it was an evil that could be turned, dexterously, into good. This style of thinking has been encountered already, in the earlier discussion of resignation bonds; it comes as no surprise to encounter it again. On this occasion the casuistical sword was wielded by Edward Berens, an archdeacon as well as an advanced and influential church reformer. He claimed, in grandiloquent prose, that pluralism might well enable a busy priest to 'enlarge his own sphere of professional activity',[80] a statement with which it is hard to disagree. This notion, on the part of Berens, may well strike the reader as an instance of special pleading with a vengeance; nevertheless it claimed a wide following among the author's clerical contemporaries. It was not uncommon for conscientious clergy - even, may it be said, for conscientious Evangelical clergy - to justify their plurality on the grounds that it promoted godliness.[81]

A further argument was pragmatic. It was possible to look at the state of the church, and in particular to consider the plight of the poor curate, and then to conclude that tampering with the existing system was a tricky, possibly even ill-advised, course of action. Would not thousands of curates be deprived of their livelihood, were droves of lax incumbents now to reside? These reflections occurred to Edward Burton,[82] Regius Professor of Divinity at Oxford, and, together with Thomas Arnold and Lord Henley, the most discussed church reformer of the age. Burton, it has to be said, voiced genuine disquiet; there was a risk that, in getting the beneficed clergy to mend their ways, reformers would also succeed in making life extremely difficult for many of the beneficed clergy's employees, the curates.[83]

The last word on this subject belongs with William Howley, promoted to primate on the death of Manners-Sutton in 1828. Manners-Sutton had not been noted for over-activity during his tenure at Canterbury, a happy precedent Howley was determined to follow. Mild and ineffectual, his mind was steeped in traditional attitudes. These were to the fore in 1832, when he addressed the Canterbury clergy on the subject of pluralism and non-residence. 'The holding of more Benefices than one by the same individual', he told ·them, 'has been always allowed under certain restrictions in our Church, with a view to the more liberal maintenance of its ministers, the encouragement of sacred learning, and the remuneration of professional merit'.[84] Such sentiments as these do little to enhance Howley's reputation.

Although ecclesiastical leaders showed, at times, a less than tepid enthusiasm for the cause of reform, much improvement was achieved during the 1830s. The contrast with the situation earlier in the century is stark. In the fourteen years between 1813 and 1827, residents rose in number by 230, equivalent to a rate of increase of 16 a year; and in the eleven years between 1827 and 1838 the improvement was 1,446, or 131 a year. Such is the measure of change and reform. Also - and this point is equally important - there is a sense of gathering pace, an accelerated momentum. Between 1827 and 1831 the increase in residents was 236; between 1831 and 1835 it was 497; and between 1835 and 1838 it was 713.[85]

As might be expected, the margins of England - extensive areas of mountain and forest - were less affected by the spirit of the times than the centre. No whisper of alteration reached Carlisle, northerly and remote; or, if it did, bishop and clergy chose to ignore it. In 1810 there were 78 resident incumbents; in 1838 there were 78 resident incumbents; and, in the years between, there was an infuriating consistency: never more than the magic figure of 78 and never less than 73; between 1831 and 1838 the overall improvement was three.[86] In Wales things were not much better. In Llandaff the number of residents went up by five between 1831 and 1838; in St Asaph by ten; and in Bangor by thirteen. This makes an aggregate improvement of twenty-eight, matching with perfect statistical neatness the decline in residents recorded for St David's, still the epitome of administrative chaos at its most rampant.[87] Wales did no better during the 1830s than did the Cumberland and Westmorland fells.

The history of the church prior to 1830 shows that the clerical horse needed to be whipped before it would move. Since this was the case, the expertise and determination of the rider was of paramount importance. The 'new breed' of bishop was more effective and persistent than the old; and, among this new breed, two men - Henry Phillpotts and Charles James Blomfield - towered over the others. Phillpotts and Blomfield differed in most things. They differed in churchmanship, in political attitudes and in mentality, Blomfield being much the more flexible of the two. They also differed in their views as to the shape and direction the coming Victorian church should take. Blomfield defended the Ecclesiastical Commission, newly-founded in 1835, and all that it stood for: the pruning of cathedral establishments, levelling of episcopal incomes, simplifying of diocesan geography, and the like. Phillpotts, as predictably, detested the Ecclesiastical Commission and all that it stood for. In one important respect, however, they were alike. They were both reformers, set upon substantially reducing non-residence in their dioceses. Henry Phillpotts, we have previously noted, was prepared to offer public justification of pluralism.[88] What he said in private was different. His appointment to Exeter in 1830 caused a stir among the local radical press, and also a stir among the Devonian and Cornish clergy. In 1810 there were 269 residents in the diocese of Exeter; and in 1831 only seven more. By 1835, however, the figure had risen to 364, and by 1838 it was up to 430. Within the space of only seven years, Phillpotts had increased the number of residents by 154.[89]

Blomfield and Phillpotts were alike in one other way - neither was a man who enjoyed being beaten. What 'Henry of Exeter' could do, 'Blomfield of London' would strive to match. Phillpotts was raised to Exeter in 1830; Blomfield had moved to the metropolis from Chester two years earlier.[90] Like Phillpotts, he found his diocese in a sad state of disarray; and, again like him, he achieved much of the reform that was needed. According to the official return for 1827, there were 255 resident incumbents among 577 benefices in the diocese of London. Within four years the number of residents had risen to 287, within another four it was up to 325, and within three more it had reached 409. Phillpotts increased the number of resident incumbents in his diocese by 154 between 1831 and 1838: Blomfield over the same period increased the number in his by 122.[91] Their efforts show how large a measure of change a really strong-minded diocesan could bring about.

The successes of Phillpotts and Blomfield make it necessary to revise perceptions of the pre-1830 church. Scott's Act of 1803 put the onus for improving clerical residence upon the shoulders of the episcopate, a burden which the majority of the Bench proved singularly unable to bear. It was, ultimately, a question of will and of priorities. The will was not there, and the priorities lay elsewhere - principally, in fulfilling a defined parliamentary role, and in upholding, as against Dissent, the church's authority and power. The bishops who emerged in the 1820s - Kaye, Blomfield, Monk, and so on - agreed with the aim of maintaining, and if possible strengthening, the church's position in the nation. But they were also wise enough to perceive that it was necessary to disarm the church's enemies, and that the major weapon in the hands of anti-clericals was laxity in the ranks of the church's army. Each man must not only be on the ramparts, he must be seen to be there. Hence the new Bishop of London's single-minded effort to secure the residence of those clergy committed to his charge.

It might be tempting to conclude, on the basis of the excellent performance put in by bishops of the 'new breed', that the Georgian church was not only capable of self-reform but achieved it. To argue in this way would be, however, to ignore one vital factor - timing. Without intense external pressure, nothing was done. With intense external pressure, everything was done. The likes of Kaye and Monk were moulded by the age in which they lived, and by the cultural and political environment in which they moved. Insistence upon clerical residence was raised to the status of an imperative because it was 'impossible' that the church could 'go on as it is',[92] because the 'days of the establishment' were 'numbered'.[93] In the 1830s, a bishop needed to be quite exceptionally insensitive - as insensitive, one might say, as Bishop Percy of Carlisle[94] - in order not to perceive that something had to be done. Church reform was no longer an optional matter, the kind of thing suitable for periodic exhortation and occasional remonstrance; it was, now, crucial and critical. The future of the church, indeed its very existence, was widely believed to be at stake. With the 'Gaul at the gates', the time for wordy discussion was over and the time for decisive action had begun.

External pressures for reform were paramount in the 1830s, although this must not be taken to imply that internal pressures were easing. To begin with, the incontrovertible fact of rising clerical numbers, a subject already mentioned in this Chapter.[95] The point which needs to be forcefully made in the context of the present discussion is that ordination numbers did not rise overnight. Because overcrowding of the clerical profession was a cumulative process, it made for steady reform; yet it is not a sufficient explanation of the swift change that overtook the church in the years after 1830. Clerical overcrowding, moreover, is an explanatory tool with more than one edge; in so far as advances achieved in the 1830s are traced to this source, it must equally be said that the static situation earlier was, in reality, less defensible than might otherwise be thought.

Similar arguments apply to the influence of Evangelicalism. If the increase in residents in the 1830s is put down to the fact that there were more Evangelical clergy, it has to be asked why things did not get any better during the second and third decades of the century, when Evangelical numbers were also rising.[96] Sudden changes, I am arguing, require sudden causes. Evangelical influence within the church, like the effects of clerical overcrowding, was not sudden.

What about the Oxford movement? This, Newman thought, dated from the day of Keble's famous Assize Sermon of 14 July, 1833. Contemporaries, with accurate insight, spoke of Tractarianism. The Oxford movement was, in origin, intellectual: a matter of new minds searching for new roots, in old soil. As already pointed out, the movement could, in the 1830s, claim only a few supporters among the beneficed clergy - W.F. Hook at Leeds; Keble himself at Hursley in Hampshire.[97] Parochial mission was to come; but its time had not yet arrived.

A final point needs to be made. The initial reforming impetus was not provided by changes in the law. It is true that effective anti-pluralistic legislation was enacted during the 1830s, but not until 1838 - a decade after the transformation of clerical residence had been set in train. To trace the history of the 1838 Act is to become aware of how ecclesiastical statesmen reacted to contemporary events. They resisted pressure for change exerted during times of intense public excitement, but then subsequently conceded much of what had earlier been demanded. A tentative start was made in the early 1830s, with two abortive bills introduced into the Lords by Archbishop Howley, the first in 1831, and the second the following year. Both were superficially radical, in that they contained a clause prohibiting incumbents from taking a second living if their first was worth over £400 a year. This radical element was, however, more apparent than real; a sub-section, allowing dispensations to all Masters of Arts, brought about a fully effective emasculation.[98] The cause of reform, frustrated in the early years of the decade, triumphed after public clamour had died down. The 1838 Pluralities Act[99] had three main aims. Its first objective was to put a stop to excessive pluralism, by restricting each incumbent to a maximum of two benefices. This was less draconian than might at first be thought; as has been seen, only 6% or so of the clergy held three livings or more.[100] It was also the few who stood to lose from fulfilment of the Act's second objective: the curbing of clerical opulence. The maximum aggregate value of the two permissible benefices was set at £1,000 a year: it is interesting to note that there were only 386 incumbents (5% of the total) with ecclesiastical incomes in excess of this amount.[101] There was also a degree of flexibility. The special circumstances of poor benefices were recognised in a clause relaxing the joint wealth limit of £1,000 a year in cases where one of the livings held in plurality was worth under £150 and had a population of less than 2,000. The third aim of the Act was to confine legitimate pluralism to localised areas. It did this by replacing the canonical limit of thirty miles by a new limit of ten. This had wider implications than the other clauses in the Act; a third of the clergy held a second living,[102] and the canonical limit had not previously been taken notice of. Here was a shackle placed on the legs of the many, not of the few.

The force of the Act was not felt by the clergy immediately. As with the Deans and Chapters Act, life-interests were respected, an exercise in ecclesiastical decorum that allowed the Sparkes and Pretymans of the Establishment to linger on after mid-century. This, it can scarcely be denied, blunted the Act's effectiveness, but is probably less important than the fact that two major points of principle had been won. Parliament had shown itself willing to restrict the freedom of action of the great and powerful among the clergy; and, secondly, it was now coming to be accepted that pastoral logic was the sole justification for legitimate pluralism.

iv. *Tail-piece*

It remains to be said that there was no turning back the clock. The scale of improvement achieved in the 1830s was matched in the 1840s. The similarity is impressive. Between 1827 and 1838 the proportion of parishes with residents rose by 12.7%, and between 1838 and 1848 the proportion rose by a further 12.4%. The overall rise, during the 1830s and 1840s, was thus a shade over 25%.[103] The transformation reached remote localities. In 1851, in South Lindsey, just under 50% of livings had resident incumbents;[104] in the same district, two decades earlier, the proportion of residents had been, as already noted,[105] no more than 25%. Bearing in mind the increase in non-residence and pluralism which took place during the eighteenth century, and recalling, also, the minimal improvement registered between 1775 and 1830, the consistent progress characteristic of the 1830s and 1840s can only be regarded as remarkable.

The Pluralities Act of 1838 was followed by another in 1850,[106] reducing the limit for permissible pluralism from ten miles to three, and stipulating that the value of one of the two livings to be held in plurality should not exceed £100 a year. The passing of this Act meant that considerations to do with the fulfilment of pastoral ministry became, and not before time, the determining factor as to where clergy lived and worked. Incumbents could no longer enrich themselves by means of the simple, and elegant, tactic of acquiring a pair of livings, either one of which would have been perfectly adequate to maintain both themselves and their families in wealth and comfort; and the three-mile rule put a stop to the widespread practice of holding two benefices which were too distant from each other to permit either to be served vigorously and successfully. After mid-century, only two classes of parish were still held in plurality. The first comprised places where there was a pastoral justification for holding the living in conjunction with another somewhere else; set in remote countryside, and often with a dwindling population, these livings were so poor that they did not provide sufficient income for a beneficed clergyman. The second class was altogether different. They were made up of places held by a hard core of determined pluralists: Sparke, son of Sparke, and so on; these men, of course, were not easily moved. Nor was there any immediate solution to the problems of depopulated, penurious, livings. Despite these difficulties, progress continued to be made. Regular returns on residence cease in 1850, and the idea was only taken up again on one occasion, in 1879. By then there were 11,186 parishes with residents, and only 1,509 without; the proportion with resident incumbents was now approaching 90%, which needs to be compared with a figure of a little under 70% in 1850.[107]

At this point it is appropriate to pause, and to reflect. A traveller passing through the English countryside, either in the years around 1780 or towards the end of the first quarter of the new century, saw as he went numerous instances of clerical neglect; at both periods only four parishes in every ten had resident incumbents. But a different scene met the eyes of a traveller through the late-Victorian countryside; now, not four in every ten, but nine in every ten parishes had resident incumbents. Change was sudden but, once it got under way, it refused to be halted. The crucial period is from 1827 until 1838. Between these years, figures for residence rose by an eighth. A similar rate of change occurred in the 1840s, and there was then a gradual improvement during the mid-Victorian years.

Chapter 8 Notes

1. Samuel Horsley, *Charge* (1796), p.30.
2. Invidious, but not impossible - see above, pp.153-7, for analysis of the two Norfolk deaneries of Waxham and Repps.
3. Beilby Porteus, Bishop of Chester, 1776-87; and of London, 1787-1808.
4. See above, p.70ff.
5. The title of an article by W.M. Jacob, in *Studies in Church History*, XVI (1979), 315-26.
6. 'Bishops returns of poor livings under £80 made in 1705', Q.A.B., Bundles 1-3.
7. In Salisbury there were 12 pluralists among 52 incumbents; in Carlisle, 12 among 62; in Peterborough, 10 among 60; and in Exeter, 38 among 271. It was in Exeter that we came across the only triple pluralist. In some regions in the early eighteenth century, pluralism was even less frequent than it was in our sample. In the archdeaconry of Northumberland in 1721, there were 71 incumbents for 77 benefices - see Shuler, 'The Pastoral and Ecclesiastical Administration of the Diocese of Durham', p.26.
8. 'Bishops returns of poor livings under £80 made in 1705', Q.A.B., Bundles 1-3.
9. Warne, *Church and Society*, p.39. Residents were 231, non-residents 159.
10. Jacob, *Studies in Church History*, XVI, 322.
11. Austin, 'The Church of England', Table 6, p.93. 48 were residents, non-residents 44.
12. Ransome, *Wiltshire Returns*, p.9. 232 parishes made returns; 90 had resident incumbents.
13. Ransome, *The State of the Bishopric of Worcester*, p.14. Among 212 vicarages, rectories and perpetual curacies, there were 82 resident incumbents.
14. McClatchey, *Oxfordshire Clergy*, Table, p.31. On this topic, note also the comment in

John Addy, 'Two eighteenth century bishops of Chester and their diocese 1771-1787', p.264: 'abundant evidence survives to show that the clergy found excuses for non-residence'.

15. This calculation assumes that there were around 10,550 parishes in Georgian England, the figure given in early nineteenth-century returns on clerical residence, for which see below, Table XVIII.

16. See below, Table XVIII.

17. See below, p.203.

18. In some places in the later eighteenth century, a lot more than 36% of the beneficed clergy were pluralists. In the archdeaconry of Durham in 1774, visitation returns show 38 pluralists among 69 incumbents; the proportion of pluralists works out at 55% - Maynard, 'The Ecclesiastical Administration of the Archdeaconry of Durham', p.436. These statistics are in dramatic contrast with those of Shuler for 1721, for which see above, note 7.

19. Bezodis, 'The English Parish Clergy', I, 74-5.

20. Marshall, 'The Administration of the Dioceses of Hereford and Oxford', p.103.

21. Bezodis, *op.cit.*, I, 74-5.

22. See above, p.93.

23. See above, pp.174-8.

24. See above, pp.146-7.

25. See above, p.146.

26. See above, pp.160-1

27. Best, *Temporal Pillars*, pp. 200-1.

28. Ransome, *The State of the Bishopric of Worcester*, p. 2; quoted in Best, *op.cit.*, p.201.

29. Cook, *The Diocese of Exeter in 1821*, II, xi.

30. Bernard Falk, *The Bridgewater Millions*, p. 185.

31. *ibid.*, pp. 212-13. On one occasion his dentist charged Egerton 15,000 francs for seven sets of dentures; Egerton sued, and the bill was reduced to 7,500 francs (*ibid*).

32. *ibid.*, p. 186.

33. *ibid.*, pp. 121-2, 187.

34. *ibid.*, p. 119.

35. *ibid.*, pp. 200-1.

36. *ibid.*, pp. 211-12.

37. *ibid.*, pp. 209-10. Among his other foibles was a love of shoes. His bootmaker was kept rather busy. Egerton wore a different pair on each day of the year, and insisted that the whole collection should be kept in pristine condition (*ibid.*, p. 209). A brief sketch of Egerton can be found in Chadwick, *The Victorian Church*, I, 560-1.

38. Particularly amusing are some remarks made in Y. Brilioth, *The Anglican Revival*, p. 13. He only cites a single return on clerical residence - that for 1811 - which is said to have stated that '3,611 incumbents were non-residents'. Such widespread dereliction of duty led Brilioth 'to a comparison with the state of things in the later Middle Ages; offices which implied responsibility for the eternal welfare of human souls, were treated almost as lightly as then, as a desirable prey for covetousness and insatiableness'. One is forced to wonder what the comment would have been, if Brilioth had taken the trouble to transcribe the return correctly. For he seems to have suffered a brief attack of arithmetical dyslexia: the return showed there to be 6,311 non-residents, not 3,611.

39. See below, Table XVIII.

40. See below, Table XIX.

41. See below, Table XIX. Some interesting comments on Bathurst are to be found in Whitfield, 'Change and Continuity', p.40. The bishop spent most of his time in London and Bath, was 'inordinately fond' of whist, liked the company of Roman Catholics and Dissenters, and left the management of the diocese to his son, Archdeacon Henry Bathurst.

42. See below, Table XIX.

43. It is not entirely irrelevant tthat C.J. Blomfield became Bishop of Chester in 1824.

44. See below, Table XVIII.

45. See above, p.193.

46. In 1813 this held on 1,641 occasions (16% of the total); and in 1827 it held on 1,590 (15% of the whole). See below, Table XVIII.

47. See above, p.154.

48. James Obelkevich, *Religion and Rural Society*, p.2.

49. *ibid.*, p.9.

50. *ibid.*, p.117, note 1.

51. *ibid.*, Table, p.116 .

52. See above, pp.161-2.

53. See above, p.144.

54. See above, pp.162-3.

55. See below, p.214, notes 66 and 67.

56. See above, p.136.

57. According to Stone, *The university in society*, Appendix IV, Table 1A, p.91 and Appendix IV, Table 1B, p.92 the aggregate figure for admissions to Oxford and Cambridge in the 1790s averaged 407 a year. It is assumed that 50% of these students subsequently became ordained, and that, in the 1790s, Oxbridge-trained ordinands were 75% of the whole.

58. See above, p.136.

59. See above, p.135.

60. See above, p.90.

61. See above, pp.161-2.

62. On Simeon's trust, see Balda, 'Spheres of Influence'.

63. Richard Cecil, *Discourses of the Hon and Revd W.B. Cadogan*, pp. xviii-xix.

64. His clerical brother, J.B. Sumner, subsequently Archbishop of Canterbury, was raised to Chester just two years later. See above, p.21.

65. Best, *op.cit.*, p, 326.

66. Full figures for England are: 4,654 beneficed clergy (67.0%) with one living; 1,892 (27.3%) with two; 342 (4.9%) with three; 46 (0.7%) with four; and 6 (0.1%) with five. The total works out at 6,940.

67. For Wales: 363 incumbents (66.0%) with one benefice; 147 (26.7%) with two; 34 (6.2%) with three; and 6 (1.1%) with four. The total number of Welsh clergy was 550.

68. Three livings in twenty were served by non-residents living nearby. Some of these clergy would have served more than one place. Hence the conclusion that rather less than three in twenty of the beneficed clergy can be described as non-residents doing duty.

69. From *P.P.*, 1835, XXII, 111-1060.

70. [J. Wade], *Extraordinary Black Book* p. 79.

71. [J. Wade], *Supplement to the Black Book*, p. 212.

72. *ibid.*, p. 284.

73. Although conspicuous by lack of mention in the contemporary 'great debate', John Jones

has fared somewhat better in works of ecclesiastical history. The avarice adumbrated in the *Supplement of the Black Book* attracts the attention of S.C. Carpenter, *Church and People, 1789-1889*, p.56. In fairness to this learned historian, it should be pointed out that he is sceptical of the claim that Jones, in addition to his numerous livings, was also Rector of Exeter College, Oxford, having received information that although a certain Dr Jones was, indeed, Rector from 1819 until 1838, he does not appear to have been a pluralist.

74. See above, p.120.

75. This series of incidents is described in Best, *op.cit.*, pp. 245-50.

76. See Hobsbawm and Rudé, *Captain Swing*.

77. There is an extended account of the contemporary political and ecclesiastical crisis in Chadwick, *op.cit.*, I, 7-166.

78. See above, p.24.

79. Henry Phillpotts, *Charge* (1833), p.41.

80. [E. Berens], *Church Reform*, p.81. On Berens, see Best, *Temporal Pillars*, pp. 279-80.

81. See above, pp.202-3.

82. Edward Burton, *Sequel to Remarks upon Church Reform*, p.47. See, also, for instance, Bloomfield, *An Analytical View*, p. 42. Some very interesting remarks about Burton are to be found in Best, *op.cit.*, pp. 281-3.

83. This matter is discussed in more detail in Chapter IX, below, pp.215-41.

84. William Howley, *Charge* (1832), p.42.

85. Full figures are in Table XVIII.

86. See below, Table XIX.

87. *ibid.*

88. See above, pp.205-6.

89. Full figures are in Table XIX.

90. We have already pointed out (see above, p.200.) that the number of residents in the diocese of Chester rose strongly in the years prior to 1827.

91. Diocesan figures are in Table XX, below.

92. See above, p.19.

93. See above, p.19.

94. After a rather short stay at Rochester, during a few months of 1827, Percy was translated to Carlisle, where he remained until his death in 1856.

95. See above, p.202.

96. See above, pp.202-3.

97. See above, p.23.

98. Lord King, House of Lords, 5 March 1832, *Hansard*, Third Series, IX, 1108; Lord Suffield, House of Lords, 23 March 1832, *ibid.*, XI, 795.

99. 1 and 2 Vic. c. 106.

100. See above, notes 66 and 67.

101. See above, p.90. See also Table VI.

102. See above, notes 66 and 67.

103. See below, Table XVIII.

104. The figure was 101 among 209 (48%) - see Obelkevich, *op.cit.*, Table, p.116.

105. See above, p.201.

106. 13 and 14 Vic. c. 98.

107. See below, Table XVIII.

9

The Lives of the Subalterns

'As to those who court this *genteel* profession, with no other prospect but of being "journey-men" - "soles" - not "upper-leathers" - which is (being interpreted) poor curates - they are truly to be pitied. If they regard present circumstances, without "having respect unto the recompense of future reward", they would, I am sure, do better for themselves, and for their families, by making interest for upper-servants' places in a genteel family, than by being mere *"soles or understrappers"* in the Church'.[1]

'We may divide the clergy into generals, field officers, and subalterns'.[2]

i. *Career Structure*

The career structure of the Georgian church was like a pyramid; a pyramid, moreover, with an unusually long base and gently tapered sides that steadily ascended to meet at a distant apex. Along the base stood several thousand curates, all looking apprehensively upwards, while at the apex was a select group of wealthy incumbents and cathedral dignitaries. Curates had good reasons for their troubled state of mind. Their problems, at bottom, flowed from their status: and this was defined by their position as the employee of the incumbent of the parish (or parishes) they served. It was difficult for them to be independently-minded or to show initiative. Indeed, it was all too often the case that, as a class, they were subservient; their spinelessness, and lack of ambition, receive frequent mention in contemporary literature. One series of complaints, among others, was voiced by one of their own number, who wrote anonymously to the *Morning Herald* in 1831.[3] He had, he explained, been a curate for twenty years, during which time he had become increasingly embittered. Recently, he had tried to persuade some of his brethren to sign a statement of grievances, to be sent to the bishops, but all had refused. The anonymous correspondent despaired at this lack of support. The curates of England, he averred, were 'in as complete a state of bondage to our Very Rev and titled Masters as ever the Jews were to the arbitrary despotism of Pharaoh'.

Despite the obvious overstatement, he had a valid point. As proof of this, it is necessary to look no further than the treatment curates could receive at the hands of incumbents. Consider, for example, the behaviour of Harry West, the eccentric and parsimonious non-resident rector of Berwick, in Sussex. West's activities, reprehensible though they were, would probably never have come to light had not one of his curates, E.B. Ellman, later published some delightful *Reminiscences* - an apt illustration of the difficulty of obtaining reliable information concerning relations between the 'inferior' and 'higher' clergy. The story began in 1837, when Ellman's father was persuaded to purchase the advowson to Berwick by a clerical friend.[4] A year passed, and then Ellman received a letter from West, asking him to call. At their subsequent meeting, West explained that he had been having 'much trouble' with his curates; knowing that Ellman was to succeed him as rector, he pressed him to take the curacy. The terms offered were the same as those that had been agreed to by the present holder of the curacy at Berwick; Ellman was to live in the furnished rectory and receive £40 a year, free of all rates and taxes.[5] The prospective rector hesitated and then accepted.

In September 1838 Ellman was duly ordained. A week later he rode over to Berwick, took the prayers and the former curate preached his farewell sermon. On the following Tuesday the new curate installed himself in Berwick rectory, bringing a widow from a neighbouring village to act as general servant.[6] Life was not easy. To live on £40 a year required constant vigilance. He bought pigs instead of books, and spent his leisure working in the rectory garden, and sending vegetables to Lewes market.[7] Harry West lived at a distance in the same salubrious market town, but kept up a war of nerves with his curate. On several occasions, he tried to make Ellman pay the rates on the rectory, a favourite ploy among incumbents with West's cast of mind. The rector of Berwick was also willing to enter contests over minutiae. Ellman gives a fine example of his petty-mindedness. In the autumn of 1843, West sent a letter stating that it was not usual to supply clocks in furnished houses, and that on turning to his accounts he found that the one in the rectory had cost five guineas. If Ellman was prepared to pay the same amount, he could keep it; if not, it would be taken away. A watchmaker was duly sent to take it away. The next year, after Ellman had left the curacy, the clock was returned to the rectory.[8] All in all, it is difficult to describe West as other than obstructive and troublesome. Although his home in Lewes was only eight miles away, he never once rode over to see Ellman during the six and a half years he held the curacy at Berwick.[9]

John Smith, curate of Banham in Norfolk, also claimed to have been badly treated by his rector. He set out his complaints in a letter to Henry Brougham, then Lord Chancellor, in August, 1832.[10] Banham was a rich Crown living, and the rector, a pluralist, was a nephew of Lord Eldon[11] - a detail that Brougham would have relished. Smith had been curate since 1824. His stipend of £100 a year was small enough.[12] What made matters worse was that no house was provided. For five years Smith had been forced to rent lodgings, at a cost of £40 a year. His situation, he explained, was desperate. He had a wife, who was constantly ill; there was a child, a son; he had to provide for his sister-in-law; and he had, as was only natural, a servant. The bill for medicine alone, came to £10 a year. Smith feared for the likely consequences of his plight - 'had not the Almighty graciously raised me up some friends, who have kept me free from debt, I must long since have been in gaol'. There is a measure of special pleading in all of this - Smith, after all, was a self-confessed plaintiff at the bar of ecclesiastical patronage - but the tenor is clear enough and was found elsewhere.

If Brougham was unimpressed by the clumsy blatancy of Smith's advocacy, he kept such thoughts to himself. His public answer came swiftly, in the form of the promotion of the curate of Banham to the Crown living of Baldock in Hertfordshire, where a thankful Smith was to remain until his death in 1870. There are several reasons for the Lord Chancellor's prompt response to Smith's appeal. As Smith reminded him in the letter, they had met the previous year and Brougham had promised to do something on his behalf. Also, Smith could justly claim scholarly attainment, often a fact likely to weigh heavily with a potential patron, but in his case the circumstances were special. He had entered St John's College, Cambridge as a poor sizar in 1817, already married and already with a son. Two years later, he had been assigned the massive task of deciphering Pepys' diaries, with little to guide him. Smith laboured twelve or fourteen hours a day for three years, completing the fifty-four volume transcription by the spring of 1822. Though his scholarship was impressive, his reward was not. The fee - a lump sum of £200 for the whole transcription - can only be regarded as less than generous, when computed on an hourly basis; and, instead of fulsome acknowledgement of the brilliance of his expertise in decoding one of the major documents of English history, Smith had to suffer the indignity of receiving, in the Preface of the published work, a grudging note of condescending thanks from the editor, Lord Braybrooke: 'he appears', wrote the noble Lord - and how the word 'appears' must have grated - 'to have performed the task allotted to him ... with dilligence and fidelity'.[13] The transcriber of Pepys deserved a more wholehearted commendation than this; he also deserved something a little more substantial than his meagre Banham curacy. Poor while working on Pepys, and still poor afterwards, it is easy enough to understand Smith's annoyance at the rough treatment he had received at the hands of his non-resident rector. Brougham gave him the public recognition he richly deserved.

There is a further reason for Smith's promotion to Baldock. In 1828, he had published an anonymous hard-hitting pamphlet on church reform, which had as its theme *The State of the Curates of the Church of England*; a copy had been sent to Brougham,[14] who doubtless liked its radical tone. Following in the footsteps of Richard Yates,[15] Smith asserted that the church was 'in danger'. The numerous 'labouring' clergy, otherwise known as the 'journeymen' parsons, were not doing their work properly. And they were not doing their work properly because they were not being paid properly. If married, they were 'compelled' to spend the 'greater part' of their time teaching private pupils, in order to eke out income.[16] A second point, also made vigorously, was that pastoral ministry was suffering because the ill-paid curate had developed 'migratory habits'; he was, in Smith's phrase, a mere 'bird of passage' that flitted from curacy to curacy.[17] Many curates, he went on to declare, were weighed down by their poor career prospects. In this regard, the church was unfavourably compared with the army. Commissioned ranks, Smith contended, often complained of the slowness of promotion; but there 'never yet was an instance of an officer dying a subaltern after fifty years of service'.[18] He ended with a plea for help; the 'inferior' clergy needed to know that there was a 'helping hand ready to raise them out of the state of genteel beggary in which they have been hitherto doomed to pass their days'.[19]

ii. *Pressure of Numbers*

It is difficult to assess the accuracy of Smith's portrayal of the country curate. The historian, when dealing with the 'non-commissioned' ranks of the clergy, lacks the abundant information available for the officers. Even such an apparently straightforward matter as the number of curates does not easily lend itself to analysis. Most useful in this regard are parliamentary returns on residence among curates;[20] but these, unhappily, do not generally distinguish between stipendiaries (curates looking after parishes where the incumbent was non-resident) and assistants (curates helping either a resident incumbent or a resident stipendiary). An exception to this rule is a parliamentary return for 1838; this gives the number of stipendiaries as 3,088, with a further 1,725 assistants, making a grand total of 4,813.[21]

The goal of discovering the size of the curate workforce will be reached once two further statistical obstacles have been overcome. One of these has already been glimpsed in an earlier chapter. Many curates, it has been found, were not curates at all, but incumbents giving a helping hand to brother beneficed clergy. Indeed it is very difficult to quantify curates as such. Parliamentary returns do not distinguish between *bona fide* curates and incumbents acting as curates, and the study of the Georgian diocesan archive has not as yet yielded enough facts upon which to base confident conclusions. My own work on the deaneries of Waxham and Repps showed, it will be remembered, that incumbents were serving as curates in 21 places out of 72 (29% of the sample) in 1794, and at 8 (11%) in 1834; but this part of Norfolk is both too remote and too small to be useful in a general context. Some other scholars have tackled the problem. Their work has, for present purposes, one major advantage and one major disadvantage. The advantage is that energy has been concentrated upon a narrow time-scale, making it easy to compare results. The disadvantage is that the period which has been chosen - the late 1770s and early 1780s - is remote from the late 1830s, the time of the relevant parliamentary return. Having made this caveat, we can now present the findings. In Devon, in 1779, 17% of parishes were being looked after by incumbent-curates, a startling statistic; but if Devon was bad, the diocese of Worcester and the county of Oxfordshire were worse. In Worcester, in 1782, incumbents were trying to disguise themselves as curates in 23% of the parishes in the diocese; while in Oxfordshire, four years earlier, the comparable figure was 24%.[22] Two things are impressive about this body of research: the sample is large - in aggregate, 767 places are included - and the evidence is reasonably consistent. It looks as if, in about 1780, between 15% and 25% of the parishes in England and Wales were pastorally cared for by neighbouring incumbents. This is a lot. It would seem to imply that, among 10,500 places, incumbent-curates would have numbered between 1,575 and 2,625. The incidence fell sharply during the succeeding half-century - there were many more genuine curates, the by-product of university expansion; and a further reduction brought about by legislation. The number of incumbents acting as curates in the late 1830s can only be guessed at. Perhaps, among the 3,100 or so stipendiaries mentioned in parliamentary returns for 1838, there may have been between 500 and 750 rectors and vicars.

Secondly, there is the issue of pluralism. The parliamentary returns on residence among curates are misleading, because they fail to acknowledge the elementary philosophical distinction between persons and things. The claim to be, for instance, 'An abstract showing the Number of Curates serving Benefices, on which the Incumbents are Non-Resident'[23] is false; better would be 'An Abstract showing the Number of Benefices, on which the Incumbent is Non-Resident, and where service is done by a Curate in his stead'. The relevance of this to the present discussion will be readily appreciated. Parliamentary returns on residence of curates can be used to set an *upper limit* to the number of curates in any given year, but they cannot be employed to ascertain what the number of such curates *actually was*. The latter figure will depend upon the level of pluralism, which must be calculated separately.

This is easier said than done. There is no source material for curates comparable to the complexity and refinement of data contained in the 1835 Report. What we have to rely on, therefore, is a number of general considerations. The principal one of these has to do with a topic - namely, clerical recruitment - already discussed at several points in this book. We reckon that, during the middle decades of the eighteenth century, ordinations were running at around 245 a year.[24] After 1770, there was a modest increase; for the 1770s, 1780s, and 1790s, together with the first decade of the nineteenth century, the average is calculated at 270 a year, higher by 10%.[25] As from the close of the Napoleonic Wars, there was dramatic change. Ordination numbers leapt to 400 a year, and in the 1820s the figure was over 500 a year.[26] According to official returns, ordinations in the decade 1834-43 averaged 535 a year.[27] Twice as many men were now being ordained each year as in the later decades of the eighteenth century.

This development carried ominous implications for the race of curates. Some Georgian clerics might rise very fast, and some not at all; but most of them did at least start in the same way, with a year spent in the diaconate, usually as a stipendiary. It follows, therefore, that a rise in the number of ordinations was virtually synonymous with a rise in the number of curates. This was a state of affairs which could be viewed with equanimity, provided that one or other (or preferably both) of two things acted as a counterbalance: there would need to be an increase in the number of parishes served by curates, and there would need, also, to be a substantial change in career patterns, with more men either leaving the profession altogether or obtaining quick promotion into a first incumbency.

Unfortunately, neither of these counterbalances worked effectively. Evidence concerning the number of parishes served by curates is provided by parliamentary returns. In the years prior to 1840, there are five complete sets of these, namely returns for 1813, 1814, 1827, 1831, and 1838.[28] Between 1813 and 1831, the number of parishes served by curates altered scarcely at all; there is a low of 4,254 (in 1827) and a high of 4,405 (in 1814). There was then a reasonable increase during the 1830s, with the total reaching 4,813 by 1838. The parochial system, on this evidence, did expand modestly, but change was too little and too late. The flow of men into the clerical profession had after all begun to gather pace around 1815, and it had sustained its momentum since that time. With every year, the contrast with the situation in the eighteenth century became more marked. In 1796-1800, about 1,350 men were ordained;[29] in 1826-30, a figure of around 2,650, as many as 1,300 more.[30] Against a background such as this, the increase of 400-500 in the number of parishes served by curates - an increase delayed until the 1830s - was, quite simply, not enough

Until the District Churches Act of 1843, the curates of England could look to a rapid expansion of the parochial system in vain, and they could also look to an improvement in their career prospects in vain. The difficulty of obtaining a first incumbency is a subject that has already been discussed, and it is necessary to do no more than summarise earlier findings.[31] Two groups of clergy attract attention for present purposes. The first comprises those who, for one reason or another, never were (or who ceased to be) contenders for ecclesiastical promotion: they either emigrated, died young, entered academic life, or became schoolmasters. Throughout the early nineteenth century, it always was the case that somewhere between a fifth and a quarter of the clergy came within one or other of these four categories. Some did not run the race; others ran, but kept coming last. It might be expected that, as the number of clergy rose, the proportion doomed to permanent exclusion from the ranks of the beneficed clergy would have risen as well, but this expectation is, in this instance, not fulfilled. Some 20% of those ordained around 1805 either remained assistant or stipendiary curates throughout their careers, vanished into obscurity, or only managed to obtain a perpetual curacy - an appointment generally short on social position and even shorter on financial reward. One or other of these three fates also awaited 20% of those who were ordained in 1815, and the same proportion among the ordinands of 1825 and 1835.

A further finding causes less surprise. The rise in the number of curates intensified competition for clerical employment; and the effect of this intensification was that it became more difficult to obtain a first incumbency within a short space of time. This, once again, is a subject that has already been discussed.[32] It was found that, among those ordained soon after the turn of the nineteenth century, 20% got a first vicarage or rectory within five years; but that among the ordinands of 1825, and also of 1835, this was true of only 15% or so. It would have been strange had things turned out otherwise.

Although the restriction of career prospects that this contrast implies was real enough, it does not provide a sufficient explanation of how the late-Georgian ecclesiastical system coped with the great influx of clergy which characterised the period. The nature of the problem may be glimpsed by a comparison between the number of ordinands of 1796-1800: about 1,350 men; and those of 1826-30: about 2,650 men. This gives an indication of the difficulty. It is now necessary to distinguish those who spent a material proportion of their working lives as curates from those who did not. The latter grouping, it can be argued, is broadly represented by those who either gave up the struggle to get an incumbency - they emigrated, died young, entered academic life, or became schoolmasters - or else succeeded in obtaining one within five years. This distinction can now be applied to the ordinands of 1796-1800 and also to those of 1826-30. Among the former, there were at most 608 (45%) who quickly passed through their curacies on the way to something better (or at least different), compared with 742 (55%) who might be described as career-curates. Among the latter, there were about 1,590 (60%) who were career-curates, and about 1,060 (40%) who were not.

Viewing things this way makes the point with some force: 1,590 is a lot more than 742. When combined with a static parochial system, the increase in the number of career-curates can mean only one thing: if the number of parishes served by curates remains the same, but the number of curates rises with every year, then the conclusion must be that pluralism among the subalterns was on the wane. Logic, moreover, finds a staunch ally in another quarter. In the early years of the century, there was increasing concern that the sight of curates 'galloping about from church to church' was bringing the Establishment 'into contempt'. In 1813 legislative action was taken to amend matters: obstacles were placed in the way of those wishing to acquire a string of curacies, and the argument that pluralism was a financial necessity was torpedoed by introducing, for the first time, a decent scale for all stipends paid to stipendiaries. This piece of legislation, known as the Stipendiary Curates Act, is fully discussed in the next section of the present Chapter.[33]

To quantify the decline in the incidence of pluralism among the 'inferior' clergy is difficult. Once again, we come up against the lack of any nationwide survey comparable to the 1835 Report. The best that can be done is to suggest some sensible upper and lower limits for pluralism, based upon known facts regarding the influx into the ranks of the clergy, prevalence of the practice of incumbents acting as curates, and patterns of clerical residence. We can start from figures for the number of curates, as given in parliamentary returns. In the second and third decades of the nineteenth century, there was little change in this regard: the total hovered around 4,300.[34] In the 1830s there was a reasonable increase, with the complement reaching 4,800 by 1838.[35] The next step is to analyse the numbers of assistants, since, by definition, these were not pluralists. In 1838, assistants amounted to 1,725,[36] but it was a regiment within the clerical army which was putting forth fresh ranks all the time: by 1841 there were around 2,025,[37] an increase of 300 within three years. The rise in the overall number of curates during the 1830s can probably be put down to the growth in assistants. On this basis, assistants will have numbered about 1,300 in 1830. With regard to the situation earlier in the century, there is, unfortunately, no information; in these circumstances one is forced to assume that assistants probably also amounted to about 1,300 in 1810.

The major quandary is the figures to do with incumbents acting as curates. It has been suggested that, in 1780, the number of parishes receiving spiritual ministrations from neighbouring incumbents was between 1,575 and 2,625.[38] There is no evidence that the beneficed clergy changed their pluralistic and non-resident habits, in any material way, between 1780 and 1810.[39] It is therefore reasonable to conclude that they did not alter their co-operative habits either: they certainly did not in Waxham and Repps.[40] At the end of the first decade of the nineteenth century, there were probably between 1,600 and 2,600 parishes in the hands of neighbouring incumbents. A figure of 2,000 is as good an estimate as any.

Finally, there are *bona fide* stipendiaries to contend with. According to parliamentary returns for 1813, there were 4,325 curates of every type and description.[41] I have argued that 1,300 were assistants - all of them non-pluralists- and that 2,000 were incumbents acting as curates. Thus, in that year, no more than 1,025 parishes had (according to this analysis) a *bona fide* stipendiary as minister. It is here that, in contrast to assistants, pluralism enters the lists. Every incumbent who acted as a curate served more than a single cure, a fine example followed by most stipendiaries. Possibly, the 1,025 parishes which we have estimated were being looked after by stipendiaries in 1813 were ministered to by 500 or so individuals, making a ratio of places served to curates serving of 2:1. This conclusion is, inevitably, very tentative.

In 1813, legislative steps were taken to curb pluralism among stipendiaries. Meanwhile, within a year or so, university expansion started to lead to an increase in newly ordained curates.[42] Against this background, two things happened: the incidence of plurality fell sharply, while the number of stipendiaries sharply rose. The change, it would seem, was dramatic. In 1838 the number of curates, as given in parliamentary returns, was around 4,800. There were 1,725 assistants; and I have calculated that incumbent-curates amounted to 500-750.[43] Parishes served by *bona fide* stipendiaries were, therefore, in the range of 2,325-2,575, a far cry from the estimated figure of 1,025 a quarter of a century earlier. We would not be surprised if the ratio of parishes served to curates serving had, by now, fallen to 3:2. By implication, *bona fide* stipendiaries in the late 1830s numbered between 1,550 and 1,715. This estimate, it scarcely needs to be stated, is to be treated with extreme caution. The fragmentary and disparate nature of the evidence means that conclusions on this matter necessarily contain a wide margin of error.

iii. *The Stipendiary Curates Act*

Between the incumbent and the curate stood the law. As with most other ecclesiastical matters, regulation of relationships between incumbents and curates was within the bounds of parliament's legitimate interest and concern. The first piece of legislation to deal with the matter was an Act of 1713.[44] This was a threadbare enactment; the clauses were neither numerous nor tightly drawn. The Act started encouragingly, by forging a link between the poverty of a curate's stipend and the poverty of religious provision - 'for want of sufficient maintenance', it argued, there were places in the land which were 'meanly supplied'. Its weakness did not lie in diagnosis, but in the remedy that was prescribed. It stopped short of fixing a scale for stipends; instead, it did no more than draw up what amounted to a number of guidelines, which were to be applied by the bishops. Eighteenth-century episcopal administration being what it was, this was a hazardous way of seeking betterment. The central statement in the Act was clear enough. Non-residents were to nominate curates to serve parishes in their absence; and these curates were to be licensed by the bishops, who were to fix 'sufficient' stipends. The difficulty lay in the vagueness of the definition of sufficient; it was a sum 'not exceeding Fifty Pounds per Annum nor less than Twenty Pounds per Annum'. Too much was left to episcopal discretion.

In two other respects, however, the 1713 Act had something to commend it. Bishops could award salaries of between £20 a year and £50 a year to curates who were already licensed; it was thus of general, not merely prospective, application. Secondly, when fixing stipends, the bishops were to bear in mind both the value of the living which the curate was to serve and the pecuniary means of the incumbent who was to employ him; they were, in the words of the Act, to have regard to 'the greatness of the Cure and the Value of the Ecclesiastical Benefices of such Rector or Vicar'. The interesting point is the use of the plural, 'Benefices', the clear implication being that the bishops, when setting an appropriate level for curates' stipends, should take into account the worth of each and every living in the possession of the employing incumbent, not just that of the living to which the curate was being nominated. Here was a genuinely radical proposal, that was well ahead of its time; or, perhaps, more accurately, a proposal very far ahead of its time. Even a century later, Queen Anne's Bounty could not quite bring itself to penalise pluralists, when allocating sums from the Parliamentary Grants Fund;[45] and subsequent legislation on the subject of curates' pay also evaded the issue. It is extremely doubtful, however, whether the clause had any practical significance. What was demanded of the members of the episcopal Bench - namely, to keep a watchful eye on clerical appointments to benefices throughout the length and breadth of the land - was beyond them. Most eighteenth-century bishops were hard-pressed to keep track of what was happening among the beneficed clergy within the confines of their own dioceses; they had neither the inclination nor the administrative capability to monitor the accumulation of benefices in Cumbria and Kent, or in Norfolk and Northumberland.

Nor was it only in this regard that the 1713 Act was to be stretched upon the rack of practicality and be found wanting. Fault can also be found with the discretionary limit of £20 to £50 a year for stipends. The appropriate context here is Ecton's recently published survey of benefice values. According to Ecton, there were 3,826 livings - more than a third of the total - which did not bring in £50 a year.[46] In reality, as has already been pointed out, the number of these 'small' livings was appreciably higher.[47] Parliament, in setting a maximum of £50 a year for curates' stipends, was giving diocesans considerable power: they could allocate to the curate the full value of every living in Ecton's survey. The problem with the legislation, however, was that it did not reckon with the steep climb in benefice values that characterised the eighteenth century; and although £50 did not appear excessive by 1750, by the end of the century it was beginning to look decidedly paltry.

As inflation gathered pace, and as the rise in benefice values gathered greater momentum, it came to be recognised that something had to be done. Parliament acted in 1796, on the eve of the Napoleonic inflation. The preamble to the new Act[48] shows an awareness of the developing situation; 'in many places', it states, the provision made under 13 Anne c.11 has become 'insufficient'. In other respects, the 1796 Act was a disappointment. No important new principle was enunciated; all that was done was that the limit of £20 to £50 a year for stipends was replaced by a maximum of £75 a year. The only novel proposal was that the bishop was empowered to permit the curate to live in the parsonage, in cases where the incumbent was non-resident for at least eight months of the year. If there was not a parsonage, or if 'it shall appear to the Bishop ... not to be convenient to allot and assign' the parsonage to the curate, a cash sum not exceeding £15 a year could be given in lieu. The 1796 Act was not an exciting piece of legislation.

How did the curates of the eighteenth century, unprotected by strong laws, manage to fare? Norman Sykes thought they did reasonably well. Up until 1750, he claimed, there was a 'marked tendency towards an average of £30-£40 per year'; and, 'in the later years of the century the standard of emolument rose to an average of £70'.[49] The latter judgment implies that the 1796 Act, in setting a maximum of £75 a year for stipends, did not strive to improve the financial position of the average curate but rather to curb the opulence to which, on the logic of Sykes' arithmetic, a section of the subalterns had by now become accustomed. It scarcely needs stating that this was not the intention of the legislation, nor, also, that Sykes is wrong. Research carried out for a number of areas has exposed errors in both his calculations. There are, firstly, figures for the mountainous Welsh diocese of St Asaph: 130 parishes and chapelries in the counties of Denbigh, Merioneth, Montgomery, and Flint, with a scattering of livings in Shropshire. At a visitation held in 1738, the average curate's stipend was found to be a little over £22.[50] Judging by the information for Carlisle, the pay of curates in mountainous districts did not progress at all during the succeeding half-century; in the late 1780s, in Cumberland and Westmorland, the average stipend seems to have been £20.[51] In the diocese of Durham, much richer than either St Asaph or Carlisle, the picture is brighter but still, for the most part, bleak. In the archdeaconry of Northumberland, in the early 1730s, ordination papers mention an average of £28.[52] Forty years later, in the archdeaconry of Durham, there is a similar average figure of £30 a year, but there is then a strong advance, with the average rising to £56 by 1810.[53] It was better to be a curate in the archdeaconry of Durham than in the diocese of

Worcester. Under Isaac Maddox (Bishop, 1743-59), the average payment was £29.[54] Under Richard Hurd (Bishop, 1782-1808), things did not materially improve: the values of stipends are mentioned in 212 curates' licences, and on 130 occasions (61% of the sample) the sum was fixed at an amount between £21 and £40.[55] There are, also, figures for Oxfordshire in 1793, 1796, and 1799. In parochial returns for these years, curates' stipends are specified in 57 instances. Only once was over £60 a year paid. On the other hand, one curate had to make do with £19; there were 19 with between £20 and £29; and a further 16 got less than £40.[56] This implies that half the curates in Oxfordshire in the 1790s had to get by on stipends of £34 a year or less. Finally, there are two impressive arrays of statistics for Norfolk, the first for 1784 and the second for 1806. In the former year the median is calculated at £23, and in the latter at £30.[57] It look as if, at the start of the eighteenth century, a curate could count himself lucky if his stipend was much over £25; while, by the 1790s, he was doing well if his stipend was over £35.

Parliament, in framing the 1796 legislation, did not benefit from the guidance given by statistical sophistication; it was more a matter of considering general economic conditions - rising prices, higher tithe incomes, and the like - and then making a decision based on these. There was a feeling that the 1796 Act did not go far enough. Parliament, soon after the turn of the nineteenth century, began to give fresh thought to the problem. It was proposed to include a clause in the 1803 Residence Bill on the subject, a plan wisely abandoned in favour of a separate Act. Getting something on to the statute book did not prove easy. A Bill was introduced in 1805, passed its third reading in the Lords, and was then lost because the Commons could not agree to the Lords' amendments. The following year, another attempt was made. This made even less headway, and the second reading in the Commons was defeated by 25 votes to 13.[58] Nothing was done in 1807, but a new effort was made in 1808. This Bill met a similar fate to the first two; it was lost in the Lords on third reading, without a division. Beilby Porteus, the forward-looking and reforming Bishop of London, spoke in favour of the motion; but the Bishops of Rochester, Hereford, and Carlisle spoke against, as did Charles Manners-Sutton, Archbishop of Canterbury. This timely show of episcopal enthusiasm did little to promote the project. The wonder is that reformers did not throw up their hands in despair and turn to something else.

However, they did not give up. Battle was renewed in 1812, with Lord Harrowby introducing a fourth Bill in the Lords, later abandoned at the committee stage. Perseverance pays, and Harrowby tried again in 1813. This time the Bill cleared every hurdle in four months, passing its crucial third reading in the Commons by 66 votes to 9, a majority of 57.[59] Once again, the bishops did everything they could to prevent change. Only three of them spoke in the debate on third reading in the Lords, and none was in favour. Lord Harrowby, however, had the last word. He was crushing and effective. 'Curates discharging the duties of four parishes, and galloping about from church to church, was what brought the church into contempt', he declared.[60]

The most succinct defence of the proposed legislation had been made by Beilby

Porteus in his speech on the second reading of the 1808 Bill. The Bishop of London brought forward, in quick succession, four main arguments. First of all, there was inflation; the cost of the 'necessaries of life', he rightly pointed out, was now 'high'. Secondly, curates had a position in society, and this must be maintained: they were 'accustomed to support a decent appearance in the world'. Thirdly, parliament must remember that it was not dealing with nobodies; most curates were men of 'taste and literature', graduates of one of the two ancient universities. Finally, Porteus played his trump card: an appeal to sympathy. The curates of England, he declared, were men with responsibilities; many of them were married, with seven or eight children.[61] Theirs was a human problem, urgently requiring relief.

The attack came from many directions. There were, predictably, those who objected to raising curates' stipends on principle; the various bills were described as an 'invasion of ecclesiastical property'.[62] The tone will be familiar to anyone acquainted with the contemporary literature, as will the contention that, if the curates' Bill was passed, 'the subordination of the different ranks, so necessary to the well being of the ecclesiastical government, would be destroyed'.[63] More subtly, it was suggested that reform would harm those it was designed to help; feather-bedded by the legislature, curates would lose all drive and ambition and sink into a sort of quiescent inertia. This was well wide of the mark. The career prospects of curates being what they were, the last thing that was likely was that they would feel feather-bedded by the legislature. Some bishops viewed the intended enactment as an example of 'interference' in ecclesiastical affairs by the legislature.[64] To these objectors, it was necessary to do no more than politely enquire whether the parliamentary grants of £100,000, then being received annually by the Bounty, caused equal alarm and despondency.

Other criticisms were more cogent. As with previous legislation, parliament proposed to act through the bishops, and the resultant increase in episcopal power aroused protests in some quarters. Speaking of the 1805 Bill Lord Porchester had been both more aggressive in his stance, and also more picturesque in his language, than most; if the Bill were to become law he feared that 'a bishop within his diocese would become a more uncontroulable despot than any first consul or emperor of the French'.[65] Charles James Fox made a good point. He felt that curates' stipends should be related to the scale and extent of their public duties, not to the value of the benefice, or benefices, served.[66] Then there were the sceptics, who thought that legislation would be circumvented by means of private agreements between incumbents and curates. Some of the bishops feared that the structure of the church was too complex to permit parliament to formulate effective reform. Archbishop Manners-Sutton argued this with considerable force - 'to apply a general Act to the making [of] provisions for curates without leaving any discretion as to the numberless circumstances that arose would be like making a suit of clothes to fit the moon in all its changes'.[67] As will be seen, this statement was prophetic.

Given the strength of feeling - especially of episcopal feeling - against the measure, it is perhaps surprising that anything was achieved. The main reason for success was publication of information regarding the current level of curates' stipends. Parliament had had no facts and figures to go on when discussing the proposed legislation in 1805, 1806, or 1808, but by 1812 the omission had been rectified. On the table, now, were parliamentary returns, for 1810, giving the stipends of curates serving parishes where the incumbent was non-resident by licence.[68] It was a large sample - returns were obtained from 1,745 parishes - and it was also an illuminating sample. The speech by Lord Grenville is an excellent barometer by which to judge its effect. 'It was', he began, 'impossible for any person to see the returns of the state of the parochial clergy in this country ... and not to feel, that if parliament ... did not carefully enter into the examination of the subject, they would omit one of the most important of their duties'.[69]

Lord Grenville was right. Parliament was now fully justified in 'interfering' in ecclesiastical affairs. The returns painted an appalling picture of neglect and decay. Salary bands were used to give an indication of the level of each of the 1,745 stipends included in the survey; one band was for stipends of under £10 a year, another for stipends of under £20 a year, and so on. The most crowded band was the range of £20-£30 a year; there were 428 stipends (25% of the sample) in this category. Rarely did it happen that a stipend was over £80 a year; indeed, this was the case on only 52 occasions (a meagre 3% of the total). An alternative way of viewing the figures is to apply the 'Ecton test': to see how many incumbents were paying their curates more than £50 a year, which had been the maximum value for livings in Ecton's published survey and also the maximum that bishops had been permitted to appoint as stipends under the 1713 Act. No churchman could be proud of the result. In 1810, only 455 curates serving parishes where the incumbent was non-resident by licence received over £50 a year, whereas 1,290 received less than this amount. The median value for stipends was set at the exceptionally low figure of £37 a year. In other words, the jibe about the curate 'passing rich on £40 a year' was true. The figures did not make any allowance for pluralism among the subalterns, but this in no way weakened Lord Harrowby's case; it was, as he put it, the sight of curates 'galloping about' that brought the church 'into contempt'. Lord Grenville's reaction to publication of the statistics for 1810 is as good an example as there could be of the interrelation between investigation and reform in early nineteenth-century England.

All the bills made a clear distinction between assistants and stipendiaries, and only the latter were to benefit from the proposed measures. As a consequence, a lot of curates - almost certainly the great majority - saw no improvement in their status.[70] This was a pity. On the other hand, it was much easier to get a bill through parliament if it could be presented as a scheme to penalise non-resident clergy - perhaps inducing a number of rectors and vicars to desist from this activity - without at the same time damaging the financial interests of those incumbents who did reside. This is why assistants had to be left out. An assistant was, by definition, a cleric lending a hand to a resident, not a non-resident.

A third ingredient in the recipe for success was reliance upon the prospective principle. In early nineteenth-century England, reforming measures stood a far better chance of making the statute book if present holders of offices were left undisturbed. The Deans and Chapters Act is a good example of the prospective principle in operation,[71] as is the Stipendiary Curates Act. Lord Harrowby made the point crisply and well. Upon induction to a benefice, an incumbent should 'clearly understand what was to be the result in case he did not reside'.[72]

Finally, the measure was modified in order to reduce opposition from vested interests. The first version, in 1805, had been directed against the rich clergy. On livings worth over £400 a year, the stipendiary was to receive a fifth of the value. No upper limit for a stipendiary's stipend was laid down. This bill was not calculated to please a Sparke or a Pretyman. An acolyte of one or other of these two venerable prelates would have been even less amused by the proposals put before parliament in 1806. The stipendiary was still to get a fifth of the proceeds, but this was now to be the case on all livings, not, as before, only on those producing more than £400 a year. In 1808, there was a return to the proposals made in 1805, with the modest addition of a clause placing a ceiling of £250 a year upon a stipend. This alteration was designed to mollify the opposition, but failed in its purpose. In 1810, and also in 1812, there was a radical shift in emphasis; in place of the negative objective of hurting the pocket of the wealthy incumbent there was put the positive objective of filling the stomach of the poor stipendiary. The mechanism that was chosen to bring this about was the guaranteed wage: in future all stipendiaries would, in normal circumstances, receive at least £80 a year. This abrupt about-turn on the part of ecclesiastical reformers drew a sharp and witty aphorism from a speaker in the Commons; the Curates Bill, he declared, was no longer 'a tax upon opulence to support indigence; but it was a tax upon indigence to support indigence'.[73] Although cleverly expressed, this was beside the point. It failed to meet the objection that the 1808 version of the bill had done nothing for stipendiaries serving livings worth less than £400 or so a year. On balance, the new proposals were better than the old. They also had the solid advantage of being more practicable. In this regard, the difficulty with the earlier versions of the Curates Bill was that they looked too much as though they had been drafted by a political Radical. Their thrust had been against the lazy and the opulent rather than in favour of putting forward constructive proposals that had a real chance of success. Lord Harrowby was made of different mettle. The epitome of the cautious ecclesiastical reformer, he went out of his way to avoid offending unduly the rich and well-connected; he presented his case forcefully; and he wisely focused attention upon the need to supply every stipendiary with a living wage. Astuteness had its due reward.

The Stipendiary Curates Act[74] is a much more thorough and detailed measure than either the 1713 Act or the 1796 Act. Its starting point was the need to supply religious provision, a resident 'Moses', in every place. Non-resident incumbents must henceforth ensure that parishes deserted in their absence were looked after. Where there was not a curate, one must be nominated, and whenever a curate either died or resigned, another must be found to take his place. This, however, was all. So long as non-residents nominated curates, they were left undisturbed. The new legislation only came into effect if a curate was not nominated, or if there was a vacancy in a living previously held by a non-resident. In the former instance, the bishop was authorised to license a curate and to fix a stipend that accorded with the Act. When a vacancy occurred, everything depended upon whether the new incumbent did, or did not, serve the parish. If he did, well and good; if he did not, the curate nominated to serve the parish in his absence must be licensed by the bishop, and the curate's stipend was fixed by the Act.

The Stipendiary Curates Act was, thus, a gradualistic measure of reform. Legislators had in mind the numerous livings - 4,734 of them in 1813[75] - where the incumbent neither resided nor did duty. As each of these fell vacant, change would occur: the parish would be served either by its new incumbent, or by a curate whose stipend was fixed by law. In the nature of things, not much would happen overnight. It is well worth recalling at this point the earlier study of mobility, or rather immobility, among the beneficed clergy in Sussex.[76] Surveying the situation at the end of 1833, it was found that in 45% of parishes there had been no vacancy for close on twenty years. The situation elsewhere was probably much the same. This gives a perspective to the present discussion. About 30% of livings with non-residents would be affected by the new legislation within ten years, with a further 30% or so sharing the same fate within twenty. This is slow by any reckoning. In 1860, there were still to be a scattering of places where the incumbent was a non-resident who had held the living since before 1813.

Although the effects of the Stipendiary Curates Act were more gradual than they should have been, the one great point in the Act's favour was that it ensured there would be no going back. Once a parish had a licensed curate with a salary appointed under the Act, it would never again have to rely on the services of a 'hack' whose salary was at the discretion of the incumbent who employed him. Reform might be slow, but it was certain.

As for the scale of payment for stipendiaries laid down under the Act, the minimum, in normal circumstances, was now to be £80 a year, or the full value of the benefice if it was worth a lesser amount. The sum of £80 a year might seem, at first sight, somewhat parsimonious, but it will seem less so in the context of the parliamentary returns for 1810, which showed that the typical stipendiary, serving a parish where the incumbent was non-resident by licence, was receiving only £37 a year.

Fox, it will be remembered,[77] had complained that the proposed legislation failed to relate the pay of curates to their public duties. The 1813 Act went some way towards meeting this objection, by varying the minimum for stipends according to the population of the parish. Where a population exceeded 300, the minimum was set at £100 a year, with full value if amount was less. Where the population was above 500, the minimum was to be £120 or full value. Where it was more than 1,000, the figure for the minimum stipend was laid down as £150 a year or full value. This sub-clause is important. In most counties, more than half of all parishes had over 500 inhabitants.[78] The minimum stipend of £120 a year was thus of wide application.

Lord Harrowby also listened to Archbishop Manners-Sutton, when he complained of the difficulty of 'making a suit of clothes to fit the moon in all its changes'.[79] The bishops were given a good deal of discretion under the Act. In some instances, this favoured the curate rather than the incumbent. Where benefice income exceeded £400 a year, the bishop was permitted to assign a stipend of £100 a year, even if the population was less than 300, provided that the curate served no other cure. Where the value of the living was more than £400 a year, and where the population was in excess of 500, the bishop was also given discretion to add as much as £50 to the stipend, provided, once again, that the curate had but a single licence. This clause, the thirteenth, represents the distinctly ragged remains of the earlier proposals to penalise those non-resident incumbents who were fortunate enough to have come by a wealthy living.

Instances where the permitted exercise of episcopal discretion favoured the curate were more than outweighed by instances where such discretion favoured the incumbent. The decisive clause in this respect was the tenth. In cases where 'great Hardship and Inconvenience' would be caused to incumbents if they were to be compelled to pay the salary appointed under the Act - reference was made to those who were non-resident by reason of 'Age, Sickness, or other unavoidable Cause' - the bishop was to fix a stipend which he considered 'just and reasonable'. Here, indeed, is a fine and unblemished cameo, depicting what untrammelled episcopal power might look like. Parliament had little choice but to place confidence in the sagacity of the Bench. Whether that confidence was also well founded is not as immediately clear.

A problem arose over dilapidations. The bishop was empowered to allot the parsonage as the curate's place of residence. At the same time, the incumbent remained responsible for the parsonage's upkeep, an ambiguous situation creating an obvious source of potential unfairness and friction. The Act dealt with the matter in the following way. Where the whole income of a benefice was appointed as stipend, the bishop could permit the incumbent to deduct up to a quarter from the payment in order to meet costs laid out in repairs. Where benefice income was under £150 a year, and where sums spent on dilapidations exceeded the surplus after payment of the curate, the stipend could also be reduced by up to a quarter.

Finally, there was the issue of what to do about those curates who aped their elders and betters by indulging themselves in a little - or, in some instances, a lot of - pluralism. Towards the most serious offenders, each with four curacies or more, the Act took a straightforward stance; in future, licences were to be granted to serve three churches or less, but they were not to be granted to serve four churches or more. This was a sensible measure, clearly showing the drafting hand of Lord Harrowby. Prohibition of the most excessive forms of plurality was both the obvious, and also the necessary, *quid pro quo* for the substantial rises in stipends that were to be brought about by the Act. There was a greater degree of leniency towards those with a third curacy. A medley of factors lay behind the legislative enactments on this matter. First of all, there was a respectful regard for vested interests that was wholly characteristic of the period; those who already had a third curacy would not be required to give it up. Legislators also took account of the gradualism inherent in their proposals. If it was impossible to apply the new scales for stipends, because there had not as yet been a vacancy, a third curacy could be kept. Finally, there were the usual worries about curates 'galloping about', to the detriment of the proper performance of their professional duties. This problem was dealt with by restricting legitimate pluralism to localities; all three of a curate's parishes must be within four miles of each other.

Minor offenders against ecclesiastical decorum - those who had done no more than add the curacy of Great Sleeping to that of Little Sleeping, without the further indulgence of Great (or maybe Little) Snoring - fared better. Once again, legislators relied upon a tender, not to say fragile, reed: that of episcopal discretion. In cases where a stipendiary held a second curacy, or, alternatively, was either an incumbent or a perpetual curate elsewhere, the bishop was empowered to deduct a sum, not exceeding £30 a year, from the relevant salary scale. The second curacy, moreover, was not to be more than five miles from the first - 'except', of course, 'in cases of necessity approved by the bishop'.

All in all, the Stipendiary Curates Act made life more difficult for pluralists among the 'inferior' clergy. A prohibition upon fourth and subsequent curacies; restriction of third curacies to the immediate locality; financial penalties against the taking of a second curacy: the legislature had not previously made such a determined effort to curb pluralism among the subalterns. The Act, moreover, would seem to have been successful; there is a good weight of indirect evidence that the curates of the 1830s were significantly less pluralistic than their counterparts of the first decade of the century.[80]

Apart from its array of reforming measures designed to meet perceived needs, the Stipendiary Curates Act has a further importance: the increase in episcopal power that it brought about. If a non-resident incumbent failed to nominate a curate, the bishop was to act in his stead. The appropriate salary, appointed under the Act, was written down and included in each curate's licence by the bishop. It was the bishop, once again, who could vary that salary, according to the population and wealth of the benefice mentioned in the licence. If a non-resident incumbent was old or sick he had to rely totally upon his diocesan's sense of fair play; in these instances the bishop could fix a stipend that he considered 'just and reasonable'. On the vexed issue of clerical accommodation, it was the bishop who was to decide whether the curate should, or should not, live in the parsonage. The incumbent, for his part, could use part of the curate's stipend to meet the cost of repairs - provided he obtained his diocesan's agreement. Episcopal discretion also held sway in the two blighted regions of pluralism and non-residence. A curate's second living could be more than five miles from the first, if the bishop agreed to the plan; and the Bench was also given powers to vary stipends if curates served more than a single cure.

The proposed increase in the bishops' powers caused apprehension in some clerical quarters. Relations between the Bench and the clergy were, at the best of times, awkward and abrasive. Incumbents strove to assert their freehold while bishops strove to enforce canon and parliamentary law. In this situation, enlargement of the bishop's sphere of influence inevitably provoked animosity. As far as the Stipendiary Curates Bill is concerned, the case against reform was argued by none other than the clergy's polemical champion: Sydney Smith. As a propagandist, the 'Smith of Smiths' had few equals among his contemporaries. His typically eighteenth-century mind possessed a truly marvellous power to simplify and clarify issues; and, what is equally to the point, he had a fine talent for wit, irony, and downright sarcasm. He turned the considerable fire-power of his verbal artillery upon the bishops in an article for the *Ediburgh Review* in 1808, attacking the abortive third version of the Curates' Bill. With an unerring instinct, Sydney Smith concentrated upon two areas in which many Georgian prelates were particularly vulnerable: lack of intellectual ability, and an absence of administrative capacity. The members of the Bench, readers of the *Review* were reminded, were not 'always the wisest of men'; nor were they 'always preferred for eminent virtues and talents, or for any good reason whatever, known to the public'.[81] There was certainly a kernel of truth in these statements; some of the bishoprics were customarily reserved for men of 'family and fashion'. Sydney Smith also made much of the point, equally indisputable, that too many of their lordships were rather long in the tooth. The prelates of England, he asserted, 'are subject to the infirmities of old age, like other men; and, in the decay of strength and understanding, will be governed as other men are, by daughters and wives, and whoever ministers to their daily comforts'.[82]

To claim that many of the bishops were men of modest ability, and that they were, like as not, much too old to function effectively, was scarcely startling. The strength of Sydney Smith's position was that he rested his case on known facts. Parliamentarians were as aware as anyone else of the shortcomings of the episcopal Bench, but they were also aware of the constraints imposed upon them by necessity. The structure of the Georgian church being what it was, plans of reform could only be put into effect by the bishops. Thus it had been with the Residence Act of 1803; and thus it was with the Stipendiary Curates Act.

It made no difference that, among their lordships, only Beilby Porteus had spoken with any warmth in favour of the proposal. The bishops were there; the bishops would continue to be there; and that was that. It meant that implementation of the Stipendiary Curates Act was, by a supreme irony, left to the group that had most vigorously opposed its enactment all along; but this unhappy position could not, in the circumstances of the time, be avoided. It was thus against a less than optimistic background with hostile storm-clouds whipped up by Sydney Smith, and the episcopal officer class, by now well past their best and whispering under their breath about being dragooned into undertaking the voyage, that the good ship stipendiary edged out of port.

iv. *The Case against the Act*

Clerical irritation at the newly-imposed changes in curates' pay and working conditions continued after 1813. The continuing strength of feeling is evident from a number of protests made three years later against a proposed Consolidation Bill containing, *inter alia*, the provisions of the Stipendiary Curates Act. A printed paper - purporting to be a 'humble address' from the clergy of the diocese of Bath and Wells to their bishop - found its way into circulation. An address it was, humble it was not. Humility, on this occasion, adopted the curious disguise of arrogant assertion: the payment of the full proceeds of a living to a mere curate, it was contended, was tantamount to applying the nefarious principle of equalising the revenues of the church. The clergy of Castle Cary deanery, also in Bath and Wells, were more direct in their tactics, passing resolutions against the bill. Displays of bravado were not confined to the west country. Further afield, in Wales, the stance taken by the clergy of Castle Cary deanery was supported by the archdeacon of Brecon. At a public meeting, he was unwise enough to propose a vote of thanks to his west country brethren, but in this he overplayed his hand. Stout opposition arose in the shape of a certain Major Price, a 'highly distinguished officer' who had served for over twenty years in the East Indies where, amongst other exploits, he had managed to lose a leg. Words of military command proved more than a match for anything that his opponent could offer. Major Price declared that he was 'decidedly for subordination', the meeting agreed, and the archdeacon's proposal was unanimously rejected.[83]

Once the Consolidation Bill became law, it is difficult to find any examples of overt clerical opposition to the new salary scales for curates, but this does not preclude covert opposition. The spirit of rebellion did not die; rather did it become subterranean, occasionally erupting into caustic comment or bitter words. Particularly striking is the force and impish dry humour of a little-known pamphlet that came out in 1819. This work was based upon an imaginary dialogue between a vicar, Eusebius, and a rector, Theophilus, who had been together at university thirty years previously and had met again by chance. Eusebius told his friend that he had started clerical life as the curate of a laborious parish, receiving only £40 a year from a living worth between £500 and £600. Somehow, he had found time to marry and produce six children. Recently, he had become the incumbent of a populous parish, but joy at this well-earned promotion had not lasted for long. Soon, elation had given way to depression as ill-health, brought about by overwork, had set in. A curate had had to be employed to do duty, and he received the whole value of the living, worth £150 a year. The deputy lived in fine style - he 'keeps his hunter, a brace of pointers, and a footman in livery!'

Theophilus was sympathetic. He had spent many years trying to provide for his wife and seven children on a curate's stipend of £50. Eventually he, too, had risen into the ranks of the beneficed clergy; but a 'cold' on the lung had forced him to take on a curate, who also received the full income of the living. 'My preferment', he said bitterly, 'proves nothing else than a portico to a prison, and after that to a charnel-house, where my bones will soon be mouldering'.[84]

In distress, the two friends knelt down and said prayers together from the Liturgy. Theophilus then sent for a copy of the 1813 Act, and found a clause in it which offered a way of deliverance to them both. Little imagination is required to guess which clause it was: it was the tenth, permitting diocesans to fix 'just and reasonable' stipends in cases of 'great Hardship' - sickness and so on - among the beneficed clergy. Armed with their copy of the Act, Eusebius and Theophilus waited upon their bishop.

The two clergymen received what can only be described as an exceptionally warm welcome. Their diocesan was most anxious to make amends for his earlier ineptitude. The licences of the two curates were revoked, and the stipends were reduced from £150 to £40; a circular was sent to all the clergy in the diocese reminding them of the 'benign clauses' in the 1813 Act; and, as a gesture of goodwill, the two supplicants were given cheques for £50 out of the diocesan fund for the relief of indigent clergy.[85] Heirarchial principles were thus speedily reasserted.

The message of *The Sufferings of the Clergy* is clear. The world, it was feared, was becoming a puzzling place. The hierarchical structure of clerical society was becoming disturbed; privates were turning themselves into officers, with the result that officers were, willy-nilly, being turned into privates. This intolerable state of affairs should not be allowed to continue. The officers must rally themselves, bring into action the heavily armoured episcopal battalions - which should be, but currently were not, fighting on their behalf - and force the non-commissioned ranks back into the position they had occupied in the late eighteenth century. Curates cannot be allowed to keep hunters, pointers and footmen in livery; such joys must be reserved for their superiors.

A lot of this is more droll than it is serious, but the anonymous author nevertheless had a valid argument. A good number of poor beneficed clergy did suffer as a result of the maladministration of the Stipendiary Curates Act. This fact was discovered through detailed examination of the 1835 Report, that mine of information which has been so unashamedly plundered throughout this book. The Report provides, among other things, a profile of the clergy as at 31 December 1833, twenty years after the Stipendiary Curates Act became law. I managed to trace, from its pages, a previously unrecognised phenomenon: the existence of a group of incumbents who were earning less than, or only as much as, one or other of their own curates. In 1833, there were at least 322 beneficed clergy, a little under 4% of the total, who were in this invidious position. After payment of taxes and curates' stipends, every one of the 322 was left with an ecclesiastical income which did not exceed £100 a year.[86]

Almost all the members of this strange group of clergy shared two things in common: they were not pluralists, and they were not resident. Only twenty-eight of them - less than 10% of the whole - had another living or livings; and about the same number were described in the Report as resident.[87] This is compelling evidence of their plight. After all, it was pluralism that was the *fons et origo* of non-residence. For a rector not to live in his parish because he was living in another of his parishes was perfectly understandable; for him not to reside when he had but a single living was an event calling for intellectual effort at explanation. Why, then, should it have been that nearly all these poor incumbents were non-resident? Was it not that 'great Hardship' - sickness, old age, and so on - forced them to take this course of action? It is, indeed, difficult to escape this conclusion. The evidence suggests that there was a submerged 'proletariat' among the poor beneficed clergy, made up of men who all employed curates, were all beggared by employing curates, and who did this, not because they were looking after another living elsewhere but because they were unable, for whatever reason, to do duty themselves.

How much blame should be placed at the door of the Stipendiary Curates Act? In order to answer this question, it is necessary to find out the extent to which the 1813 Act affected these poor clerics' lives. The prospective, not retrospective, nature of the legislation must be borne in mind; the new salary scales did not come into force until there was a vacancy in a living served by a non-resident. It is therefore important to know how many of these poor beneficed clergy had obtained their incumbencies since the passing of the Stipendiary Curates Act, thus obliging them to pay their curates at the new rates. The answer to this question is that a lot had. Among the group of 322, there were 223 (69%) who had risen into the ranks of the beneficed clergy since 1813, leaving only 99 (31%) who had held preferment for longer. The plea of mitigation, entered on behalf of the 1813 Act, therefore largely falls to the ground. Its failure is not surprising. Poor livings were generally held by poor clergy, and a major distinguishing characteristic of the latter is that they had often not acquired their first, and probably last, benefice until they were already well into middle age.[88] It follows that vacancies brought about by death or (much less often) by resignation, occurred in poor livings at more regular intervals than in others. It was not long before aged Snoggins holding the penurious benefice of Little Blithering departed this life, to be succeeded by nearly-aged Sniggins. This explains why nearly 70% of the group of 322 had obtained their incumbencies since the Stipendiary Curates Act had been passed, a statistic implying a higher level of mobility than was the case among the body of the clergy as a whole.

In the light of this evidence, it must be concluded that the Stipendiary Curates Act was seriously flawed. Legislators failed to take sufficient account of the life led by many poor clergy; they mouldered in a curacy (or curacies) for decades, enjoyed late, and partial, relief from their plight upon promotion to a living, and then, often quite soon afterwards, submitted to relief of a more dubious and drastic kind: they died. The Stipendiary Curates Act did two things. Firstly, by failing to forge a sufficiently strong connection between wealth of benefice and size of curate's stipend, it had the unfortunate effect of increasing the number of incumbents earning less than one or other of their own employees. Secondly, by restricting itself to future appointments, it placed the poor beneficed clergy at a relative disadvantage as against the rich. Although the rich generally became incumbents at a young age,[89] the poor often did not do so until they were already well into middle age; whenever this happened, length of tenure was inevitably restricted. Here, indeed, was the rub: for it was precisely at the point where tenure ended that enforcement of the Stipendiary Curates Act began.

A caveat is necessary at this point. In some cases, the poverty of the group of 322 was more apparent than real. Take, for instance, the vicar of St Mary the Virgin, Oxford, a cleric with whom the reader is likely to be familiar. According to the Report, Newman's incumbency was worth £38; the curate was paid £30. Newman was one well-known clerical don, Charles Simeon, leader of the Cambridge Evangelicals, was another. Simeon received £96 a year from his perpetual curacy at Holy Trinity, but paid his curate £100. This left him with the princely ecclesiastical income of minus £4. Simeon was, we know, frugal; but he was somewhat less frugal than this rather dire arithmetic might, at first glance, imply. Descended from an Oxfordshire land-owning family, he had considerable private means. The extent of these is hinted at in a private memoir, written in 1813; 'my income', he writes, 'is now very great'.[90] Apart from Newman and Simeon, there was only one other clerical academic among the group of 322: Adam Sedgwick, fellow of Trinity College, Cambridge, and vicar of the Cambridgeshire living of Shudy Camps.

Of greater interest is the miscellaneous group of clergy which imitated Simeon in apparently living off berries in the hedgerows. Simeon was one of 44 incumbents with a decidedly paltry ecclesiastical income, after payment of taxes and curates' stipends. Thirty-three members of this exclusive club did not make a profit at all from their preferments, while the remaining eleven, of whom Simeon was one, all made a loss. Several anomalous individuals are to be found on the list, and it is even possible to come across a sprinkling of pluralists. William Williams deserves mention. He had been perpetual curate of two Oxfordshire livings - Ascott-under-Wychwood and Leafield - since 1826; the full proceeds of both, £55 in each case, were given to curates. Thomas Gilbert suffered a similar fate, the only difference being that he had endured it rather longer. He had been perpetual curate of Cotton, in Staffordshire, since 1795. The living was worth £44, and the curate also received £44. Gilbert had been perpetual curate of Cockshutt, this time in Shropshire, for a year longer. The value of Cockshutt was £86 a year, and the full proceeds - as at Cotton - went to the curate.

In some instances, the financial arrangements between incumbent and curate look a little odd, and odder than most was the deal that had been clinched at Whittlingdon, in Staffordshire. Thomas Lovett had held this perpetual curacy for nearly forty years, since 1795. The value of Whittlingdon, according to the Report, was £251 a year - not a bad sum for a perpetual curacy - and the stipendiary received the whole amount. This arouses the suspicion that Lovett and his curate conducted their business relations at a distance somewhat shorter than the proverbial arm's length.

Clearly, there are compelling reasons for not always taking the poverty of the group of 322 at face value. In at least three instances, incumbencies were held by academics deriving ample income from posts at either Oxford or Cambridge. Conversely, it could happen that net ecclesiastical income dwindled to zero, or even reached a minus figure. This brings that stalwart old argument - *reductio ad absurdum* - into play. Those with nothing from their benefices must have had something from some other quarter, a private nest-egg, say, or maybe a lucrative appointment as private tutor to some nobleman's son. Thirdly, it is necessary to take into account that intricate web of family interest, and paternal concern, that is met with everywhere in the Georgian church. Curates might well be sons; or, if not sons, close relatives or firm friends.

These are important qualifications, but they are merely qualifications. The claim that maladministration of the Stipendiary Curates Act caused hardship to a section of the beneficed clergy has not been compromised. It is not difficult to gather examples by way of illustration. The plight of Henry Berkin is one such. Berkin was a multi-pluralist, being perpetual curate of Trinity Church in the Forest of Dean, and also of Kilgwrwg and Penterry, both in Monmouthshire. He did not reside at any of his three livings. Trinity Church had been held since 1817, and the level of the appointed stipend was therefore determined by the terms of the 1813 Act. The living was worth £80, and the curate was paid £80; but Kilgwrwg and Penterry had both been held since 1810, and consequently, being outside the scope of the new legislation, the curate in each case received no more than £30. Berkin's income, after deduction of curates' stipends, was a meagre £62.

Robert Vernon was in similar straits. He, like Berkin, had three livings - the perpetual curacy of Huddington, and the rectory of Grafton Flyford, both in Worcestershire; as well as the Oxfordshire rectory of Heythrop. Like Berkin, he did not reside at any of them, and he, too, had gained preferment before the Act was passed as well as acquiring it afterwards, so that apt comparisons between stipends can be made. The most recent acquisition was Grafton Flyford, which Vernon had entered in 1831. Somewhat strangely, the living was valued at £75 although the curate received £100. At Heythrop, on the other hand, Vernon's since 1800, the curate's stipend was £40. Huddington had been his for ten years longer and the stipend, once again, was £40. After paying his three curates, Vernon's income amounted to £70 a year, just £8 more than Henry Berkin's.

It becomes clear what Archbishop Manners-Sutton meant, when he spoke of the difficulty of 'making a suit of clothes to fit the moon in all its changes'. Parliament had no option but to employ the bishops to be tailors; there simply was no one else qualified for the job. The difficulty, however, was that most of their lordships were not keen on the work, and nor were they competent. The important discretionary tenth clause, allowing the Bench to fix 'just and reasonable' curates' stipends in cases of 'great Hardship' among incumbents, was not applied properly. In the early 1830s, slightly under 4% of the beneficed clergy were earning as little as one or other of their own curates, a neat defeat for hierarchical principles. A few of these poor incumbents were dons; others had livings not covered by the Stipendiary Curates Act; a further group employed sons or relatives to help them out; and some had ecclesiastical incomes so low that they must have had alternative sources of livelihood; but none of these facts destroys the strength of the case that the new legislation was badly administered. This analysis has after all focussed only on those incumbents who were, by way of income, effectively curates themselves. If they suffered as a result of the insensitive implementation of the Stipendiary Curates Act, it is reasonable to assume that a good number of other clergymen, with ecclesias*:-`¹ incomes of, say, £100-£250 a year after payment of curates' stipends, suffered as well. Reforming the Georgian church was not, as the Stipendiary Curates Act shows us, always as easy as it looked.

v. *The Case for the Act*

The Stipendiary Curates Act was not without merit. It may have had defects but was, nonetheless, a reforming measure that substantially achieved its primary aim of radically improving curates' stipends. Although parliamentary returns dealing with curates' pay generally fail to distinguish between stipendiaries (who were covered by the new legislation) and assistants (who were not), and despite the uncertainty brought about by this unfortunate conflation, the changes that occurred in curates' financial fortunes are great enough to enable us to assert confidently that the Act had, in this regard, a profound effect. It is easiest to compare figures for 1813 - the year in which the Act came into force - with those for 1838, a quarter of a century later.[91] The situation in 1813 was bleak. In nearly four cases out of ten, curacies did not bring in £50 a year, and there was a scattering of derisory stipends - two curates were paid £4 a year, four others got £8, and two more got £9. In a further 45 instances, it is worth noting that the payment did not amount to as much as £20 a year, and there were 263 stipends for sums between £20 and £30.

The Georgian church, one may be tempted to conclude, took a positive delight in the preservation of anomalies, and the figures on curates' pay in 1813 support this contention. Some stipends were scarcely enough to satisfy the appetite of a hungry mouse, while others would have sated a greedy lion: best off was a curate in the diocese of Winchester, whose incumbent allowed him £700 a year, the kind of sum that a Norfolk rector would have regarded as wholly acceptable. Three other curates received between £300 and £350 a year, and thirteen received between £200 and £260. These were exceptions, however. The most crowded band was for stipends in the range of £40-£50 a year: there were 871 payments in this category. The median was set at £55 a year.[92]

There are two main reasons why things were so bad. Firstly, it was exceptionally difficult to break through the thick accretions of custom. Once a stipend had been fixed at £40 a year, it tended to remain at this level. A given rate was considered appropriate for the task in hand, both sides to the bargain gave it their stamp of approval, and it occurred to neither subsequently to attempt to change what had been agreed. The principle of the customary payment was the more powerful, in that it was in no way confined to matters ecclesiastical. On the contrary it was, in the direct sense, a social norm. This is clear from the payments made by Parson Woodforde to his servants; cooks may come and cooks may go, but the rate for the job, in this case £8 a year, went on for ever.[93] For most of the eighteenth century, maintenance of custom was made easier by lack of inflationary pressure. The inflation of 1799-1801 changed all this. Beilby Porteus, a perceptive prelate, was among the first to sense its significance. In his speech on the Curates' Bill in the House of Lords in 1808, he emphasized that the cost of the 'necessaries of life' made reform an urgent and imperative matter.[94] Porteus was right. It was inflation that paved the way for legislation.

The second reason why things were so bad has to do with the nature of much Georgian clerical work, and with attitudes towards that work. It is a recurring theme in this book.[95] All too often, it seems, being a cleric was reduced, virtually, to a matter of taking services. Non-residence was tolerated, and pluralism was not frowned upon. In places where a clergyman's work was viewed in this way, the stipends paid to curates were likely to be low. To understand why this was so, it is necessary to consider things from the incumbent's point of view. He would assume that his stipendiary was serving two or three churches, and was therefore receiving two or three stipends; and he would think to himself that, in each case, he was doing no more than paying for 'duty' to be done: by no means an arduous task. That such attitudes were widespread is evident from parliamentary returns for 1813. One curate in the diocese of Ely received '15s when he does the duty'; another, in York, received the same sum on the same basis; there was a curate in Exeter with '10s 6d every Sunday', and another 'inferior' clergyman, this time from Bangor, who received twice as much - '£1 1s per Sunday'.[96] It was against all of this that the Stipendiary Curates Act was directed.

Within a quarter of a century, the curate's lot - for stipendiaries as for assistants - had, as a result of the Act, substantially improved. The degree of easement was particularly marked at the bottom end of the salary scale, among those who had previously been 'passing rich' on less than £40 a year. In 1813 there were 868 stipends which failed to meet the £40 mark, but by 1838 this modest target proved too much on only 161 occasions, a decline of over four-fifths; 161 is not many among 4,813 payments. Equally important is the pattern that emerges of a reasonably even regional distribution. There was, it is true, one maverick diocese - the reader may, perhaps, be amused to learn that this was St David's - where poverty-stricken curacies were still quite numerous; there were thirty-two in all. In other places, however, even where episcopal jurisdiction covered several counties, between five and fifteen was the norm: there were five instances among 227 curacies in Chester, and sixteen among 496 in Lincoln. The failure wholly to do away with stipends of less than £40 a year is not a surprise. There were numerous nooks and crannies in the ecclesiastical Establish-ment, and it was in these that the most neglected clergy often sought shelter. To find them was one thing, helping them was another.

An alternative way of assessing change is to look at the number of stipends that had, as the contemporary phrase put it, been 'raised into respectability'. For present purposes, we will define respectability as a stipend of £100 a year or more. According to this definition, respectable stipends were by no means numerous in 1813, when the Stipendiary Curates Act came into force; they amounted to 482, well over half of which were for sums of between £100 a year and £110.[97] A quarter of a century later, the much-maligned race of curates had come up in the world. There were now 901 stipendiaries and assistants with stipends in the range of £100 to £110 a year; 355 with between £120 a year and £130; and even 301 with £150 a year or over. Taken in the round, stipends in three figures amounted to 1,679, a far cry from the 482 in 1813.[98]

The Stipendiary Curates Act achieved two main things: poverty-stricken curacies were more or less eliminated, and the number of curates with 'respectable' stipends was greatly increased. In one other respect, however, the Act was less successful. It is clear from its detailed provisions that legislators wanted to increase all stipends to at least £80 a year. Hence the requirement that stipends for less than this amount could only be permitted in four sets of circumstances: when the holder of the curacy was an incumbent acting as a curate; when he was a *bona fide* curate who was a pluralist; when the incumbent of the living being served was a man facing 'great Hardship'; and when the income from the benefice did not reach the stipulated figure of £80 a year. They were four impediments in the way of achieving the laudable aim of raising every curate's stipend to the £80 a year mark, and it must be admitted that some of the hindrances were considerable. The number of incumbents acting as curates was numerous; curates who were pluralists were also numerous; quite a few rectors or vicars faced hardship; there was still a scattering of benefices worth less than £80 a year.[99] As though all this was not enough, there were two further difficulties. The Act applied only to parishes where there were stipendiaries. This was a serious defect in the legislation; in 1838, parishes served by assistants amounted to 1,725. More importantly, the figure for assistants was rising all the time, partly because of pressure of numbers within the clerical profession and partly because the campaign to extend urban ministry was starting to get off the ground.[100] The second source of further difficulty, whilst diminishing every year, was as yet neither paltry nor insignificant. This was the prospective - not retrospective - nature of the 1813 Act. Because vacancies were infrequent, the benign attitude towards the existing holders of rectories and vicarages was a substantial barrier to quick improvement. In a quarter of all the parishes in England and Wales, it was probably the case that the rector or vicar who was incumbent in 1838 had also been incumbent in 1813.[101] In a few instances, those sitting in the pews looked up at the same face in the pulpit for over half a century.

For all these reasons, a large wedge of stipends still brought in less than £80 a year in 1838. To receive less than £40 a year had become demeaning, but £50 or £60 a year was a different matter. All in all, there were 2,000 stipends that failed to make the £80 a year mark.[102] This was rather a lot: the median was now £83 a year.[103] Although a substantial improvement on the situation in 1813 - when the median had been £55 a year - church reformers were still well short of their target of providing every curate with a stipend sufficient enough to enable him to devote all of his energies to a single parish, without having to resort to pluralism in order to make ends meet.

The fact that the median value for curacies in 1838 was £83 a year does not mean that there was, at that date, widespread evasion of the Stipendiary Curates Act. Among the 2,000 curacies that failed to bring in £80 a year, 600 were held by assistants, leaving 1,400 in the hands of stipendiaries.[104] Although this might, at first sight, seem to establish a strong case that widespread evasion was, indeed, taking place, this assumption is quickly eroded, as soon as the limitations of the 1813 Act are taken into account. Especially pertinent is the gradualism inherent in the prospective nature of the Act. Incumbents were legally permitted to go on paying miserly stipends of £30 or £40 a year until such time as they either died or resigned their livings. In order to assess the extent to which the legislation of 1813 was evaded, a very large sample of beneficed clergy, made up of every incumbent with an income of more than £300 a year, was studied. It was found that, about 1830, 287 rectors or vicars, each earning over £6 a week, themselves were paying stipends of £50 a year or less on 326 occasions.[105] What is particularly interesting is the second layer of investigation. Of the 326 livings whose stipends were £50 or less, I divided them between places where there had been a vacancy since 1813, thus bringing the benefice within the scope of the 1813 Act, and places where there had not. In 246 instances, three-quarters of the sample, there had been no vacancy. Among the 80 remaining, moreover, there were 15 places where an assistant, not a stipendiary, was employed. In other words, among 326 low stipends, only 65 (20%) were being paid to stipendiaries whose terms and conditions of employment were laid down in the 1813 Act.[106] This is conclusive. Clerical diehards did not always obstruct reform in early nineteenth-century England.

vi. *An Individual Life*

A lot more is known about Georgian beneficed clergy than about Georgian curates. A curate was in most areas likely to be a stipendiary, and stipendiaries, as John Smith noted, were nomadic: they were 'birds of passage' that flitted from curacy to curacy.[107] A peripatetic is rarely one who keeps interesting or important records. Those who served as curates longest, and there were, as has been seen, a good number who were condemned to being assistants or stipendiaries for a very long time indeed,[108] were also among the least enterprising and least well-connected; and were also the least likely to leave any recorded trace of themselves. Diaries, letters and other biographical sources to do with the beneficed clergy are easy enough to come by, but documenting the lives of the subalterns is a different matter; here a vignette is as precious as gold. Generally one finds what can best be described as scattered literary remains; only on one occasion was I fortunate enough to come across a collection of unpublished material that was graphic and had any real life.

James Layton,[109] by way of coincidence, was a Norfolk curate working in the deanery of Waxham, a small corner of the ecclesiastical firmament which already has been written about at some length.[110] Ordained in 1802, he started his clerical life as a stipendiary at Catfield, a marshy area about four miles from the sea.[111] Immediately, a piece of luck came his way. His rector, George Lucas, had been promoted to Catfield a year earlier.[112] He did not think much of the parsonage, regarding it as 'unfit', so he went to live in his wife's house at Little Ormesby near Yarmouth.[113] The rector being an absentee, Layton was permitted to take over the parsonage at Catfield for himself. Very soon, the new curate enjoyed a further piece of fortune; in the same year that he obtained the curacy at Catfield, he also acquired the curacy at Sutton, a small village two miles away.[114] Fortune, we know, always comes in threes. In this instance, however, the third was a little slower in arriving than the first two. It was not until 1805 that Layton obtained his third curacy. As with Sutton, it was in the immediate vicinity of Catfield, at Potter Heigham.[115] James Layton, then, was in many ways typical of the curates of his time; a stipendiary, he looked after three contiguous rural parishes. His was an isolated life, in small communities: the population of Catfield in 1801 was 476, with a further 267 at Sutton, and 321 at Potter Heigham.[116]

Catfield seems to have been a peaceable place, with no 'very great difficulties' over collection of tithe[117]. Opposition to the church, in the shape of Dissent, seems to have been muted - at a visitation, held in 1806, Dissenters in the parish were described as being 'few and of low rank'. The new stipendiary curate cannot be accused of over-exerting himself. There was no church school, no parochial clubs of any kind, and catechising was left to the local schoolmaster.[118] Services were held weekly, and Communion was only three times a year; getting parishioners to come to the Sacrament was not easy and in 1820 attenders numbered no more than about twenty-five.

Sutton could, on occasion, be turbulent. The parish had enjoyed, for most of the eighteenth century, an exceptionally long incumbency. Thomas Williams became rector in 1732, and was still rector on his death, in 1796, at the age of ninety-four, a long innings even for a Georgian clergyman. He had found the parishioners inclined to be restive. When he entered the living he set a fixed sum for compositions, which was not subsequently altered. This act of magnanimity on his part was not, it would seem, appreciated. In the 1760s, some farmers withheld payment of their tithes. The rector was required to take in kind, and was then threatened with a legal suit for failing to collect with sufficient promptness! This dispute, which seems to have been rather silly, was soon resolved. It says a good deal for Williams that, when the dust had settled, he did not go back on his original policy of not raising his tithes.[119]

In about 1778, Thomas Williams, then well into his seventies, left Sutton and entrusted the care of the parish to a succession of curates. Among these, for a time, was William Ivory, vicar of the nearby living of Horsey.[120] This did not prove a good plan. The flower of the Establishment withered, and the flower of Dissent flourished. In the 1790s, 'many' of the families in the parish were Baptists. They frequented a chapel at Ingham, and also held Sunday-evening meetings in Sutton, gathering at the house of a 'respectable miller'. There was still a regular, though by no means constant, attendance at church on the part of the farmers and 'principal people' within the parish, but things were bad with the 'lower classes'. They 'very seldom' attended, and the frequency of 'desertions' was increasing.

The parish of Sutton scarcely features in James Layton's correspondence. The succession of curates since the late 1770s had bred the feeling that attending to the needs of the parishioners could conveniently be reduced to a simple matter of 'doing duty'. In this regard, James Layton differed not at all from his predecessors. Among diocesan records there is a paucity of information regarding Layton's ministry, usually a clear sign that a parish was neither well-organised nor well cared for. At the visitation held in 1806, it was noted that Communion was held three times a year, with 'few' coming; there was no school; and there was also no catechism.[121] No returns were made in 1813, a precedent which was devoutly followed seven years later.

Potter Heigham was also a neglected parish. Richard Lockwood had come by the living in 1803. The next year, he had done even better, obtaining not only the vicarage of Lowestoft but also another Suffolk benefice, Kessingland.[122] He described the parsonage at Potter Heigham as 'very poor', preferring to live at Lowestoft. Earlier, the parish had been looked after by Benjamin Cubitt, later vicar of Stalham, who had served Potter Heigham along with Ludham.[123] As at Sutton, Communion was held three times a year. Communicants, in 1806, were described as 'few and in general poor'; in 1813 the number was put at 'about ten'; and by 1820 the figure had crept up to 'about twenty'. James Layton seems to have regarded the parish much in the same way as he regarded Sutton; duty had to be done because duty had been paid for, but that is all.

The portrait of James Layton that emerges from his letters makes up with honesty what it lacks in attractiveness. His own laziness is a constant theme. 'My activity', he once wrote, 'is only that of [a] bottled small bee which flies about and plentifully if shaken, but otherwise is still enough'.[124] On another occasion, he complained bitterly that he lived according to the 'lawyer-maxim of "Never do today what can by any means be put off 'till tomorrow'"'.[125] He was destined to remain long in his curacy at Catfield, and this bred a crippling fatalism. Relations with the Almightly became distant, not to say cool - 'I am afraid now to ask anything of God, but resignation to that which is - for He has frequently granted my prayer, but always with a vengeance'.[126] Life was quite without zest, and his correspondence is pervaded by a sense of pessimism and impending doom. In a word, he plumbed the depths. Of the reality of this, we must let him speak for himself. He summed up his position in a letter written in 1816, after he had been at Catfield for fourteen years without any sign of promotion coming his way. 'How frequently', he wrote, 'do I wish that I had gone from my cradle directly to my coffin'.[127]

Ecclesiastical promotion might be slow in arriving, but promotion of a different kind was soon to be his. Whether this worked for his good or whether it did not is open to question. Layton was convinced in his own mind, and was characteristically forthright. His wife, he wrote - he married in 1817 - was 'a woman nearly my own age, very plain, very deformed, without an accomplishment or a guinea'.[128] Marriage changed James Layton's life in two ways. Firstly, he was pressured into paying more attention to his parochial duties - 'my wife has extorted a promise from me to compile a new Sermon every week and to preach it too'.[129] Secondly, he became desperately short of cash.

Writing a weekly sermon was an easier matter than resolving his financial difficulties. His friends urged him to take pupils, a course of action he was most reluctant to pursue. What stood in the way was his sense that he was unequal to the task - 'whatever my talents may have been, from neglect they have become so rusted and wasted as to be of no use to me now'.[130] His resistance, however, was soon broken down. Within a few months of his marriage, he received a visit from a cattle-drover of Catfield, looking for a tutor for his nephew. Layton took a long look at the visitor, and came rapidly to the conclusion that his general demeanour was not propitious. Judging from the cattle-drover the prospective pupil, recently turned sixteen, was unlikely to be as intelligent as an average twelve-year-old. Were this to be the case, he would, thought Layton, 'be a great lout & a troublesome one'. On the other hand, if the cattle-drover's nephew was up to the mark intellectually, how would he, James Layton, manage to keep ahead?[131]

Richard Daniel, nephew to the cattle-drover of Catfield, duly arrived as Layton's first pupil early in 1818. He was, indeed, slow; but, happily, he was not a lout. Layton's initial apprehensions melted. He still felt unworthy as a teacher, but he also found, much to his own surprise, that he enjoyed being with young men and that his experience was of benefit to them. Richard Daniel was soon joined by other pupils, and a new career was begun.

Layton's time was now wholly consumed. Teaching, he said, was occupying him from 8 a.m. until 10 p.m., apart from a two-hour break in the middle of the day.[132] Such time as was not spent with his pupils was spent with his wife. As with a lot of married couples, there was a degree of incompatibility to overcome. Analysing the source of the difficulty was easier than finding a remedy for it. It was, indeed, an age-old problem: 'she hates to be alone, I hate to be in company'.[133] By way of necessary compromise, Layton was, whenever possible, attentive to her emotional needs. He attended to his pupils and he attended to his wife, but he did not attend to his three parishes: there simply was not the time. Enforced dereliction of clerical functions brought, in its train, remorse and a touch of despair. He ceased to believe that it was either good or right to be in Orders. His views on the matter were expressed forcefully in a letter written in 1820. 'If', he wrote, 'there is a good living in this world & a judgement day in the next, when every man shall be dealt with according to his work, the clergy I fear will come off sadly, they doing very little of their duty. I do believe it would go against my conscience to put a son into the church: how much worldly considerations may produce this feeling, myself perhaps does not fully know'.[134]

Taking pupils was not good for pastoral ministry, and it also failed to resolve the financial problems that came with marriage. Requests for money are found throughout Layton's correspondence. In May 1819, after he had been teaching for over a year, he put in a request for £20 - 'how terribly fast it melts!'[135] Later on, in 1822, we find him comparing himself with the cuckoo: like that bird, he has 'but two notes'.[136] These difficulties should not have assailed him. Private tutoring might be hard, but it was also lucrative - Layton charged £100 a year for boys up to fifteen, and £150 a year for those who were sixteen or over.[137] It is not known how many pupils he had at any one time but, as a guideline, there is mention of at least four in a letter written in 1821.[138] His three curacies also brought him in a reasonable income. The stipend at Catfield was fixed at £50 a year; because the rector, George Lucas, remained throughout Layton's curacy, the living never came within the scope of the Stipendiary Curates Act. For a brief period, Layton did rather better out of Potter Heigham. Richard Lockwood paid him £40 a year in 1806, and raised this to £50 a year in 1814. Much later, in 1829, Lockwood died, the Stipendiary Curates Act came into play, and the curate's stipend was raised without delay to £70 a year. Layton did not benefit from the new rate for long; in April 1832, Francis Baker was licensed to the curacy. Finally, there is Sutton. Here, Layton received £40 a year in 1806, and he received the same sum in 1829.[139] Layton's ecclesiastical income, in the years around 1820, works out at £140 a year: £50 from Catfield, £50 from Potter Heigham, and £40 from Sutton. Two pupils, both paying £100 a year, would have increased his income to £340. A lot of curates, it is certain, got by on much less. Layton had a young and growing family - he ended up with five children - but he still should have been able to cope adequately. It is hard to escape the conclusion that he was one of those people, the reader will doubtless know others, for whom expenditure is always destined to rise and surpass income.

Layton carried on teaching at Catfield for ten or so years. He would have carried on for longer had the rhythm of his life not been disturbed by trauma. He explained what happened in a letter - 'sad has been my week, but sad especially the event of this day. I have no longer a wife - or my five blessed children a mother: she died at 8 this evening with inflammation of the lungs having been confined four days to her bed'.[140] His wife gone, his mother came to live with him. This arrangement, unhappily, did not work well; her constant complaints only added to his severe sorrow. Desperate, he sought a way out of his predicament. An opportunity seemed to offer itself towards the end of 1829, with the death of Richard Lockwood, rector of Potter Heigham. James Layton now sat himself down and wrote a petition to Bishop Bathurst.[141] He had, he wrote, been curate of Catfield and Sutton for twenty-eight years, and of Potter Heigham for twenty-five. He was past his fiftieth birthday, and had four small children to support (the fifth had recently died). His health was poor, and he had but a 'scanty precarious' income. Would it, he wondered, be possible for the bishop to let him have 'some portion' of Mr Lockwood's preferments?

It was not. The petition met with a chilly response. Nothing daunted, Layton tried again. This time he employed direct tactics, arranging an interview. Layton, according to his own account,[142] began by suggesting a kind of compact. George Lucas (rector of Catfield) was, he rightly pointed out, becoming elderly; he was, in fact, sixty-two. If Bathurst were to outlive Lucas,[143] and if he, James Layton, were also to outlive Lucas, would his Lordship make a promise of the living? Bathurst feigned deafness. James Layton repeated the proposal. Repetition proved too much for the bishop; he arose, and he spoke. The proposal was ''absurd: the most absurd request he ever heard in his life - it was worth £500 or £600 per annum[144] & what should he give it [to] me for''. Layton then mentioned his needs and referred, also, to the length of his service. The storm became a tempest - ''there were 100 curates in his diocese more deserving than myself ... he had nephews who were *starving*''.[145] The bishop left the room, banging the door behind him, without saying goodbye.

Thus died James Layton's hopes of preferment within the diocese of Norwich. Failure had been anticipated, and he had already started to look elsewhere. He had connections at Sandwich in Kent, which he had begun to exploit, applying for the mastership of Sandwich School.[146] Although this came to nothing, he did not give up. In 1830, he put his name forward for the rectory of St Peter's, Sandwich. This parish was, in one respect, highly unusual; rights of presentation were vested alternately in the Crown, and in the corporation of Sandwich.[147] Thus there was, from time to time, a popular election. This, indeed, was what was happening in 1830. Layton was initially enthusiastic, but then withdrew when he realised there would be a contest - 'I hate a contest for shopkeepers favor - I hate a struggle as it were upon the very stairs of a Pulpit - & most of all to be beaten in the struggle and kick'd down'.[148] His withdrawal, as it happens, took place less than a week before his fateful interview with Bishop Bathurst. Humiliation, on this occasion, proved a tonic. Within two days James Layton was back in Sandwich, campaigning vigorously in what had turned into a three-cornered fight. He did not pull any punches - 'I have applied for votes in Hospitals, Almshouses, Workhouses & Alehouses - In Tanyards & in Coalships; have stayed the labourer with his barrow or mortar hod - have discussed points of Creed with an Unitarian Brewer's-servant ... & a Methodist-barber'.[149] His clerical career might have advanced had such enthusiasm and evident self-confidence appeared earlier.

In the first week of January 1831, the result of the poll was declared. The third candidate having withdrawn, Layton was victorious by fifty-seven votes.[150] Thraldom was now at an end. He had obtained a rectory worth £150 a year; there was a school, bringing in a further £40 a year or so; and the school included, also, a spacious house and large garden.[151] He had hopes of holding on to his curacy at Catfield,[152] but these were soon dashed. In March 1832, another cleric was licensed to serve the living. After nearly thirty years, his career in Norfolk lay behind him, and his career in Sandwich lay ahead. In financial terms, Layton was not now substantially better off - the living and school in Kent were worth £190 or so a year, whereas the three Norfolk curacies were now producing £160 a year - but he felt that his status had improved, and he was glad to leave Norfolk.

With the move to Kent, we are forced to part from Layton; his regular correspondence ceases in 1831. Thereafter, there is only a short letter written in 1848;[153] and also a further brief note penned in 1851.[154] He hoped to meet up with an old friend early in 1852, but was hesitant about the reception he would receive after the lapse of years. As always, he spoke directly and from the heart - 'you will see me very much weakened both in body & mind - deaf - near blind'.

Chapter 9 Notes

1. Diary entry of the Revd William Jones of Broxbourne in Hertfordshire, dated 27 January 1803, quoted in Christie, *The Diary of the Revd William Jones*, pp. 148-9. Jones was curate of Broxbourne, 1781-1801, and also vicar there, 1801-21. Italics in text.

2. Addison, *The Spectator*, 24 March 1710-11, quoted in Sykes, *Church and State*, p. 147.

3. *Morning Herald*, 22 October 1831.

4. E.B. Ellman, *Recollections of a Sussex Parson*, p. 132.

5. *ibid.*, p. 133.

6. *ibid.*, pp. 137-8.

7. *ibid.*, p. 160.

8. *ibid.*, p. 165.

9. *ibid.*, p. 138.

10. Revd John Smith to Henry Brougham, Lord Chancellor, 8 August 1832. This letter is to be found at the Pepys Library, Magdalene College, Cambridge.

11. The rector of Banham at this time was John Surtees; he was also rector of Taverham in Norfolk, as well as holding a prebend at Bristol. According to the 1835 Report (*P.P.*, 1835, XXII, 710-11), Banham was worth £800 a year, while its population was 1,297.

12. The 1835 Report (*P.P.*, 1835, XXII, 710-11) confirms this figure.

13. R. Latham and W. Matthews, *The Diary of Samuel Pepys*, I, LXXVI-LXXXIII.

14. See Smith's letter to Brougham, 8 August 1832, referred to above.

15. See above, pp.23-4.

16. *The State of the Curates*, p. 15.

17. *ibid.*, pp. 23-4.

18. *ibid.*, p. 29.

19. *ibid.*, p. 57.

20. For 1810, *P.P.*, 1812, X, 157; for 1813, *P.P.*, 1817, XV, 150-1; for 1814, *P.P.*, 1817, XV, 152-3; for 1827, *P.P.*, 1830, XIX, 40-1; for 1831, *P.P.*, 1833, XXVII, 334-7; for 1838, *P.P.*, 1840, XXXIX, 62-5; for 1841, *P.P.*, 1843, XL, 6-7. See below, Table XX, p.000.

21. *P.P.*, 1840, XXXIX, 62-5.

22. See above, pp.152-5, and note 103, p.168.

23. *P.P.*, 1840, XXXIX, 62-3. Modern historians also blur the distinction between the number of parishes served and the number of curates serving; see, e.g., Haig, *The Victorian Clergy*, p.241, note 15, where it is stated that, in 1812, there were 3,694 curates to non-residents. There were not; all that the return in that year tells us is that in 3,694 places duty was performed by stipendiaries.

24. See above, p.136.

25. According to Stone, *The university in society*, Appendix IV, Table 1A, p.91 and Table 1B, p.92 admissions to Oxford and Cambridge, over these four decades, averaged 406 a year. Assuming that 50% of matriculants subsequently became ordained, and surmising, also, that 75% of ordinands were Oxbridge-trained, the average annual figure for ordinations works out at 270.

26. See above, p136.

27. See above, p.135.

28. In 1835, returns were only made out for stipendiaries, not for assistants (see *P.P.*, 1837,

XLI, 220-1); while, in 1810, no figures were received from St David's.

29. According to Stone, *op.cit.*, university admissions in the 1790s averaged 407 a year. Assuming that half of all matriculants took Orders, the number of ordinations in the second half of the decade would have been 1,357. (This calculation is based on the premise that 75% of all ordinands had signed college registers).

30. According to *ibid.*, admissions to Oxford and Cambridge in the 1820s averaged 850 a year. If 80% of all ordinands were Oxbridge-trained, and if 50% of all matriculants became clergy, ordinations in the second half of the decade would have amounted to 2,656.

31. See above, pp.138-42.

32. See above, p.139.

33. See below, pp.224-43.

34. See above, p.222.

35. See above, p.220.

36. See above, p.220.

37. The figure given in parliamentary returns was 2,032 - see *P.P.*, 1843, XL, 6-7.

38. See above, pp.219-21.

39. See above, pp.191-205.

40. See above, pp.153-5.

41. The figure given in the return is 4,327 - see *P.P.*, 1817, XV, 150-1.

42. See above, p.135.

43. See above, p.221.

44 13 Anne c. 11.

45. See above, p.68.

46. See above, p.70.

47. See above, p.71.

48. 36 George III c. 83.

49. Sykes, *Church and State*, p.206, 208.

50. Salter, 'Isaac Maddox', p.58.

51. C.M.L. Bouch, *Prelates and people*, p.367.

52. Shuler, 'The Pastoral and Ecclesiastical Administration of the Diocese of Durham', Table VI, p.21.

53. Maynard, 'The Ecclesiastical Administration of the Archdeaconry of Durham', p.354. In 1832, the average was £88.

54. Salter, 'Isaac Maddox', pp.105-6.

55. Ransome, *The State of the Bishopric of Worcester*, p.11. On scholarly Richard Hurd, see above, p.196.

56. McClatchey, *Oxfordshire Clergy*, p.71. The returns are incomplete.

57. Jacob, 'Clergy and Society', Table, p.167.

58. House of Commons, 25 April 1805, *Hansard*, VI, 927.

59. House of Commons, 13 July 1813, *Hansard*, XXVI, 1197-98.

60. Lord Harrowby, House of Lords, 21 May 1813, *Hansard*, XXVI, 301.

61. Beilby Porteus, Bishop of London, House of Lords, 27 June 1808, *Hansard*, XI, 1087.

62. See, e.g., House of Commons, 6 May 1805, *Hansard*, IV, 611.

63. Bishop of London, House of Lords, 21 May 1813, *Hansard*, XXVI, 295.

64. See, e.g., Bishop of Worcester, House of Lords, 21 May 1813, *Hansard*, XXVI, 298.

65. Lord Porchester, House of Lords, 21 May 1805, *Hansard*, V, 42.

66. Charles James Fox, House of Commons, 25 April 1806, *Hansard*, VI, 926.

67. Charles Manners-Sutton, Archbishop of Canterbury, House of Lords, 23 March 1813, *Hansard*, XXV, 257.

68. *P.P.*, 1812, X, 157.

69. Lord Grenville, House of Lords, 1 July 1812, *Hansard*, XXIII, 871.

70. See above, pp. 220-4.

71. See above, p.102. The same, incidentally, applies to the 1838 Pluaralities Act.

72. Lord Harrowby, House of Lords, 18 June 1812, *Hansard*, XXIII, 592-3.

73. Charles Wetherall, House of Commons, 5 July 1813, *Hansard*, XXVI, 1117.

74. 53 George III c. 149.

75. See below, Table XVIII.

76. See above, p.150.

77. See above, p.228.

78. See above, p.144.

79. See above, p.228.

80. See above, pp.220-4.

81. [Sydney Smith], 'Letter on the Curates' Salary Bill', *E.R.*, XIII (October, 1808), 28.

82. *ibid.*

83. *Observations on the new Residence Bill*, pp. iii-iv, vi, viii, 1, 4.

84. *The Sufferings of the Clergy disclosed*, pp. 6-9.

85. *ibid.*, pp. 12-16.

86. In my analysis, I have restricted myself to those incumbents who, after payment of taxes and curates' stipends, had incomes of £100 a year or less. There may also have been a few beneficed clergy with higher net incomes who found themselves in the situation of earning less than one or other of their own curates.

87. The 1835 Report used a capital 'A' to distinguish between a stipendiary (a curate serving a parish with a non-resident incumbent) and an assistant (a curate working in a place where the incumbent was resident). It follows that, provided an incumbent employed a curate at each of his livings, it is possible to discover his whereabouts. The group of 322 clergy now under discussion only held eight livings where curates were not employed. Among the remainder, there were 25 assistant curates, indicating the same number of resident incumbents.

88. See above, pp. 138-42.

89. See above, p.139.

90. On the subject of Simeon's finances, see William Carus, ed., *Memoirs of the Life of the Revd Charles Simeon*, pp. 2, 17, 433-5, 589-91.

91. Figures for 1813 are in *P.P.*, 1817, XV, 150-1; for 1838 in *P.P.*, 1840, XXXIX, 62-5.

92. It will be noted that this sum of £55 a year is 50% above the median payment of £37 made only three years earlier to stipendiaries serving livings whose incumbents were non-resident by licence (for which, see above, p.229.). The main reason for the disparity is that parliamentary returns for 1813 include assistants, and assistants, always non-pluralistic, received higher stipends at this period than stipendiaries.

93. See above, pp. 96-7.

94. See above, p.228.

95. See above, pp. 115-16, 151-2.

96. *P.P.*, 1817, XV, 150-151.

97. The number between £100 a year and £110 was 278 - *P.P.*, 1817, XV, 150-1.

98. *P.P.*, 1840, XXXIX, 62-5.

99. According to the 1835 Report, the number of livings valued at under £80 a year was 876 (*P.P.*, 1835, XXII, 1053).

100. See above, p.223. There is illuminating comment on assistant curates in the Victorian era in Haig, *The Victorian Clergy*, pp.218-40.

101. This calculation is based on the earlier analysis of mobility among the beneficed clergy in Sussex (see above, p.150). In Sussex, vacancies did not occur in 45% of parishes over the eighteen-year period 1815-33. This is consistent with vacancies not occurring in about 24% of parishes over the quarter-century spanning 1813 and 1838.

102. The figure was 2,017.

103. In all, returns were obtained from 4,813 parishes in 1838. In 282 instances, the figure for the curate's stipend was not given. Among the 4,531 parishes remaining, the median works out at £83 a year - £84 a year for assistants and £82 a year for stipendiaries.

104. The figure was 2,017.

105. Stipendiaries held 1,398; assistants had 619.

106. There may have been a few more incumbents who behaved in this way, but successfully concealed the fact by failing to make a return. This, at any rate, is how Harry West seems to have acted. Although he was non-resident at Berwick, no curate's stipend is given in the 1835 Report.

107. See above, pp.216-8.

108. See above, pp.138-42.

109. Layton's letters are to be found among the Dawson Turner Papers, at the Wren Library, Trinity College, Cambridge. Details of this collection are in the Bibliography.

110. See above, pp.153-7.

111. See above, p.153.

112. George Lucas (1768-1833) was rector of Catfield, 1801-33 (Venn, *Alumni*, Part II, IV, 227).

113. *ibid*. See also visitation returns for 1806.

114. See letter, 06/11/1829, *D.T.P.*, XXXVIII, 79.

115. *ibid*.

116. *P.P.*, 1801-2, VI, 234.

117. See visitation returns for the deanery of Waxham in 1794. Information about these can be found in the Bibliography.

118. See visitation returns for 1806.

119. See visitation returns for 1794.

120. *ibid*.

121. See visitation returns for 1806.

122. Richard Lockwood, rector of Potter Heigham, 1803-29; vicar of Lowestoft, 1804-29; vicar of Kessingland, 1804-29; prebendary of Peterborough, 1824-29.

123. See visitation returns for 1794.

124. 18/12/1813, *D.T.P.*, X, 181.

125. 13/06/1817, *D.T.P.*, XIII, 80.

126. 17/10/1828, *D.T.P.*, XXXIV, 157.

127. 19/01/1816, *D.T.P.*, XII, 17.

128. 01/07/1817, *D.T.P.*, XIV, 1.

129. 18/07/1817, *D.T.P.*, XIV, 16.

130. 09/09/1817, *D.T.P.*, XIV, 59.

131. 24/12/1817, *D.T.P.*, XIV, 152.

132. 20/02/1818, *D.T.P.*, XV, 49.

133. 01/09/1820, *D.T.P.*, XX, 32.

134. 28/01/1820, *D.T.P.*, XIX, 24.

135. 28/05/1819, *D.T.P.*, XVII, 101.

136. 21/03/1822, *D.T.P.*, XXIII, 62.

137. 16/10/1818, *D.T.P.*, XVI, 43.

138. 03?/08/1821, *D.T.P.*, XXII, 21.

139. 06/11/1830, *D.T.P.*, XXXVIII, 79.

140. 20/04/1829, *D.T.P.*, XXXV, 89.

141. 06/11/1830, *D.T.P.*, XXXVIII, 79.

142. 29/11/1830, *D.T.P.*, XXXVIII, 107.

143. The bishop, at this time, was already eighty-six; he was destined to survive for another seven years, dying in 1837 at the age of ninety-three.

144. According to the 1835 Report (*P.P.*, 1835, XXII, 725) the gross value of Catfield was £500 a year, and the net value was £467.

145. Italics in text. Bathurst's rapid appeal to the 'nephews in Orders syndrome' was standard episcopal behaviour, when faced with the need to find some easy way of refusing pleas by clergy for promotion or higher stipends. The ploy was also used by George Pelham, Bishop of Lincoln, when confronted by importunings on the part of James Plumptre. 'Two of Mrs Pelham's nephews', he told the vicar of Great Gransden, 'are gone into the church with no other expectation of being provided for in it, but by me, & many others, I know, look up to me & reasonably too expect I should do something for them' - a letter, dated 15 October 1822, C.U.L., Add. Mss. 5864, f.200.

146. 16/04/1830, *D.T.P.*, XXXVII, 81.

147. *P.P.*, 1835, XXII, 232-3.

148. 23/11/1830, *D.T.P.*, XXXVIII, 97.

149. 01/12/1830, *D.T.P.*, XXXVIII, 109.

150. 03/01/1831, *D.T.P.*, XXXIX, 1.

151. 01/12/1830, *D.T.P.*, XXXVIII, 109.

152. 03/06/1831, *D.T.P.*, XXXIX, 69.

153. 19/11/1848, *D.T.P.*, LXXVII, 155.

154. 31/12/1851, *D.T.P.*, LXXXII, 155.

10

Conclusion

To draw together the threads, to arrive at a statement of the case that takes full account of the facts, is neither simple nor straightforward. The varieties of Georgian clerical experience defy easy generalisation. The life of a well-connected 'squarson' such as Benjamin Newton[1] - the riding to hounds, the prompt purchases of canal shares, the lavish dinners with menus mentioning turtle and champagne - was in every way different from the determined drabness, and dutiful sadness, characteristic of a reclusive scholar in the mould of John Skinner.[2] Differences arising from temperament and background were reinforced by the effects of regional disparities. England, unhappily, was cleft in two. There was the south, affluent, effortless and elegant, a place of tall rectories with a high culture; and there was the north, rugged, poor, and rough in manner, with a 'working' clergy close to toil. In 1830, the ecclesiastical income of the typical Norfolk incumbent was £395 a year; whereas in Cumbria the comparable figure was only £108 a year.[3] It is exceptionally difficult to forge any point of contact between Parson Woodforde, affably entertaining local incumbents and gentry in his snug Norfolk rectory, and the numerous 'peasant' clergy of the likes of William Sewell,[4] found tending the cuts and sores of his neighbours'sheep.

Despite these necessary caveats, it is still possible to make general statements that seem to ring true. The first, and one of the most important, is that the beneficed clergy of the 1830s enjoyed incomes which would have seemed wondrous to their late seventeenth-century predecessors. In the intervening period, a handful of things had come to the clergy's assistance. There had been improvements in agricultural techniques; there had been extensive land reclamation; there had been Napoleon's gift to English farmers - the Napoleonic boom in agriculture; there had been enclosure; clerical estate management had improved; and Queen Anne's Bounty had been founded, with the policies of that body being implemented and developed. On the other side, as counterweight, there was only the post-war agrarian depression; and it would seem that this produced nothing worse than modest reductions in benefice incomes in some areas.[5]

The accuracy of statements regarding rising clerical wealth can be statistically verified. Two national surveys of benefice values were carried out in the first decade of the eighteenth century, and the exercise was repeated in the 1830s, so that results can be compared. Because of errors in the two earlier surveys, the extent of change will never be precisely known; but it was concluded that, for England and Wales as a whole, the rise in benefice values as between the first decade of the eighteenth century and the fourth decade of the nineteenth was at least 400%.[6] Placing this finding in context, the domestic inflation rate probably did not rise by much more than 100% over the same period.[7]

This is interesting enough, but is only part of the truth. Equally important is relative performance: did rich livings do better than poor, or was the opposite the case? Contrary to expectation, rises in values of poor livings were greater than rises in values of rich. For vicarages and rectories bringing in over £50 a year in the first decade of the eighteenth century, the increase was 325%; and for vicarages and rectories bringing in £50 a year or less, the increase was 462%; for perpetual curacies, less well-endowed than either vicarages or rectories, the increase was 686%.[8] This leaves in tatters the conventional view, which holds that the chasm separating rich clergy from poor, already wide by the end of the seventeenth century, widened still further between 1700 and 1840. Wide it may have been; widen it did not.

Although the generally held view of the Georgian church is false in this respect, in another regard it is sound. Biography reveals that opulent clergy, mostly with aristocratic connections, had extensive sources of extra-ecclesiastical income. Often, wealth from privately-owned land far surpassed what was obtained from a rectory or two.[9] The majority of clergy, less well-placed socially, had to manage as best they could. Teaching in one guise or another was the most popular means of supplementing income. Most teachers, either in public schools or in private establishments, were clergy; but the numbers were few.[10]

Anti-clerical propagandists grossly, and unfairly, exaggerated the extent of the clergy's wealth.[11] The facts are now revealed, by the detailed consideration of the findings of Grey's famous commission of inquiry, which reported in 1835. There were, according to the Report, 7,500 beneficed clergy. Of these, only 76 drew more than £2,000 a year from their livings; a further 310 incumbents managed to make in excess of £1,000 a year. Although, on this evidence, there were a few clerical incomes that were, so to speak, in the clear air, many more drifted in a dense mist at ground level. In the early 1830s, 1,222 beneficed clergy (16% of the total) got £100 a year or less, after payment of taxes and curates' stipends. The figure for the first quartile was £138 a year, and the median was set at £265 a year.[12]

It was widely held among contemporaries that £150 a year was a reasonable minimum income for an incumbent, if he was to fulfil his many social, as well as family, obligations. In order to test out the truth of this claim, clerical account books were studied. The claim, it was found, was broadly justified. A reclusive clerical bachelor could in the 1830s meet his basic requirements out of about £100 a year, whereas an incumbent with a household of seven needed twice as much to achieve the same end.[13] This shows how easy life was for those with more than £1,000 a year. Two cultures existed among the Georgian clergy: on the one hand, a clerical élite able to sustain what an earlier generation described as 'high port'; and, on the other, a large group of incumbents who had to teach, farm, or otherwise employ themselves, if they were to maintain their place in society.

Failure to eliminate clerical poverty places the activity of Queen Anne's Bounty in context. Despite all the Bounty's work of steady augmentation, the eleven parliamentary grants of £100,000 each, and the Board's special effort, as from 1810, to help the most penurious livings[14] - and despite, also, the economic advantages that the clergy gained from agricultural improvement, the Napoleonic boom in agriculture, and so on - there still remained a large group of beneficed clergy with net incomes of £100 a year or less. This, arguably, should not have been the case.

The economic position of the clergy improved during the Georgian era, and with it their social standing - there was, P.A. Bezodis has noted, an 'easing and transfusing of a professional dignity into a status of genuine social emancipation'.[15] It is important, however, not to exaggerate how far the advance was taken. By 1830, a fifth of the beneficed clergy could claim a link, forged either by marriage or by birth, with the peerage and gentry; on the other hand, the social origins of 45% of incumbents were either lowly or obscure.[16] The members of the Georgian clergy were not a homogeneous social class.

The clergy's rising social status was by no means a wholly untarnished good. On the contrary, it is indicative of certain developments whose benefits were more than a little dubious from the church's point of view. Reference is made, here, to a tightening in lay control. It is not only that more clergy were successful in winning the hands of squires' daughters; it is also that such marriages were increasingly welcomed by the gentry themselves. A clerical career was deemed to demand little by way of work and to offer much by way of remuneration. Such attitudes wrought considerable havoc. It is the powerful laity which, in parliament, defended its vested financial interests in the church by successfully resisting pressure for necessary reform; and it is the powerful laity, once again, which controlled half of all ecclesiastical patronage and held most impropriated tithes. The perpetual curate, forced to subsist upon a fixed pension paid by a lay impropriator drawing all of the tithe-income from the parish that the perpetual curate served, was one of the worst victims of the prevailing ecclesiastical system. The extent of this abuse - for abuse it was - is clarified by further analysis of the 1,222 beneficed clergy with net incomes of £100 a year or less. 141 were Welsh, and 1,081 were English. Among the English contingent were four chaplains and 432 rectors or vicars, leaving 645 unaccounted for. Each and every one of the 645 was a perpetual curate. This shows how heavy the incubus of private patronage was. On the credit side, the church's educational effort would have been less effective without lay support, the Bounty would have received less by way of private donations, and Anglicanism would have been less potent in the national life.

Although the Georgian church was highly laicised, Georgian culture and society were also highly clericalised. The clergy's contribution to learning, across a wide range of subjects, was formidable - Butler and Berkeley in philosophy; Sterne in literature; Malthus and Whately in political economy; Crabbe in poetry; Stephen Hales in chemistry; William Buckland in geology and mineralogy; Thomas Arnold in ancient history; Gilbert White in natural history; and Burn in law.[17] These were among the most original and gifted, but there was also plenty of talent lower down the intellectual ladder; after all, one in six of the parish clergy had been, at some time, a don.[18]

The clergy's contribution to society did not end with its cultural exploits, great though these were; it played, also, a crucial role in rural local government. Sidney and Beatrice Webb thought that clerical participation in the magistracy was 'for the most part abandoned' until the middle of the eighteenth century.[19] Their view established an orthodoxy, which has only recently been overturned. In 1761, 1,038 clergy were appointed to commissions; probably, over 400 of these took an active part in magisterial work.[20] The clerical magistracy, by no means negligible at the start of George III's reign, was significantly stronger by the close of George IV's. In 1831, there were 1,321 active clerical JPs, a figure equivalent to 25% of the magisterial Bench. Geographical distribution, though, was far from even. There were no active clerical magistrates in either Sussex or Derbyshire. On the other hand, clergy made up a majority in Carnarvonshire, and were over 40% of the total in Cambridgeshire, Lincolnshire, and Northamptonshire[21]. Of equal importance is the fact that, in many places, clergy did more than their fair share of the work. Research supports this contention for a good number of areas - for instance, Gloucestershire, Oxfordshire, Breconshire, and the East Riding and West Riding of Yorkshire[22] - and there is no reason to believe that the same does not hold for many other counties where there was significant clerical participation. The clergy were the work-horses of the magistracy.

Maintenance of the crucial role played by the clergy in society owed much to an obdurate conservatism, embodied in the career choices of alumni. Although Oxford and Cambridge both expanded rapidly as from the second decade of the nineteenth century, it still remained true that half of all matriculants subsequently sought Orders. In 1800, a total of 143 men entered Cambridge, of whom 73 (51%) later became ordained. Thirty years later the figure for entrants had climbed to 405, with subsequent ordinations numbering 203 (50%).[23]

Not surprisingly, the 'ladder' of clerical preferment was unable to take the weight of the increasing number of men striving to climb it. Finding a first incumbency was not easy during the eighteenth century; and the task did not become any easier in the years after 1800. The facts make sombre reading: 45% of those ordained around 1805 were never beneficed, and 45% of those ordained in the mid 1830s were never beneficed.[24] Since the number of ordinands was rising virtually every year, the ranks of the unbeneficed inevitably swelled.

In another way, overcrowding of the clerical profession assisted reform. In the late eighteenth century, a fortunate group among the clergy - numbering about a fifth of the whole - managed to obtain a first incumbency within five years of ordination.

The usual method of achieving this happy result was by obtaining access to convenient, and preferably powerful, patronage. Unfortunately for the few, the rise in clerical numbers which occurred after 1815 eroded their privileged position by increasing competition for employment. From the mid 1820s, it became harder to obtain a first incumbency quickly.[25] Thus it was that distortions in the career structure, which would not have occurred if the career choices of alumni had been more adventurous, acted as an unseen 'engine of reform'.

Once a living *was* found, the odds were that it was situated in the countryside. The Georgian clergy were born in the countryside, brought up in the countryside, and worked and died in the countryside. Few incumbents heeded the call to serve the urban masses. Most of the new towns, that sprang up in the wake of the industrial revolution, were still single parishes in 1840.[26] Even in the late-Georgian period, the typical incumbent was a man serving a rural parish with a population of around 500.[27]

Finding a living was one problem, finding a parsonage was another. The Georgian church did not exercise any corporate responsibility for the upkeep of its buildings. As far as parsonages were concerned, improvement largely depended upon the efforts of the occupying incumbent. This was unfortunate. The clergy did not own their parsonages; they had, at best, a life-interest in them, and where incentive to improvement was lacking, the will to improvement was lacking too. The Georgian clergy did not build many new parsonages, and, often enough, did not keep those they had in a good state of repair. Queen Anne's Bounty made a concerted effort to improve matters, as from 1803; but, despite the Bounty's campaign, the situation remained appalling. In 1830, among about 10,500 parishes, there were 2,900 or so without parsonages at all, with a further 1,700 having residence-houses in varying degrees of 'unfitness'. In any circumstances, this was neither defensible nor right. In the context of benefice values having risen by at least 400% since 1700, and of the clergy's improved social standing, it was not far short of scandalous.[28]

Having found (at least) a living, and having found somewhere to live, the Georgian incumbent could set about the task of caring for the people committed to his charge. Not that the issue was always perceived by him in quite this light. There was a strong emphasis upon formality; serving a parish was often reduced to a matter of taking Sunday services, baptisms, and funerals. Thus it was that the 'co-operative neighbouring incumbent syndrome' developed. It quite frequently happened that incumbents served neighbouring parishes as well as, or even instead of, their own. In Devon, in 1779, one parish in every six was being looked after by an incumbent who did not hold the cure.[29] This was bad, but there was worse: a reflection that applies with particular force to the situation prevailing in the isolated deaneries of Waxham and Repps, on the wind-swept coast of north-east Norfolk. There were 72 places with churches in the two deaneries, and, at a visitation held in 1806, it was discovered that duty in twenty-three instances (nearly a third of the total) was being done by neighbouring beneficed clergy.[30]

Yet, paradoxically, it was also from the deaneries of Waxham and Repps that information of an altogether different kind, running counter to the conclusions of the previous paragraph, was gathered. In Waxham and Repps, formalism was on the retreat in the early nineteenth century. Although twenty-three parishes were served by neighbouring incumbents in 1806, the comparable figure in 1834 was only eight. More significantly, there was a vigorous revival in every aspect of church life: more Sunday services, more communicants, more teaching of the catechism, and, above all, more schools.[31] This discovery, like much else, was unexpected; and is, potentially, of great importance. If the experience in Waxham and Repps was replicated elsewhere, historians will need to reassess the time-scale of parochial renewal in nineteenth-century rural England, locating that renewal in the years around Waterloo, not, as currently, in the early and mid-Victorian period. The difficulty, however, is that the two deaneries are not large enough - or representative enough - to be used as a valid basis for generalisation. A decisive judgement regarding this matter cannot be made until such time as the visitation returns of late-Georgian England have been studied in depth, a task which lies outside the scope of this book. As things now stand, we can only bring forward the strong *prima facie* argument that if there was a revival among the parishes in the isolated coastlands of Norfolk, there was, in all probability at least, an equally impressive spiritual resurgence in the numerous places that were neither isolated nor sparsely populated.

Unhappily, little ambivalence surrounds the subject of episcopal administration. Dioceses were mostly large and unwieldy; bishops were promoted late in life and did not retire; travelling around the eighteenth-century countryside was a cumbersome and difficult task; political duties kept the bishops in London for most of the year; episcopal translations were frequent; recalcitrant clergy used the parson's freehold to good effect; and the considerable costs associated with disciplinary proceedings had to be met by the bishops out of their own pockets. It was not until the late 1820s that the Bench started to be more effective, largely through the activities of a 'new breed' of bishop of an altogether different mettle from the old.

It is symptomatic of much episcopal thinking, or rather lack of thinking, that little or no consideration was given to a major problem of church reform - the difficulties faced by senescent, or ageing, incumbents. Retirement, on the part of the beneficed clergy, led to a double financial penalty: payment of dilapidations, and loss of benefice income without any compensating pension. Unsurprisingly, it was not popular among them. Incumbents lingered on in their parishes, some of them for a considerable time. As at the end of 1833, 10% of the beneficed clergy were over seventy, and 40% were in their fifties and sixties.[32] Something should have been done about the problem, but nothing was.

With regard to ecclesiastical patronage, there are two main conclusions. First, patrons with two advowsons or more promoted pluralism more frequently than patrons with only one; there is a direct correlation between the accumulation of rights of presentation on the part of patrons, and the accumulation of livings on the part of the beneficed clergy. Second, the exercise of rights of patronage was in no way affected by the status of the patron, whether he happened to be, a bishop, a corporate body, or a peer. This latter point is conclusively proved by the fact that, on a nationwide scale, it is impossible to distinguish between the practice of the Bench and the practice of wealthy laity. In a large sample of 597 livings, laity fostered pluralism on 380 occasions (63.7%), whereas bishops had done the same thing in 155 instances among 247 (62.8%). The market in advowsons, it would seem, was active in some districts but not in others. Where there was activity, lesser gentry accumulated livings, as did clergy. Use of open resignation bonds was made illegal in the 1780s, and further restrictions were imposed by statute in 1828; but obliging incumbents still continued to 'keep livings warm' in the years after 1830.

Incidence of pluralism and non-residence in the Georgian period has not previously been systematically studied by historians, an omission this work has striven to rectify. From a sample of 445 beneficed clergy, active in the first decade of the eighteenth century, it is clear that these practices ' of a very hurtful tendency' were not frequent when the period opens: 72 (16%) of the sample held more than one living and, among these, only one incumbent had compounded the offence by adding a third benefice to the second.[33] It is indisputably the case that there was a very substantial increase in pluralism during the first three quarters of the eighteenth century. By the mid 1770s we reckon that somewhere in the region of 36% of the beneficed clergy held more than one living, a statistic implying that pluralism was at least twice as prevalent as it had been in the age of Anne.[34] A major cause of rising plurality was the decline in manpower. During the first three decades of the eighteenth century ordinations averaged around 320 a year; whereas, in the 1740s, 1750s and 1760s, the figure slumped to 245, down by 23%.[35] The reduced flow of ordinands, over the span of working lives, reduced competition for benefice appointments and facilitated the accumulation of livings by incumbents.

Around 1780, pluralism and non-residence entered a phase of consolidation, lasting for half a century. There were forces working for change, but these made no headway. Three main 'engines of reform' can be identified. Firstly, there was the Evangelical movement, led from the 1780s by Wilberforce, who did much to enlist support. The difficulty with early Evangelicalism, however, is that it was largely an urban movement,[36] whereas the vast majority of clergy worked in the countryside. Secondly, there was the mastering of much clerical indigence. Queen Anne's Bounty sprang to life in the first decade of the nineteenth century. Its energies, moreover, were concentrated upon raising the values of livings that were hopelessly inadequate; places, in other words, where pluralism was a necessity rather than an option. The Bounty, acting quickly and decisively, searched out and put to rights many of the worst pockets of poverty: livings bringing in less than £50 a year numbered 1,061 in the period 1810-15, and 297 in 1829-31;[37] but pluralism and non-residence did not, despite the Board's efforts, decline. There was also successful resistance to pressure exerted by rising clerical numbers. At first this pressure was very gentle - ordinations in the period 1770-1810 ran at around 270 a year[38] - but it then became very fierce. I calculate that ordinations averaged 530 a year in the 1820s. Between 1834 and 1843, according to official statistics, the average was 535 a year.[39] The lives of the pluralistic clergy were becoming increasingly precarious.

It was not until the late 1820s that reform made progress. Steadily, and inexorably, the defences of the negligent clergy crumbled; between 1827 and 1838 the number of parishes with resident incumbents rose by an eighth, and between 1838 and 1848 the number rose by a further eighth.[40] There was now no turning back. Improvement continued throughout the high Victorian years, and by 1880 only one in ten parishes had an incumbent who was non-resident.[41] Fifty years earlier the figure had been eleven in twenty.[42]

The lot of the eighteenth-century curate was not enviable. As with much else, the views of historians on this matter require revision. Norman Sykes thought that, up until 1750, there was a 'marked tendency' for stipends to average £30 to £40 a year, and that the figure rose to £70 a year by 1800.[43] This estimate is wildly optimistic. It was found that, at the start of the period, the median figure for stipends was probably between £20 and £25 a year; while, by the century's end, the median had crept up to £35 or so.[44] In the context of the eighteenth-century boom in benefice values, the parsimony of most Georgian incumbents, and the ineffectiveness of most Georgian bishops, is hard to justify. Episcopal cajoling having failed, legislation was required. An act of 1813 established a sliding scale of payment for all curates serving livings where the incumbent was non-resident. The legal minimun, in normal circumstances, was set at £80 a year.[45] This piece of legislation succeeded in its stated intention of significantly raising curates' stipends - the median figure in 1838 was £83 a year,[46] more than twice as much as in 1800. Of equal importance is the fact that the Stipendiary Curates Act created a new momentum which was carried through. Advertisements of the salaries of assistant curates, given in the *Ecclesiastical Gazette*, have been studied. On the basis of these, the average payment is calculated at £82 2s 10d in 1843, rising to £97 10s 0d in 1863 and then to £129 5s 8d in 1873.[47] But although the 1813 Act achieved much long-term good, it was also seriously flawed. Its most obvious limitation is that it did not come into force until a vacancy occurred, and vacancies, among the livings held by the Georgian clergy, were not as frequent as might be thought. This is one measure of the Act's failure, but there is also another. The Act, it was discovered, was ineffectively administered. There were clauses in the legislation permitting episcopal discretion to be used, in cases where payment of full stipends would be likely to cause hardship to incumbents; but these were not applied consistently by the Bench. A rather alarming consequence flowed from episcopal incompetence. We have identified the existence of a strange, and hitherto unrecognised, phenomenon: a group of incumbents earning less than one or other of their own curates. Because of the maladministration of the Stipendiary Curates Act, the size of this 'proletariat' among the beneficed clergy swelled; by 1830, there were at least 322 incumbents (4% of the total) who found themselves in this invidious position.[48] Reforming the Georgian church was not as easy as it looked.

Conclusion

There is much in our research that emphasises the centrality and importance of the 1830s, particularly of the critical reforming period 1828-32. Recently, another historian has put forward a strong argument to the same effect, but from an angle different to our own. Writing of the Repeal of the Test and Corporation Acts (1828), Roman Catholic Emancipation (1829), and the Reform Act (1832), J.C.D. Clark makes an ideological point: 'what was lost', he claims, 'was not merely a constitutional arrangement, but the intellectual ascendancy of a world view, the cultural hegemony of the old élite'.[49] The accuracy of these insights can, clearly, only be verified within the history of ideas. This book is not the place for such a task. My research does, however, carry profound implications for an understanding of the structures of power through which the ideology of the 'old élite' was expressed; and it also carries implications for the superseding of the 'world view' of that elite by an alternative set of values and beliefs. What has been shown - I hope conclusively - is that the structures of power through which a dominant ideology could be expressed remained intact in 1830. The role of the clergy within the magistracy had not been challenged; the tradition of an eclectic clerical culture was still strong; and the body of beneficed clergy, or at any rate the wealthier sections of it, were able to view with peculiar satisfaction the wholeheartedness with which they were now accepted as social equals by the great and powerful throughout the land.

If the relevant structures of power were demonstrably still in place in 1830, these same structures were also demonstrably beginning to be shifted out of place ten years later. In Sussex, and also in Derbyshire, the clergy had traditionally been excluded from the magistracy, but the effect of this within a nationwide context was immaterial. Not so the change in mood that took place in the years after 1830. Firstly, there was a growing unease among 'those who counted' about the suitability of placing clergy in commissions; and this unease is reflected in the fact that, for the first time, there is a spate of parliamentary returns monitoring both the number of clergy already serving and the number of clergy newly appointed to serve.[50] Secondly, a reaction against the magisterial role became fashionable among the clergy. The problem resolved itself, ultimately, into a matter of visibility: the clergyman who was also a magistrate declared himself to be a 'squarson', behaved like a squarson, and indeed was a squarson. On the other hand, the number of clergy who were influenced either by Hackney, Clapham, or Oxford was steadily increasing; and those who took their spiritual authority seriously - who, in Newman's phrase, 'magnified their office' - could not but question the efficacy of continuing to act both as judge and as pastor. 'By the beginning of the 1840s', another historian has written, 'the opposition to the union of the ministerial and magisterial character ... was increasingly heard among the clergy';[51] and there is no reason to doubt the truth in this claim. The combination of a lack of enthusiasm on the part of the clergy and doubt on the part of government proved very powerful. Clerical representation on the Bench started to decline. In the six-year period 1836-42 there were 401 clergy appointed to act, a figure dwarfed by the total of 2,689 laymen. What had been started was carried through. Although 401 clergy were appointed to act between 1836 and 1842, the number placed in commissions over the much longer twenty-year period 1843-63 was no more than 839.[52] Change was, moreover, more than a matter of implementing new policies towards recruitment; the period when the number of clerical admissions to the magistracy started to tail off coincided with a marked reduction in the workload of those clergy who were already JPs. Some figures to do with this matter are available for Oxfordshire. Up until 1830, clergy dealt with over 70% of prosecutions; but the proportion then dropped both suddenly and permanently. In 1840, clerical magistrates in Oxfordshire dealt with 19% of prosecutions, and in 1850 they dealt with only 26%.[53] The available evidence points in the same direction: there was initiation of radical change in the fourth decade of the nineteenth century, and no going back thereafter.

Magisterial power meshed with social and economic power: it was the rising values of tithes, aided and abetted by the commutation movement, that had transformed a section of the beneficed clergy into a landowning class, with the added consequence that entry into the magistracy had been considerably eased. The clergy's incomes increased sharply during the Napoleonic boom in agriculture, but they did not rise anything like as strongly during the mid-Victorian boom. In the way, now, was the Tithes Commutation Act of 1836. This, in essence, abolished those aspects of tithe that had rendered it a tax on increases in agricultural production. Growth in tithe-income could now only come about through rises in cereal prices, and not, as before, through higher crop yields, expansion of the area under cultivation, enclosure, and the like. The long-term significance of the 1836 Act was not immediately grasped. The prosperity characteristic of mid-Victorian agriculture kept the tithe rent-charge at, or around, the level established at the time of commutation; it was not until the 1870s and 1880s that disaster struck. The catastrophe may have been long in coming, but its arrival was decisive. English agriculture, for centuries pre-eminent, was now faced with formidable North American competition. The Canadian prairies were opened up; production on those same prairies was greatly increased by the introduction of the newly invented combine-harvester; and the grain thus gathered could then be brought to London by steam, not by sail. This was a happy turn of circumstances for Canadian farmers, if not for the English. Cereal prices went into free fall, and it was not long before the tithe rent-charge followed suit. In 1881, the rent-charge stood at slightly over £107, but by 1901 the figure was down to £66 10s 9d, a collapse approaching 40%.[54]

If the beneficed clergy of the 1830s had only had the Tithes Commutation Act to contend with, all might have been well. Unfortunately, they faced a further foe. In 1838, the first effective Pluralities Act became law. This did not initiate change - the crisis of the early 1830s had already seen to that - but it did ensure that momentum was maintained. A further, more tightly drawn, Pluralities Act, passed in 1850, worked a similar effect. The holes made in the clergy's pockets were large. In 1830, pluralism had been virile, with nearly three livings for every two clergy. Ten years later it was visibly weakening; by 1860 it was decrepit; and by 1880 it was virtually dead.

Conclusion

Close on the heels of this little-lamented event came agrarian depression, with the consequent fall in the tithe rent-charge. This means that, after 1830, the clergy's economic standing suffered a severe decline. Strangulation of pluralism cut the ecclesiastical incomes of the beneficed clergy by about a third between 1830 and 1880. Then, during the last two decades of the century, the disappearance of a prosperous English agriculture produced a further cut that proved, unhappily, more serious.

There was, arguably, also an economic dimension to the weakening of the church's stranglehold upon Oxford and Cambridge. It was widely held among contemporaries that a major reason for the declining influence within the ancient universities was that the fleecy parts of the church had been comprehensively shorn, with the result that a clerical career became a less attractive prospect to many of the sons of the peerage and gentry.[55] Whatever the merits of this particular line of argument, the fact of change is clear enough. Two things occurred: there was a reduction in the number of matriculants subsequently seeking Orders, and there was an increasing tendency for the best intellectual talent to choose not to be ordained. We will deal first with the changing educational background of the body of clergy. It would not be surprising if there was, after 1840, a relative decline in the number of Oxbridge students entering the church, with the proportion choosing alternative careers rising, but the total opting for Orders increasing as well. This, however, was not what happened: the decline was not relative, it was absolute. In the decade 1834-43, there were 4,383 Oxbridge men who took Orders; but between 1854 and 1863 the figure was 3,978, a reduction of 405 (9.2%).[56] By way of counterbalance, the number of literates rapidly increased - 565 in 1834-43, and 1,403 in 1854-63.[57]

It was also after 1840 that a clerical career began to attract fewer of the best minds. Among those who obtained first class degrees in the years 1841-3, 65% later became ordained; by 1851-3 the proportion was down to 58%; by 1861-3 it had fallen to 50%; and in 1871-3 it was 30%.[58] There was, as a consequence, a weakening of the marvellously varied and long-standing tradition of an eclectic clerical culture. Among the factors that contributed to the tradition's partial demise was the growth of alternative professions and the increasing importance of secularising trends within society; and probably, too, the growth of doctrinal doubts in many sensitive minds, a result of the mid-Victorian crisis of faith.

On the basis of all this evidence, the conclusion seems inescapable that the position of the clergy within society began to alter radically in the 1830s. There were to be fewer parsons in the mould of the vicar of Glascwm, ruling parishes like the patriarchs of old. Young graduates, especially bright young graduates, no longer regarded ordination as a virtually certain career option; and the beneficed clergy found entry into the landowning class was made more difficult by the failure of their ecclesiastical incomes to continue increasing year by year. The clergy had earlier been invited to dine at the rich man's table; they had been asked to occupy the place of honour, at the rich man's side; now they were being requested to move further down.

It is now time to address the fundamental questions that were posed, during discussion of the historical context of ecclesiastical change, towards the close of the first Chapter.[59] England, in the late-Georgian period, experienced what no human community had experienced before - the onrush of the process that has become known as industrialisation. The ramifications were as varied as they were profound. The printing industry was transformed, leading to the growth of a Radical press in the years after Waterloo; the rising unemployment and social dislocation that are common characteristics of industrial revolutions in their earliest phase heightened social tensions: 'Captain Ludd' stalked the towns, while 'Captain Swing' roamed the countryside; and massive problems were posed by the likes of Bradford and Leeds - sanitation, street lighting, policing, and so on. All of this affected the church. Bishops and clergy came under attack in the Radical press; those incumbents who were also JPs were involved in problems of maintaining social order; and the basis of the church's pastoral ministry was challenged and threatened by the sudden emergence of the new industrial towns. The church faced further difficulties. The rise of Dissent began to undermine the comfortable eighteenth-century assumption that Anglicanism was the religion of the nation; and, from within, Evangelicalism was emerging as a major movement of spiritual renewal, with increasing numbers of clergy voicing their discontent in a spate of pamphlets on church reform. The question at issue is the church's response to the ferment of changing times. Did it gradually change, Probeus-like, with society, or did it stoutly resist renovation and reform, until events forced its hand? The answers to these questions, it was suggested, carry implications for the debate among historians over the methods, and means, of historical change in Georgian England. On the one side, there is the 'cataclysmic' school that believes English institutions successfully resisted pressure for reform until the 1830s; while, on the other, there are the gradualists, who see reform as a continuing process, starting in the 1780s.

As far as the church is concerned, a strong case can be made out for gradualism. The foundations of the argument were first laid, in a systematic and convincing fashion, by Geoffrey Best in *Temporal Pillars*, published in 1964. He rightly places emphasis upon the period of the Bounty's renewed activity, which can be dated from the 1780s onwards. There are several aspects to this. The most important is the setting up of the Parliamentary Grants Fund, in order to utilise the grants of 1809-20, and the subsequent formation of a new path for policy. From studies of the Bounty's files, it is clear that a Herculean effort was made to raise the values of many of the poorest benefices in the years after 1809.[60] Although the reservoir of clerical poverty was not drained by the Bounty, it is undeniably the case that, without the Board's drive and leadership, things would have been much worse.

A second pillar upon which to rest the gradualist case is the Stipendiary Curates Act. This piece of legislation can be criticised on the ground that it did not go far enough - the payment of assistant curates was outside its scope, and the bishops were only empowered to fix the salaries of stipendiaries appointed to livings where the incumbent was instituted after the passing of the Act; and it can also be criticised on the ground that it went too far. The Act was not always well administered, with the result that a good number of poor (and probably ageing) incumbents found themselves at the wrong end of some decidedly rough justice. Nevertheless, the Act succeeded in its stated intention of significantly raising the pay of stipendiaries. It did this, moreover, by means of a scheme which amounted to a redistribution of clerical wealth, with money being taken out of the pockets of the beneficed clergy and being put into those of the beneficed clergy's employees, the curates. This 'invasion of ecclesiastical property', as some irate contemporaries described it, occurred a little before the battle of Waterloo and well before the reforming era of the 1830s.

Further grist is added to the gradualist mill by research on the Norfolk deaneries of Waxham and Repps. The discovery of a vigorous parochial revival in this isolated area was certainly among the findings that could least easily be predicted. What was going on in Waxham and Repps is important in several respects. Parochial renewal was achieved despite the fact that most places in the two deaneries lacked what was generally regarded as a precondition of such renewal - the constant presence of a resident incumbent. There were 72 places with churches in Waxham and Repps. In 1794 residents numbered 8; by 1820 the figure had reached 9; and there was then a brisk advance, with 17 being recorded in 1834. Although this was better, there remained room for further improvement; after all, 55 places in the two deaneries (76% of the total) were still being looked after either by neighbouring incumbents or by stipendiary curates. What is remarkable is that, despite such potent evidence of pastoral neglect, there should have been a surge in the number of services, a strong rise in the number of communicants, and a flowering of Anglican schools. The salutary and important lesson to be drawn from this is that whatever its faults - and these were many - the Georgian church had within it a capacity for new life, and for new growth, that must not be underestimated. The case for gradualism is strong.

The gradualist case is not, though, overwhelming, and fails to take account of major problems that were never tackled. The system of ecclesiastical patronage heads the list in this regard. Moves to restrict the use of resignation bonds - Lowth's successful attack upon open bonds in the 1780s, and the further strengthening of legislation in 1828 - did not affect matters much. What was needed was a determined assault upon the citadel of private patronage, but this never came. Many plans for reform made little or no headway. The best example is the Bounty's effort, starting in 1803, to increase the number of parsonages. There were also serious problems - the difficulties faced by ageing clergy, for instance - which were not perceived as problems at all. Only four livings in ten enjoyed the presence of a resident incumbent;there were nearly 2,900 parishes without parsonages; and at a further 1,700 places the parsonage was 'unfit'. Half the beneficed clergy were aged over fifty; 45% of those who were ordained never found a living; the practice of incumbents acting as curates was prevalent; and lay patronage was undisturbed. The church of 1830 was not, in many major respects, a particularly fine example of a reformed institution.

The Church in an Age of Negligence

The failures of gradualism offer opportunity for the cataclysmists; and the latter have the consolation of knowing that they can rest a further part of their case upon solid and unshifting ground. Reference has been made to the improvement in clerical residence that began in the late 1820s and continued throughout the 1830s and beyond. This chronology could scarcely be better from the cataclysmists' point of view: nothing achieved before the 'Age of Reform'; everything achieved during the 'Age of Reform'. The case against gradualism is strengthened by the cogency in the argument that securing the residence of the beneficed clergy was the most crucial issue of ecclesiastical reform; for it was residence that constituted the litmus test of the clergy's rectitude. Parliament attached great importance to the subject. Hence the 1803 Residence Act, and hence, too, the shape and formulation of the various curates' bills that were placed on the table during the first decade of the nineteenth century, culminating in the Stipendiary Curates Act. These bills, it will be remembered, differed widely from each other, but had a common theme: new salary scales were to be paid by non-resident incumbents, but not by resident incumbents. The message is clear: everything must be done to discourage non-residence, if need be by imposing a 'tax' in the form of higher payments to those curates who discharged the clerical duties which non-residents could not, or would not, discharge themselves. Most of the bishops, at any rate in their public utterances, shared parliament's concern. This is understandable enough. After all, the non-residence of the clergy was the church's Achilles' heel, an easy target for the Radical Press and for politicians in the mould of Henry Brougham and Joseph Hume. Exhortations to reside abound in those most prolix of publications, the numerous *Charges* published by the Georgian Bench. The characteristic episcopal attitude, whether in 1780 or in 1820, was two-fold: things are not really too bad and, in any case, things are improving. To arrive at the truth, it is only necessary to stand these statements on their heads: things, as a matter of fact, *were* bad - six livings in ten were without resident incumbents - and things, again as a matter of fact, were *not* improving. Experience at Waxham and Repps shows that parochial renewal could be achieved despite non-residence of beneficed clergy; but this recognition must not be taken to imply either that such non-residence was a light and inconsequential matter, or that a reduction in it would not have significantly strengthened the church's pastoral ministry. The beneficed clergy could have, and should have, done better in this regard in the years prior to 1830.

There is a further fact that deserves emphasis. The improvement in residence achieved during the 1830s was particularly marked in those dioceses where determined bishops were at the helm. This is especially true of Exeter under Henry Phillpotts, and of London under C.J. Blomfield. Both were men who were well able to 'read the signs of the times'; Phillpotts had 'ratted' over Roman Catholic emancipation, while Blomfield had been diplomatically absent from the House of Lords during the crucial debate on the Reform Bill in November, 1831. Both men were well aware of the strength of contemporary 'pressure from without', and both had responded to that pressure. They knew that the church needed to put its house in order, and they set about doing just that. Equally, both the rapidity and the extent of their success throws into sharp relief the earlier failure of the Bench to get much done. Figures for non-residence improved after 1830 because 'pressure from without' became stronger, and because a section of the leadership of the church, sensitive to the changed climate of public opinion, acted with new urgency and drive.

Although there is strength in the case of the cataclysmists, it does not follow that gradualism is discredited. Its monuments, massive and impressive, continue to stand. Gradualism, it would be truer to say, is not so much discredited as circumscribed; its limitations are now marked out. What is required is a sense of balance, a recognition of the achievements of the church in the era prior to the 'Age of Reform', and a recognition, also, of the contribution to ecclesiastical change made by the ferment of the 1830s. It is this sense of balance which has previously been lacking. The accepted view of the Georgian church has been, too often, crude and ill-informed. Scarcity of accurate information has not stood in the way of confident assertion. This situation is now rectified. It has been my task in this book to develop, for the first time, a comprehensive portrait of the church of the eighteenth and early nineteenth centuries, 'warts and all'. It is no longer appropriate for historians to argue about the wealth of the clergy in the Georgian period; about the incidence of pluralism and non-residence; about the practice of ecclesiastical patronage; and about the beneficed clergy's social composition. These matters are, one hopes, now resolved. Collecting and collating the data has not always been easy, but it has been worthwhile. Through the swirling and often dense mists of historical misconception, it is my hope - as it is also my belief - that a new vision of the Georgian ecclesiastical polity - its strengths and weaknesses, its ambiguities and clarities - has at last begun to appear. One holds fast to that hope and to that belief, sure in the knowledge that, as the historical endeavour advances, the vision will become easier to grasp and the misconceptions harder to make.

Conclusion Notes

1. See above, pp. 81-2.
2. See above, p.83.
3. See below, Table VIII.
4. See above, p.86.
5. See above, pp. 51-4.
6. See above, pp. 71-4.
7. See above, p.74.
8. See above, p.71.
9. See above, pp. 81-5.
10. See above, pp. 87-9.
11. See above, pp. 91-3.
12. See below, Table V.
13. See above, pp. 93-9.
14. See above, pp. 64*ff.*, 146-7, 195.

15. See above, p.86, 109.
16. See below, Table X.
17. See above, p.119, 133.
18. See above, p.133.
19. See above, p.116.
20. See above, pp. 116-18.
21. See below, Table XIV.
22. See above, pp. 120-1.
23. See above, p.135.
24. See below, Table XIII.
25. See below, Table XIII.
26. See above, pp. 142-3.
27. See above, p.144.
28. See above, p.151.
29. See above, pp. 152-3.
30. See above, p.153.
31. See above, pp. 153-7.
32. See above, pp. 161-3, 259.
33. See above, p.192.
34. See above, pp. 193-4.
35. See above, pp. 135-7, 221.
36. See above, pp. 20-2, 200.
37. See above, pp. 67-9.
38. See above, p.135, 202.
39. See above, pp. 135-7, 202.
40. See below, Table XIX.
41. See below, Table XIX.
42. *ibid*.
43. See above, pp. 224-5.
44. See above, p.225.
45. See above, pp. 228-9.
46. See above, pp. 239-40.
47. J.J. Halcombe, *The Church and her Curates*, p.96.
48. See above, p.234.
49. Clark, *English Society*, p. 90.
50. See below, Table XIV.
51. Russell, *The Clerical Profession*, p. 160.
52. See below, Table XIV.
53. McClatchey, *Oxfordshire Clergy*, Table, p. 191.
54. See above, pp. 100-2.
55. Heeney, *A Different Kind of Gentleman*, p. 28.
56. Haig, *The Victorian Clergy*, Table 2.2, p.32. Haig shows that, after 1860, the number of Oxbridge ordinands stabilised.
57. *ibid*. In this source, 'literate' includes some men who had been to London university.
58. *ibid*., p.49.
59. See above, pp. 15*ff*.
60. See above, pp. 15, 65-8.

Statistical Appendix

A NOTE ON METHOD

I have calculated the wealth of the English beneficed clergy in this manner. A separate sum has been worked out for each incumbent, by adding up the values of each of his livings together with the annual worth of a cathedral post, if any. Incomes are net, not gross - curates' stipends, taxes, and benefice expenses having been deducted. Some preferments held by English clergy were excluded. Fourteen cathedral posts and nine livings held by bishops fall into this category, as do sixty-six prebends and canonries in the possession of non-parochial clergy, and also seventy livings omitted either because they were vacant or because another living held by the incumbent was not returned. A similar procedure was adopted for Welsh clergy, except that no preferments or livings held by them needed to be excluded. According to the Report of the Ecclesiastical Revenues Commission (1835), returns were received from 10,540 livings. Seventy-nine, for reasons stated above, have been omitted, leaving a total of 10,461.

The figures, unfortunately, are not precise. Study of the Report reveals two main types of error in it. Marginal cross-references, indicating that benefices were held in plurality, are sometimes given for one entry but not for the other, or others, which should be linked with it. On other occasions, appropriate cross-references are not given at all. Both types of error disguise the prevalence of pluralism. To overcome the first is relatively easy since it only involves constant checking of all cross-references, but the second is much more obdurate and can only be effectively combated by comparing the Report with other reference books, notably *Clerical Guide* for 1829 and 1836, J.A. Venn's *Alumni Cantabrienses,* and Joseph Foster's *Alumni Oxonienses.* Of these, Venn's *Alumni* is undoubtedly the most reliable, and Foster's *Alumni* undoubtedly the least. The task of using these various reference books is time-consuming and has only been carried out for poor clergy earning less than £100 a year, for very rich with incomes of over £2,000 a year, and for all those in the five counties studied in depth. These together number 2,187; reference sources other than the Report have been followed in seventy-five occasions. This is a large sample, so it can be assumed with some confidence that the margin of error among the remaining 5,395 clergy was broadly similar. In all probability, therefore, there are about a further 185 instances where the Report treats pluralists as though they were not. The statistics have been revised accordingly, reducing the number of English clergy by 85, and of Welsh by 7. It was assumed, in the process of revision, that these errors were weighted as between the various categories, under £200 a year, under £300 a year, and so on.

In working out statistics for pluralism (see above, pp. 192-4), the Report was studied again, using similar methods. These figures are also adjusted. The number of English non-pluralists has been reduced by 170, increasing the total holding two livings by 85, and fourteen Welsh non-pluralists have been replaced by seven pluralists.

TABLE 1

The monetary value of tithes, both lay and clerical, in England and Wales, 1806-1812

(Source: Parliamentary Returns on Property Tax)

ENGLAND	1806 £	1808 £	1810 £	1812 £	1806-12 % change
1. Rutland	2,416	3,805	3,963	4,862	101.2
2. Middlesex	11,093	17,574	19,270	20,511	84.9
3. Warwickshire	15,977	21,132	26,123	26,485	65.8
4. Herefordshire	33,439	39,616	49,090	53,801	60.9
5. Wiltshire	62,232	70,321	88,497	96,686	55.4
6. Lancashire	36,043	38,649	44,328	55,408	53.7
7. Cambridgeshire	26,591	35,539	36,780	38,755	46.7
8. Cornwall	46,066	47,780	57,463	67,481	46.5
9. Kent	104,174	116,739	132,640	151,196	45.1
10. Lincolnshire	42,458	43,472	49,507	60,493	42.5
11. Durham	20,241	22,748	24,813	28,327	39.9
12. Cheshire	39,045	40,324	43,427	54,267	39.0
13. Derbyshire	14,278	15,149	19,009	19,290	35.1
14. Oxfordshire	28,174	30,343	35,530	37,642	33.6
15. Gloucestershire	42,449	46,689	48,692	56,622	33.4
16. Surrey	39,451	43,782	47,320	52,638	33.4
17. Somersetshire	71,829	76,626	83,823	95,099	32.4
18. Hampshire	95,697	100,337	114,625	126,205	31.9
19. Sussex	82,406	89,590	100,499	108,457	31.6
20. Shropshire	67,067	63,048	79,515	85,900	28.1
21. Yorkshire	93,313	96,953	114,108	119,268	27.8
22. Dorsetshire	45,236	46,883	51,931	57,157	26.4
23. Leicestershire	11,908	13,034	13,820	14,947	25.5
24. Essex	135,346	145,262	155,334	169,565	25.3
25. Berkshire	52,797	53,372	56,846	66,038	25.1
26. Devonshire	103,227	107,299	112,933	128,525	24.5
27. Norfolk	122,328	126,593	133,393	150,790	23.3
28. Staffordshire	31,952	35,756	38,780	38,761	21.3
29. Hertfordshire	41,401	44,319	45,292	47,780	15.4
30. Suffolk	106,318	110,661	117,401	122,129	14.9
31. Huntingdonshire	9,226	8,092	10,166	10,327	11.9
32. Buckinghamshire	27,321	26,926	28,949	30,119	10.2
33. Northumberland	59,913	64,189	65,371	65,342	9.1
34. Northamptonshire	16,282	16,404	17,490	17,626	8.3
35. Westmorland	5,414	5,203	6,602	5,845	8.0
36. Cumberland	13,261	15,300	14,332	14,057	6.0
37. Nottinghamshire	14,877	15,835	16,434	15,371	3.3
38. Bedfordshire	14,236	14,455	14,090	14,307	0.5
39. Worcestershire	49,681	50,094	46,901	40,552	-18.4
40. London	22,557	14,629	15,443	16,510	-26.8
TOTAL	1,857,720	1,974,522	2,180,530	2,385,141	
Percentage increase	-	6.3	10.4	9.4	

WALES	1806	1808	1810	1812	1806-12 % change
1. Cardiganshire	11,297	13,745	15,793	22,509	99.2
2. Flintshire	9,813	9,507	12,236	13,839	41.0
3. Monmouthshire	11,678	12,451	13,468	15,933	36.4
4. Pembrokeshire	10,861	13,148	12,709	14,576	34.2
5. Carnarvonshire	11,587	14,195	13,356	14,803	27.8
6. Merionethshire	5,939	6,088	6,380	7,277	22.5
7. Radnorshire	8,310	8,041	9,373	9,985	20.2
8. Carmarthenshire	11,864	13,315	13,161	14,033	18.3
9. Denbighshire	24,689	22,944	26,919	29,065	17.7
10. Glamorganshire	13,373	14,263	14,472	14,765	10.4
11. Montgomeryshire	13,398	13,628	13,966	14,457	7.9
12. Anglesey	12,691	14,461	12,994	13,392	5.5
13. Breconshire	8,844	9,635	7,896	8,898	0.6
TOTAL	154,344	165,421	172,723	193,532	
Percentage rise over previous year	-	7.2	4.4	12.0	
JOINT TOTAL	2,012,064	2,139,943	2,353,253	2,578,673	
Joint percentage rise over previous year	-	6.4	10.0	9.6	

Rise in England, 1806-1812 : 28.4%
Rise in Wales, 1806-1812 : 25.4%
Joint rise, 1806-1812 : 28.2%

(All figures in this Table are given to the nearest £)

There is a difficulty about the estimates for 1812. The figure given in the summary of the return is £2,583,673, but the sums for individual counties amount to £5,000 less. The explanation is probably the misprint of a '3' for an '8' somewhere in the Table. This is impossible to locate, so for reasons of general coherence and tidiness, we have taken the lower sum, computed from the figures for each county, and included that in the summary.

TABLE II

The Values of poor Rectories and Vicarages in selected Counties of England and Wales, in 1708 compared with 1830

(Sources: Ecton, *Liber Valorum; P.P.*, 1835, XXII, 15-1060).

	Number of Parishes in Sample	Average Value 1708	Average Value 1830	Percentage Rise 1708-1830
1. Carnarvon, Denbigh, Flint, Merioneth, Montgomery	92	£34	£237	597
2. Northumberland	15	£31	£198	539
3. Hampshire	45	£31	£190	513
4. Derbyshire	51	£31	£181	484
5. Devonshire	109	£36	£158	339
TOTAL	312	£34	£191	462

The statistics from the 1835 Report are in each case net values, but no deductions have been made for payments to curates. Livings which were amalgamated with others whose value is not given in Ecton, and also benefices which failed to make any return to the Ecclesiastical Revenues Commission, have been excluded.

Statistical Appendix and Tables

TABLE III

The Values of poor Perpetual Curacies in selected Counties of England and Wales, in 1708 as compared with 1830.

(Sources: Ecton, *Liber Valorum; P.P.*, 1835, XXII, 15-1060).

	Number of Parishes in Sample	Average value in 1708	Average value in 1830	Percentage rise 1708-1830
1. Carnarvon, Denbigh, Flint, Merioneth, Montgomery	31	£11	£ 93	745%
2. Northumberland	11	£12	£138	1050%
3. Hampshire	2	£31	£ 88	184%
4. Derbyshire	46	£12	£106	783%
5. Devonshire	29	£21	£122	481%
TOTAL	119	£14	£110	686%

The analytical methods applicable to Table III apply also to Table IV.

TABLE IV

The number of livings worth less than £80 a year in each diocese in England and Wales, in 1708 as compared with 1830

(Sources: 'Values of Livings under £80' in records of Queen Anne's Bounty; *P.P.*, 1835, XXII, 1053.

Diocese	Under £10 a year		£10-£20 a year		£20-£30 a year		£30-£40 a year		£40-£50 a year		£50-£60 a year		£60-£70 a year		Under £80 a year		Decline No.'s	Decline %
	1708	1830	1708	1830	1708	1830	1708	1830	1708	1830	1708	1830	1708	1830	1708	1830	1708-1830	1708-1830
St Asaph	4	0	3	0	10	0	21	0	17	1	8	2	17	1	11	1	86 (91 to 5)	94.5
Bangor	10	0	18	0	14	0	22	0	9	2	7	1	10	3	1	4	81 (91 to 10)	89.0
Bath and Wells	0	0	29	2	46	2	70	4	47	4	44	8	21	7	23	11	242 (280 to 38)	86.4
Bristol	2	0	2	1	8	1	8	1	7	2	5	8	0	7	0	4	8 (32 to 24)	25.0
Canterbury	4	0	9	0	32	0	24	2	31	4	18	8	18	5	3	6	114 (139 to 25)	82.0
Carlisle	19	0	14	0	13	0	11	0	7	4	4	10	0	6	0	8	40 (68 to 28)	58.8
Chester	99	0	69	0	53	0	26	2	15	17	13	25	9	27	4	28	189 (288 to 99)	65.6
Chichester	11	0	15	0	23	1	23	1	30	0	34	9	43	11	13	1	169 (192 to 23)	88.0
St David's	62	1	75	0	70	3	48	0	26	7	32	21	7	36	4	28	228 (324 to 96)	70.4
Durham	22	0	39	0	19	1	21	1	7	1	9	6	11	11	1	6	103 (129 to 26)	79.8
Ely	1	0	4	0	16	1	12	0	17	1	6	2	1	6	1	5	43 (58 to 15)	74.1
Exeter	27	0	26	1	32	1	48	1	71	4	75	9	51	9	15	9	311 (345 to 34)	90.1
Gloucester	13	1	19	1	19	0	2	3	0	6	0	10	0	9	0	6	17 (53 to 36)	32.1
Hereford	9	1	16	2	37	0	18	2	11	7	11	15	8	4	4	9	74 (114 to 40)	64.9
Lichfield	40	1	44	0	34	4	24	4	30	13	10	21	5	28	3	18	101 (190 to 89)	53.2
Lincoln	26	0	53	1	100	4	84	8	75	27	42	26	27	43	14	27	285 (421 to 136)	67.7
Llandaff	7	1	26	0	25	0	24	1	12	6	8	8	9	13	2	7	77 (113 to 36)	68.1
London	8	1	19	0	37	2	48	2	52	2	44	6	41	7	23	5	247 (272 to 25)	90.8
Norwich	21	3	73	5	117	2	201	8	166	17	116	24	89	30	62	24	732 (845 to 113)	86.6
Oxford	4	0	6	2	15	1	19	1	14	2	9	7	2	8	2	1	49 (71 to 22)	69.0
Peterborough	2	1	11	0	14	0	22	0	11	1	18	2	3	1	1	5	72 (82 to 10)	87.8

Rochester	0	0	0	0	6	0	3	0	4	0	7	0	1	1	0	0	20	95.2
																	(21 to 1)	
Salisbury	2	0	11	1	13	1	28	4	21	2	20	9	15	1	5	4	93	80.9
																	(115 to 22)	
Winchester	2	0	7	2	7	3	11	6	7	6	9	8	3	6	0	11	4	8.7
																	(46 to 42)	
Worcester	19	0	21	0	17	1	21	0	29	4	21	5	20	1	9	5	141	89.8
																	(157 to 16)	
York	57	1	136	1	129	4	82	12	67	32	50	55	14	36	10	21	383	70.3
																	(545 to 162)	
TOTAL	471	11	745	19	906	32	921	63	783	172	620	305	425	317	211	254		
																	3909	76.9
																	(5082 to 1173)	

Figures for Sodor and Man have been amalgamated with those for York

TABLE V

The Structure of the Annual Ecclesiastical Income of the Beneficed Clergy,
both English and Welsh, in the year 1830

(Source: *P.P.*, 1835, XXII, 15-1060)

£100		Percentage	£700		Percentage
and			and		
Under	1,222	16.3	Under	315	4.2
£200			£800		
and			and		
Under	1,708	22.8	Under	211	2.8
£300			£900		
and			and		
Under	1,261	16.8	Under	166	2.2
£400			£1,000		
and			and		
Under	933	12.5	Under	92	1.2
£500			£1,000		
and			to		
Under	707	9.5	£2,000	310	4.2
£600			Over		
and			£2,000	76	1.0
Under	489	6.5			

TOTAL: 7,490
First Quartile: £138 a year
Median: £265 a year
Third Quartile: £470 a year

TABLE VI

The Structure of the Annual Ecclesiastical Income of the English Beneficed Clergy in the Year 1830

(Source: *P.P.*, 1835, XXII, 15-1060)

		Percentage			Percentage
£100 and Under	1,081	15.6	£700 and Under	305	4.4
£200 and Under	1,523	21.9	£800 and Under	206	3.0
£300 and Under	1,156	16.7	£900 and Under	160	2.3
£400 and Under	877	12.6	£1,000 and Under	92	1.3
£500 and Under	683	9.8	£1,000 to £2,000	310	4.5
£600 and Under	471	6.8	Over £2,000	76	1.1

TOTAL: 6,940
First Quartile: £143 a year
Median: £275 a year
Third Quartile: £483 a year

277

TABLE VII

The Structure of the Annual Ecclesiastical Income of the Welsh Beneficed Clergy in the Year 1830

(Source: *P.P.*, 1835, XXII, 15-1060)

£100 and Under	141	Percentage 25.6	£600 and Under	18	Percentage 3.3
£200 and Under	185	33.6	£700 and Under	10	1.8
£300 and Under	105	19.1	£800 and Under	5	0.9
£400 and Under	56	10.2	Over £800	6	1.1
£500 and Under	24	4.4			

TOTAL: 550
First Quartile: £98 a year
Median: £172 a year
Third Quartile: £283 a year

TABLE VIII

The Annual Incomes of the Beneficed Clergy in selected Counties in the year 1830

(Source: *P.P.*, 1835, XXII, 15-1060).

	Cumberland and Westmorland	Per centage	Kent	Per centage	Norfolk	Per centage	Sussex	Per centage
£100 and under	78	46.7	23	8.1	45	11.0	23	10.8
£200 and under	50	29.9	42	14.7	53	13.0	47	22.0
£300 and under	14	8.4	48	16.8	60	14.7	28	13.1
£400 and under	12	7.2	46	16.1	51	12.5	27	12.6
£500 and under	4	2.4	35	12.3	43	10.5	27	12.6
£600 and under	4	2.4	22	7.7	37	9.1	14	6.5
£700 and under	1	0.6	21	7.4	26	6.4	10	4.7
£800 and under	1	0.6	9	3.2	26	6.4	11	5.1
£900 and under	0	0.0	10	3.5	24	5.9	6	2.8
£1000 and under	0	0.0	3	1.0	13	3.2	2	0.9
£1,000-£2,000	3	1.8	19	6.7	22	5.4	18	8.4
Over £2,000	0	0.0	7	2.5	8	1.9	1	0.5
TOTALS	167	100.0	285	100.0	408	100.0	214	100.0

	Cumberland and Westmorland	Kent	Norfolk	Sussex
First Quartile	£ 70 a year	£216 a year	£211 a year	£160 a year
Median	£108 a year	£353 a year	£395 a year	£340 a year
Third Quartile	£192 a year	£590 a year	£625 a year	£551 a year

The Ecclesiastical Revenues Commission gave the average net value of the benefices in each diocese. The national average was £285 a year, and the figure for Carlisle, the diocese of the Fells, was only £175 a year. Rochester, which formed part of Kent, had an average of £414 a year; and the figure for Canterbury, the other Kent diocese, was £318 a year. Norwich, of which Norfolk formed a large part, had an average of £313 a year; and Chichester, almost conterminous with Sussex, had an average of £282 a year (*P.P.*, 1835, XXII, 1052). Thirty-four Norfolk livings were not returned, two were vacant and a further four have been omitted because other livings held by their incumbents were not returned. Only two Kent livings were not returned, two were vacant, and three were held by clergy who did not return the value of their other preferments. Four Sussex livings were not returned, and one was held by an incumbent who did not disclose his other source of ecclesiastical income. All the Lakeland livings were returned, and none was vacant.

Twelve clergy held livings both in Kent and in Sussex; two held them in Norfolk and in Sussex; and one held a living in Westmorland and another in Kent. Each has been assigned to the county in which he did not employ a curate.

TABLE IX

Account Books of the Revd James Woodforde, Rector of Weston Longeville, Norfolk (for 1799), and of the Revd James Plumptre, Vicar of Hinxton, Cambridgeshire (for 1802)

	Woodforde		Plumptre	
Item	Amount	% of total expenditure	Amount	% of total expenditure
1. Housekeeping	£146 17s 4½d	58.4	£73 1s 8d	35.7
2. Clothes	£20 4s 8d	8.1	£12 13s 2d	6.2
3. 'Private'	£36 15s 6d	14.6	£35 11s 6½d	17.4
4. 'Sundries' and repairs	£6 3s 5d	2.5	£5 19s 6½d	2.9
5. Charity	£13 8s 4d	5.3	£22 13s 8½d	11.1
6. Books (1) Their			£34 7s 7d	16.8
(2) To give away	3s 6d	0.1	£6 16s 1½d	3.3
7. Gardening expenses	£10 18s 0d	4.3	£5 14s 5½d	2.8
8. Letters and Parcels	£5 13s 11d	2.8		
9. 'Physic'	£16 18s 7d	6.7	£2 2s 6½d	1.0
TOTAL	£251 9 s 4½d	100.0	£204 14s 3d	100.0

The sources used here are the Plumptre Papers, C.U.L., Add. Mss. 5820, f.26-46; and *The Diary of a Country Parson.*

Plumptre meticulously records each payment, Woodforde does not. In some instances, no bill for 1799 in given in the *Diary* for a particular item, so we have been forced to use bills for the nearest available year. Thus the flour bill is that for 1798, as are the tailor's and woollen-draper's; the wine bills run from September 1799 to the same month of the next year; and the nearest doctor's bill, for fifteen months, is for 1797, of which we have taken four-fifths. Such necessary guesswork inevitably leads to inaccuracies. There are also some omissions. Woodforde's expenditure was, probably, £40 or £50 more than is stated. A good proportion of this omitted expenditure would have gone on housekeeping.

Statistical Appendix and Tables

TABLE X

The Social Composition of the Beneficed Clergy in selected Counties as at the end of 1833

(Sources: *P.P.*, 1835, XXII, 111-1052; Venn, *Alumni Cantabrienses*; standard works of reference on the peerage and landed gentry)

| | Norfolk | | Kent | | Sussex | | | |
	No.	% of sample	No.	% of sample	No.	% of sample	No. in whole sample	% of whole sample
1. Peerage	31	9.6	16	12.9	7	8.2	54	10.2
2. Landed Gentry	42	13.0	15	12.1	5	5.9	62	11.7
3. Episcopal	2	0.6	1	0.8	1	1.2	4	0.8
4. Clerical	67	20.8	22	17.7	18	21.1	107	20.1
5. Miscellaneous *	44	13.7	13	10.5	17	20.0	74	13.9
6. Tradesmen and Artisans	18	5.6	3	2.4	2	2.4	23	4.3
7. Unknown	118	36.7	54	43.6	35	41.2	207	39.0
TOTALS	322	100.0	124	100.0	85	100.0	531	100.0

Note: Because Joseph Foster, *Alumni Oxonienses* is defective, this Table includes only Cambridge alumni.

* This section includes the sons of army and naval officers, merchants, doctors, schoolmasters, lawyers, and MPs.

In cases where clergy married into a higher social class than their parentage, we have taken the status achieved by marriage as indicative of the place occupied within the social hierarchy.

If a clergyman's father was also a member of the gentry, we have included the clergyman concerned under one of the first two classifications.

It is possible to reach conclusions on this matter materially different to our own. This is, indeed, the case with Mary Ransome, *The State of the Bishopric of Worcester*, pp.7-8, which analyses the social origins of 532 clergy working in the diocese between 1782 and 1808. Ransome finds that 205 of these men (38.5%) were the sons of peerage and gentry - much higher than our estimate of 21.9%. The reason for divergence is that Ransome uses Foster, *Alumni Oxonienses*, as well as Venn, *Alumni Cantabrienses*. Unhappily, Foster's use of the term 'gent' to describe parentage is excessively liberal and also, often, exceedingly misleading.

The Church in an Age of Negligence

TABLE XI

The career choices of Cambridge graduate alumni, matriculating in selected years, 1800-1830

(Sources: Venn, *Alumni Cantabrienses*; college admissions' books)

	1800		1810		1820		1830		No. in	% in
	No.	% of Year	No.	% of Year	No.	% of Year	No.	% of Year	whole sample	whole sample
Clergy	73	64.6	113	65.7	230	70.8	203	66.1	619	67.5
Lawyers	12	10.6	19	11.0	36	11.1	38	12.4	105	11.5
Landed Gentry	3	2.6	15	8.7	12	3.7	18	5.9	48	5.2
Doctors	3	2.6	5	2.9	6	1.8	8	2.6	22	2.4
MPs	5	4.5	5	2.9	8	2.5	2	0.7	20	2.2
Army and Naval Officers	1	0.9	2	1.2	5	1.5	3	1.0	11	1.2
Non-ordained	3	2.6	2	1.2	2	0.6	3	1.0	10	1.1
Schoolmasters	0	0.0	1	0.6	0	0.0	1	0.3	2	0.2
Civil Servants	1	0.9	0	0.0	0	0.0	0	0.0	1	0.1
Diplomats	0	0.0	0	0.0	0	0.0	1	0.3	1	0.1
Bankers	0	0.0	1	0.6	0	0.0	0	0.0	1	0.1
Merchants	0	0.0	0	0.0	0	0.0	1	0.3	1	0.1
Manufacturers	0	0.0	0	0.0	1	0.3	0	0.0	1	0.1
'Adventurers'	0	0.0	0	0.0	1	0.3	0	0.0	1	0.1
Antiquaries	0	0.0	0	0.0	0	0.0	1	0.3	1	0.1
Musicians	1	0.9	0	0.0	0	0.0	0	0.0	1	0.1
Artists	0	0.0	0	0.0	0	0.0	1	0.3	1	0.1
Died Young	2	1.8	1	0.6	6	1.8	7	2.3	16	1.8
Unknown	9	8.0	8	4.6	18	5.6	20	6.5	55	6.0
TOTALS	113	100.0	172	100.0	325	100.0	307	100.0	917	100.0

See, also, Haig, *The Victorian Clergy*, Table 2.4, p.38 which analyses the occupational choices of samples of Cambridge Honours men in the period 1841-3 to 1871-3. Among the 348 graduates included in Haig's sample for 1841-3, there were 235 (67.5%) who took Orders. This is the same proportion as in our sample of matriculants, 1800-30.

TABLE XII

The number of those matriculating at the University of Cambridge in selected years, showing the percentage subsequently becoming ordained

(Sources: Venn, *Alumni Cantabrienses*; the various college admissions books)

	Number of Matriculations	Number subsequently becoming Ordained	Percentage becoming Ordained
1800	143	73	51.0
1810	208	113	54.3
1820	394	230	58.3
1830	405	203	50.1
TOTAL	1,150	619	53.8

TABLE XIII

The career prospects of future clergy admitted at the University of Cambridge in selected years, 1800-1830

(Sources: Venn, *Alumni*; college admissions' books)

	1800		1810		1820		1830		Total sample	
	No.	% of sample	No.	% of sample	No.	% of sample	No.	% of sample	No. in	% of
1. Beneficed within 5 years	17	23.3	30	26.3	37	15.8	45	21.6	129	20.5
2. Beneficed in over 5 years, but within 15	14	19.2	20	17.6	52	22.2	46	22.0	132	21.0
3. Beneficed in over 15 years	8	11.0	17	14.9	30	12.8	31	14.8	86	13.6
4. Never beneficed*	15	20.6	23	20.2	53	22.7	45	21.6	136	21.6
5. Became Fellows	9	12.3	11	9.7	20	8.6	5	2.4	45	7.1
6. Became Schoolmasters	1	1.4	3	2.6	16	6.8	17	8.1	37	5.9
7. Emigrated	2	2.7	3	2.6	11	4.7	11	5.2	27	4.3
8. Became army or naval chaplains	2	2.7	0	0.0	2	0.9	0	0.0	4	0.6
9. Became Dissenters	0	0.0	0	0.0	1	0.4	0	0.0	1	0.2
10. Died, unbeneficed, within 15 years of ordination	5	6.8	7	6.1	12	5.1	9	4.3	33	5.2
TOTAL	73	100.0	114	100.0	234	100.0	209	100.0	630	100.0

*Clergy whose later careers are untraceable have been included under this classification. In every case these clergy were curates for at least 15 years, and were not subsequently beneficed.

Statistical Appendix and Tables

TABLE XIV

A Digest of Parliamentary Returns on the Number of Clerical JPs in the various Counties of England and Wales, 1831-1863

ENGLAND

County	Qualified JPs in 1831	JPs appointed, 1831-34	JPs appointed, in 1836	JPs appointed, 1836-42	JPs appointed, 1843-63
	Clergy/laity	Clergy/laity	Clergy	Clergy/laity	Clergy
Bedfordshire	19/ 27	0/ 6	66	4/ 11	10
Berkshire	28/ 95	1/ 21	76	6/ 70	6
Buckinghamshire	54/ 90	No commission	84	17/ 77	24
Cambridgeshire	23/ 28	5/ 1	56	15/ 10	5
Cheshire	16/ 58	1/ 11	69	14/ 67	9
Cornwall	36/ 54	15/ 21	82	8/ 52	19
Cumberland	15/ 39	4/ 32	36	6/ 44	36
Derbyshire	0/ 79	No commission	0	0/ 41	0
Devonshire	42/ 144	No commission	84	10/ 38	25
Dorsetshire	25/ 43	No commission	79	2/ 60	9
Durham	23/ 59	63/ 188	54	1/ 17	16
Essex	51/ 119	5/ 30	116	14/ 68	N.R.
Gloucestershire	49/ 127	13/ 44	83	10/ 60	16
Hampshire	19/ 131	1/ 16	43	5/ 118	6
Herefordshire	58/ 97	5/ 10	106	15/ 51	61
Hertfordshire	44/ 102	0/ 15	79	10/ 106	41
Huntingdonshire	7/ 18	1/ 1	18	2/ 22	6
Kent	2/ 145	2/ 8	62	4/ 94	8
Lancashire	24/ 112	3/ 30	40	9/ 140	25
Leicestershire	17/ 27	5/ 6	71	2/ 22	8
Lincolnshire	52/ 59	2/ 8	160	20/ 38	67
Middlesex	16/ 153	24/ 517	19	1/ 110	0
Monmouthshire	13/ 44	2/ 2	36	12/ 34	13
Norfolk	78/ 119	No commission	135	4/ 58	39
Northamptonshire	35/ 49	5/ 10	183	15/ 38	14
Northumberland	6/ 40	No commission	16	7/ 45	12
Nottinghamshire	10/ 44	0/ 4	23	8/ 49	9
Oxfordshire	18/ 53	1/ 10	62	9/ 39	16
Rutland	3/ 6	No commission	9	4/ 14	4
Shropshire	36/ 85	0/ 1	100	9/ 53	53
Somersetshire	53/ 97	2/ 19	99	1/ 67	0
Staffordshire	16/ 70	2/ 21	55	5/ 79	14
Suffolk	58/ 98	10/ 12	110	43/ 56	8
Surrey	39/ 215	No commission	60	3/ 98	0
Sussex	0/ 189	0/ 32	0	0/ 73	3
Warwickshire	24/ 42	4/ 42	74	2/ 69	13
Westmorland	12/ 18	2/ 20	20	8/ 19	11
Wiltshire	18/ 71	7/ 21	42	7/ 58	21
Worcestershire	44/ 92	10/ 21	76	5/ 45	18
Yorkshire	71/ 234	10/ 62	160	28/ 180	49
TOTALS	1154/3372	205/1242	2743	345/2390	694

WALES

Anglesey	6/ 14	0/ 2	36	2/ 10	9
Breconshire	24/ 37	No commission	44	4/ 40	2
Cardiganshire	11/ 53	1/ 9	31	1/ 5	2
Carmarthenshire	9/ 75	21/199	26	0/ 38	10
Carnarvonshire	17/ 14	71/139	70	9/ 9	6
Denbighshire	24/ 41	2/ 5	59	2/ 55	4
Flintshire	15/ 26	1/ 2	39	1/ 28	11
Glamorganshire	25/ 65	0/ 1	44	5/ 29	44
Merionethshire	9/ 14	28/ 60	28	20/ 26	2
Montgomeryshire	13/ 31	No commission	51	4/ 20	14
Pembrokeshire	10/ 35	4/ 14	66	2/ 22	29
Radnorshire	4/ 29	0/ 1	29	6/ 17	12
TOTALS	167/434	128/432	523	56/ 299	145
JOINT TOTAL FOR ENGLAND AND WALES	1321/3806	333/1674	3266	401/2689	839
Percentage of Clergy	25.8	16.6		13.0	

A digest of the relevant parliamentary return for 1831 (*P.P.*, 1831-2, XXXV, 231-72) appeared in *The Church Reformer's Magazine*, I (March, 1832), 63. Numerous historians have used this source in preference to the more arduous task of compiling statistics from the parliamentary return (see, e.g., Webb, *The Parish and the County*, p. 383, note 1; W.L. Mathieson, *English Church Reform, 1815-1840*, p. 27, note 2; and Soloway, *Prelates and People*, p. 88, note 3). This is not a sensible thing to do. The compilation in *The Church Reformer's Magazine* is riddled with error. Worst are statistics for Yorkshire. The parliamentary return has 71 clerical magistrates and 234 lay magistrates: *The Church Reformer's Magazine* manages to come up with totals of 103 and 311. The only way in which it is possible to arrive at the strange estimate of 103 clerical JPs is by double counting the clergy who had qualified in the North Riding. By adopting the same procedure, the band of 234 lay JPs is, also, miraculously transformed into a larger band of 311. Figures derived from *The Church Reformer's Magazine* can safely be discarded.

Other historians have done better. Statistics based upon the original parliamentary return can be found in Kitson Clark, *Churchmen and the Condition of England* (p. 146), and in Zangerl, 'The Social Composition of the County Magistracy in England and Wales, 1831-1887', *J.B.S.*, XI, Table 2, 118. Both sources calculate qualified English clerical JPs at 1,154; but figures for Welsh magistrates differ. Kitson Clark puts the total at 166, and Zangerl expresses a preference for 168. Also on offer is our own estimate of 167. We would be willing, in a spirit of academic ecumenism, to agree either with Kitson Clark or with Zangerl; but, having rechecked the figures, stay with 167.

TABLE XV

The age distribution of the beneficed clergy in selected counties, as at the end of 1833.

	Kent	%	Norfolk	%	Sussex	%	Sample total	% of whole sample
Under 30	26	10.0	45	11.9	17	9.0	88	10.6
31-35	29	11.1	43	11.4	19	10.0	91	11.0
36-40	30	11.5	35	9.3	28	14.8	93	11.2
41-45	33	12.6	27	7.2	22	11.6	82	9.9
46-50	26	10.0	26	6.9	27	14.3	79	9.6
51-55	34	13.0	43	11.4	13	6.9	90	10.9
56-60	26	10.0	44	11.7	18	9.5	88	10.6
61-65	20	7.7	50	13.3	16	8.5	86	10.4
66-70	22	8.4	25	6.6	11	5.8	58	7.0
71-75	8	3.0	20	5.3	9	4.8	37	4.5
76-80	6	2.3	11	2.9	6	3.2	23	2.8
Over 80	1	0.4	8	2.1	3	1.6	12	1.5
TOTALS	261	100.0	377	100.0	189	100.0	827	100.0

The median was 46 in Kent, 52 in Norfolk, and 47 in Sussex. The sources used here were: *P.P.*, 1835, XXII, 111-1052; Foster, *Alumni*; Venn, *Alumni*; *Clerical Guide*, 1829 and 1836; and the *Gentleman's Magazine*.

TABLE XVIII

A Digest of Parliamentary Returns on the Residence of the Beneficed Clergy, 1805-1879

(Source: Parliamentary Returns)

Year	Parishes with Resident Incumbents	%	Parishes with Non-Residents doing duty	%	Parishes with Non-Residents not doing duty	%	Number of Benefices
1805	No Return	0.0	No Return	0.0	4,506	0.0	No Return
1806	No Return	0.0	No Return	0.0	4,132	0.0	No Return
1807	No Return	0.0	No Return	0.0	6,145	0.0	No Return
1808	No Return	0.0	No Return	0.0	6,120	0.0	No Return
1809	3,836	34.3	No Return	-	7,358	65.7	11,194
1810	4,421	43.1	622	6.1	5,218	50.8	10,261
1811	4,490	41.6	1,164	10.8	5,147	47.6	10,801
1813	4,183	39.6	1,641	15.6	4,734	44.8	10,558
1814	3,798	35.8	1,990	18.8	4,814	45.4	10,602
1827	4,413	41.9	1,590	15.1	4,530	43.0	10,533
1831	4,649	44.0	1,684	16.0	4,227	40.0	10,560
1835	5,146	48.7	1,646	15.6	3,779	35.7	10,571
1838	5,859	54.6	1,184	11.0	3,699	34.4	10,742
1841	6,699	61.0	1,059	9.6	3,229	29.4	10,987
1844	7,246	65.1	1,061	9.5	2,820	25.4	11,127
1846	7,445	65.4	1,177	10.3	2,764	24.3	11,386
1848	7,779	67.0	1,119	9.6	2,713	23.4	11,611
1850	8,077	68.9	1,137	9.7	2,514	21.4	11,728
1879	11,186	88.1	0	0.0	1,509	11.9	12,695

All miscellaneous cases (e.g. vacancies, recent institutions, sequestrations, suspensions, no returns) are included in the column 'non-resident not doing duty'.

TABLE XIX

Parishes classified by residence and duty, according to the Parliamentary Returns on the residence of the beneficed clergy

The figures for each diocese are shown under four headings: resident incumbents, non-residents doing duty, non-residents not doing duty, and the total number of benefices in the diocese. A dash indicates that no information is available and may be read as zero.

Year	Bath & Wells				Bristol				Canterbury			
1810	163	29	232	424	111	17	131	259	144	0	205	349
1811	159	39	233	431	125	10	131	266	145	28	178	351
1813	178	58	247	483	103	39	110	252	129	53	155	337
1814	159	69	257	485	99	47	105	251	124	65	148	337
1827	178	61	201	440	98	52	105	255	132	45	166	343
1831	186	58	196	440	113	47	92	252	139	50	151	340
1835	199	55	186	440	126	48	78	252	162	53	123	338
1838	265	28	141	434					202	26	110	338
1841	266	36	140	442					237	22	86	345
1844	283	40	124	447					239	12	95	346
1846	307	37	116	460					240	15	86	341
1848	310	40	111	461					251	23	74	348
1850	311	40	111	462					258	18	76	352
1879	434	-	32	466					373	-	30	403

Year	Carlisle				Chester				Chichester			
1810	78	0	56	134	317	0	265	582	108	34	123	265
1811	77	18	36	131	314	33	237	584	109	14	137	260
1813	78	14	37	129	299	83	201	583	105	50	112	267
1814	74	19	36	129	302	117	168	587	98	52	117	267
1827	73	11	44	128	383	55	178	616	114	42	110	266
1831	75	17	38	130	426	53	145	624	119	42	104	265
1835	74	15	42	131	442	60	132	634	130	47	86	263
1838	78	17	35	130	459	28	86	573	134	42	86	262
1841	95	4	35	134	489	45	90	624	151	39	71	261
1844	96	7	29	132	548	7	70	625	162	40	58	260
1846	94	17	23	134	519	22	80	621	189	42	66	297
1848	97	14	23	134	307	18	111	436	194	32	79	305
1850	99	19	19	137	330	27	74	431	204	32	75	311
1879	262	-	22	284	374	-	34	408	285	-	53	338

Year	Durham				Ely				Exeter			
1810	87	most	107	194	51	34	63	148	269	0	335	604
1811	89	19	83	191	49	36	63	148	258	10	336	604
1813	94	26	75	195	47	27	82	156	283	69	290	642
1814	85	29	83	197	47	34	74	155	250	88	317	655
1827	90	10	75	175	51	22	83	156	282	61	264	607
1831	111	22	51	184	52	28	71	151	276	71	283	630
1835	116	14	58	188	56	29	65	150	364	47	225	636
1838	137	11	61	209	246	68	232	515	430	11	198	639
1841	151	14	49	214	273	88	159	520	459	9	166	634
1844	179	9	36	224	320	70	132	522	444	26	167	637
1846	186	14	33	233	315	68	147	530	454	28	170	652

1810	31	0	100	131
1811	26	0	168	194
1813	41	52	99	192
1814	34	54	108	196
1827	61	36	97	194
1831	64	42	86	192
1835	66	36	91	193
1838	69	42	84	195
1841	82	31	81	194
1844	102	34	70	206
1846	105	36	74	215
1848	124	38	60	222
1850	131	41	50	222
1879	193	-	25	218

1. Many of those without exemptions or licences do duty.

In this, as in the previous Table, all miscellaneous cases are placed under the classification 'non-resident not doing duty'.

Statistical Appendix and Tables

TABLE XX

The number of parishes with resident curates, both assistant and stipendiary, in each of the dioceses of England and Wales, 1810-1841.

(Source : Parliamentary Returns)

	1810	1813	1814	1827	1831	1838	1841
St Asaph	38	42	39	22	26	34	41
Bangor	27	29	38	31	38	49	48
St David's	N.R.	62	64	67	75	64	78
Llandaff	18	33	20	31	42	52	49
Bath and Wells	76	90	85	100	120	170	172
Bristol	36	29	30	53	60	N.R.	N.R.
Canterbury	59	66	66	66	73	117	109
Carlisle	26	26	33	35	39	31	27
Chester	116	117	151	121	120	202	230
Chichester	59	51	51	53	66	85	79
Durham	45	56	57	56	61	92	97
Ely	18	23	21	36	38	151	142
Exeter	112	131	131	145	174	232	255
Gloucester	42	51	54	67	78	128	151
Hereford	44	49	53	52	81	100	94
Lichfield and Coventry	98	135	134	157	162	169	167
Lincoln	182	193	187	248	320	306	304
London	84	97	102	133	144	237	285
Norwich	112	122	127	176	183	243	245
Oxford	33	42	50	41	48	118	96
Peterborough	41	51	50	64	65	79	155
Rochester	18	19	16	27	29	41	31
Salisbury	70	72	81	100	116	138	137
Winchester	85	101	93	114	167	177	205
Worcester	31	34	36	51	51	119	146
York	117	163	179	152	161	309	269
TOTAL	1,587	1,884	1,948	2,198	2,537	3,443	3,612

In 1835, returns were made for stipendiaries alone; these have therefore been omitted. In 1838, a new format was adopted, and this precedent was followed in 1841: there are figures for resident stipendiaries, but not for resident assistants. What is given, instead, is the number of assistants in each diocese. This alteration in presentation is not, fortunately, material: an assistant was, by definition, resident.

As with figures for residence among the beneficed clergy, reorganisation of diocesan geography means that returns for 1838 and 1841 are not strictly comparable with those for prior years: Bristol was absorbed into Gloucester, Ely was greatly expanded, and so on. We have conflated figures for the diocese of Ripon, and also for Sodor and Man, with those for the diocese of York.

Finally, it should be noted that, with regard to statistics (for 1838, there is a minor error in the relevant parliamentary return. According to *P.P.*, 1840, XXXIX, 64 the number of parishes with assistant curates in that year was 1,725. However, when aggregating figures from each diocese (as given in the same return) the total works out at 1,723, two less. We have taken the lower of the two sums.

JPs appointed in 1836 - *P.P.*, 1836, XLIII, 161-262.

JPs appointed, 1836-42 - *P.P.*, 1842, XXXIII, 445-70.

JPs appointed, 1843-63 - *P.P.*, 1863, XLVIII, 259-79.

Other returns on Clerical Magistrates:

Names of clergy qualified to serve in 1840 - *P.P.*, 1840, XLI, 351-94.

The number of JPs in commissions in 1853 - *P.P.*, 1852-3, LXXVIII, 329.

Clergy serving in 1861 - *P.P.*, 1861, LI, 665.

Clergy serving in 1873, with date of appointment - *P.P.*, 1873, LIV, 33-57.

The number of JPs, both qualified and non-qualified, in 1887 - *P.P.*, 1888, LXXXII, 193-406.

Returns on the Residence of the Beneficed Clergy (as used in Tables XVIII and XIX):

1805, 1806, 1807 and 1808 - *P.P.*, 1809, IX, 23-31.

1809 and 1810 - *P.P.*, 1812, X, 152-3, 160-1.

1811 - *P.P.*, 1812-13, XIII, 48-9.

1813 and 1814 - *P.P.*, 1817, XV, 142-9.

1827 - *P.P.*, 1830, XIX, 36-7.

1831 - *P.P.*, 1833, XXVII, 329-33.

1835 - *P.P.*, 1837, XLI, 218-19.

1838 - *P.P.*, 1840, XXXIX, 56-7.

1841 - *P.P.*, 1843, XL, 2-3.

1844 - *P.P.*, 1846, XXXII, 10-11.

1846 - *P.P.*, 1847-8, XLIX, 58-9.

1848 - *P.P.*, 1850, XLII, 132-3.

1850 - *P.P.*, 1852-3, LXXVIII, 2-3.

1879 - *P.P.*, 1881, LXXII, 19.

Returns on the Residence of Curates (as used in Table XX):

1810 - *P.P.*, 1812, X, 157.

1813 and 1814 - *P.P.*, 1817, XV, 150-3.

1827 - *P.P.*, 1830, XIX, 40-1.

1831 - *P.P.*, 1833, XXVII, 334-7.

1838 - *P.P.*, 1840, XXXIX, 62-5.

1841 - *P.P.*, 1843, XL, 6-7.

Other returns on the Residence of Curates:

1835 - *P.P.*, 1837, XLI, 220-1.

Further parliamentary returns:

Advowson of Marylebone - *P.P.*, 1817, XV, 127-131.

Berkhamstead School - *P.P.*, 1833, XVIII, 289-303.

Capitular clergy - *P.P.*, 1835, XXII, 35-121; *P.P.*, 1836, XXXVI, 20-4.

Corn Laws - *P.P.*, 1814-15, V, 1098-9.

Ecclesiastical Duties and Revenues Commission (Second Report) - *P.P.*, 1836, XXXVI, 1-44.

Ecclesiastical Patronage - *P.P.*, 1835, XXII, 1058; *P.P.*, 1836, XL, 25.

Ecclesiastical Revenues Commission (Report) - *P.P.*, 1835, XXII, 15-1060.

Enclosures - *P.P.*, 1836, VIII, Pt II, 505; *P.P.*, 1836, XLIV, 1-293.

Episcopal Revenues - *P.P.*, 1851, XLII, 93-503.

Income Tax Payers in 1801 - *P.P.*, 1852, IX, Appendix, Table I, 964.
Parsonages - *P.P.*, 1818, XVIII, 145-358.
State of Agriculture, 1821 - *P.P.*, 1821, IX, 33-376.
State of Agriculture, 1833 - *P.P.*, 1833, V, 3-631.
State of Agriculture, 1836 - *P.P.*, 1836, VIII, Pt II, 5-502; *P.P.*, 1837, V, 5-365.
Surplice Fees of City of London incumbents - *P.P.*, 1834, XLIII, 41-154.
Tithe Commutation - *P.P.*, 1887, LXIV, 532-3.
Values of Livings, 1809 - *P.P.*, 1809, IX, 37.
Values of Livings, 1810 - *P.P.*, 1810, XIV, 92-3.
Values of Livings, 1815 - *P.P.*, 1818, XVIII, 361.
Values of Livings, 1829-31 - *P.P.*, 1835, XXII, 1053-6.

REVIEWS AND MAGAZINES

Agricultural History Review.
Blackwood's Magazine.
British Critic.
British Journal of Sociology.
Economic History.
Economic History Review.
Edinburgh Review.
Gentleman's Magazine.
Historical Journal.
Journal of British Studies.
Journal of Ecclesiastical History.
Journal of the Royal Statistical Society.
Past and Present.
Quarterly Review.
Review of Economic Staticties.
Social History.
Studies in Church History.
Theology.
Tracts for the Times.

NEWSPAPERS

Bury and Norwich Post.
Cambridge Chronicle.
John Bull.
Kentish Gazette.
Morning Herald.
Norfolk Chronicle.
Norwich Mercury.
Spectator.
The Times.

1938), 21-37

Thompson, R.J. 'An Inquiry into the Rent of Agricultural Land in England and Wales during the Nineteenth Century', *J.R.S.S.*, LXX (1907), 587-624

Ward, W.R. 'The Tithe Question in England in the Early Nineteenth Century', *J.E.H.*, XVI (1965), 67-81

Williams, J.E. 'The British Standard of Living, 1750-1850', *E.H.R.*, Second Series, XIX (1966), 581-9

Zangerl, Carl H.E., 'The Social Composition of the County Magistracy in England and Wales, 1831-1887', *J.B.S.*, XI (November, 1971), 113-25

UNPUBLISHED DISSERTATIONS AND THESES

Addy, John 'Two eighteenth century bishops of Chester and their diocese 1771-1787' (Leeds Ph.D., 1972)

Austin, M.R. 'The Church of England in the County of Derbyshire, 1772-1832' (London Ph.D., 1969)

Balda, W.D. 'Spheres of Influence: Simeon's trust and its implications for evangelical patronage' (Cambridge Ph.D., 1981)

Bezodis, P.A. 'The English Parish Clergy and their Place in Society, 1660-1800' (Trinity College, Cambridge dissertation, 1949)

Coolidge, C.W. 'The Finances of the Church of England 1830-1880' (Trinity College, Dublin Ph.D., 1958)

Foskett, R. 'John Kaye and the Diocese of Lincoln' (Nottingham Ph.D., 1957)

Jacob, W.M. 'Clergy and Society in Norfolk 1707-1806' (Exeter Ph.D., 1982)

Leatherbarrow, J.S. 'The Rise and Decline of the Squarson (with special reference to the Diocese of Worcester)' (Birmingham Ph.D., 1976)

Marshall, W.M. 'The Administration of the Dioceses of Hereford and Oxford, 1660-1760' (Bristol Ph.D., 1978)

Maynard, W.B. 'The Ecclesiastical Administration of the Archdeaconry of Durham, 1774-1856' (Durham Ph.D., 1973)

Moir, E.A.L. 'Local Government in Gloucestershire 1775-1800; a study of the Justices of the Peace and their work' (Cambridge Ph.D., 1955)

Murray, N.U. 'The Influence of the French Revolution on the Church of England and its Rivals, 1789-1802' (Oxford D.Phil., 1975)

Nockles, P.B. 'Continuity and Change in Anglican High Churchmanship in Britain, 1792-1850' (Oxford D.Phil., 1982)

O'Brien, P.K. 'Government Revenue, 1793-1815' (Oxford D.Phil., 1967)

Salter, J.L. 'Isaac Maddox and the dioceses of St Asaph and Worcester, 1736-1759' (Birmingham MA, 1962)

Shuler, J.C. 'The Pastoral and Ecclesiastical Administration of the Diocese of Durham 1721-1771; with particular reference to the Archdeaconry of Northumberland' (Durham Ph.D., 1975)

Whitfield, P.W. 'Change and Continuity in the rural church: Norfolk 1760-1840' (St Andrews Ph.D., 1977)

Bibliography

SECONDARY WORKS

[A beneficed clergyman], *What will the bishops do?* 1833

[A clergyman of the Church of England], *Safe and easy steps towards an efficient church reform* 1832

[A College Incumbent], *Ecclesiastical Taxation and Augmentation of Small Benefices: considered in six letters from a college incumbent to a friend in Oxford,* 1832

[A Country Gentleman], *Hints for Church Reform,* 1832

A Letter to the Right Honourable Sir Robert Peel, Bart, MP, on the present condition and prospects of the established church, 1832

[A Non-Beneficed Clergyman], *A Letter to His Grace the Archbishop of Canterbury on Church Reform, in which is suggested a plan of alterations both safe and efficient,* 1833

Addison, William, *The English Country Parson,* 1947

Arnold, Thomas *Principles of Church Reform,* 2nd edn., 1833

Aspinall, A. *Politics and the Press, c.1780-1850,* 1949

Bateman, Josiah *The Life of the Right Revd Daniel Wilson* 2 vols., 1860

[Berens, E.] *Church-Reform. By a Churchman,* 1828

Beresford, John, (ed.) *The Diary of a Country Parson,* 5 vols, 1924-31

Best, G.F.A. *Temporal Pillars. Queen Anne's Bounty, the Ecclesiastical Commissioners, and the Church of England* 1964

Beverley, R.M. *A Letter to His Grace The Archbishop of York, on the Present Corrupt State Of The Church of England,* Beverley, 1831

Blomfield, Alfred (ed.) *A Memoir of Charles James Blomfield, D.D., Bishop of London with Selections from his correspondence,* 2 vols., 1863

Bloomfield, S.T. *An Analytical View of the Principal Plans of Church Reform,* 1833

Bossy, John *T he English Catholic community, 1570-1850,* 1975

Bouch, C.M.L. *Prelates and people of the Lake-Counties: a history of the diocese of Carlisle, 1133-1933,* Kendal, 1948

Bowen, D.G. *The idea of the Victorian Church; a study of the Church of England, 1833-89,* Montreal, 1968

Bowles, W.L. *A Word on Cathedral Oratorios, and Clergy-Magistrates, Addressed to Lord Mount Cashel,* 1830

Bradley, A.G. *Our Centenarian Grandfather, 1790-1890,* 1922

Brilioth, Y. *The Anglican Revival. Studies in the Oxford Movement,* 1925

Brown, A.W. *Recollections of the conversation parties of the Revd Charles Simeon,* 1863

Brown, Ford K. *Fathers of the Victorians,* 1961

Bullock, F.W.B. *The History of Ridley Hall, Cambridge,* 2 vols., 1953

Burton, Edward *Sequel to Remarks upon Church Reform, with observations upon the plan proposed by Lord Henley,* 1832

Butler, John *The Bishop of Hereford's Charge to the Clergy of his Diocese, at his triennial visitation in the year 1792,* Hereford, 1792

Butler, J.R.M. *The Passing of the Great Reform Bill,* 1914

Butler, S. *Thoughts on Church Dignities,* 1833

Butler, Samuel *The Life and Letters of Dr Samuel Butler* 2 vols., 1896

Carpenter, S.C. *Church and People, 1789-1889,* 1933

Churchmen and the Condition of England, 1832-1885. A study in the development of social ideas and practice from the Old Regime to the Modern State, 1973

Latham, R. and Matthews, W. *The Diary of Samuel Pepys*, 11 vols., 1970-83

Letter to R.M. Beverley Esq.. in Defence of his Strictures on the University of Cambridge. By An Undergraduate, 1834

Lloyd Jukes, H.A. (ed.) *Articles of Enquiry addressed to Clergy of the Diocese of Oxford at the Primary Visitation of Dr Thomas Secker, 1738*, Banbury, 1957

McClatchey, Diana *Oxfordshire Clergy, 1777-1869. A study of the Established Church and of the role of the Clergy in local society*, 1960

Marsden, J.B. *Memoirs of the life and labours of the Revd Hugh Stowell*, 1868

Marsh, P.T. *The Victorian Church in Decline. Archbishop Tait and the Church of England*, 1969

Martin, Frederick *The Property and Revenues of the English Church Establishment*, 1877

Mathieson, W.L. *English Church Reform, 1815-1840*, 1923

Maxwell Lyte, H.C. *A History of Eton College, 1440-1875*, 1875

Mingay, G.E. *English Landed Society in the Eighteenth Century*, 1963

Mitchell, B.R. and Deane, Phyllis *Abstract of British Historical Statistics*, 1962

Moir, Esther *Local Government in Gloucestershire 1775-1800. A Study of the Justice of the Peace*, Bristol, 1969

Monk, J.H. *A Charge delivered to the Clergy of the Diocese of Gloucester, in August and September. MDCCCXXXV, at the Triennial Visitation of the Right Reverend James Henry, Lord Bishop of Gloucester*, 1835

Mozley, Thomas *Reminiscences, chiefly of Oriel College and the Oxford Movement*, 2nd edn., 2 vols., 1882

Norman, E.R. *Church and Society in England 1770-1970*, 1976

Obelkevich, James *Religion and Rural Society: South Lindsey 1825-1875*, 1976

Observations on the new Residence Bill, and on Objections which have been made to it, Carmarthen, 1817

Ollard, S.L., and Walker, P.C., (eds.) *Archbishop Herring's Visitation Returns, 1743*, The Yorkshire Archaeological Society, Record Series, Vols. LXXI, LXXII, LXXV, LXXVII Wakefield, 1928-30

[One of the priesthood], *The outline of an efficient plan of Church Reform*, 1833

Park, T. *St Bees College, 1816-1895: a short history*, Dalton-in-Furness, 1982

Peacock, A.J. *Bread or Blood*, 1965

Pearson, Hesketh *The Smith of Smiths, being the Life, Wit and Humour of Sydney Smith*, 1934

Phillpotts, Henry *Charge delivered to the Clergy of the Diocese of Exeter, by the Bishop of Exeter, at his Primary Charge in 1833*, 1833

　　'Correspondence between the Lord Bishop of Exeter and Members of the Commission of Ecclesiastical Enquiry, 1840

Plain words addressed to members of the Church of England. By one of themselves, 1833

Plomer, William (ed.) *Kilvert's Diary*, 3 vols., 1938-40

Pius, Revd Father *Life of Father Ignatius of St Paul*, 1866

Porter, G.R. *The Progress of the Nation, in its various social and economical relations, from the beginning of the nineteenth century to the present time*, 1836-43

Price, D.T.W. *A history of Saint David's University College Lampeter, I, to 1898*, 1977

Purcell, E.S. *Life of Cardinal Manning*, 2 vols., 1895

Pusey, E.B. *Remarks on the Prospective and Past Benefits of Cathedral Institutions, in the promotion of sound religious knowledge, occasioned by Lord Henley's plan for their abolition*, 1833

Quinault, Roland and Stevenson, John (eds.) *Popular protest and public order. Six studies in British history, 1790-1920*, 1974

Ransome, Mary (ed.) *The State of the Bishopric of Worcester 1782-1808*, Leeds, 1968
    Wiltshire Returns to the Bishop's Visitation Queries 1783, Devizes, 1972

Ranson, S., Bryman, A., and Hinings, R. *Clergy, ministers and priests*, 1977

Ravitch, Norman *Sword and mitre. Government and episcopate in France and England in the age of aristocracy*, The Hague, 1966

Read, Donald *Peterloo. The 'Massacre' and its Background*, 1958

Report from the Clergy of a district in the Diocese of Lincoln, 1800

Riland, John *Ecclesiae Decus et Tutamen. The Extension, Security and Moral Influence of the United Church of England and Ireland*, 1830

Robson, Robert *The Attorney in Eighteenth-Century England*, 1959

Rule, John *The Experience of Labour in Eighteenth-Century Industry*, 1981

Russell, Anthony *The Clerical Profession*, 1980

Savidge, Alan *The Parsonage in England, its history and architecture*, 1964

Smith, George *Bishop Heber*, 1895

Smith, Nowell C. *The Letters of Sydney Smith*, 2 vols., 1953

Smyth, C.H.E. *Simeon and Church Order. A Study of the Origins of the Evangelical Revival in Cambridge in the Eighteenth Century*, 1940

Soloway, R.A. *Prelates and People: Ecclesiastical Social Thought in England 1783-1852*, 1969

Southey, C.C. (ed.) *The Life and Correspondence of Robert Southey*, 6 vols., 1849-50

Stanley, A.P. *The Life and Correspondence of Thomas Arnold*, 2 vols., 1844

Stephens, W.R.W. *The Life and Letters of Walter Farquhar Hook*, 2 vols., 1878
    A Memoir of Richard Durnford, 1899

Stephenson, H.F. *A Letter to Lord Henley on his Plan of Church Reform*, 1833

Stone, Lawrence (ed.) *The university in society: Oxford and Cambridge from the 14th to the early 19th century*, Princeton, 1975

Strachey, Lytton, and Fulford, Roger (eds.) *The Greville Memoirs, 1814-1860*, 8 vols., 1938

Suggestions on Clerical Education: by a Late Fellow of Balliol, 1833

Sykes, Norman *Church and State in England in the XVIIIth Century*, 1934

Tate, W.E. *The Parish Chest. A Study of the Records of Parochial Administration in England*, 1946

Taylor, A.J.P. *English History, 1914-1945*, 1965

Thackeray, Francis *A Defence of the Clergy of the Church of England*, 1822

The State of the Curates of the Church of England: by a Parish Priest, 1828

The State of the Established Church: in a series of Letters to Spencer Perceval, 1809

The Sufferings of the Clergy disclosed, in a dialogue between a Rector and a Vicar, 1819

Thompson, E.P. *The Making of the English Working Class*, 1963

Thompson, F.M.L. *English Landed Society in the Nineteenth Century*, 1963

Thornton, Percy M. *Harrow School and its Surroundings*, 1885

Index